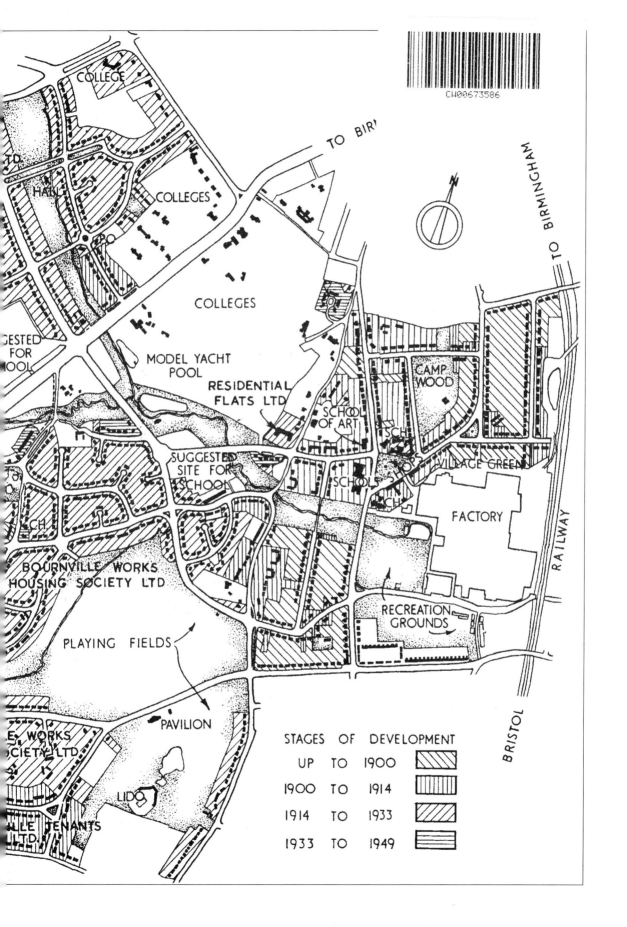

STAGES OF DEVELOPMENT

UP TO 1900		
1900 TO 1914		
1914 TO 1933		
1933 TO 1949		

BOURNVILLE:
MODEL VILLAGE
TO GARDEN SUBURB

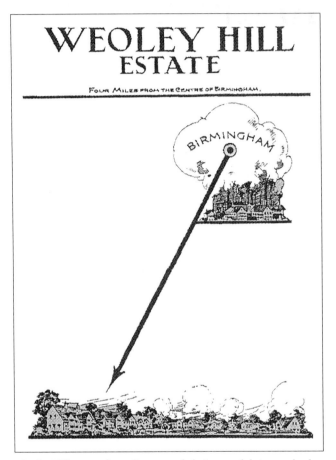

Weoley Hill estate: from dirty, crowded city to salubrious suburb.

BOURNVILLE:
MODEL VILLAGE
TO GARDEN SUBURB

Michael Harrison

Phillimore

1999

Published by
PHILLIMORE & CO. LTD.
Shopwyke Manor Barn, Chichester, West Sussex

ISBN 1 86077 117 3

Printed and bound in Great Britain by
BOOKCRAFT LTD.
Midsomer Norton

CONTENTS

In memory of

J.G.H., L.S. and M.S.

LIST OF ILLUSTRATIONS

Frontispiece: Weoley Hill Estate

ILLUSTRATION ACKNOWLEDGEMENTS

I would like to thank the following for giving permission for the reproduction of these illustrations: British Association, 6; Bournville Village Trust, frontispiece, xvi, 1, 2, 4, 5, 8-14, 20, 22, 23, 26-32, 34-37, 39-47, 49-59, 61-64, 66-68, 69-74, 76, 81-92, 94-98, 101-111, 113-123, 125-156; *Bournville Works Magazine*, 15-19, 24, 25, 65, 93, 99; W.A. Harvey, *The Model Village and its Cottages: Bournville*, 33, 48; Bournville Tenants Ltd., 67; Jonathan Woodley, 60; *Garden City and Town Planning*, 77; Weoley Hill Limited, 100. All other illustrations were supplied by myself.

ACKNOWLEDGEMENTS

This book could not have been written if I had not been given full and free access to the records of Bournville Village Trust. I have received practical and financial assistance from the Trust in producing this study and two earlier exhibitions about the early history of the Estate. The Chief Executive of the Bournville Village Trust, James Wilson, and his Personal Assistant, Diane Thornton, have been particularly helpful. Several Trustees and a number of the Trust's present and former members of staff have been willing to speak to me: I would like to thank Janet Denley, Tom Greeves, Veronica Wootten and John Dakin, Gloria Gain, Steve Gray, Philip and Liz Henslowe, Alan Kelly, William Muirhead, Les Pankhurst, Sue Maneffa, Alan Shrimpton, Bob Stanton, John Walker and Colin Wright. Representatives of some of the residents and tenants groups and a few longstanding residents on the Estate have also shared their memories with me: Mrs Joan Barlow, John Bridgeman, Dennis and Terry Carson, John Clarke, Herbert Davey, G.O. Jones, Mr. and Mrs. J. Taylor and Jim Wilson. Dennis Carson and John Clarke kindly lent me books and ephemera relating to the history of the Estate. Tom Hill was good enough to let me see his collection of postcards relating to Bournville.

Academically, I owe a great debt to my colleague, Professor Mick Durman, Dean of the Birmingham Institute of Art and Design at the University of Central England. Mick Durman had already completed a Master's dissertation on Bournville before we collaborated on two exhibitions on the Bournville Estate. It had been our intention to work on the book together, but due to pressure of work he had to take a back seat. He has continued to show an interest in the progress of the book and he has been supportive of my work (even though a joint volume might have had a slightly different emphasis).

Professor John Swift, the head of the Art Education Research Group in the Birmingham Institute of Art and Design, supported my application for funds which enabled me to take a period of sabbatical leave to complete the manuscript. In the latter stages of my research, Ken Taylor at the Cadbury Limited Archives and Fiona Tait and the staff at the Birmingham Central Reference Library Archives helped me to locate, and relocate, important material. (Fiona Tait had responsibility for the transfer and cataloguing of the vast body of archival material from the Bournville Village Trust which is now in the keeping of the professional archivists at Birmingham Central Reference Library.) The late Gordon Cherry, a key figure in the world of planning history and the first non-Cadbury Chairman of the Bournville Village Trust, gave me much encouragement over the years.

At home, Sandra, Tom, Ruth and John have patiently put up with my preoccupation with Bournville. They too have been supportive, and Tom helped me when I had problems with the computer. My colleagues, Ruth Levy and Alice Crompton, have also offered me technical assistance.

This book is better for the help I have received from those mentioned here (and from colleagues at U.C.E. and members of the International Planning History Society); they bear no responsibility for any of its shortcomings.

INTRODUCTION

'Birmingham's townscape is still a matter of bits and pieces', Gordon Cherry wrote in one of his last books. 'Its main pleasures lie in the suburbs.'[1] This is a study of one of the city's 'environmentally privileged' suburbs, Bournville. It seeks to explore the building history of the Estate, its management and its social complexion.

Begun as a 'Model Village' in 1895, Bournville has grown into a large garden suburb. The scheme was started by George Cadbury, but the management of the Estate was handed over to a charitable trust in 1900. At that time there were 313 houses in the village. Since then the development of the Estate has been in the hands of the Bournville Village Trust. The Trustees (the majority of whom have been members of the extended Cadbury family) have carefully watched over the steady growth of the Estate, which now covers 1,000 acres and contains around 7,600 houses. The Bournville Village Trust owns and manages 3,000 acres of farmland and woodland just outside the city's south-west boundary, owns 500 homes in Shropshire, and is increasingly involved in urban regeneration, especially in Birmingham Heartlands, but these aspects of the Trust's work are beyond the scope of this study. This book is solely about the Bournville Estate in south-west Birmingham. Its development will, however, be related to local and national events. The Trustees have always been aware of the wider context, just as those interested in housing and town planning (in Britain and elsewhere) have understood the importance of the Bournville Estate.

Bournville was, and is, renowned for its good quality housing and excellent landscaping. 'The landscape of Bournville, the balance of buildings and open spaces, the presence of trees, grassed areas and hedges', it has been rightly claimed, 'these are the features of the Estate that distinguish Bournville from other suburbs.'[2] The Trustees have repeatedly emphasised that Bournville was more than just an exercise in housebuilding and site planning; it was also a community building scheme. In the early days of the Estate there was a commitment to social mix and a desire to provide communal facilities. In recent decades the Trustees have reaffirmed their willingness 'to provide support to establish and maintain communities'.[3]

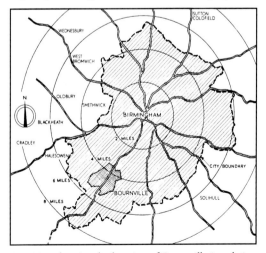

1 Map showing the location of Bournville in relation to Birmingham and surrounding towns.

The development of the Estate has taken place over more than one hundred years, but the basic aims of the Trust remain broadly similar to those established by George Cadbury in 1900. 'The same strands of policy and ideals', it was stated in 1986, 'are pursued by today's Trustees.'[4] If the ends have remained broadly the same, the means by which the Trustees sought to achieve them have changed over the years. They have had to respond to the evolving social, economic, political and architectural context in which the Trust operated.

The legislative framework within which the Trust operated has also changed. This has meant, among other things, that the forms of tenure on the Estate have been extended. Initially, Bournville was populated by leaseholders and tenants. Later members of co-partnership tenants societies and public utility societies were welcomed onto the expanding Estate. In recent decades shared ownership schemes and special leasehold agreements have further expanded the range of tenure groups. The 1967 Leasehold Reform Act allowed leaseholders to purchase their freeholds, and 1,466 Bournville residents had done so by 1993.[5] A Scheme of Management was introduced in 1972 to allow the Trust to preserve the amenity of the Estate.

The ways in which the Estate was financed and developed have changed over the years. In the first instance, various members of the Cadbury family and other individuals built houses on long leases. After the formation of the Bournville Village Trust in 1900, the emphasis was on building houses for rent, although individuals were allowed to build properties on 99-year leases. In 1906, Bournville Tenants Limited, a co-partnership society, leased land from the Trust and started to build an estate of 145 houses.

2   George Cadbury (1839-1922).

The 1909 Housing and Town Planning Act made it easier for public utility societies to borrow money and build housing estates. Two such societies, Weoley Hill Limited and the Woodlands Housing Society Limited, played an important part in the development of the Estate in the inter-war years. Cadbury Brothers Limited made a more obvious contribution to the expansion of the Estate at this time. They funded a post-war housing experiment aimed at investigating the effectiveness of different building materials, paid for the construction of some houses and bungalows for their workers and ex-employees and supported, through their pension fund, the Bournville Works Housing Society. This society built houses, predominantly for rent, for Cadbury employees and their families. Despite the contribution of the firm to the building of the Estate, it should always be remembered that Bournville was never a factory village housing just Cadbury workers.

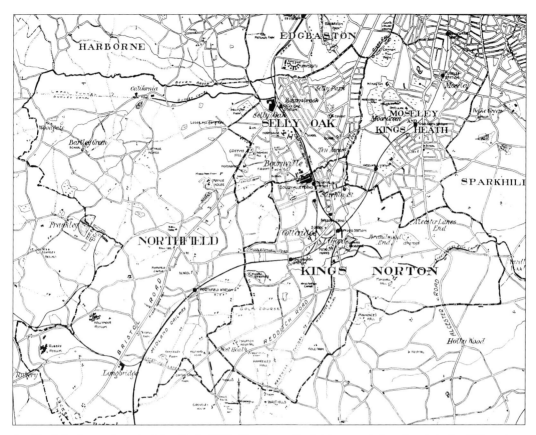

3   Wards in the south west of the City in 1911. The Bournville Estate expanded westwards in the 20th century.

This has become even more obvious since the Second World War. The Bournville Village Trust has received funds from the local authority and the Housing Corporation to build and modernise rented properties. The receipt of public money has meant that an increasing number of tenants have been Council nominees, whilst the Trust has been required to select tenants according to housing need. Charitable and non-charitable housing societies have constructed various forms of accommodation on the Estate. A significant contribution to the development of the Estate was made by self-build groups in the 1950s and 1960s. Private builders have also leased plots from the Trust and built houses for sale. In exceptional circumstances, land has been sold to developers. Much of the Trust's income from rents goes on the maintenance of the Estate, so for new developments in recent years it has sometimes borrowed money from commercial banks to finance its own schemes (a pattern encouraged by Conservative governments).

Just as the means of developing the Estate have been varied, so, to a lesser extent, has the housing and landscaping. The housing stock at Bournville has altered over the years, as the Trust and other providers sought to meet the changing needs of the local population. Bungalows and flats had been built for the retired and single female workers before 1939. After 1945 an increasing number of maisonettes and flats were built on the Estate. Housing densities had to increase in this period too. From the earliest days provision has been made for groups with special needs, especially the elderly.

The perceived needs of various groups, and the ways in which they have been met, have altered over the years. Standards and styles have changed since the 1890s. The earliest cottages on the Estate were rather self-consciously varied. Later dwellings were often simpler, with economy triumphing over art. Because the Trust's architects (who have designed the vast majority of the dwellings on the Estate) have largely clung to traditional designs and used mainly brick and tile there is a greater degree of coherence at Bournville than one finds in other areas developed over such a long period. The visual impact of even the most austere post-war dwellings has been softened, in the vast majority of cases, by careful landscaping. Even here there have been changes, as large native trees have frequently been replaced by smaller flowering varieties.

The Trust has always prided itself on providing practical examples for others to follow. The original Village was seen as an exemplary scheme. It is clear that a considerable number of developers followed the Bournville lead, and some admitted that they had been directly influenced by the Model Village. Although the impact of later developments at Bournville has been less obvious, the Trustees have continued to sponsor practical experiments (in landscaping, building, furnishing and energy conservation) as well as research in the fields of housing, town planning and landscaping. The results of much of this work have been published and have thus encouraged good practice elsewhere. Some of their best-known publications, such as *When we build again* (1941), were significant contributions to ongoing debates about the shape of urban Britain.[6]

Of course, parts of the Bournville story are reasonably well-known, but no full-scale study of the Estate has been published since the 1950s.[7] General histories of British planning inevitably mention this important development, but most just concentrate on the early pioneering days before the First World War.[8] Although the comments made in such works can be perceptive, they are inevitably brief.[9] The best and fullest accounts of the early history of the Estate are to be found in two unpublished theses by Michael Durman and Joel Hoffmann.[10] Both are well-researched and offer new perspectives on the early history of Bournville. A number of recent articles and studies add a little to our knowledge of the history of the Estate and its background and offer new insights and suggest lines of approach.[11]

Most of these accounts of Bournville concentrate on the early history of the Estate. Few studies of Bournville explore the inter-war years, and still fewer mention the post-war period.[12] This study seeks to provide a full, thoroughly researched and well-illustrated history of the Estate from 1895 through to 1998. This work is based on the very large collection of material belonging to the Bournville Village Trust (most of whose records have now been deposited in the Archives at Birmingham Central Reference Library).[13] This extensive collection includes books, pamphlets, minute books, reports, plans and photographs relating to the Bournville Village Trust and other societies operating on the Estate. A certain amount of archival material relating to the history of Bournville can be found elsewhere.[14] Specialist journals, newspapers and surveys offer a different perspective on the Estate. Yearbooks, the published reports of Bournville's community groups and local newsletters can provide useful information on the activities and concerns of the residents. Reminiscences, whether published or recorded on tape, can be revealing. Those memories should, however, be tested against other sources, but they contribute to a study which seeks to gauge the residents' responses to Bournville.[15]

Bournville Village Trust is one of the oldest and best-known housing trusts. It is an organisation that is aware of its own traditions. Significantly, most of the Estate's residents are aware of them too. This means that many of them have taken on board the ethos of the place and effectively help to 'police' it. Communal values may be strong on the Estate, but they are not immune to change. 'It is the Trustees' constant endeavour to see that old traditions are used not as a handcuff to the past', the Trust's Chief Executive explained in 1986, 'but as a handrail to the future.'[16] There have been occasions throughout the history of the Estate when new developments, or policies, have been resisted. The tension has not just been between the residents and the Trust. Occasional signs of conflict between neighbours, between established residents and 'newcomers', and between generations have been noted.

At the beginning of the 20th century Bournville was characterised as 'the modern Utopia'.[17] By the middle decades of the century Bournville was no longer regarded as 'a unique experiment'.[18] Despite the growing legislative constraints under which they worked, the Trustees have continued to encourage the planning of pleasant residential areas with good landscaping and plenty of open spaces. They also remain committed to their social role: 'The aim of the Trust is to provide houses in a balanced community to improve the housing conditions of those in housing need regardless of race, colour, religion or politics.'[19]

Bournville may no longer be regarded as 'Utopia in practice', but it is still a pleasant and popular suburb; one which can be studied with profit for its past successes and its more recent experiments.

The emerging town planning movement in Britain can be characterised as a reactive development. The motives of its theorists and practitioners were often complex. 'A planned environment', Helen Meller recently reminded us, 'is an indication of the social values of the planners and the society in which they work.'[20] The particular schemes put forward as solutions to the late Victorian housing crisis owed much to the distinctive nature of the local problems the reformers faced and sought to counter. This study, therefore, begins with a brief review of the Birmingham scene and the cultural context in which George Cadbury grew up and from which he emerged to develop the family business and build a model village. The following chapters are arranged broadly in chronological order. The first section deals with the growth of Bournville up to 1914. This is followed by a study of the Estate in the inter-war period. The penultimate sections cover the post-war decades and the final part deals with the period since 1979. Throughout attention will be paid to the national framework and the local context. The development of the Bournville Estate will be assessed against this background. The Trust's policies will be reviewed, the buildings and site planning of the Estate will be assessed, and social and communal trends will be identified.

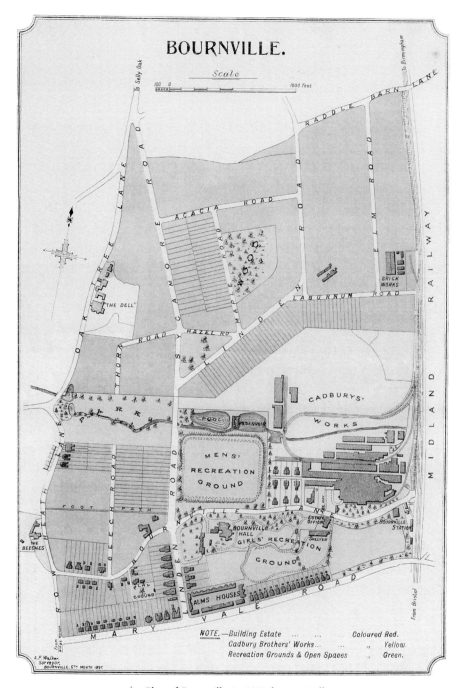

4 Plan of Bournville in 1897 by A.P. Walker.

Town planning was once described as 'a continuous and positive attempt to shape the urban environment and provide for community needs'.[21] Within the confines of the Bournville Estate, this is precisely what George Cadbury and his fellow Trustees attempted to do.

Chapter One

THE BIRMINGHAM BACKGROUND

From Saxon Hamlet to 'City of a Thousand Trades'

Birmingham grew from insignificant beginnings to become the Second City of Great Britain.[1] It began life as an obscure Saxon hamlet. Situated in an impoverished area of low productivity, Birmingham and the surrounding region was of little importance at the time of the Domesday Survey in 1086. By the 14th century, however, Birmingham had become the most populous and prosperous place in the district, but it was still overshadowed by Warwick, Stratford and Coventry. Birmingham's modest success was largely due to the efforts of the lords of the manor, the de Birmingham family, in getting market rights in the mid-12th century and the right to hold an annual fair a century later. Increased trade led to Birmingham being viewed as 'a good market toune' by Leland in the second quarter of the 16th century. Besides the cloth and leather workers, there were 'smiths and cutlers' and 'lorimers' and 'naylors' in the town at this time.[2] By the 1580s Birmingham was said to be 'swarming with inhabitants and echoing with the noise of anvils'.[3]

Birmingham's population grew further during the 17th century, reaching almost 5,500 at the Restoration and expanding more rapidly thereafter. It profited from its position as 'the natural gateway to the South Staffordshire coalfield' and the development of the gun trade.[4] Birmingham continued to expand even more rapidly in the early 18th century. Although textiles and tanning remained important, Birmingham was becoming a significant metal-working centre. The late 18th and early 19th centuries saw the development of a number of specialist trades in the town: gun making, button making, silversmithing and jewellery, and the brass trade. The raw material for most of these trades lay close at hand in the Black Country. Turnpike roads and canals (from 1769) provided the means of communication. Banking facilities were available locally and thus helped to facilitate the industrial development of the area. The town also benefited from its lack of trade restrictions, its religious tolerance and its acceptance of immigrants. While allowing for these factors, historians tend to explain Birmingham's industrial growth in terms of human factors: they stress the industry, inventiveness and entrepreneurship of the people of the town.[5]

In the last quarter of the 18th century Birmingham became the third largest town in England and Wales; only London and Bristol were more populous. Birmingham's population had tripled in the half-century before 1801, from an estimated 23,600 in 1750 to 73,670 at the time of the first census. The growth rate continued in the early 19th century as Birmingham underwent an urban explosion, its population reaching 182,922 by 1841. Well before this date Arthur Young had called Birmingham 'the first manufacturing town in the world'. Others were to characterise the town as 'the workshop of the world' or 'the city of a 1000 trades'.[6]

These events had a significant impact on the built environment and social and political relations within Birmingham. As a centre of workshop production, Birmingham had few 'dark satanic mills' or palatial warehouses like Manchester.[7] Workshops and small factory units, intermingled with working-class dwellings, were the norm. The relative ease with which a worker could start up a business and the close contact between employer and worker in the small workshops, helps to explain the more amicable relations between the classes in Birmingham than elsewhere. Although there were disturbances and moments of unease in Birmingham in the late 18th and early 19th centuries, Hopkins has concluded that 'the stereotyped picture of Birmingham as a scene of class co-operation rather than class conflict seems to be substantially accurate'.[8] Such a state was no doubt reinforced by the commitment of sections of the working classes to the ideals of self-reliance and respectability that were so much admired by the middle classes. Birmingham was a centre of working-class self-help, and many friendly societies, savings institutions and building societies were found there.[9] The viability of such institutions was underpinned by the reasonable earnings of Birmingham's skilled artisans and the diversified and flexible nature of the local economy which made it better able to withstand trade fluctuations.

Although a substantial town by 1801, Birmingham still had the administration of a rural parish. From 1768 Town (or Street) Commissioners were appointed with powers to levy a rate for the cleansing and lighting of the streets of the manor, the regulation of traffic, the removal of obstructions and control of the markets. Subsequent local Acts of Parliament widened their powers, but these were never sufficient to ensure the orderly and healthy development of the town. Birmingham did not become a corporate borough until 1838, and the Town Council did not take over the powers of the oligarchic Street Commissioners until 1851.[10] By that date the population of the borough was 232,841.

Given the almost total absence of planning legislation and environmental controls, Birmingham's physical growth was largely the result of market forces and the cumulative actions of numerous landlords, developers and builders. In only a few cases did landlords establish clear guidelines and tight controls over developments on their land. Even then, they were as dependent on market forces as much as the lie of the land and the direction of the prevailing winds for the success or failure of their schemes. For every successful exclusive estate, like that at Edgbaston, there were schemes, like that at Ashted, which quickly deteriorated, despite the aims of its promoters. There were few attempts to control the numerous speculative builders who constructed the many small dwellings built at high densities on virtually every piece of spare ground in the rapidly expanding districts around the centre of Birmingham.[11]

At mid-century, small workshops still outnumbered factories employing large numbers of workers and using steam power. Guns, jewellery, buttons and brass products remained important to the local economy, but as the century progressed industrial output diversified. Allen and others have identified a shift away from hardware to engineering.[12] The newer industries included electro-plating, chemicals, bedsteads, plate glass, steel pens, screws, hydraulic machinery and railway rolling stock. In 1870 *Kelly's Directory* listed 953 types of firm in Birmingham.[13]

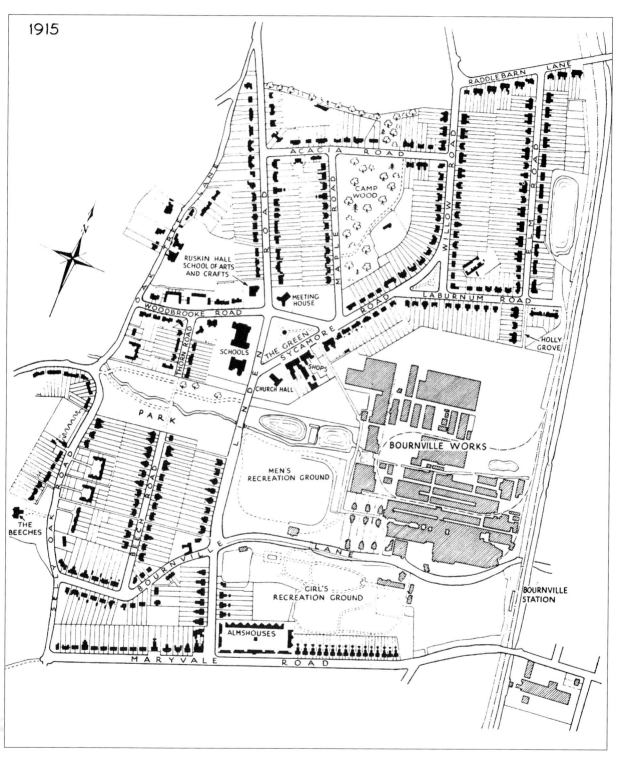

5 Bournville in 1915.

By the last quarter of the 19th century it was clear that the spatial pattern of Birmingham was beginning to change. New industries, often based in larger factories, began to emerge. More frequently than not, they occupied peripheral sites, where there was room for expansion and land was cheaper. Machine tool and engineering firms began to challenge the dominance of the hardware trades, and even newer products like cycles, cars and electrical apparatus started to be manufactured in the city. Other products, not hitherto closely associated with the city, such as rubber, food and drink were becoming more significant. The local firms of Dunlop and Cadbury, for example, were to become household names.[14]

The signs of peripheral growth were clear. There was expansion towards the north west beyond Ladywood, along the banks of the Birmingham Canal. To the south east, alongside the canal and the railway, the districts of Small Heath, Greet and Hay Mills were expanding. (At the latter place, James Horsfall built a church, a school and houses alongside his works.) Large industrial units were constructed in the Tame Valley (including the G.E.C. factory at Witton) and in the Rea Valley, where the gas works and carriage works of Nechells and Saltley were prominent examples of industrial decentralisation. In the south west of the city, businesses were attracted to sites at Stirchley, Selly Oak and Kings Norton alongside the canal and railway. The opening of the Birmingham West Suburban Railway in 1876 helped to stimulate the development of this area. A few firms had already settled in this district before the Cadbury Brothers moved to Bournville in 1879.[15]

Equally important was Birmingham's emergence as a regional commercial and retailing centre, 'the market place of the Midlands'.[16] A commercial district emerged around Colmore Row, which was redeveloped in the 1860s. The building of the Council House from 1874 (and the municipal Gas Offices and Art Gallery a decade later) added further to the architectural distinction of Colmore Row and provided a monument to the 'Civic Gospel' which brought many of Birmingham's leading manufacturers (including George Cadbury) onto the Town Council. This ushered in a period of 'municipal socialism' (or, more accurately, municipal capitalism) when the Council, led by Joseph Chamberlain, took over the supply of water and gas, and pushed through other far-reaching reforms. The most significant of these was the Birmingham Improvement Scheme which resulted in the creation of that great central 'boulevard', Corporation Street. Using slum clearance legislation, the Council drove a great thoroughfare through the heart of the city to provide much needed sites for the town's expanding retail and service sector.[17] Unfortunately, the City Council was averse to building dwellings for those displaced, and the land was too expensive for private builders to consider erecting working-class houses on such central sites.

Whilst the richer citizens of Birmingham continued to live in their suburban villas and large detached houses, the pattern of housing of the skilled artisans and the ever-increasing lower middle class changed. The introduction in Birmingham of new building bye-laws in 1876 brought an end to the building of back-to-backs and led to the creation of the bye-law terrace. Birmingham's suburbs expanded rapidly in the late 19th and early 20th centuries. Some of these new residential (and industrial) areas were served by trams and, to a lesser extent, by suburban railways. Gradually, these districts began to develop a character of their own, for there were subtle but important differences between the new suburbs.

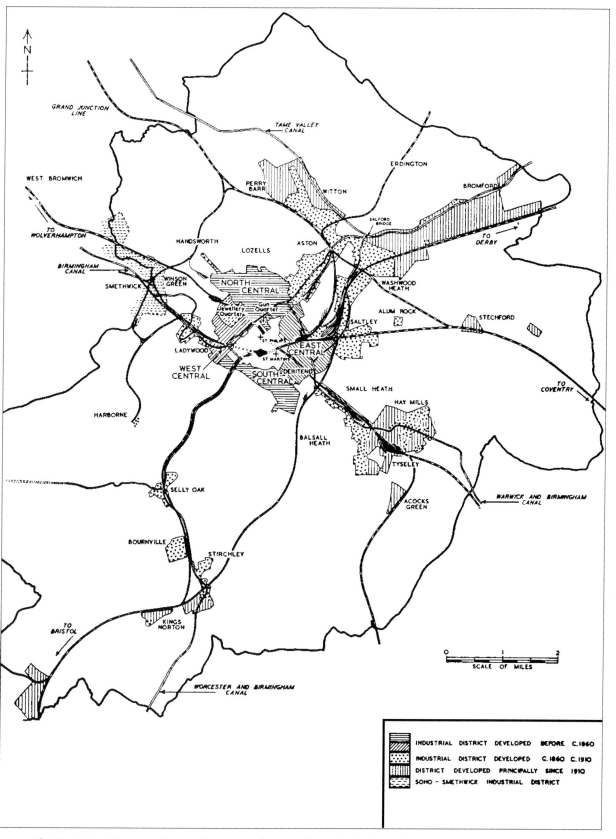

6 The industrial pattern of Birmingham, 1950. The areas of peripheral industrial expansion are apparent on this map.

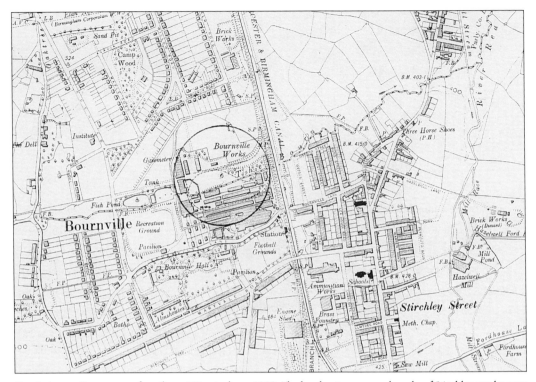

7   Ordnance Survey map of south-west Birmingham, 1902. The bye-law terraces and works of Stirchley can be seen on the other side of the canal and railway line from Bournville.

As these new industrial and residential suburbs began to engulf, or threaten the calm of, previously exclusive suburbs, such as Edgbaston, some of the city's more affluent citizens began to move to more distant semi-rural retreats. Some developments, for example, at Four Oaks and Barnt Green, where the houses were designed by Birmingham's leading Arts and Crafts architects, could be architecturally distinguished, but they further contributed to the social segregation within the district.[18]

By 1881, Birmingham's population had risen to 400,774. The population of the central wards had begun to fall and the distribution of the population bore less and less relationship to the administrative boundaries of the area. Between 1891 and 1911 significant boundary extensions took place. As a consequence of these changes, Birmingham took control of an area three times the size of Glasgow and twice the size of Manchester and Liverpool. By 1911 the population of 'Greater Birmingham' stood at about 840,000 and its area was approximately 43,600 acres.[19] This opened up the prospect of more building land becoming available on the fringes of the city. Far-sighted and thoughtful promoters, such as George Cadbury and the Bournville Village Trust, were by that time setting new standards of suburban estate development. The Model Village of Bournville was seen as a more attractive alternative to the slums and bye-law terraces of Birmingham.[20]

Chapter Two

THE HOUSING PROBLEM

Birmingham grew most rapidly at a time when most gave little thought to the development of the town. Local government was undeveloped and, in an age when *laissez-faire* ideas were dominant, controls were few. Consequently, the town, for the most part, grew in an unregulated, haphazard and piecemeal way.

The rapidly expanding working-class population of late 18th- and early 19th-century Birmingham had to be housed. Very few industrialists built houses for their workers, except where there was a need to attract skilled labour to isolated works. As elsewhere, it was the speculative developers and small-scale builders who responded to the demand for accommodation, and built town houses and suburban villas for the few, and cheap, low-rise dwellings at high density for the many. The low earnings of large sections of the urban working classes ensured that they could only afford a minimal form of dwelling. This varied from one part of Britain to another. In Birmingham, the back-to-back became the most common type of working-class house.

8 Congested districts in the older parts of the city, showing the admixture of industry and housing and the presence of many back-to-back houses. *When we Build Again*, 1941.

Back-to-back and Courtyard Dwellings

Availability of land was not a problem in Birmingham; builders took up land on infill sites in the town centre and on peripheral estates, released for development from the mid-18th century.[1] By 1796 more than one-third of the houses in Birmingham were described as 'back' houses.[2] Chapman sees this as the period in which the pattern for courtyard development was established:

> The lining of yards with workmen's cottages seems to have been more highly developed than elsewhere, and is most readily identifiable as the source of the proliferation of tiny courts of blind back houses that became so common in Birmingham.[3]

A group of local doctors reported in 1836 that there were 2,030 courts, containing 12,254 tenements, in the manor of Birmingham.[4] Another official report, five years later, provides a clear picture of these courtyard dwellings:

> The courts vary in the number of houses which they contain from 4 to 20, and most of these houses are three stories high and built back-to-back. There is a wash house, an ash pit and a privy at the end, or one side of the court, and not infrequently one or more pigsties or heaps of manure.[5]

Three-roomed houses were to become 'a striking feature of working class housing in Birmingham'.[6] The great bulk of these were also built back-to-back. The prevalent type was a three-storey house which consisted of an all-purpose living room/kitchen on the ground floor, with a bedroom on each of the floors above. A two-storey variation included a ground-floor living room/kitchen with two bedrooms on the floor above. The four-roomed tenement ('two up and two down') was much less common in Birmingham than in the textile towns of the north of England.

9   *Left*. A courtyard containing workshops and back-to-back houses.

10   *Below*. A street of three-storey back-to-back dwellings.

Back-to-back dwellings, the bugbear of later reformers, housed perhaps two-thirds of Birmingham's population in the mid-19th century.[7] The prevalence of the three-roomed type can be gauged from the fact that as late as 1908 nearly thirty per cent of the population of the city still lived in this type of dwelling.[8] A year later national legislation was finally introduced to ban the back-to-back, although many towns had independently taken this step much earlier, Manchester in 1844 and Birmingham in 1876.

Building and Freehold Land Societies

Whilst most working-class housing was the result of the actions of speculative developers and small-scale builders seeking to make a profit, it has been calculated that in Birmingham one in ten of the houses built in the 1780s was provided by terminating building societies.[9] Chapman concluded that the local societies 'catered only for the artisan elite and the middle classes'.[10]

The 1832 Reform Act, which gave the vote to 40-shilling freeholders, stimulated another attempt to promote home ownership. Drawing on the local tradition of class co-operation, the Freehold Land Society was set up to create 'Freeholds for the People' and 'county votes for Working Men'. They built small estates of houses in Aston, Lozells and Perry Barr in the period through to the 1860s.[11] Given that the weekly subscriptions ranged from 5s. 2d. to 15s. 6d., one must agree with Chapman that 'those who benefited from the Freehold Land Society were hardly working class'.[12]

One interesting aspect of their work was that covenants were introduced into the building agreements to ensure that 'no back or small dwelling house' or 'any workshop ... any beerhouse [or] public house' be constructed on their sites. The distance from the footpath to the houses and the price of the properties (from £160 to £400) was also specified in the Freehold Land Society scheme at Aston Park in the 1850s. Chapman concluded that the achievement of the Freehold Land Society in their Aston scheme was, besides increasing the number of voters, 'to set a superior standard of housing, and because they had been able to buy land at bargain prices, to obtain this better quality at a lower price.'[13] The use of covenants to control estate development was a key element in the management of the Calthorpe Estate at Edgbaston and was to be a feature of the Bournville Estate at the turn of the century.

Health and Housing

The overall consensus was that the housing of the working classes in Birmingham was better than in most other large towns. Its back-to-back houses were regarded as being superior to the overcrowded tenements of Glasgow or the cellar dwellings of Liverpool and Manchester:

> The great town of Birmingham ... appears to form a rather favourable contrast, in several particulars, with the state of other large towns ... the general custom of each family living in separate dwellings is conducive to comfort and cleanliness, and the good site of the town, and the dry absorbive nature of the soil, are very great natural advantages.[14]

The report submitted to Edwin Chadwick by a group of local doctors did, however, identify a few blackspots. Lodging houses were, in particular, condemned. They were said to 'abound' in Birmingham, and nearly all were in a 'filthy condition'. Reflecting the moral as well as the physical concerns of most commentators in the 19th century, the local physicians claimed that the lodging houses were full of 'the most abandoned characters'.

Undoubtedly, the lodging houses and central courts represented the worst of Birmingham's housing stock. When the town was still relatively small in extent, the working classes could still walk out into the country, or even tend an allotment. Robert Rawlinson had been impressed by the number he found in the area in 1849. As the town grew, however, these 'guinea gardens' were swallowed up by builders. Bunce recorded in 1878 that they had 'almost been swept away by the extension of the town'.[15] Until the 1870s, there was little in the way of park provision to compensate for the loss of these allotments, as the City Council was committed to a policy of 'negative parsimony'.[16]

'Sanitary evils' were to be found in early Victorian Birmingham, but some contemporaries suggested that the houses there were being built 'on an improved plan'.[17] Individual houses may have become a little more spacious, but the layout of those houses changed little before the 1870s. When the inner suburbs of Lozells, Ladywood, Newtown, Duddeston, Nechells, Highgate and other working-class districts were built up in the mid-Victorian period, the layout, as Chapman and Bartlett have shown, 'preserved the familiar traditions of the workshop courts'.[18] The typical pattern produced was one of long terraces with 'front houses' built back-to-back with tunnel entries to numbered courts, each containing six to eight houses.[19]

'Slum-Land'

Some of the worst houses in the city centre were demolished to make way for new railway stations and the Corporation Street development. Some were sceptical about the impact of such 'improvements'. As Rev. Michael Hill explained:

> The progress of improvement in the town was letting in light and air into quarters which had been hotbeds of disease and crime; but the classes were not improved—they were merely displaced to other localities which had hitherto enjoyed a more healthy reputation.[20]

Many overcrowded and insanitary houses were thus to be found in the surrounding districts. These houses were known to local clergymen, campaigning reporters and Quaker Adult School teachers (for example, Councillor William White and George Cadbury). There were a number of local figures who drew attention to the housing problem in the city. Rev. T.J. Bass highlighted the problems of the 'East End' of Birmingham and, in particular, the poor and run down parish of St Laurence. His work complemented that of a local journalist, J. Cuming Walters, whose 'Scenes in Slum-Land' were published in the *Birmingham Daily Gazette*.

Walters wrote graphically about 'the poorest class of decrepit and frowning houses and unlit courts'.[21] He was especially concerned about the 'contamination' that resulted from 'the unavoidable mixing of the respectable poor with the criminal classes'. He recognised the need of the poor to live near to their place of work. He believed that 'the advocacy of self-contained suburban dwellings, though excellent for the artisan, is mere idealism in regard to the humbler classes'. His 'Scenes in Slum-Land' were published as 'a protest against apathy in the past and an appeal for greater municipal activity in the future'. Walters drew attention to the low number of tenements provided by Birmingham Corporation compared with Manchester and Liverpool.[22]

The Municipal Response

The campaign that followed Walters' revelations resulted in a change in the political complexion of the Council and some administrative restructuring. A new Housing Committee, under the chairmanship of John Sutton Nettlefold, was set up. Mayne has shown that the Council's supposedly revitalised housing policy was merely a restatement of the old belief in private builders and the piecemeal improvement of slum properties.

The Council continued to put its faith in private enterprise and the movement of the population to the suburbs. They believed that, as the better paid artisans moved to the suburbs, a filtering up process would follow:

> The empty houses they have left will be filled by those who now inhabit the lower grades of dwellings, each class will have moved one step up and the worst properties will be unlettable. Then it will be possible to bring about a gradual reconstruction of the old city on better lines.[23]

Unfortunately, by 1914 there was a house famine. 'No new houses were being provided for the very poor', it was reported, 'and not enough for the better off.' By this time critics of the Unionist and Conservative-led Council were claiming that Birmingham had 'one of the worst names with regard to slums among the cities of this country'.[24] The 1914 Housing Inquiry revealed that there were no less than 43,366 back-to-back dwellings in the city, and that 27,518 were situated in courtyards. Furthermore 40,020 of the city's houses had no water supply inside the dwelling and 55,028 had no separate w.c. Well might they conclude that 'a large proportion of the poor in Birmingham are living under conditions which are detrimental both to their health and their morals'.[25]

Whilst recognising the magnitude of the problem, the Council remained unwilling to contemplate either large-scale municipal housing projects or the Garden City model. Influenced by 'the example of Germany', the Council came out in favour of town extension planning and municipal land purchase in 1906. Nettlefold claimed that if councils could buy up suburban land they could control development and encourage either public utility societies or private contractors to build on carefully zoned plots.[26]

Nettlefold's lead in this area was followed by Neville Chamberlain and by George Cadbury Jnr., both of whom were on the Special Housing Inquiry Committee in 1914 which concluded:

> The Committee consider the best way of aiding the resumption [of building in the suburbs] is for the Council to purchase estates in the undeveloped areas, and, after developing them by constructing roads, laying sewers and mains, and providing easy access, to let off the building plots to public utility societies and builders, imposing suitable restrictions on ground rents.[27]

The bye-law suburb

Birmingham Corporation had, by late 19th century, become aware of the need for some environmental controls. The introduction of new building bye-laws in 1876 not only brought a ban on back-to-back housing but also resulted in a new type of urban landscape—the bye-law terrace with its 'tunnel back houses'. Long rows of seemingly uniform terraces, with tunnel access to the rear of these 'through' houses, were an ubiquitous feature of the late Victorian and Edwardian townscape. They filled an arc of territory from Perry Barr in the north of the city to Selly Oak in the south west. More isolated developments along these lines were also to be found at Yardley and Kings Heath.[28]

The outer parts of Birmingham came to be covered with long, straight streets (sometimes built regardless of the lie of the land). Most contained five-roomed houses, with a sitting room, kitchen and scullery on the ground floor and three bedrooms above, one each over the two living rooms and a smaller one over the scullery. Narrow rear gardens were the norm in these developments.

A 1908 Board of Trade Enquiry indicated that the rents of five-roomed properties in Birmingham at that time varied according to the age, situation and type of house (as well as the character of the area). The newer five-roomed houses in the outer districts of the city were let at from 5s. 9d. upwards, with the

11 Late 19th-century bye-law housing laid out in long, straight terraces. Housing reformers complained about the monotony of these developments and disliked the back projections of these tunnel-backed dwellings.

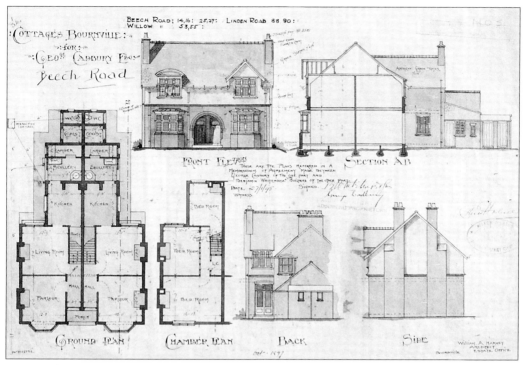

12 14-16 Beech Road, Bournville, was designed by W.A. Harvey in the late 1890s. Although having long back projections typical of Birmingham tunnel-back dwellings, the façade was treated in a simpler and freer manner.

majority at 6s. 6d. inclusive of rates. The rent for 'superior' five-roomed houses possessing an entrance passage and larger rooms was about 7s. 6d. Houses of this type with a bathroom let at up to 8s. 6d., and were said to be occupied by 'clerks, foremen, insurance agents, shop assistants, etc.' Clearly, these houses were beyond the means of the poor earning £1 per week or less. They were more likely to be found living in the three-roomed back-to-back properties paying rents of between 3s. 6d. and 5s., with the cheaper properties being found in the courts and the more expensive facing the street.[29]

Suburbs and slums

Local commentators and government officials noted the tendency to migrate to the suburbs of Birmingham. 'Natural desires for healthier conditions', it was suggested, 'are already drawing a large proportion of the population out of the central areas into the outlying suburbs.'[30] The City Council's own housing survey in 1914 not only identified a desire for a healthier environment; it also noted a growing interest in gardening amongst the city's artisans:

> The artisan of today desires to bring up his family in a fresher atmosphere and amid more attractive surroundings than are to be found in the heart of the city. He likes to indulge the taste for gardening which is becoming general among his class, and which often adds to his income as well as his enjoyment.[31]

There was, however, a growing recognition that there was 'a large class of workmen who cannot afford, in many cases, to move into the more healthful conditions in the suburbs'.[32] They remained trapped in the overcrowded central districts—trapped by poverty and the need to be near their places of work. This was clearly expressed by one woman to J. Cuming Walters in 1901:

> Why don't I leave? Because I can't get a house any better near to my husband's work, or near the school the children go to. We've got no choice. We're obliged to take the houses we can afford.[33]

Such families existed in districts of the city where there were the worst housing, the poorest sanitary facilities and the greatest amount of pollution. Not surprisingly, death rates were higher than in the suburbs.

Many felt the new suburbs to be a healthier and socially superior alternative to the slum (which was regarded as morally and physically repugnant).[34] Reformers, such as George Cadbury, were also coming to regard the ugly and monotonous bye-law streets as the potential slums of the future. They looked to town planning 'to save the country from being built over with closely packed masses of houses which in future may develop into slums'.[35] More careful control of the future development of the towns of Britain would allow for lower density layouts, and more health-giving light and air.

The village and cottage ideal

Those who wanted to get 'back to the land' saw the bye-law suburb as a travesty. They believed rapacious builders and developers were still producing an atmosphere of dull monotony lacking in natural beauty or the picturesqueness of the pre-industrial village.[36] They extolled the benefits of nature and advocated cottage homes, based on the English vernacular. 'The majority of men would accept Mr. Ruskin's ideal of a house ...' Raymond Unwin argued, 'a cottage all of our own, with its little garden, its healthy air, its clean kitchen, parlour and bedrooms.'[37]

Arts and Crafts architects had helped bring about 'the revival of domestic architecture'.[38] Whilst much of the pioneering work in the domestic field had been on small country houses, there were those who believed that the lessons learned there could, and should, be applied to working-class cottages. The task was not an easy one. 'To design a comfortable and beautiful house for a limited sum of money', M.H. Baillie-Scott later wrote, 'is perhaps one of the most difficult problems the modern architect has to solve. It is also one of the most important—for the housing question as applied to the great majority of the people is still a question which remains unanswered in an intelligent way.'[39] The challenge was to be taken up by architects like W.A. Harvey at Bournville and Parker and Unwin at New Earswick, Letchworth and Hampstead Garden Suburb.[40]

Cottage homes not only had a strong visual appeal, they also symbolised the desire among reformers to create organic (but still hierarchical) communities to replace the segregated settlements of industrial Britain.[41] The village and its cottages (lovingly portrayed by Helen Allingham and Kate Greenaway) came to be seen as an antidote to the segregated and slum-ridden city.

The aesthetic reaction against the squalor of the cities was reinforced by a more general belief in the power of nature to soothe and heal, and a feeling that the separation of the classes was harmful.

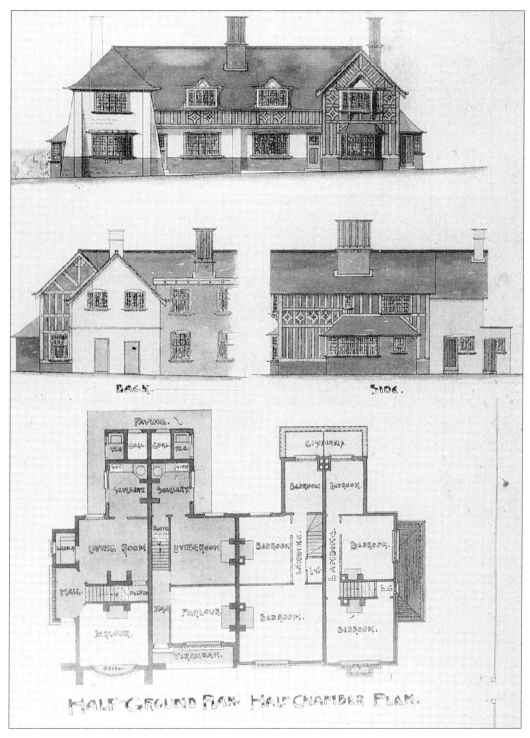

13 A picturesque group in Holly Grove designed by W.A. Harvey in 1900. This block, with its half-timbering and elaborate chimney stacks, is one of the most appealing evocations of the cottage ideal.

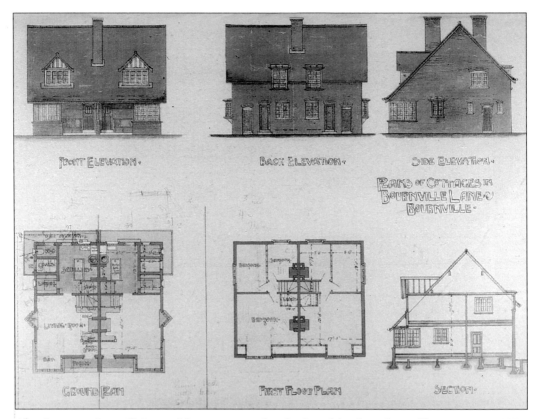

14   Cottages on Bournville Lane with low sweeping roofs and inglenook fireplaces designed by W.A. Harvey in 1901.

Social integration, whether in university settlements or in model villages, was seen as a means of achieving social peace and social improvement.[42] The potential health benefits of such communities were also widely touted at a time of great concern about the challenges to Britain's military and economic supremacy. These fears were heightened by the growing number of reports about the degeneration of the urban population from the 1860s onwards. These fears came to a head in the early years of the 20th century, in the wake of revelations about the poor physical state of those seeking to enlist in the army during the Boer War.[43] Even the Quaker pacifist George Cadbury was worried about 'the diminution in the size and lack of physique in our town workers'. He believed it was his patriotic duty to raise the physique of the nation. He believed, however, that model villages and garden cities were a better way of achieving that aim than national military service.[44]

Chapter Three

FRIENDS, PHILANTHROPISTS AND BUSINESSMEN

Quakers

Birmingham did not become a corporate borough until 1838. Historians have suggested that this was one of the reasons not only for the town's industrial success but also its religious freedom. A small but significant group of Quakers played an important part in the development of Birmingham from the late 18th century. Among the town's leading Friends were the Lloyds, the Galtons, Joseph Sturge, William White and, later, the Tangyes. There was already a welcoming group of Quakers, based at the Bull Street Meeting House, when the Cadburys first moved to Birmingham in 1794.

The scale of the achievements of the Quakers in the fields of business and social welfare, both nationally and locally, was disproportionate to their numbers.[1] What was it that made this numerically insignificant and somewhat isolated group so successful? The isolation of the 'peculiar people' is part of the explanation. Their mode of dress and speech and rigid rules about conduct, marriage and morality contributed to their separateness. Excluded from the armed forces, the universities and politics for many years, 'plain' Friends also frowned on frivolous activities and tended to ignore the arts. Not surprisingly, they turned to business, where their commitment to hard work, self-discipline, frugality and honest dealing stood them in good stead. The fact that they formed a close-knit and inter-related circle of prosperous families also contributed to their success. Advice, introductions and funds were often provided by Friends to their co-religionists.[2]

Like their contemporaries, Quakers did not usually question the pursuit of wealth (although they increasingly began to accept that their businesses should benefit rather than harm people). In many ways, their religious beliefs reinforced the prevalent notions about the work ethic, thrift and self-help.[3] Business success was usually explained in terms of these values. It brought fulfilment, satisfaction and status (in the eyes of man and God). It also brought wealth and power. A key question for many Quakers was how to use this wealth and power.[4]

Quakerism emphasised the potential and value of each individual person and thus encouraged some to undertake a review of the human consequences of capitalism, industrialisation and urban growth by the late 19th century. As a result a number of prominent Quakers became involved in philanthropic works and movements for social, industrial and environmental reform (whilst usually maintaining their commitment to religious activities). This work enabled Quaker reformers to use their wealth in a conscientious manner and fulfilled 'the gospel of duty'.[5]

Victorian social commentators, from Carlyle to Ruskin, were keen to urge their readers to rediscover their souls and their consciences. Carlyle reminded Victorians of their 'duties to serve God and society in [their] rank and calling'.[6] John Ruskin reinforced these ideas and called upon the rich to provide all those things which would promote the physical, mental and moral well-being of the populace. He powerfully reminded contemporaries about the degradation and waste of life in Victorian England. 'There is no wealth but life,' Ruskin proclaimed. 'That man is richest, who, having perfected the functions of his own life to the utmost, has also the widest helpful influence, both personal, and by means of his possessions, over the lives of others.'[7] This message combined well with the increasingly powerful belief in 'practical Christianity' among late Victorian Quakers. It encouraged Friends like George Cadbury and Joseph and Seebohm Rowntree to seek ways of 'combining social progress with commercial success'.[8] They were men who showed astuteness in their business dealings but also displayed a concern for others and a commitment to personal and public service. In the case of George Cadbury these were lessons also learned (by word and deed) from members of his family.

The Cadburys

The Cadbury family came originally from the West Country. It was Richard Tapper Cadbury (1768-1860) who established the Birmingham branch of the family. In partnership with Joseph Rutter, he began trading in 1794 as a silk merchant and linen draper at 92 Bull Street. Richard Tapper Cadbury married Elizabeth Head in 1796. They lived for a time in Old Square and their first three children were born there. In 1800, after Joseph Rutter had returned to London, the family moved to 92 Bull Street. Between 1800 and 1811 another six children were born to Richard and Elizabeth Cadbury. Although they were brought up strictly by their 'plain' Quaker parents, the children seem to have been happy.[9]

In 1812 Richard Tapper Cadbury rented a house for his enlarged family at Islington Row, Edgbaston. It is clear that the children loved to play in the garden and in the open country near the house. Twenty years later, Richard Tapper Cadbury moved to Calthorpe Road, Edgbaston. Once again, the garden, with its flowers and fruit, was a source of joy to the members of the family. The house was often full of visitors and Richard Tapper Cadbury came to be known, among other things, as 'the Earl of Edgbaston'.[10]

As a result of his many contacts with the leading citizens of Birmingham, his reputation for probity, the quality of his products and his effective window displays, Richard Tapper Cadbury's business prospered. He retired at 60, and the business was taken over by his eldest son, Benjamin. In 1824, Richard Tapper Cadbury had helped his third son, John, to set up in business as a tea dealer and coffee roaster at 93 Bull Street (next door to his brother Benjamin). He too attracted some of the best known families in Birmingham.[11]

15 Bull Street in the 1820s, showing the shops of John and Benjamin Cadbury, from a sketch by E. Wallcousins, 1956.

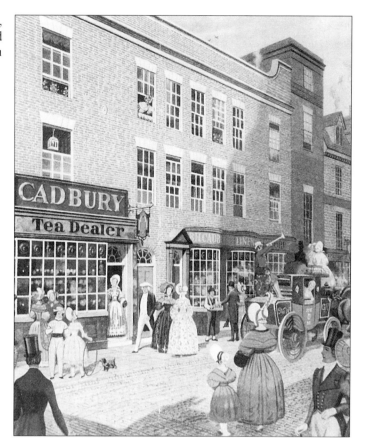

Richard Tapper Cadbury devoted much of his life to religious and public work. He was a devout Friend, and played an active part in the Bull Street Meeting. A member of the Bible Society, he also supported Joseph Sturge's Peace and Anti-Slavery campaigns. He was an advocate of the abolition of capital punishment and leader of the campaign against the employment of climbing boys for sweeping chimneys. A local newspaper later described 'his untiring industry and earnestness in philanthropic movements'.[12] In addition to the support he gave to a wide range of voluntary institutions, Richard Tapper Cadbury served on two important public bodies: he was an Overseer of the Parish of Birmingham and a Street Commissioner. He was Chairman of the Street Commissioners when their powers were handed over to the Council in 1851.[13]

Richard Tapper Cadbury was a widely respected and commanding figure, but not everyone agreed with his views. 'He was dignified, both in speech and action, somewhat dogmatic in manner, and occasionally obstinate in endeavouring to enforce his views;' one commentator noted, 'but his undeviating kindness and unvarying courtesy made him very popular.'[14] He was sometimes called 'King Richard' and 'the Prince of Quakers'. Like later generations of Birmingham Cadburys, his religion seems to have guided his private and his public life. He also sought to balance his business interests with good works and public service.

16   Bridge Street Works from an engraving in the *Bournville Works Magazine*, September 1909.

As his father before him, John Cadbury (1801-1889) not only achieved commercial success; he also became actively involved in the public life of Birmingham. The early prosperity of the tea and coffee business led to further expansion. In 1835 John Cadbury rented a warehouse in Crooked Lane where he experimented in making cocoa and chocolate. In 1847 the property was demolished to make way for a new railway line. After a few months in temporary premises John Cadbury established himself in Bridge Street. In 1849 he handed over the Bull Street business to his nephew, Richard Cadbury Barrow, and began to concentrate on his cocoa and chocolate business. He achieved further success and was awarded the Royal Warrant for his products in 1853.

John's first wife had died, after two years of marriage, in 1828. His marriage to Candia Barrow in 1832 produced six children. At first, they lived at Bull Street, but eventually they settled at 51 Calthorpe Road, Edgbaston, and this remained the family home for 40 years. The house was said to be 'cottage-like', but extra rooms were added as the family expanded. John Cadbury was remembered as 'a fine type of the old Puritan'. He refused to sit in an armchair until he was 70 years old, and there was little in the way of art, literature and music allowed. (A couple of musical boxes and jew's harps seem to have been the only exceptions.) Family life, with its simple pleasures, was not cheerless, though it was circumscribed. Candia Cadbury was a quiet but caring mother. On her death, her husband wrote, 'The duty of a mother she always felt to be most important ... inculcating habits of restraint, and the maintenance of simplicity and plainness in language and attire ... encouraging thoughtfulness and reflection.'[15]

The children were allowed to play in the garden and walk and ride in the surrounding countryside. Maria, John and Candia Cadbury's eldest daughter, remembered these early days:

> House and garden were full of charms, and the children were taught from babyhood to love Nature and all living creatures ... Flowers and fruit, trees and fields, were the rich sources of study and enjoyment for the young folks ... Many were the games we had on the square lawn. The boys played a game on gymnastic poles of various kinds ... The roads round Edgbaston were very country-like then, with rambles across fields, and pools of water where the dogs enjoyed a swim.[16]

This passion for gardening and enthusiasm for nature, picked up in childhood, was to play a significant part in the creation of Bournville.

John Cadbury's religion was not confined to the Meeting House. Prayers were part of family life and were also introduced at the works. A similar pattern of firmness and care seems to have pervaded both places. An 1852 report on the Bridge Street works clearly establishes the system employed:

> The score or more girls, who work under the superintendence of a forewoman, are all dressed in clean Holland pinafores—an industrial uniform ... No girl is employed who is not of known good character ... The men employed exhibit the good effects of proper management not less than the girls. Some have acquired a steady habit of saving, and with nearly all, from the mere force of example, teetotalism is the rule ... Factories conducted on such a system must be at once schools of morality and industry.[17]

'Morality' and 'industry' were central to the belief system of John Cadbury and his children, and were clearly values to be inculcated in the working classes. Whilst some members of the working classes resented what seemed like indoctrination, for others, sobriety and self-help seemed important elements in the quest for working-class respectability.

John Cadbury, in the steps of his father, was also an Overseer of the Poor and a Street Commissioner. In the latter capacity, he was instrumental in the building of the town's Market Hall in the 1830s and significantly involved in the transfer of the Commissioners' powers to the Town Council in 1851. Richard Tapper and John Cadbury were founder members of the Birmingham Temperance Society in 1830. Four years later they were converted to teetotalism by Joseph Livesey. John Cadbury also sought, by practical and other means, to encourage smoke abatement. He found it sad and disappointing that some of the worst offenders were leading citizens of Birmingham. He did, however, get more support from fellow employers for the promotion of thrift and the encouragement of savings banks.

John Cadbury was on the committees of a number of humanitarian and educational institutions, including the Birmingham General Hospital and the Birmingham Infant School Society. He also set up the Animal Friends Society and took an interest in the Ann Street kindergarten founded by his father. He was also an active member of the Bull Street Meeting all his life.[18]

John Cadbury was badly affected by the death of his wife in 1855. Shortly after, his own health began to deteriorate (although he was to live on until 1889). He began gradually to withdraw from the running of the business. As early as 1856, John had written to his son, Richard:

> I wish to encourage thee quietly and steadily to place thyself in my position ... I ... conclude with the earnest and serious hope that neither business nor pleasure, nor any other lawful pursuit, may interfere with the performance of thy civil and religious duties.[19]

The Cadbury Brothers

The Cadbury household was a strictly religious one, but the children benefited from the warmth and attention of their mother. Unlike his elder brothers, George was not sent away to school. This seems to have reinforced his beliefs in the value of family life. 'God has placed men in families,' he said, 'and there is no influence like that of parents upon their children.'[20]

It is also clear that Richard and George Cadbury enjoyed their early morning walks and rides with their father in the then undeveloped area of Ladywood. They nurtured an early interest in gardening, a love of nature, and a strong attachment to athletics and sports. These childhood passions remained with the brothers and both continued to be active in later life. George Cadbury, for instance, learned to play tennis in his 50s and took up golf in his 70s. Both were keen providers of recreational facilities for their workers and tenants during their lifetimes.[21]

Both boys served apprenticeships with other Quaker firms (in George's case with Joseph Rowntree of York) before joining the family firm in the 1850s. John Cadbury believed that his sons should acquire business knowledge early. The ill-health of his father and elder brother, and the intermittent presence of his uncle Benjamin, meant that Richard Cadbury was forced to take responsibility at an early age.[22] George and Richard formally took over Cadbury Brothers in 1861. The company was in a parlous

17   Richard and George Cadbury, from the *Bournville Works Magazine*, September 1909.

situation. 'The business was rapidly vanishing,' George later recalled. 'Only eleven girls were employed.'[23] But by 1861 they also had other responsibilities. Richard had married Elizabeth Adlington in that year, and both brothers were already actively involved in the Adult School movement in Birmingham. They managed to turn the fortunes of the company around at the same time as they fulfilled their family and religious commitments.

By hard work, economy, good human management, new products and advertising, George and Richard Cadbury managed to rescue the firm, although not without losing almost all their inheritances from their mother. 'We had ten depressing stocktakings,' George recalled, 'but every time we went back again to our work with vigour.' They believed they had learned valuable lessons rescuing the firm: 'It was splendid training, especially for young men, and I sometimes pity those who have never had to go through it: success is infinitely sweeter after struggle.'[24]

George Cadbury also believed that his Quaker training gave him, and others like him, the sort of qualities required to succeed in business: 'They were taught self-denial, rigid abstinence from all luxury and self-indulgence.'[25] Whilst acknowledging their own hard work and restraint, the Cadbury brothers also recognised the value of a healthy, efficient and committed workforce. Like their father, they recruited their staff personally. When Richard engaged a new employee, he laid great stress on the importance of pure morals and practical Christianity.[26] The brothers showed a genuine concern for their workforce, and they and their successors became well-known for their enlightened management policies.

Having saved the company, the brothers sought to improve its fortunes further. They changed the emphasis of the business by concentrating on cocoa and chocolate. They introduced technical innovations, like the Dutch press, which produced a purer cocoa essence. This in turn enabled them to stress the purity of their products at a time when concern was being expressed about the adulteration of food. Improved marketing and the advertising of their products, like the 'Pure Cocoa Essence' introduced in 1866, led to increased sales and profits. The upsurge in sales led to a growth in the workforce. By 1870, Cadbury Brothers were employing some 200 workers.[27]

A Factory in a Garden

By this time the firm was outgrowing its city centre site. There was limited scope for expansion in this densely-packed and smoke-laden area, and the Bridge Street works were increasingly being seen as unsuitable for the 'pure' products being promoted by the firm. After much soul-searching and some prospecting, the Cadbury brothers bought a 14½-acre site four miles south-west of Birmingham in 1878. Apart from Bournbrook Hall, there were just a few farms and cottages in the area, although there were some larger mansions a little further away near the Bristol Road. (George Cadbury was to take up residence in one, Woodbrooke.) The plot was divided by the Bourn Brook. It was essentially a 'greenfield' site with plenty of room for expansion. Although road connections were not good and the site was not traversed by trams, it was adjacent to the Birmingham West Suburban railway and the Birmingham and Worcester Canal, thus allowing access for goods and people. The nearby station at Stirchley Street (later Bournville) had opened in 1876.

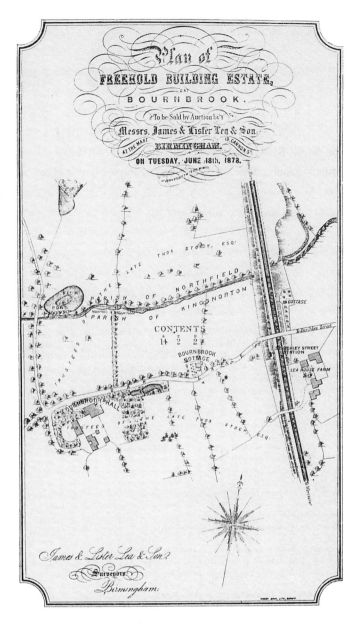

18 Auctioneer's notice advertising the sale of the land at Bournbrook on which the Bournville Works was built in 1879.

Work began on the new factory in March 1879. The planning of the factory was largely the responsibility of George Cadbury, although he was assisted by the architect, George Gadd. George Cadbury took a small cottage at Lifford during the construction of the works. In October the move was made to the new factory at Bournville. The Cadbury brothers chose a deliberately French-sounding name for the location as the French were regarded as the market leaders in chocolate at the time.[28]

Some people had reservations about the move, and George Cadbury always recalled the messages of doom which he received on announcing their decision to transfer their works to the outskirts of the expanding town.[29] There were precedents for such a move, and it was not, perhaps, as risky a venture as they suggested. Some of the pioneers of the industrial revolution had set up factories in isolated situations and succeeded. In the mid-Victorian period, the textile manufacturer, Titus Salt, had moved his business from the centre of Bradford and built a factory and model village at Saltaire, on a site which was not greatly dissimilar to that chosen by the Cadbury brothers some quarter of a century later.[30] In Birmingham itself, many factories were constructed alongside the railway lines and canals that ran outwards from the centre of Birmingham. The firms of Nettlefold, Chamberlain and the Tangyes were to be found on the Wolverhampton line, whilst B.S.A. established their new works on the Oxford line at Small Heath in the early 1860s. Industrial colonies were also growing up in the south west of the city by the 1870s. Albright and Sturge had built a factory in Selly Oak by the 1840s and were later to erect another works at nearby Lifford. Other well-known firms were to occupy sites at Hazelwell, Breedon and Kings Norton. In the latter district, there was an important group of new establishments by 1865, including G.R. Wilson's India rubber works and James Baldwin's Sherborne paper factory. Indeed, by 1871, the parish of Kings Norton (which included the districts of Balsall Heath, Moseley, Kings Heath, Stirchley and Kings Norton) had more than 11,000 industrial workers. The adjacent parish of Northfield (which included Bournbrook, Selly Oak and Northfield) was not so well populated, having 4,609 residents as opposed to Kings Norton's 21,845 in 1871.[31]

What was significant about the new Cadbury works was not its novelty, but its quality. The site was developed in such a way that the area did not entirely lose its rural character. It was indeed (as the

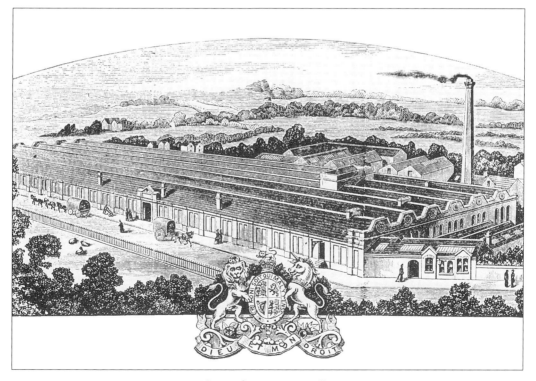

19 The new factory at Bournville, 1879.

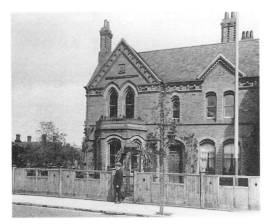

20   The cottages built for key workers at Bournville in 1879.

company's later publicity proclaimed) 'a factory in a garden'.[32] An early visitor confirmed its aesthetic appeal:

> Messrs. Cadbury's factory is a plain brick structure, but the creepers which are being coaxed along its walls, the grassy slope with shrubs evidently glorying in the pure air, the green relieved by snowdrops and crocuses in the winter and bright coloured flowering plants in the summer, the well-dressed happy looking girls trooping in at the door, all tend to give it the appearance of a high class school or branch of South Kensington and one hesitates to call it a factory.[33]

Conditions at the factory were, by the standards of the day, exemplary. 'We consider', the brothers said, 'that our people spend the greater part of their lives at their work, and we wish to make it less irksome by environing them with pleasant and wholesome sights, sounds and conditions.'[34] This was a product of an approach to business which combined Christianity and commerce, altruism and financial astuteness. 'Although undoubtedly keen businessmen', a local journalist reported, 'these men regard those in their employ not as part of the machinery, but as human beings for whose well-being they are in large measure responsible.'[35] Richard and George Cadbury and their immediate successors believed business efficiency and industrial betterment could, and should, run hand in hand.[36]

When the workers first arrived at Bournville they found a small playground for the girls laid out alongside the factory. (The recreation grounds came later, the men's grounds not being finished until 1897.)[37] At that point, only 17 houses had been constructed on site. With the exception of a detached house for William Tallis, the works manager, they were semi-detached dwellings. These houses were designed by George Gadd (probably under instructions from George Cadbury). They were fairly typical late 19th-century dwellings with some Gothic detailing. They did, however, have quite generous gardens to the front and the rear (with w.c.s at the bottom of the garden). An early description gives us an idea of the contemporary reaction to the first houses built at Bournville:

> In the sixteen semi-detached cottages reside the foremen, and their well-to-do appearance and neat gardens are in keeping with the place. Nearby is the beautiful home occupied by the foreman of the works.[38]

This meant, of course, that the vast majority of the workforce had to walk, cycle or catch a train to work, as the factory could not be reached by tram. Although Cadbury Brothers made special arrangements with the railway company and even provided overnight accommodation in Bournbrook Hall for some of the women workers who lived at a distance, the journey to and from work was an extra burden for the employees at Bournville. In bad weather the local roads turned into quagmires, while there were no road lamps in the nearby 'straggling village' of Stirchley. 'On the other hand,' it was reported, 'the Bourn stream was noted for its trout, and sports and outdoor games amid country conditions were no small compensation for the workers' journey from town.'[39]

With rising real wages in the late 19th century, demand for cocoa and chocolate increased. With new products (like Dairy Milk and Bournville chocolate) and effective advertising (for which Richard Cadbury must take much credit), Cadbury Brothers prospered and the firm expanded. This is reflected in the phenomenal increase in the size of the workforce. By the time they left Bridge Street, Cadbury Brothers were employing 230 workers. By 1899 some 1,200 workers were employed at Bournville. A decade later 2,700 women and men were working there, and the figures rose even more dramatically after the First World War.[40]

The growth of industry in the surrounding area and the expansion of the works at Bournville stimulated a demand for houses in the vicinity. The population of the parishes of Kings Norton and Northfield (and Bournville was partly situated in both districts) rose significantly from 1881 to 1911, when both were incorporated in the extended City of Birmingham. The population of Kings Norton grew from 34, 071 to 89,044 in that period, whilst that of Northfield expanded from 7,190 to 31,395.[41] Many took up residence in the characteristic bye-law terraces lined with 'tunnel back' houses that were being built in large numbers on the ever-expanding periphery of Greater Birmingham. After 1895, the opportunity to live in the Model Village became available.

21   Bournbrook Hall and female workers at the Bournville Works.

22   Aerial view of Bournville Lane, Cadbury Brothers works and recreation grounds and the bye-law terraces of Stirchley.

George Cadbury: the 'practical mystic'

George Cadbury was clearly an enlightened entrepreneur. He believed in the classic Victorian virtues of thrift, sobriety and hard work, but he was also deeply imbued with a belief in practical Christianity. He not only saw religion as a basis for personal conduct; he argued that Christian beliefs should be applied to social questions. He held that it was his duty to apply himself and his wealth to improve the moral and physical condition of his employees and fellow citizens. Religion was central to his ideals; wealth gave him the means to pursue some of his more ambitious schemes.

There can be little doubt that George Cadbury was a deeply religious man. Contemporaries often described his faith as being 'simple' and 'childlike'. It was a faith concerned more with conduct than theological debate: 'Religion does not consist in outward show or outward profession, but in feeding the hungry, giving drink to the thirsty, and taking in the stranger.'[42] It was a faith that coloured George Cadbury's life and work. It produced in him an exceedingly strong sense of duty and a belief in 'the joy of service'.[43] Even though he refused many honours, George Cadbury must have felt satisfaction and pride when his work was recognised by employees, tenants or dignitaries. Affection and respect were often accorded this worthy philanthropist, but the relationship between donor and recipient was (despite George Cadbury's kindness and simplicity) never an equal one.

Many contemporaries noted that George Cadbury's approach combined idealism and practicality. Several described him as a 'practical mystic'.[44] He was sensitive to the problems of the poor, he had the vision to produce grand schemes, and he was sufficiently practical and pragmatic to carry them through. He supported radical land reform policies, started to promote industrial democracy in his factory, carefully distributed some of his wealth so as to promote healthy living and the relief of human suffering and over a lifetime engaged in personal, self-denying work.[45] Although he was sympathetic to the emerging Labour Party, it was suggested that George Cadbury might have achieved less if he had taken to preaching Socialism. His second wife, Elizabeth, who had also read Carlyle and Ruskin and engaged in voluntary work before her marriage, was of the opinion that philanthropists got on with the job of helping people whilst the Socialists merely offered them utopian dreams. She wrote to the Quaker and Fabian, Edward Pease:

> What seems to me wrong about all these Socialist reforms is first, that the day is always coming, people of the future will have the benefit, if it comes at all, but those of the present who require help, they have to listen to lectures and poems, and their pressing need is untouched. That is looked after by philanthropists, at whom and whose beliefs the revolutionists scoff.[46]

Although his business brought him wealth, George Cadbury believed it should be used during his lifetime to benefit others: 'A man should do what he can for the world while he is in it, and not leave it for others to do when he is gone and when it is not his to give.'[47] Despite his generosity during his lifetime, and his belief that wealth could be a curse on those inheriting it, George Cadbury still left a large fortune. His widow and his children did, however, continue his schemes and became prominent philanthropists and Trust founders in their own rights. Besides their religious activities, they became active figures in the fields of education, industrial betterment, pensions, public health, juvenile crime and town planning. It was appropriate that George Cadbury Jnr. had carved in his study at Primrose Hill William Blake's famous words:

> I will not cease from mental fight
> Nor shall my sword sleep in my hand,
> Till we have built Jerusalem
> In England's green and pleasant land.[48]

The starting point for George Cadbury's own public work was, Gardiner suggested, a belief in 'the supreme value of human life and character'. He began by trying to improve 'the standard of thought and conduct'.[49] He soon came to realise that, before raising people's ideals, it was necessary to improve the environment in which they lived. This he learned through his Adult School experiences. Bournville Village can be seen as 'the sequel to George Cadbury's Adult School work'.[50]

Adult Schools

Quakers were relatively late in embarking on Sunday School activity. One area in which they did make a mark was with Adult Schools. Started in Nottingham, they were introduced into Birmingham in 1842 by Joseph Sturge, and then strongly promoted by William White from the Severn Street Schools.[51]

Quakers were prominent in the Adult School movement, but the approach adopted in the Adult Schools was an undenominational one. The objective was both educational and religious—to promote literacy and spirituality. Put simply, the aim was to transform people's lives. An Adult School was, to its supporters, 'a centre of citizenship' which helped men (and women) 'to live Christian lives'.[52]

The promoters of the Adult Schools sought to recruit not only the 'respectable' poor; they also made efforts to attract the 'degraded' sections of the working classes by operating from old factories and disused pubs as well as schools and (Quaker) Institutes.[53] J.F. Crosfield is probably correct to suggest that 'the majority were intelligent working men from self-respecting homes', although there is some evidence that a small number came 'from the slums and even from prison'.[54]

The Adult Schools had a strongly religious flavour, and a Bible lesson was the central feature of the meetings. The schools were said to be 'essentially democratic'. The teachers were expected to 'neither patronise nor pauperise' and members were expected to make a financial contribution each week. The Adult Schools were intended to be 'co-operative in action' and 'foster a spirit of unselfishness and self-reliance'. They sought to promote sympathy and encourage a belief in service. Essentially they were concerned with helping men 'to live Christian lives'.[55]

Besides the moral and religious teaching, the Adult Schools also established Savings Funds, Sick Clubs and Mutual Aid Societies. Thrift and self-help were clearly encouraged, but so also was 'rational recreation'. Football, cricket and fishing clubs were formed, as was an ambulance society. By such means it was believed a healthy, morally upright, self-reliant and respectable citizenry could be created—a citizenry whose values reflected those of their middle-class promoters.[56] Making Christians, raising ideals and promoting citizenship was not easy in the depressing central districts of Victorian Birmingham. Although resistance or apathy were common, the appeals of the Adult School promoters struck a chord with small sections of the local working class.[57] Isichei notes that William White's writings are full of stories about scholars who had reached 'the plateau of respectability' as a result of 'the exercise of the bourgeois virtues of sobriety, thrift and self-improvement'. George Cadbury used to tell similar stories. 'For forty years I have had a class in Birmingham,' he told Garden City delegates in 1901, 'many of whom have been drunkards and profligates, have come into my class in ragged coats, but who have become well-to-do now.'[58]

George Cadbury first helped with the classes at the Severn Street Adult School when he was 20 years old. After four years he was given his own class, Class XIV. He was to remain committed to this class for 50 years. It has been estimated that between 4,000 and 5,000 men passed through the class in that time.[59]

By 1877, George Cadbury's class had grown so large that it had to move to rooms in the Bristol Street Board School. In the ensuing years Class XIV became something of a 'missionary exercise' as its former scholars founded offshoots elsewhere in the city.[60] Some of those in the southern suburbs of Birmingham, at Northfield, Selly Oak and Stirchley, were founded with the help (financial and otherwise) of the Cadburys.

There can be no doubt that this work gave George Cadbury a good deal of satisfaction. He loved to recall the more dramatic 'conversions'. Among the converts at the Coppersmiths Arms (which George Cadbury acquired as an Adult School and social club) were 'at least two men whose right to be regarded as the worst drunkards in Birmingham might at one time have passed almost unchallenged'.[61] He also enjoyed the 'gatherings' of old scholars that he arranged at the Manor House. The attendances were large, and contemporary accounts stress the respect that the scholars had for their former teacher. George Cadbury was especially happy that some of his scholars had followed his lead and engaged in Adult School work. Some also moved to Bournville.[62] A more recent authority on Victorian Quakers has suggested that 'scholars were flattered by the attentions of their middle-class and often wealthy teachers, and repaid them with a devotion which often lasted many years'.[63]

The Adult Schools brought Quakers like William White and George Cadbury face to face with the harsh realities of life in the inner city areas of Birmingham. They both became aware of 'the misery and degradation caused by the conditions under which thousands of their fellow townsmen had to live'.[64] William White sought, when he was Chairman of the Improvement Committee, to sweep away some of these slums. George Cadbury attributed his interest in housing reform to his knowledge of conditions in the city gained when visiting the homes of Adult School students. He was stunned by the horrors of the slum dwellings, the misery of the women and children and the sorrows of the aged poor. Although he was a teetotaller and a temperance advocate, he understood why men and women tried 'to find solace or forgetfulness in the public house'.[65] Recalling this work some years later, George Cadbury explained:

> If I had not been brought into contact with the people in my Adult Class in Birmingham and found from visiting the poor how difficult it was to lead a good life in a back street, I should probably never have built Bournville Village.[66]

Whilst believing in the potential for good in mankind, George Cadbury was realistic enough to accept that it was difficult for a man to raise his ideals in a slum environment. Even a sober and respectable man had difficulties in 'providing suitable and healthy recreation for himself and his family'. Cadbury saw how 'the stuffy, sunless, badly-built houses undermined the health and subsequently the will power' of many living in the slums. 'If a man works in a factory all day and sits in a public house by night what can you expect', he asked, 'but a poor emaciated creature without physical or moral strength.'[67]

George Cadbury was among that growing band of reformers who reacted with alarm at the apparent degeneration of the urban population of Britain in the late 19th and early 20th centuries. Evidence, of varying reliability, was produced to highlight the physical and moral deterioration of the inhabitants of the poorest districts in the towns and cities. George Cadbury's hopes and fears were apparent in his justification of a move 'back to the land':[68]

> Largely through my own personal experiences among the back streets of Birmingham I have been brought to the conclusion that it is impossible to raise a nation, morally, physically and spiritually in such surroundings, and that the only effective way is to bring men out of the cities into the country and to give every man his garden where he can come into touch with nature and thus know more of nature's God.[69]

Whether he was aware of Jesse Collings' smallholdings scheme for 'three acres and a cow' is unclear, but Cadbury moved in the same political circles.

23   Woodbrooke, the home of George Cadbury and later one of the Selly Oak Colleges.

Public service

George Cadbury's sense of public duty, his interest in the physical environment and his own radical Liberal political beliefs led to his standing for election to the Town Council. He served as a Councillor for the Rotton Park Ward for a short period between 1875 and 1881. It was a time when clergymen and politicians were proclaiming 'the Civic Gospel'.[70] Recalling the situation in 1921, George Cadbury wrote:

> Some sixty years ago a large majority of the Birmingham City Council was non-progressive. There were no parks, no free libraries and only one bath. The gas and water undertakings were monopolies carried on for private gain. This state of things was absolutely changed in a few years by a band of young men, of whom at that time I was one, who did individual work, canvassing, holding meetings, etc., and securing a majority of votes in favour of progress. We were led by ministers of religion, Dale, Dawson, Croskey, etc., and Joseph Chamberlain, a magnificent leader of young men, was just coming to the front.[71]

It is interesting to note that, in his 1878 election address, George Cadbury promised not only 'to promote the interests of my fellow citizens' but also claimed he would take 'a perfectly independent course'. He indicated his interest in, and knowledge of, working-class housing. He deplored the fact that 'in the past there was not more supervision exercised by the Town Council over the construction, position and sanitary arrangement of their dwellings'.[72]

George Cadbury did not make a great name for himself on the Council, but he did work conscientiously in committee, even though he was heavily involved in the building of Bournville works at that time. He served rather appropriately on the Baths and Parks Committee of the Council. He did not find the work congenial, and he did not seek re-election after his move to Woodbrooke in 1881.[73] Fourteen years later he was to embark on a housing venture that was far in advance of anything the Council had considered.

Chapter Four

THE MODEL VILLAGE

The Bournville Experiment

While the predominantly Nonconformist promoters of the 'Civic Gospel', led by Joseph Chamberlain, set about improving the city centre from the mid-1870s, a few years later the Quakers, George and Richard Cadbury, began work on their 'Factory in a Garden' on the southern edge of Birmingham.[1] In 1895, they started to construct a model village alongside their expanding cocoa and chocolate factory. This was to be their contribution to the housing problem in Birmingham. They also saw it as an exemplary model for other developers.

The Bournville experiment arose out of George Cadbury's religious beliefs, his educational efforts and his business concerns. Some saw it as the product of 'the union of industrial enterprise and wise philanthropy'.[2] Cadbury's long experience of teaching working-class men and youths at the Adult School had convinced him that it was 'almost impossible for a workman living in a back street of Birmingham to keep steady and bring up his children well'.[3] Cadbury was concerned not only about the moral condition of the Birmingham working classes; he was also worried about the apparent physical deterioration of the urban population. 'Those who work in close factories by day and spend their evenings, even, in Temperance Clubs or worse still public houses', he continued to argue, 'can but become a poor feeble emaciated race, physically, mentally, and morally.'[4] George Cadbury was not the only housing reformer who was anxious about the degeneration of the population of Britain's expanding towns and cities. 'The present physical condition of the people in our great towns', Ebenezer Howard maintained, 'is a serious danger, not only to our national life, but to our capacity to compete with other nations.'[5] Whilst some advocated compulsory military training as a means of improving the physical condition of the urban population, Cadbury came to see the creation of a model village as the 'peaceful path to real reform'.[6] His early experience of the 'Factory in a Garden' convinced him of the benefits of village as opposed to town life. 'The condition of our unfortunate countrymen thus situated', he wrote to T.C. Horsfall, the Manchester planning advocate, 'is a great contrast to our own workpeople who have the opportunity of living in the villages around our works.' These employees also had the chance to work the soil. 'The cultivation of a garden improves a man and his wife and family, not only physically, but morally and spiritually.'[7] George Cadbury's ideals were clearly expressed in the Deed establishing the Bournville Village Trust in 1900:

> The Founder is desirous of alleviating the evils which arise from the insufficient and insanitary accommodation supplied to large numbers of the working classes, and of securing to the worker in factories some of the advantages of the outdoor village life, with opportunities for the natural and healthful occupation of cultivating the soil.[8]

Cadbury, like many of his contemporaries, believed that village life was physically and morally beneficial. During his own childhood, spent in leafy Edgbaston and in the country, he had come to value outdoor activities, especially gardening. He wanted to create a settlement that would have the bucolic charm that the slums and expanding suburbs of Birmingham lacked. For it was not just the back-to-back houses and courtyard dwellings that filled the housing reformers with fear and dread, they also believed that it was 'the suburbs which threaten[ed] to engulf our cities'.[9] A model estate would pre-empt the speculative developers who, it was claimed, were 'building desolate row upon row of ugly and cramped villas'[10] in those expanding suburbs. 'As a landowner,' Cadbury later explained, 'he felt he ought to be blamed if he allowed a dreary row of houses to be built on land belonging to him.'[11] He therefore set about planning and building his model village: a settlement intended to combine the beauty and the social stability of a pre-industrial community. George Cadbury was anxious to see that his experiment was widely emulated, so he devoted as much energy to publicising this venture as he did to promoting his chocolate products. To ensure that others would follow his lead, Cadbury sought to demonstrate that the village was not a charitable concern but an affordable proposition; a scheme developed on sound economic lines.

The Factory in a Garden

After rescuing the ailing family firm in the 1860s, George and Richard Cadbury realised by the end of the following decade that they needed a larger site for their expanding cocoa and chocolate business. In 1879 they opened their new factory at Bournville.

At first, Cadbury Brothers only erected one detached and 16 semi-detached houses for key workers at Bournville. It was not until some years later that George Cadbury turned his attention to the provision of houses and public buildings in the surrounding area. His first efforts involved the building of a few cottages and Institutes, containing Quaker meeting houses, in Stirchley and Northfield in the 1880s and early 1890s. These can be seen as the immediate precursors of the model village at Bournville.[12]

In 1893, George Cadbury acquired 120 acres of land adjacent to the expanding factory at Bournville. Further small parcels of land were purchased in 1894 and 1895. It was on this land that the original Model Village was built. Between 1898 and 1911 yet more land was bought. The most significant acquisitions were the Woodlands Park estate in 1899, the Middle Park farm in 1903, the Middleton Hall estate in 1905 and the Park Cottage farm two years later. The Rowheath Farm estate, bought jointly by the Bournville Village Trust and Cadbury Brothers in 1911, was the last major land purchase before the First World War.[13]

24   Stirchley Institute, from *Bournville Works Magazine, c.*1929.

Factory Villages and Model Estates

Bournville was not, however, a unique venture. During the previous century a number of industrialists had built factory villages for their workers.[14] Lord Calthorpe's more exclusive estate at Edgbaston, where George Cadbury lived for many years, showed the value of restrictive covenants in leasehold development.[15] In the late 1870s, the influential and artistic suburb of Bedford Park in west London was begun.[16] At the same time as Cadbury was starting to develop the Bournville Estate, W.H. Lever, the soap manufacturer, was masterminding a grand scheme for his workforce at Port Sunlight, on the Wirral.[17]

At first George Cadbury had in mind a religious colony. 'I am rather hopeful', he wrote in March 1894, 'that this will be to a large extent a Quaker colony.'[18] Similar sectarian settlements and alternative communities had been built in Britain and America throughout the 19th century, including the Chartist colony at Great Dodford, near Bromsgrove. This venture was the model for Jesse Collings' later smallholdings scheme based on 'three acres and a cow'.[19] (Collings was a significant member of the Liberal caucus in Birmingham.) George Cadbury must soon have had second thoughts about the nature and scope of such a scheme. Perhaps he felt that a small sectarian colony could be ignored or marginalised. Given his knowledge of the extent of the housing problem, it would seem that he wanted to promote a venture that would have a greater impact. He was moving towards a scheme that would provide, both in terms of its form and organisation, an exemplary model to others. He also decided that it would be 'a much more genuine experiment' if it were not just confined to the Firm's employees.[20] There were a few twists in the plot before the Village came to fruition and the Bournville Village Trust emerged as the guiding force behind the scheme.

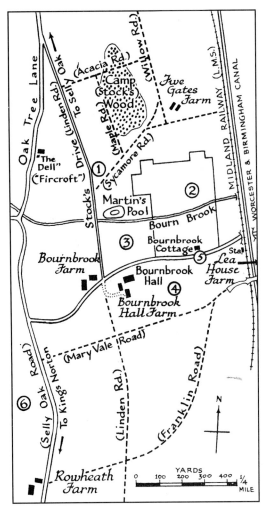

25 The local farms that occupied the site of the future developments at Bournville. The sites shown are (1) Bournville Green, (2) Bournville Works, (3) Men's Recreation Ground, (4) Girl's Recreation Ground, (5) No.1 Lodge, (6) Rowheath Grounds. From *Bournville Works Magazine*, September 1947.

George Cadbury seemed to have a clear notion of the form that the settlement would take. It is apparent that he discussed the venture not only with his brother but also his second wife, Elizabeth. Her biographer describes how they surveyed and planned the scheme:

> Morning by morning she would walk through the fields from her home to the factory with her husband as he set off for his day's work, discussing with him the development of the village—where the roads should run and the shopping centre should lie, what type of house and cottage should be built, and what labour-saving devices could be introduced.[21]

By the time that George Cadbury wrote an invitation to take part in the venture to A.P. Walker, a Quaker surveyor from Cockermouth, he was able to provide a brief outline of the kind of scheme he had in mind:

Please let me know whether you would be likely to be able to give up some years to carrying out a scheme I have in hand for laying out 120 acres in the neighbourhood of our works for cottages, each surrounded by their own garden, not more than six to the acre. I would not care for anyone to undertake it who did not enter into the spirit of the undertaking as a labour of the Lord.[22]

Development Plans

The first sketch plan of the estate was produced in April 1894 by A.P. Walker.[23] Mary Vale Road, Bournville Lane, Oak Tree Lane and Raddlebarn Lane were the only public thoroughfares on the estate at that time, although a private road ran through the centre of the plot towards Bournbrook Hall. There were two farms and a large wood on the site. In the sketch plan, the main road through the estate (later Linden Road) followed the line of the earlier private road. Another curved road skirted Camp Wood and linked the new thoroughfare with Raddlebarn Lane. The other proposed roads on the estate were of an unexceptional rectilinear pattern, and what became Beech Road and Elm Road even had short side streets running off them. (The layout of this section resembles that of the cottages built by Gadd in 1879 for key workers at the Bournville Works.) The wood and the area alongside the Bournbrook were clearly to be left undeveloped. The central feature of the sketch plan was a small grass triangle, which was to be flanked with public buildings, shops and a swimming bath. Surprisingly, the main feature of the present village, the Green, did not figure in this plan.

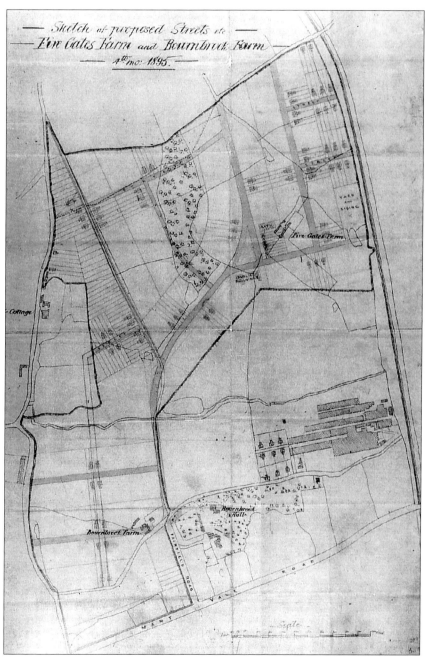

26   The original plan of the Estate produced by A.P. Walker in April 1894.

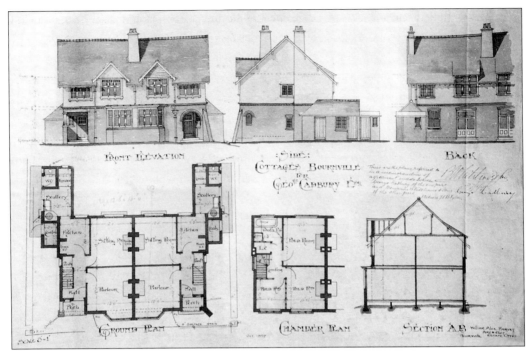

27   Drawing by W.A. Harvey of a pair of semi-detached houses on Linden Road, 1897.

28   Voyseyesque cottages on Mary Vale Road designed by W.A. Harvey in 1899.

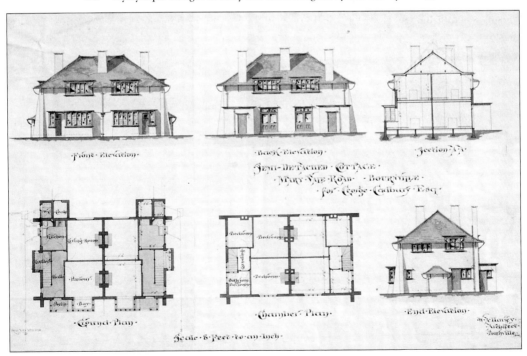

Clearly, Cadbury and Walker were not happy with this original proposal. Another plan, produced only a few months later, shows several key changes. This drawing shows the village green at the centre of the altered street layout. The street pattern was simplified and the side roads were removed. With certain minor amendments (the removal of Hazel Road and the addition of Woodbrooke Road) this plan established the layout of the road pattern for the model village. At the insistence of Kings Norton and Northfield Urban District Council, most of the roads on the estate were 42 or 45 feet wide, to comply with the bye-laws, and this undoubtedly added to the initial costs of the development. Most commentators are agreed that the street pattern of the village core lacks sophistication and that before the trees that were planted at the outset began to flourish, the roads did initially look rather wide and sometimes bare.

The Bournville Building Estate

George Cadbury's initial proposals for the new settlement were outlined in the original prospectus for the 'Bournville Building Estate'.[24] The object of the undertaking was 'to make it easy for working men to own houses with large gardens secure from the danger of being spoilt either by the building of factories or by interference of the enjoyment of sun, light and air'. Although it was clear that 'an out and out sale at cost price would have been preferred', George Cadbury decided to let the land on 999-year leases, at an annual ground rent of 1d. per yard. This enabled him to introduce restrictive covenants so that 'the rural appearance of the district and the comfort of the inhabitants may be enforced'.

The purchase of houses by the working classes was not unknown in Birmingham. Building clubs, terminating building societies and the Freehold Land Society had contributed in a small way to the housing stock of the city since the late 18th century.[25] The use of restrictive covenants to ensure that dwellings of a sufficiently high standard were initially constructed and the quality of the area was maintained had been central to the development of Edgbaston, the leafy suburb where George Cadbury had spent his formative years.

Similar controls were introduced on the Bournville Estate so as to ensure that 'the speculator will not get a footing'. None of the houses to be erected there were to be below a given size, nor were they to cost less than £150. The plans of the houses to be built at Bournville had to be approved by the architect to the Estate. There were to be strict rules controlling the amount of space in each plot occupied by the dwellings 'so that there will be no danger of gardens being overshadowed and spoiled, or that the neighbourhood will lose its pleasant rural aspect'. George Cadbury had, during his lifetime, seen how Ladywood had been transformed from an area of 'sylvan solitude' into a monotonous working-class district lacking in greenery and beauty, and he wished to guard against such an eventuality on his own land.[26]

As someone who had enjoyed outdoor activities in his childhood, Cadbury wanted to make certain that there would be a number of play areas in Bournville. Consequently he promised a seven-acre piece of land for a recreation ground and two or three small plots for use as children's playgrounds. He also stated his intention of offering a site for the erection of swimming baths. (The baths at Bournville were actually erected on the Firm's land in 1904.) Besides catering for the bodies of the future residents, Cadbury clearly wanted them to improve their minds. He thus offered to give yet more land for the construction of schools and an Institute. 'Rational recreation' in a salubrious setting was the ideal aimed for.[27]

The Estate was to be almost purely residential. Shops were to be allowed in certain places 'for the convenience of the inhabitants', but no factories or businesses of any kind were to be permitted, 'except in connection with the building of houses on the estate'.

The Bournville scheme was aimed at a 'superior class of quiet and respectable tenants'. Cadbury's solicitors were instructed to help would-be residents with mortgages. Mortgages at 2½ per cent interest were made available to those able to make a downpayment of half the cost of the property, and at 3 per cent for those only able to make a smaller downpayment. (In the latter case, George Cadbury had the house built and made a preparatory agreement for the lease and the mortgage.) He even agreed to take over the property in the event of death within ten years of a resident taking out a mortgage, paying the cost price to the next of kin provided that the former resident had 'duly performed the covenants and conditions of the lease and mortgage'.

The prospectus illustrated the advantages of buying a house in this way over renting. It showed that someone renting a £200 property would spend almost the same amount over 15 years as someone who took out a mortgage for the same type of dwelling. 'A tenant renting the house for 15 years almost pays for it and not a brick of the house is his own, while by purchase he lives in it rent free, and owns a house worth probably more than £200 at the end of the time.' The figures did not take into account the ground rent, but it was suggested that 'the ground rent should be covered by the produce of the garden, especially if poultry be kept'.[28]

The economic arguments were convincing, but were of little relevance to the poor. Nevertheless, a sufficient number of people took up the leases and the Estate grew steadily from 1895.

Members of the Cadbury family commissioned many of the early dwellings, which were then let on the long leases specified by George Cadbury. Others sought designs from the estate architects for dwellings for their own use. These early houses were constructed by local builders, such as Benjamin Whitehouse and Sons and Albert Parry.[29] Their work was carefully supervised during the first five years of development. 143 dwellings were sold on 999-year leases with the peak of the early building cycle being reached in 1898-9.

The early architects

The very first houses on the Bournville Estate were designed by Alfred Pickard Walker, the Estate's surveyor. Walker continued to work on the Estate until the early 20th century. In 1895, however, a young Birmingham designer, William Alexander Harvey, was appointed as architect to the Estate. He continued as Estate Architect until 1904, when he went into private practice. Harvey remained as a consultant architect to the Trust for some considerable time thereafter. By 1912, he had entered into partnership with his nephew, H. Graham Wicks. Harvey was largely responsible for the aesthetic impact of the model village in its early years, but two other architects were also to make their mark on the Estate during these years. The first of these was Henry Bedford Tylor, who was estate architect from 1904 to 1911. His style

29   The first houses erected on the Bournville Estate. These dwellings were designed by A.P. Walker.

could be characterised as a simpler and more economical version of that of his predecessor. The other architect and planner to emerge just before the First World War was S.A. Wilmot. He was responsible for the site plan of the Weoley Hill development, beyond Bristol Road. The building work there did not start until the First World War.

W.A. Harvey came from an artistic family. Both his father and brother were designers in stained glass. When Harvey left school it was intended that he should take up engraving, but he chose architecture instead.[30] He studied under W.H. Bidlake at Birmingham School of Art, where Harvey won prizes for his sketches of local medieval and vernacular buildings.[31] He was only just over 20 when he was appointed as Estate architect at Bournville. 'The appointment', it was later noted, 'while giving him his first big opportunity for the exercise of his gifts, proved to be of incalculable value to this pioneer housing experiment.'[32]

Harvey was to become a significant figure in the late 19th and early 20th century 'revival in domestic architecture'.[33] His increasingly secure and varied use of materials and his interest in vernacular architecture show him to be a product of the Arts and Crafts movement. Like Shaw, Baillie Scott, Voysey and Bidlake, Harvey sought 'to give a new individuality of spirit to old forms'.[34] He was also one of those architectural pioneers (like Raymond Unwin) who struggled to lift the design of 'cottages' above the level of the speculative builder's terraces. 'The two movements of housing reform and the revival of domestic architecture', Harvey argued, 'must certainly advance hand in hand.'[35] It was claimed that Harvey 'brought ... a new conception of design applied to small and medium-sized suburban houses, and to their layout in relation to their surroundings, which had no little influence over a very wide

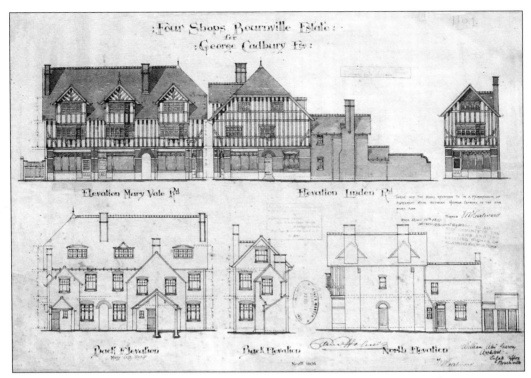

30   Plans for shops in Mary Vale Road and Linden Road by W.A. Harvey, *c*.1896-7.

field'.[36] Harvey's importance lay in his ability to develop a convenient and compact 'cottage' plan, whilst at the same time being able to avoid monotony by subtly varying his façades and by paying particular attention to the positioning of the buildings on the estate. By the outbreak of the First World War, Harvey was regarded as 'one of the greatest experts in the cheap cottage problem'.[37]

The Early Development of the Estate

A.P. Walker designed the first three pairs of dwellings on the Bournville Estate. These were situated on the west side of Mary Vale Road, and were erected in 1895. Harvey then took over, and his first houses are to be found at the southern end of Linden Road, Bournville Lane and Row Heath Lane (now Selly Oak Road). Harvey's most impressive early designs were for the shops at the junction of Linden Road and Mary Vale Road. This large timber-framed group, designed in 1897, acts as a 'gateway' building to the Village. Also executed at this time were the almshouses and large semi-detached dwellings on the east side of Linden Road and Mary Vale Road. These were controlled by the Bournville Almshouse Trust, which was set up by Richard Cadbury shortly before his death from diphtheria on a visit to Palestine. The almshouses and associated dwellings were designed in 1897 by the well-known Birmingham architect, Ewan Harper. The attractive brick Tudor-style quadrangular almshouse block looks onto a grassed quadrangle, with a small meeting place at the centre and an orchard beyond. The rents from the adjacent houses were meant to cover the costs of the almshouses.

31 The Almshouses at Bournville. These were controlled by a separate Trust set up by Richard Cadbury shortly before his death. The dwellings were designed by E. and A.J. Harper in 1897.

32 These early dwellings on Linden Road were not far removed in style from the work of speculative developers. Harvey designed the central pair of houses for a William John Bird early in 1896.

At first, building was sporadic. The pace of development did increase significantly in the late 1890s, with almost 200 dwellings being built in 1899. Unlike most settlements, the Village proceeded to grow from the outside inwards. Besides further developments along Mary Vale Road, Linden Road, Laburnum Road and Bournville Lane, rapid progress was being made along Raddlebarn Lane, Beech Road, Elm Road and Willow Road. This rate of growth was not maintained in the early years of the 20th century.[38]

George Cadbury soon realised that certain lessees were making a considerable profit from the sale of their properties. One such case related to 32 Linden Road. Originally, this house was sold to W.T. Cull for £300. It was then purchased by R.G. Cull, a relation of the original leaseholder, for £340, who then sold it on to H. Duckitt for £372 10s.[39] On hearing of such cases, George Cadbury decided to revise his scheme in order to prevent such speculation. A parallel desire to guard against overt paternalism reinforced his decision to seek an alternative form of control and development for the Estate. The result was the formation of the Bournville Village Trust in December 1900.

The Deed of Foundation

The Deed of Foundation represents a more direct attempt to tackle the housing problem than was apparent in the original prospectus for the Bournville Estate.[40] The message was soon being reinforced by the Trustees and their staff. 'The main object of the Trust', the new Secretary and Manager reported in May 1901, 'is to provide healthy dwellings for people, with plenty of air and space.'[41] The Trust Deed is equally clear:

> The object is declared to be the amelioration of the condition of the working classes and labouring population in and around Birmingham, and elsewhere in Great Britain, by the provision of improved dwellings, with gardens and open spaces to be enjoyed therewith, and by giving them facilities ... for purchasing and acquiring the necessities of life.[42]

The Deed gave the Trustees extensive powers and a reasonable degree of discretion. The original Trustees were George Cadbury, Elizabeth Cadbury, Edward Cadbury and George Cadbury Jnr. George Cadbury, the Founder and first Chairman of the Trust, had further power to change the rules of the Trust and appoint and dismiss the staff appointed by the charity.[43]

The most obvious and significant of the Trust's commitments were to acquire and develop land and erect dwellings for the working classes. The latter were to be built 'in places of easy access to centres of labour'. Although the Trust was a registered charity, it was not George Cadbury's intention to subsidise the poor or offer them a dole:

> The Founder ... desires that the rent of such dwellings may if practicable be fixed on such a basis as to make them accessible to persons of the labouring and working classes, whom it is his desire to attract from the crowded and insanitary tenements which they now inhabit, without ever placing them in the position of being recipients of a bounty.[44]

As in the earlier prospectus, there was a requirement in the Deed that dwellings should not, as far as possible, occupy more than a quarter of their plots, and that the remaining portion should be devoted to gardens or open spaces around the houses. One-tenth of the whole Estate was to be devoted to public open spaces. Shops and even factories were to be allowed, so long as the latter did not occupy more than one-fifteenth of the area of the Estate. So as to be in a position to further the development of the community the Trustees were given the power to give land for the erection of places of worship, medical establishments, convalescent homes and schools. They were to be allowed to build and fit up libraries, technical institutes, schools, museums, reading rooms, gymnasia, clubs, recreation rooms, laundries, baths and wash-houses.

The terms of the Trust Deed allowed Trustees to retain and use such profits as accrued from the estate for the benefit of the community as a whole, and so gave them freedom to initiate or support other ventures. All such bodies were, however, to be organised and run on non-sectarian lines, so as to avoid the denominational strife which was still apparent in discussions about education and politics at that time.[45]

Although George Cadbury was no longer an out-and-out prohibitionist by 1900, the Trust Deed stipulated that 'none of the houses or buildings erected on any land subject to the Trust ... shall be used for the manufacture, or sale, or co-operative distribution of any beer, wine, spirits or intoxicating liquor'. Any future change in the rule had to be with the unanimous consent of all the Trustees, and any profits arising from the sale or distribution of alcohol had to be 'devoted to the securing for the village community recreation and counter-attractions to the liquor trade as ordinarily conducted'.[46]

The Trustees were empowered to use funds to undertake research about undertakings with similar aims to their own and to subscribe to, or invest in, comparable ventures. The Trust thus assisted a number of other organisations, such as the Bournville Tenants co-partnership company, Hampstead Garden Suburb and First Garden City Limited at Letchworth.[47] They also financed lecture programmes. In April 1902, H. Budgett Meakin was appointed to give lectures 'relative to the work of the Trust and the subject generally of Social Betterment as illustrated by what is done for the employees at Bournville, and at other places'.[48] He went on to publish a major study on *Model Factories and Villages: Ideal Conditions of Labour and Housing* in 1905.[49] Six years later, Raymond Unwin (who by that time was the leading planner in the country) accepted an invitation to take up a new town planning lectureship at the University of Birmingham funded by the Trust.[50] Unwin's lectures were reported to be 'very successful'.[51] He continued to give lectures at the University until 1914, when he left to become Chief Town Planning Inspector at the Local Government Board. After Unwin's departure, the course of lectures was completed by his partner, Barry Parker.

The Deed of Foundation established clear aims and objectives, but it also gave the Trustees a certain amount of flexibility as to the means by which they could achieve their goals. Whilst the guiding principles had been established, it is apparent from the records that the Trustees gave detailed attention to the working out of those principles. It was later noted that they never lost sight of 'the importance of detail'.[52]

In terms of personnel, besides the retention of W.A. Harvey as Estate Architect and the designation of D. Jones as head of the Garden Department, the key new appointment was that of John H. Barlow as Secretary to the Trust. Along with George Cadbury, 'the guiding and creative spirit [who] largely represented the scheme to the outside world', he was to be a significant figure in both the running of the Trust and the campaign that publicised the achievements of the Village. Cadbury, Harvey and Barlow attended conferences, spoke to interested groups of reformers, professionals, industrialists and politicians, and received the many visitors to Bournville. By the end of 1901 Barlow had produced the Trust's first handbook and was reporting on the very large number of people interested in the housing question who had either visited Bournville or who had asked for particulars about the scheme. The most significant group of visitors were those who took part in the Garden City Association's meeting at Birmingham and Bournville in 1901. After this and other visits, Barlow concluded, 'It is evident that the Village has come to be regarded as a place that ought to be seen by all who are interested in housing and kindred questions.' Most of these early visitors expressed pleasure at what they saw, although it should be remembered that the Village was far from complete at that time. Nonetheless, Barlow could report that Bournville was already responsible for 'setting an example in housing which cannot fail to raise the general standard'.[53]

In order to maintain tighter control over developments on the Bournville Estate, the Trust built houses mainly for rent in the period up to the First World War. More of the houses began to be built by the Trust's Direct Labour team, who erected 149 houses between 1903 and the early part of 1908.[54] The Trust began to use their surplus funds to build cottages from 1902, but the amounts they had available were not great. 'The funds at the disposal of the Trust', it was recorded, 'though sufficient for a certain amount of building are not yet such as to allow the carrying out of any large scheme.'[55] They also sought to 'produce the cheap cottages which are so important for securing the fulfilment of the purpose of the Trust'.[56] In addition, the Trust allowed some bigger houses to be built for sale on 99-year leases in the Edwardian period. 'This work has been carried out for the lessees by the Estate architect and staff,' it was reported in 1901, 'thus ensuring its agreement with the rest of the Village.'[57]

It was somewhat ironic that little building was undertaken in the Trust's first year of operation. The two Voyseyesque shops on Mary Vale Road that were under construction when the Trust was formed were completed. A small number of plots of land were let on 99-year building leases to George, Edward and George Cadbury Jnr. and cottages were built on these. The Garden Department, which had been established on a firm basis in 1899 by George Cadbury, was more active. The laying out of the Village Green was completed and trees, hedges and open spaces were attended to.[58]

By 1906, the building plots along Acacia Road, Maple Road and Linden Road had been almost filled. Sycamore Road and Thorn Road were also partly developed. The first public buildings on the Green had also appeared by this time. Ruskin Hall, the Meeting House and the Junior School were all finished by 1905. They were all designed by W.A. Harvey. His successor as Trust Architect, Bedford Tylor, designed the range of half-timbered shops on Sycamore Road. Tylor was also responsible for the housing built in the Village between 1905 and 1911. The creation of Woodbrooke Road led to a slight amendment of the Estate plan. Building developments were concentrated there and on Thorn Road, Hay Green Lane and Selly Oak Road. One element to note is the increasing use of short terraces and quadrangles in these schemes.

The Model Village and its Cottages

The surveyor, A.P. Walker, had designed the first three pairs of semi-detached dwellings on the Bournville Estate. Both in terms of their outward appearance and their layout these houses in Mary Vale Road were backward-looking and rather unexceptional. The largest of the three pairs, with its tile-hung frontage, was the most interesting. Despite the generous plot size, the houses had the characteristic long back projections of the typical Birmingham tunnel-back dwelling. Even the young, and more adventurous, Harvey did not break away from this type of plan at the outset. Some of his early designs for houses on Linden Road, Beech Road, Elm Road and Raddlebarn Lane have similar back projections, although from the first Harvey treated the façades of his houses with greater freedom and simplicity (see illustration 12). Certain details on the façades of these houses (like the dormer windows and drip mouldings) are reminiscent of the dwellings at Bedford Park.[59]

Subsequently, Harvey began to simplify his plans for the smaller cottages on the Estate. He sought, wherever possible, to include the outbuildings, scullery and the third bedroom within the main body of the building. By removing the back projection, Harvey was able to reduce materials and costs and provide the inhabitants with a better view of the large gardens provided at Bournville. As a result, a

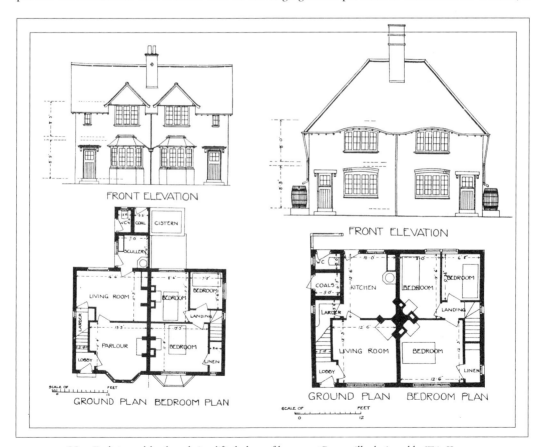

33   Early tunnel-back and simplified plans of houses at Bournville designed by W.A. Harvey.

simplified broad-fronted cottage began to emerge as one of the most characteristic early Bournville housing types. The vast majority of these early dwellings were semi-detached, and had low walls with gabled windows penetrating the roof line (see illustration 14). Such designs, while producing quite picturesque façades, generated rather awkward internal spaces in the bedrooms.

Drawings in the Trust archives show that the same designs were to be used, with subtle variations, on different streets within the estate. Even where the same, or similar, ground plans were repeated on the same road, monotony was avoided by treating the façades of the houses in a varied manner. A series of panoramic sketches of Beech Road in the Trust archives clearly show it was Harvey's intention to achieve variety in his street scenes.[60]

These early houses designed by Harvey at Bournville were predominantly brick with hand-made tiles or Welsh slate roofs. Occasionally, on unbroken roofs, Harvey used cheap pantiles to good effect. The cottages frequently had overhanging eaves and, sometimes, hipped roofs. On a number of cottages, Harvey introduced eaves that curved like eyebrows. This is, in effect, a reworking of a thatched roof in tile. Periodically, Harvey gave special treatment to chimney stacks. Bay windows, dormers and quite prominent porches were features used on some of these dwellings. Casement windows were widely employed by Harvey, although a number of houses have leaded lights. Harvey introduced Venetian windows into some of his larger blocks in the early 1900s.[61] On the whole, ornament was restricted, but half-timbering, decorative brickwork, carving, pebble-dash and pargetting were all part of Harvey's repertoire, especially on the more imposing buildings on the estate. He did, however, suggest that 'half timber should be used sparingly' on dwellings, and the way he handled this can be seen in houses on Mary Vale Road and Linden Road.[62] These more elaborate houses were often used to provide a contrast with the simpler cottages. 'We must study variety and artistic effect,' Harvey told members of the Oxford University Fabian Society in 1902. 'We must show people the beauty of architecture.'[63]

The sources for some of Harvey's designs and motifs at this early stage seem quite obvious. The larger houses on Bournville Lane and Mary Vale Road look back to Bedford Park.[64] The pebble-dashed shops and houses on Mary Vale Road, with their broad eaves and prominent buttresses, were clearly influenced by C.F.A. Voysey.[65] Shaw's 'old English' mode comes through in a number of half-timbered buildings.[66] On certain occasions, Harvey adopted a more eclectic approach. The semi-detached pair of houses on Sycamore Road, with their stepped gables, Venetian windows, elegant dormers of the kind used in the late 17th century and half-timbered porches, are among the most exotic and eclectic of his houses. The three blocks of houses in Holly Grove, built in 1900, feature a wealth of Arts and Crafts details. There, the effect was achieved by the use of hand-made bricks, half-timbering, pebble-dash and finely detailed wood and metal work (sometimes used all together). There are reminders here of Shaw, Baillie-Scott, Voysey and even Mackintosh.[67] These more exuberant designs undoubtedly have a strong visual impact, but their details are not always well resolved. It should be remembered that Harvey was a very young and inexperienced designer when he took over as Estate Architect at Bournville.

34   The timber-framed detached house was designed by Harvey for J.H. Whitehouse, editor of the *Bournville Works Magazine* and ardent follower of John Ruskin. The semi-detached dwellings on the right designed by Harvey in 1898 were clearly influenced by the work of C.F.A. Voysey.

35   A pair of large cottages in Sycamore Road was designed by W.A. Harvey for George Cadbury. The decorative plasterwork in the gables and around the windows was originally painted bright red.

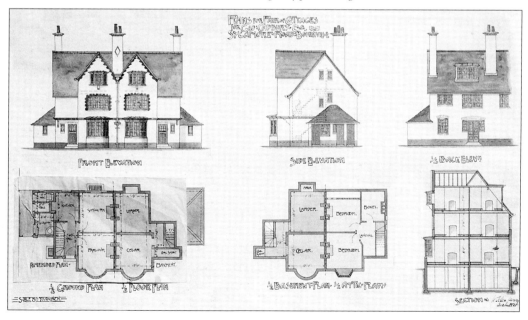

Elsewhere on the estate, Harvey occasionally used decorative plaster work to good effect. This is apparent in a number of houses at road junctions (which he felt needed special treatment) and a group of whitewashed cottages in Sycamore Road, where the effect was heightened by the use of colour.[68] Given this emphasis on variety and, occasionally, on artistic effect, it is not surprising that many of the early reports on the estate emphasise the picturesque nature of the scheme. *The Studio*, for instance, reported, 'The architect ... has introduced a large variety into his designs, which are very quaint and picturesque and revive the best traditions of country architecture.'[69] In similar vein, a 1907 review of the estate concluded, 'The village, from cottage to schools, is a remarkably varied achievement, especially for so young an architect.'[70]

These characteristics, of variety and picturesqueness, were also confirmed in Harvey's own account, *The Model Village and its Cottages: Bournville*, published in 1906.[71] There, greater emphasis was given in the plates to the more elaborately treated and heterogeneous dwellings. While Harvey's later designs remained varied, the effect of many of these works was simpler, quieter and frequently more harmonious. This trend was apparent in his work for Bournville Tenants after 1906. Certainly, Bournville was less flamboyant than Port Sunlight.[72]

36   The junction of Willow Road and Laburnum Road. Note the special treatment of the corner block and the varied treatment of the cottages along Willow Road.

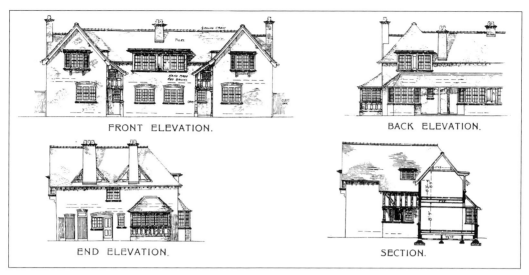

FRONT ELEVATION.

BACK ELEVATION.

END ELEVATION.

SECTION.

37   A larger pair of houses on Linden Road designed by W.A. Harvey in 1898. Note the restrained use of half-timbering, the more careful and elaborate treatment of the rear elevation.

'Art and Economy'

In trying to design pleasing small cottages, Harvey felt that the architect had to 'satisfy the demands of both art and economy'.[73] He had to try to reconcile these two potentially contradictory requirements in order to begin to fulfil the call for attractive cheap cottages at Bournville. To do this Harvey (and the Trust's building manager, L.P. Appleton) sought to save on construction costs. Compactness and regularity in the planning of dwellings were seen as means of achieving economies (though not at the expense of sacrificing privacy and homeliness of appearance in the cottages). By adapting the dimensions of dwellings to the stock sizes of building materials, waste could also be avoided.[74]

Harvey paid particular attention to the quality of materials. He believed, however, that worthy stock articles could be used to advantage. The use of inexpensive and simple internal fittings was urged in cottages to be let at low rentals. 'An excess of ornament should be avoided,' he asserted, 'especially if the aim is economy.'[75] Inglenooks and other expensive features were usually reserved for the better class of houses, though the former could occasionally be found in smaller dwellings. Harvey was not, however, one for making false economies. He stressed the importance of building homes that would last, for he recognised that the 'true cost of economy is that which will take into account the cost of repairs at the end of ten years'.[76]

38   Interior with inglenook. Dark green stain was used quite frequently by Harvey.

39　The austere block of four small dwellings built in Bournville Lane in 1902. Some leaseholders objected to the building of these cheaper cottages on the Estate.

Responding to the demand for cheaper cottages, Harvey could produce exceedingly simple cottage designs. The austere block of four dwellings on Bournville Lane, built in 1902, is a case in point. 'Economy of construction has been the main object in the design', Harvey explained.[77] He believed that privacy, homeliness of appearance and a pleasant environment, the essentials of a cottage home, had not been sacrificed in the process. Simple and cheap blocks like this one were to become the prototypes for the council houses of the inter-war period.[78]

While some of his designs displayed a greater simplicity in the 1900s, Harvey increasingly showed a talent for blending disparate elements into a harmonious whole. 'The soul of beauty is harmony', Harvey wrote in 1906, 'which may co-exist with the veriest simplicity; and it is in the harmonious treatment of parts, and not in useless and sometimes costly decoration, that a dwelling gains that homely appearance which it should be our aim to realise.'[79]

Simplicity and economy did not imply a lack of visual interest. Small cottages or simple terraced houses could be juxtaposed with larger detached and semi-detached houses to promote both social mix and architectural variety. Alternatively, by changing the street line and varying the treatment of the façades Harvey began to create a pleasing street picture from simple terrace blocks. This is especially true of his work on Kingsley Road for Bournville Tenants Limited.

With increasing confidence and maturity, Harvey seems to have felt more at ease working in this pleasing and unaffected way. There is an almost disarming simplicity about some of his designs before the First World War, as he sought to create an effect from the careful disposition of simple building blocks. At the Garden City Conference at Bournville in 1901, Raymond Unwin had declared, 'It is not to the row or the semi-detached villa that we must look for the solution to the housing problem in towns, but to the quiet quadrangle with its wide expanse of grass, or the square with its spacious garden.'[80] Harvey and his successor, Bedford Tylor, seemed to be moving in that direction after 1906. Of course, economic pressures pushed them along that path too. By 1904, the Trustees' funds were limited, and a phase of more economical house building ensued.

40   An L-shaped pair of houses at the corner of Woodbrooke Road and Thorn Road. The angled corners, the higher walls and the elaborate windows would have increased the cost of this block, which was one of the last designed by Harvey in Bournville Village.

FRONT ELEVATION.

There is some evidence to suggest that the Trustees felt that Harvey had emphasised 'art' rather than 'economy' in his house designs. Certain features of the last houses that Harvey had designed for the Trust on Thorn Road were criticised as being 'unsatisfactory and expensive'. 'Further care will be exercised in future', J.H. Barlow asserted, 'to avoid all needless outlay in planning and construction.'[81]

H. Bedford Tylor

In the quest for economy and efficiency, the new architect, Bedford Tylor, was initially instructed to repeat, as far as possible, old plans instead of preparing new ones for each block of houses. This policy did not stay in place for long, and Tylor was soon producing new, but more economical, plans. The average plot size of a number of houses built in Acacia, Linden, Maple and Thorn Roads in 1904 was considerably less than those constructed before that time.[82] No doubt this reduced costs a little, but the main reasons for the smaller plots were the presence of sand pits and the need to allow space for the new school.

Certainly, Tylor made a great effort to achieve economies. He tried to produce plans which it was hoped would 'beat all previous records for accommodation at a low inclusive rental'. Despite the rising costs of materials and wages throughout the Edwardian period, housing costs were reduced at Bournville. A block of four houses was constructed in 1908 for £959. At $5\frac{5}{8}$ d. per cubic foot, these were the lowest figures achieved on the Bournville Estate up to that time. Not satisfied with that effort, Tylor suggested that 'further economy would be attainable by building in more than one block at a time'.[83]

Eighteen new houses in short terraced blocks on Selly Oak Road and Hay Green Lane were built in 1909 for £4,179. This worked out at a cost of 5¼d. per cubic foot. A comparative survey showed that these houses cost 16 per cent less than houses constructed at Bournville in 1899. The reduction was due, in part, to the fact that the Trust were erecting simpler dwellings. The Trust's labour force was also working more quickly and efficiently by 1909.[84]

Not surprisingly, most of Tylor's houses are plainer than Harvey's. Terraced blocks and quadrangles figured more prominently in Tylor's repertoire. He was responsible for the single-storey blocks for old

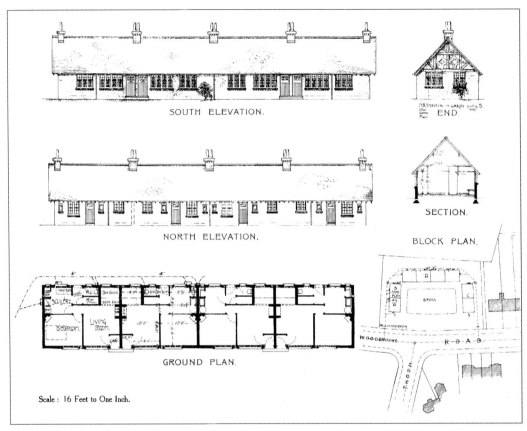

41   Single-storey blocks designed by Bedford Tylor for old people. Groups of these were erected on two grassed quadrangular plots in Woodbrooke Road in 1909-10.

people (or single women) on Woodbrooke Road, and for the quadrangles on Oak Tree Lane and Selly Oak Road. Tylor was, however, rather defensive about the latter. 'This method has been used', he reported in 1910, 'in consequence of the difficulties presented by the sites, and with the aim of securing an economical use of the land which from its contour would have been somewhat difficult to develop without waste.' These particular schemes were rather awkward and unresolved, and they were criticised at the time by some on the estate.[85]

Not all of Bedford Tylor's output was awkward, simple or austere. Some of his cottages overlooking the park are quite picturesque, while the larger blocks on Elm Road, designed by him, have elaborate rear elevations. (This was because, like some of Harvey's earlier houses, they overlooked the railway or highways, and the Trustees wanted to make a good impression on the travelling public.) Tylor also tended to design more asymmetrical blocks of houses than Harvey and these can be seen in a booklet of *Typical Plans* published by the Trust in 1911.[86] Half-timbered or rough-cast gables are the characteristically limited decorative features that Tylor allowed himself to use on a regular basis.

42 A more picturesque group overlooking the Park designed by Bedford Tylor in 1911. The mixture of flowers, shrubs and vegetables was typical of the Estate at that time.

43 One of the economical terraced blocks designed by H. Bedford Tylor and erected on Hay Green lane in 1909.

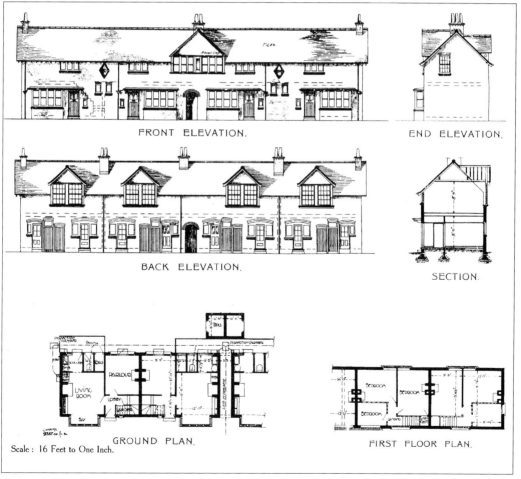

FRONT ELEVATION.

END ELEVATION.

BACK ELEVATION.

SECTION.

GROUND PLAN.

Scale : 16 Feet to One Inch.

FIRST FLOOR PLAN.

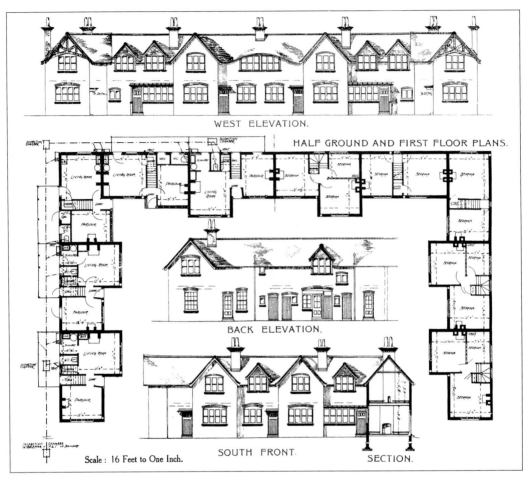

44   One of the quadrangular blocks on Selly Oak Road built in 1910. Most of the dwellings have through parlours or living rooms and a small scullery.

House Plans and layouts

While it is clear that both Harvey and Tylor sought to give the façades of their dwellings 'a pleasing appearance ... with the employment of the least costly materials', it is equally clear that they gave much thought to the internal layout of their houses.[87] This is especially true of the smaller cottages. The street pattern of the estate did not allow the architects of the original village as much freedom in terms of orientation as they would probably have liked. Harvey did design a number of larger houses where the principal rooms were placed at the back, where the aspect was favourable. Through living rooms, which allowed light and air from two sides of the house, were used by Harvey and Tylor. They also tended to place the scullery or kitchen overlooking the garden so as to offer the housewife a glimpse of nature.

Although it was rarely stated explicitly, the Bournville cottage and its garden were intended to promote domesticity. A man's place (when not at work) was in the garden and a woman's place was in the home. (The Firm's policy reinforced this because 'Cadbury's Angels' had to relinquish their jobs when they got married.) The architects seem to have paid attention to the kitchen and the hearth and tried hard to make even the most economical of cottages 'homely'.

In the smallest cottages and bungalows there was little leeway for personal design choices. When they progressed beyond these minimal dwellings, there does seem to have been a difference in outlook between Harvey and Bedford Tylor. Harvey favoured the use of one spacious living room over the parlour plan. 'For a model village or a garden city it is strongly recommended that the plan should be adopted freely', he wrote in 1906, 'and the preference for the useless front room in small cottages discouraged.'[88] This was a view shared by other reforming architects, like Parker and Unwin.[89] Although Harvey claimed that no difficulty had been found in letting these dwellings at Bournville, many lessees and tenants did not share the views of the reformers. 'Now, rightly or wrongly, there is a demand for a parlour', John H. Barlow told the National Advisory Town Planning Committee in 1913, 'and this has been recognised at Bournville.'[90] Bedford Tylor tried to solve this issue by reducing the size of the scullery and providing two living rooms in the cottages he designed between 1906 and 1911.[91]

Although they might have disagreed about certain design issues, Harvey and Bedford Tylor were clearly supportive of the broad aims and objectives of the Founder and the Trust. It is also apparent that they were happy with the Model Village and its cottages, because they (and other members of the Trust's staff) chose to live on the Estate. Indeed, Harvey, Bedford Tylor and Appleton were near neighbours on Linden Road.

In order to satisfy the demands of different classes and households, a range of house types was built in Bournville. The smallest were the one-storey cottages containing a living room, scullery, one bedroom, a tool store and w.c. These were let to single women or pensioners, and they proved very popular. Some two-bedroomed cottages were also built on the estate before 1914. The first block of these was completed in 1902 on Bournville Lane. These small, four-roomed dwellings were tenanted immediately they were ready and appeared to give satisfaction. 'The demand for houses continues unabated', the Trust's secretary noted in September 1903, 'and it seems as though an almost unlimited number of the cheaper houses can be let.'[92] The Trust used its own surplus funds to build similar simple cottages in Rowheath Lane (later renamed Selly Oak Road) and Maple Road in 1903. Although a number of larger semi-detached and detached houses were built at Bournville, three-bedroomed cottages were the most numerous group of dwellings on the Estate. The most popular of these contained a living room, scullery, a small parlour and the usual conveniences.

The Trustees believed that every home, besides having a pleasing exterior and adequate accommodation, should also have a bath. The larger houses had separate bathrooms, but other expedients had to be tried in the smaller cottages. At Bournville, wherever there was no bathroom, the bath was placed in the kitchen. This was considered the most suitable arrangement as hot water was usually to hand. As the kitchens in the small cottages were hardly spacious, various devices were employed to prevent the bath being an inconvenience when not in use. One alternative was the sunken bath. Another was the table bath, where the bath was fixed on the floor and then covered with a work surface. The Patent Adjustable Cabinet Bath, which could be raised and lowered from a built-in cupboard, was regarded as

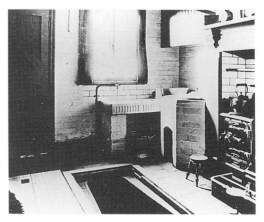

45   *Left*. The Patent Adjustable Bath.

46   *Above*. The sunken bath.

47   *Below*. The Playground and Bath-house in Laurel Grove. The latter was designed by Harvey in 1897.

more successful than the sunken or table bath. Another patent bath used at Bournville in slightly larger cottages was the Cornes' Combined Scullery-Bath-Range and Boiler. Because this used heat from the range, it was economical on fuel and saved space in dwellings still not large enough to have a separate bathroom. This particular type was used in the flamboyant pair of houses with the stepped gables on Sycamore Road. The emphasis on health and cleanliness could be taken to great lengths. One of the houses, built in 1897 adjacent to the children's playground in Laurel Grove, had bathing facilities for boys and girls. The Bath House was, however, closed in 1912. Clearly there was no real demand for such a facility when the houses of Bournville had their own baths.

The Bournville Landscape

In trying to design homes for the residents in the village, the promoters and architects of Bournville concerned themselves not just with the outward appearance and internal fittings of the cottages but also with the surrounding environment. Fresh air and healthy outdoor recreation were just as important to the planners of the model village of Bournville. Cadbury and Harvey sought to provide 'homes that are homelike in the simple harmony of their appearance, and healthy amid the free space surrounding them'.[93] Gardens, recreation grounds and open spaces were, therefore, an essential part of the overall plan. Bournville was described in 1903 as 'a place better than a town, because of its gardens; better than a village, because of its sanitary and spacious houses'.[94] Trees were an important ingredient in the landscaping of Bournville, as the street names of the Village constantly remind us. Besides the larger trees in Stocks Wood and on the main thoroughfares, smaller ornamental trees, bushes and hedges were planted near the cottages.

The Bournville Garden

The garden was regarded as being a feature of such importance in the model village that almost as much attention was paid to its layout as to the houses themselves. George Cadbury's profound interest in gardening and his preoccupation with the virtues of outdoor village life was part of his campaign to provide 'opportunities for the natural and healthful occupation of cultivating the soil'. According to Harvey, the pleasures and benefits of tending a garden were manifold:

> If it were necessary for their health that they get fresh air, it was equally to the advantage of their moral life that they should be brought into contact with nature. There was an advantage, too, in bringing the working man to the land, for, instead of losing money in the amusements usually sought in the towns, he saved it from his garden produce.[95]

In direct and obvious ways Bournville residents were encouraged to tend their large and well-stocked gardens, and discouraged, by the ban on the sale of alcohol on the estate, from seeking solace and entertainment in the public house.

As only 25 per cent of each building plot was given over to the dwelling, the average size of gardens at Bournville in the early years was 600 square yards. This was regarded as being the largest area most men could conveniently cultivate. The gardens were carefully laid out before

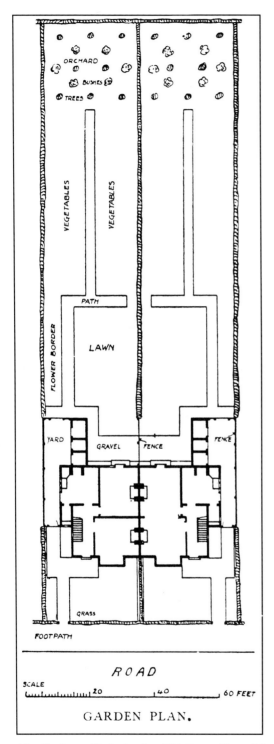

GARDEN PLAN.

48   The Bournville Garden, from W.A. Harvey, *The Model Village and its Cottages: Bournville*, 1906.

the residents moved into their houses. Fruit trees were planted at the bottom of each garden so as to provide fruit and to act as a screen between the houses. Creepers and forest trees, to frame the houses, were also introduced. Hedges were planted between the cottages, and were also used to form road boundaries (although small fences had to be erected until these hedges grew to a respectable height). The kind of garden laid out by the Trust staff allowed for a lawn and, of course, for a vegetable plot. The overall effect was captured by an Edwardian commentator: 'Flower gardens bloom in front, and kitchen gardens, heavy with fruit and vegetables, lie in the rear.' Another horticultural writer concurred, claiming that 'many of the gardens were models of usefulness and beauty'.[96]

For the uninitiated, the Trust's gardeners were available to provide advice and help for the tenants. Fruit trees were planted by the gardeners, and then pruned for three years, as were climbing plants and bush fruit. These were also replaced if adverse weather conditions, rather than negligence, could be blamed. Every encouragement was given to the residents to take up practical gardening. Lectures were arranged, gardening classes were held, and competitions were promoted. The Village Council, which bought plants and seeds on a co-operative basis, actively promoted these horticultural activities. Allotments were available for the real enthusiasts.

George Cadbury began from the premise that gardening was the ideal compensatory activity for those engaged in factory labour. As a vegetarian, he believed that increased consumption of vegetables would improve the health of the nation. He never tired of enunciating the economic benefits of gardening. Firstly, time spent productively working the soil could not be spent wastefully in the public house. Secondly, whilst being engaged in such a healthy form of activity the Bournville gardener would also be saving money on his food bill. It was calculated that in 1902 the average value of the produce of the gardens of Bournville was at least 2s. 6d. per week. Fruit, salad and vegetables were the main produce. Some people even kept fowl.[97]

It was often argued that, if the value of the garden produce were taken into account, rents at Bournville were effectively reduced to a level comparable with poorer properties in inner city areas. Whilst it was not safe to take into account the value of garden produce in every case, owing to variations in the soil and the tenants' skill, leisure and commitment, it was admitted even by the more sceptical that 'in nearly all cases there is a substantial return'.[98] By 1913 there were 1,100 gardens and 1,104 allotments on the estate.[99]

49   Front gardens in bloom.

50   'Kitchen gardens, heavy with fruit and vegetables': the productive gardens of Elm Road and Raddlebarn Road, *c*.1906.

Although some of them required training, there can be no doubt that most Bournville residents were enthusiastic gardeners. While some felt under some pressure to conform, most clearly fulfilled the hopes and desires of George Cadbury. Undoubtedly, the level of horticultural activity was exceptionally high. One American expert suggested that the gardening at Bournville was, perhaps, the finest in the world in 1913.[100] It was apparent that, beside the value of the produce, the planting of a large number of trees and shrubs also brought significant environmental, social and psychological benefits to the residents. 'Gardening plays a great, perhaps the leading, part in the social scheme of Bournville,' one commentator concluded. The generous gardens also permitted the construction of houses with wider frontages, which allowed much health-giving light and air into these homes and pleasant views from the houses.[101]

Open Spaces

Whilst all the dwellings at Bournville were given ample private gardens, the Estate as a whole was provided with substantial open spaces. These included the Green, which was grazed in the early years, the Triangle, originally a lawn with shrubs and flower beds intersected by paths, Camp Wood, a sloping area covered with old forest trees, and the land designated as a Park, alongside the Bourn Brook. In the early years, some of these were not used for active recreation. A report on the Green in 1903 clearly highlights the situation and provides a reminder of the rural atmosphere in the Village at the time:

> The paths on the Green need using badly as they are becoming weed grown. Access to the Green for tenants could be easily made by fixing swing or clap gates at the two lower entrances whilst it could still be grazed by sheep for which the upper entrance could remain locked as at present. It would also greatly improve the Green.[102]

51   The Triangle, Bournville Village.

52   The Park after 1907, when the sports facilities were provided.

A children's playground was laid out alongside the Bath House in Laurel Grove in the late 1890s. By 1907, however, one critic complained of 'the entire lack of provision for outdoor recreation'.[103] The lack of proper facilities for children in parts of the Estate meant that they might congregate and cause a nuisance where they were not wanted. In the early years of the century, the Triangle seems to have become a favoured meeting place for the children of Bournville. Their presence was not welcomed by the staff of the Garden Department:

> Since the placing of the seat in the Triangle the children have gathered there in numbers to play. They climb upon the seat, race over the grass and sometimes get amongst the shrubs, so that a playground is badly needed for these small children.[104]

A second playground was later provided in Holly Grove in 1908 for the children on the eastern side of the Estate to help rectify this situation. Unfortunately, the land on which the playground had been laid out was sold to Cadbury Brothers in 1913 for cottages for their firemen.

The extensive sports grounds and recreational areas provided for the use of Cadbury Brothers' employees contributed to the green and open aspect of the Estate, and also gave the impression that the Village was plentifully provided with facilities. They also acted as an attractive *cordon sanitaire* around the factory. Unfortunately, a majority of the residents did not work at the factory and thus did not benefit from this provision in any direct way. The laying out of play areas in the Park in 1907-8 did, however, improve matters.

Most of the old trees on the estate were retained and a large number of new trees were also planted along the roads, usually limes and planes. These soon helped to improve the streetscape of the model village (although in later years they were to cause some problems). It should also be remembered that Bournville was at this time on the edge of the built-up area of the city, and country lanes and farmland lay just beyond the western boundary of the Village.

Public Facilities

The shops on Mary Vale Road, built between 1897 and 1900, provided an early focal point for life in the Village. There could be found the retail outlets of H.W. Smith, who sold groceries and dairy produce, James Healey, a boot maker and repairer, W. Sanders, a confectioner, and Alfred Allely, the ironmonger. Two more stores were soon opened on Raddle Barn Lane, but the Green became the hub of the Village after 1905. Given the strength of George Cadbury's religious beliefs, it was hardly surprising that one of the first public buildings on the Green was the strikingly simple Y-shaped Quaker Meeting House. It was designed by W.A. Harvey and completed in 1905. It resembles in shape (though not in materials) the First Church of Christ Scientist in Manchester by Edgar Wood. Its prominent round-arched entrance and side arms draw the worshipper into the Meeting House. The timber-framed interior is striking but simple. Almost uniquely for Quaker meeting houses, it had an organ, donated by George Cadbury. The other religious building completed before the First World War, the Anglican Church Hall (1913), was designed by Harvey in an Italian Romanesque style.

53 The first shops on the Estate. These were designed by Harvey in 1897 and erected the following year on the edge of the Estate at the junction of Mary Vale Road and Linden Road.

54 The Quaker Meeting House, Bournville Green.

55   The laying of the foundation stone of the Infant School. George and Elizabeth Cadbury with their youngest daughter, Ursula. W.A. Harvey is on the right.

The west side of the Green is dominated by the Village schools and Ruskin Hall. The Junior School, with its broad, squat tower, Gothic windows and rich, didactic carvings by Benjamin Creswick, was completed in 1905 at a cost of about £20,000.[105] It was paid for by George and Elizabeth Cadbury. The demand for schools at Bournville had been mounting since the turn of the century. Unfortunately, there were long delays before the school was sanctioned and built. These were partly attributable to the restrictive and parsimonious attitude of the local Education Committee and partly to the Board of Education in London. Eventually, the latter body sanctioned George Cadbury's generous plans for the school. It consisted of 12 classrooms grouped around a large central hall. Frescoes based on scenes from the New Testament, executed on the walls of the hall by Mary Sargent Florence and Mary Creighton McDowall, were completed in 1914. The school also had a cookery room, laundry, workshop, laboratory and library, as well as about 2½ acres of land. This imposing brick and stone building could take up to 540 pupils, yet it did not fully satisfy the demand for school places in the locality. The infants had to be taught at Ruskin Hall for several years.[106]

The adjacent Infant School, with its oriel windows, half-timbering and decorative chimney stacks in the Elizabethan manner, opened in 1910. This, too, was paid for by George and Elizabeth Cadbury, who, once again, insisted on them being built to a higher standard than that thought appropriate by the local education authority.

56 The Village Schools, paid for by George and Elizabeth Cadbury and designed by W.A. Harvey. The Junior School (1905) is on the right and the Infant School (1910) is on the left.

57 The timber-framed Edwardian shops on the Green designed by Bedford Tylor. Roy's bread van figures prominently.

Letitia Haynes has left a graphic picture of life at the Infant School under the Headmistress, Miss Pumphrey. 'Discipline was firm but kind', she wrote, 'and sincerely based on character training.' She believed that the atmosphere in the school was happy and restful. Although the teaching of reading seems to have been taken very seriously, other subjects were beginning to figure significantly in the curriculum. Handwork was beginning to be taught more extensively and particular attention was given to hygiene and cleanliness. The Bournville Schools seem to have been popular with pupils, parents and teachers. In part, this is because they were so well provided. As one enthusiastic memorialist wrote:

> The Cadbury family found nothing too good for their schools, neither the Infant School, nor the adjacent 'Big School' to which the infants were promoted between the age of seven and eight, and where most of them remained until they left school at the age of 14. There were large play areas, with cover for wet weather, and shrubberies, gardens and well-kept lawns, although these latter were only accessible under supervision.[107]

The architect for both schools was W.A. Harvey, who also designed Ruskin Hall. This cultural centre, later an art school, was built as a memorial to the great Victorian art and social critic, John Ruskin, whose influence on Cadbury and other environmental reformers was considerable. Constructed between 1902 and 1905, this L-shaped brick and stone building with mullioned windows and prominent gables has the form of a 16th-century Midlands manor house.[108] Both the Junior School and Ruskin Hall were in what Pevsner called Harvey's 'early twentieth-century Tudor style'. A range of shops completed the south-east side of the Green. The timber-framed shops were designed by Bedford Tylor and completed by 1908. A further group of brick-built shops and the slightly more imposing bank were built at about the same time. The latter was a branch of Lloyds' Bank, whilst the other outlets included a Post Office, a pharmacy (O.W. Evans), a butcher's (Thomas E. Lowe), a baker's (Daniel Roy), a draper's (James Underwood), a village tailor and outfitters (Bryden and Son), a hardware store (F. Davies), a greengrocer and fishmonger's shop (John T. Payne) and a family grocery store (J.A. Shipley).[109]

One of the most noticeable features on the Green is the centrally placed Rest House. Built just before the First World War, to designs by Harvey and Wicks, this octagonal structure was erected to commemorate the Silver Wedding of George and Elizabeth Cadbury. It was paid for by Cadbury workers from around the world. It was not a typical reworking of vernacular elements, but a close copy of the 16th-century Market Hall at Dunster in Somerset.[110] Shortly after, Harvey and Wicks supervised the reconstruction and re-erection of Selly Manor. This complex but picturesque building, dating from between the 15th and 17th centuries, had originally stood on a site about a mile from the Model Village. Such reconstructions were very unusual at the time in Britain, although they have become more common in recent decades. Some 15 years later, the 14th-century cruck-framed hall house from Minworth Greaves was also rebuilt on an adjacent site. Both give an air of authenticity to the Village, and this was no doubt intentional.

The area on the north side of the Green, beyond the Meeting House, remained vacant for almost 30 years. At one point the site was earmarked for an Anglican Church. When the Church of England authorities began to build a church hall on the opposite side of the Green, plans for an impressive block

58   Selly Manor (in the foreground) and Minworth Greaves House. These original timber-framed manor houses were taken down and re-erected at Bournville. The process was overseen by the architects, Harvey and Wicks.

59   *Below left*. Ruskin Hall was completed in 1905. It was built as a memorial to John Ruskin and was the Village's early social and cultural centre. Art classes were introduced at an early date and continue to be provided in this building, which is now part of the University of Central England.

60   *Below right*. The Rest House designed by W.A. Harvey and erected to commemorate George and Elizabeth Cadbury's Silver Wedding. It was paid for by Cadbury workers from around the world and opened in 1914.

of co-operative homes were put forward by Harvey and Wicks in 1913.[111] H. Clapham Lander had advocated such a scheme at the 1901 Garden City Association conference at Bournville, and he went on to design Sollershott Hall at Letchworth in 1911.[112] The Bournville venture did not come to fruition. The north side of the Green did not get its full complement of public buildings until after the First World War, when the Day Continuation Schools were built, to designs by J.R. Armstrong.

Away from the Green, several other public buildings of note were constructed or adapted. The Beeches was built by George and Elizabeth Cadbury in 1908 to provide holidays for children from the slums of Birmingham. During the summer months 'Father and Mother Cole' washed, weighed, fed, lodged and entertained relays of city children. As a result of the fresh air, good food and regular sleep, the children usually returned home healthier and heavier than when they arrived. The children were among those who were entertained to tea by George and Elizabeth Cadbury at the Manor House.[113]

During the early years of the 20th century, the Birmingham Cripples Union used to bring some of their patients out to the fields of Manor Farm. There, groups of about 150 children could enjoy the light and air, and sight and sounds, of the countryside for a few hours. In 1909 a large house on the opposite side of Bristol Road from the Manor House fell vacant. George Cadbury purchased it for use as a hospital for crippled children. The Woodlands hospital was officially opened on 22 June 1909. At first it had 37 beds, but extensions in 1914 increased the number to 70. Elizabeth Cadbury remained Chairman of the House Committee of The Woodlands until the hospital was taken over by the state in 1948.[114]

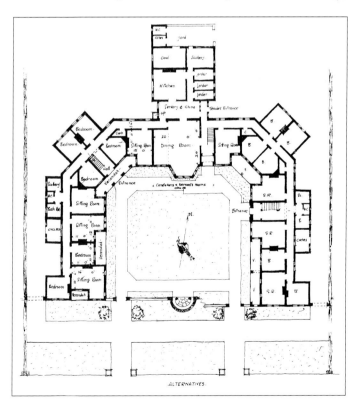

61   Harvey and Wicks 1913 plans for Co-operative Homes at Bournville.

62   The Beeches was used initially as a holiday home for city children and a convalescent home for Salvation Army officers. It later served as a continuation school and a management training centre.

Another noteworthy early building among the public and recreational facilities in the village was the *Old Farm Inn*, formerly Bourn Brook or Froggatt's Farm. This farmhouse was converted into a temperance tavern by W.A. Harvey in 1900. The *Old Farm Inn* was run by the Bodycotes. Serving non-alcoholic beverages (including, of course, drinking chocolate), food and tobacco, it embodied George Cadbury's notions of fellowship, health and temperance.

Bournville and its inn, though models of their sort, were never fully part of 'Merrie England'. Bournville was a sober and disciplined re-creation of the pre-industrial village. Although many commented on the picturesqueness of the Estate, others chafed at 'the prim tidiness of it all'. The Village certainly had an air of ordered informality.[115]

63 & 64   *The Old Farm Inn.* Harvey converted the old Bournbrook (or Froggatt's) Farm into a temperance tavern in 1900, hence the pure milk tub on the bar.

The atmosphere of calm respectability was reinforced by the creation of the Selly Oak Colleges on land on either side of the Bristol Road. They are a significant presence on the Estate, but they are separate from the Trust's activities. This group of colleges had its origin in 1903 when George Cadbury gave his former home, Woodbrooke, to become a 'Settlement for Social and Religious Study'. It was designed primarily, but not exclusively, for the Society of Friends. Kingsmead, another Quaker college, this time for the training of foreign missionaries, followed in 1905. Other institutions for the training of women missionaries were established nearby. Carey Hall, completed in 1912, served the Baptists, the Presbyterians and the London Missionary Society, while the later College of the Ascension (1923) was an Anglican foundation. Westhill College, founded in 1907 by George Hamilton Archibald, was a non-denominational centre set up to train youth leaders and welfare workers in the sphere of religious education. W.A. Harvey provided the designs for Westhill, Kingsmead and Carey Hall. Fircroft was rather different from the other religious institutions. It was a college for working men set up in 1909 in conjunction with the Workers' Educational Association, the Adult School, Labour and Co-operative movements. It eventually found a more permanent home in the half-timbered former residence of George Cadbury Jnr. This L-shaped house was built to the designs of W.A. Harvey in 1902.[116]

Bournville Tenants Limited

Between 1906 and 1913, a new development was started on the south-western boundary of the Bournville Estate. This second scheme was built on a 20-acre plot off Northfield Road, leased from the Bournville Village Trust by Bournville Tenants Limited. They were a tenants' co-partnership company registered under the Friendly Societies' Acts in August 1906. The stimulus for the venture was a meeting held in June 1906 at Ruskin Hall. The meeting was chaired by John Sutton Nettlefold, and was addressed by two other leading advocates of co-partnership housing, Sybella Gurney and Henry Vivian M.P. Assistance in starting the Bournville society was given by F. Litchfield of the Co-partnership Tenants Limited. Tom Bryan M.A. was the first chairman and David Glass was the first secretary of Bournville Tenants Limited. It was part of the co-partnership idea that residents buy shares in the societies. Loan stock was also required to launch such schemes. Bournville Tenants were no doubt helped by the fact that, at the outset, George Cadbury intimated that he was prepared to put up to £7,000 into the society.[117]

The position of the society's estate was regarded as being 'in every way desirable'. It lay on high ground with extensive views over wooded countryside midway between Cotteridge and Northfield. It was relatively close to Kings Norton railway station and within walking distance of the trams on the Pershore Road. The site plan for this co-partnership scheme was the work of W.A. Harvey. The main features of the site were the triangular green and the two recreation grounds. The number of houses on the estate was restricted to 11 per acre. The houses, as in Bournville Village itself, were not to occupy more than a quarter of the site. The majority of the dwellings were designed by Harvey, though H. Bedford Tylor and David W. Glass, the Secretary and Manager of Bournville Tenants Limited, were responsible for some of the houses on Woodlands Park Road.[118]

The society began building in November 1906. By August 1907, 35 houses were either completed or in the course of erection. The first 18 houses were put out to contract, but thereafter direct labour was used. Almost two-thirds of the 150 houses planned had been completed by the summer of 1909. The Bournville Tenant's estate was finished at a cost of £52,000 by the autumn of 1913. The costs might have been lower, but Kings Norton and Northfield Urban District Council again insisted on the provision of ordinary bye-law roads. In addition to the extra expense, it also affected the planners' ability to produce a picturesque treatment of the roadway. The tasteful arrangement of their front gardens by the tenants and the road-side planting of trees by the Tenants soon began to temper the ill-effects of the local authority's rigid stance on road-building on the estate. Local commentators soon began to comment favourably on the venture. A writer from the *Birmingham Post* was full of praise for this scheme:

> From the central tennis lawn and bowling green the village presents an attractive appearance to the onlooker; glimpses of the distant country, well-wooded and undulating, may be caught between the houses on the north side. On the south side the lawns are fringed with a belt of shrubs and trees, and all round the tenants have well stocked and charmingly laid out gardens.[119]

As the aim of Bournville Tenants Limited was 'to promote the erection, co-operative ownership and administration of houses for working men and others' there was some variety in the size and treatment

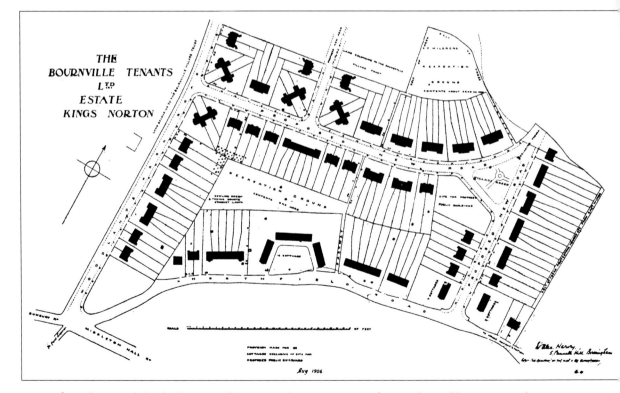

65   The original plan for the Bournville Tenants Ltd. estate, August 1906. It was designed by W.A. Harvey, but some modifications were made to the plan, most notably on Kingsley Road.

66 Semi-detached dwellings on Woodlands Park Road. The block in the centre was designed by H. Bedford Tylor in December 1906.

67 Houses at the junction of Woodlands Park Road and Kingsley Road. From a Bournville Tenants Ltd. prospectus, *c*.1907.

68   Simple, short terraced blocks on Kingsley Road designed by W.A. Harvey and set around a grassed quadrangle.

69   *Below*. The triangular open space on the Bournville Tenants' estate. Note the contrast between the more richly treated block on the right and the remaining simpler dwellings.

of the houses on their estate.[120] Whilst a significant number of semi-detached dwellings were erected on Woodlands Park Road and Northfield Road, on Kingsley Road Harvey achieved a new effect by grouping blocks of houses in a simple but effective way. Certain dwellings were treated in a more decorative manner. As in the Village itself, Harvey used these more richly detailed groups as counterpoints to the plainer terraces. He also continued to give special emphasis to corner blocks, and nowhere is this more clearly demonstrated than at the junction of Northfield Road and Hawthorne Road and at the corner of Kingsley Road and Woodlands Park Road.

In terms of accommodation, the dwellings on the Bournville Tenants' estate ranged from small two-bedroomed cottages with just a living room and a kitchen and a detached w.c. and coal shed in the rear yard, through to quite large semi-detached houses with a hall, drawing room, dining room, kitchen, scullery, coal shed and w.c. attached to the rear of the house, three bedrooms and an attic. Designs for three-bedroomed cottages with either two or three rooms downstairs were more commonly used by Harvey, Bedford Tylor and Glass. Such arrangements were found in both the larger terraced blocks and most of the semi-detached dwellings. The promoters and the architects generally described the dwellings as 'cottages with gardens'. This undoubtedly reflected their desire for 'a land of garden villages with large open spaces'. 'Kings Norton Model Village' or 'The Beauty Spot of the Midlands' was not to be covered with tenements or even mere houses. Rural terminology and arcadian imagery were drawn on to describe this outlying estate as well as the Model Village itself.[121]

A change of direction

The encouragement given to Bournville Tenants signalled a significant change of direction for the Bournville Village Trust. Shortages of funds meant that they had to limit their own building activities. 'The Trustees have now decided to discontinue building after filling up the remaining available sites in the Village,' the Secretary reported in 1911. 'The intention is to endeavour to lease building land to co-partnership or kindred societies, and to private individuals, and thus continue the development of the Estate.'[122]

One consequence of this change was the departure of the Estate Architect, Bedford Tylor. The Trustees also decided to close down the Building Department after they had completed work on the blocks in Selly Oak Road and Oak Tree Lane. By 1911 the Department had erected over 340 houses, 10 shops, a bank and the Bournville Meeting House, as well as other associated work.[123] The architectural duties of the Trust were taken over by S.A. Wilmot, who was also engaged by Cadbury Brothers at that point. Wilmot was already making a name for himself, having won prizes in site planning and cottage design competitions at Yeovil in the summer of 1911.[124]

Although there was a continuing demand for dwellings at Bournville, few houses were constructed on the Estate in the years immediately before the First World War. 'As usual', Barlow noted at the end of 1911, 'the greatest number of applications are for houses up to 6s. a week clear.'[125] Among the small number of houses constructed in 1912 and 1913 were some for H.B. Tylor's 'Home Purchase Scheme'. It was said that a certain amount of interest had been shown in this venture, which Tylor had taken up with the Trust's blessing after he left their employment in 1911. Indeed, the eight plots in Woodlands

70 Houses built on Woodlands Park Road under H. Bedford Tylor's 'Home Purchase Scheme' 1911-13.

Park Road for this scheme were the only sites leased by the Trust for building in 1912.[126] The dwellings were similar to ones that Tylor had designed for other parts of the Estate. A few more plots were leased before the outbreak of war in 1914. The only other building that took place on the Estate at this time was the construction of a group of firemen's cottages in Sycamore Road and Holly Grove for Cadbury Brothers. The site had been used for a children's playground for a number of years.[127]

The Trust's shift in policy was confirmed in 1911 when a plan to develop the Weoley Hill estate, to the north of the Bristol Road, got under way. This scheme was to be undertaken by Weoley Hill Limited, a public utility society, on land leased from the Bournville Village Trust. The society, whose draft rules were drawn up in 1913, sought to borrow money from the Public Works Loans Commissioners to develop the site. George Cadbury Jnr., who was closely involved in the scheme, explained that the aim of the promoters was 'to provide on a good business basis good houses for working men at a working man's rent, with big gardens and in an open situation such as were not obtainable under conventional housing conditions'.[128] It was originally intended that the majority of the properties would be let at rents of between 6s. 6d. and 7s. 6d. per week. Given the initial desire to produce good quality houses at relatively low rents, standardised designs were thought necessary. 'There cannot be much to spare for architectural features and individuality of design,' it was asserted. The lessons learned about 'art' and 'economy' in previous years were, once again, to be put into practice. 'Variety will have to sought', it was explained, 'in the method of grouping, the relation of the ground plan to the road line, the intermixture of the three grades of house to be built.'[129] In the end, however, the houses on the Weoley Hill estate were built for sale on 99-year leases. The pressure to economise and standardise was therefore slightly reduced.

Raymond Unwin, the leading Garden City architect and planner, was lecturing at the University of Birmingham at the time. Although he was asked to submit layout plans for the Weoley Hill estate, the scheme presented by the Trust's own architect, S.A. Wilmot, was deemed to be the most satisfactory. This estate, which has a more interesting plan than Bournville Village, was laid out on a south-facing slope. The plan features roads of varying width and culs-de-sac, elements which had visual interest and economy to recommend them and which had recently been used to good effect at Hampstead Garden Suburb.[130] The layout provided for playing fields and open spaces for recreation, as well as the obligatory large gardens. Building did begin during the war, but most of the estate was completed in the 1920s.

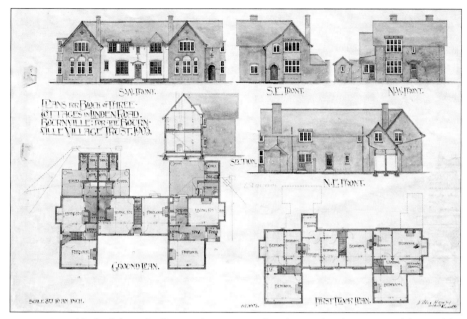

71 A block of three dwellings at the junction of Linden Road and Acacia Road designed by Harvey. The central cottage has a through living room and parlour and has a pebble-dashed exterior. The outer blocks are faced with brick and have more elaborate windows. The bays and the roof were covered with green Westmorland slate.

72 10-12 Sycamore Road, designed by W.A. Harvey in the early 1900s. One of the more unusual larger pairs of houses with Dutch gables, Venetian windows, Renaissance dormers and timber-framed porches.

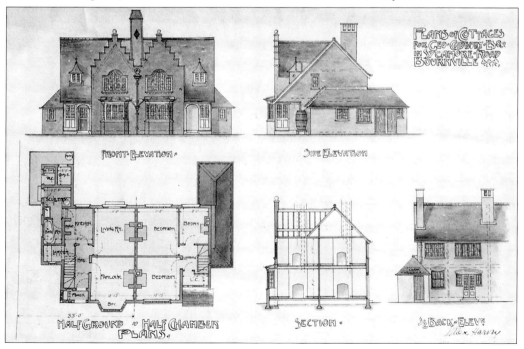

The social complexion of the Village

The Cadburys gave much time, effort and money to ensure the success of Bournville. If W.A. Harvey gave the estate its aesthetic character, George and Elizabeth Cadbury did much to establish the social tone of the Village. Their message was clear: they wanted to encourage the residents to live clean, healthy and respectable lives. Although George Cadbury claimed that he set up the Bournville Village Trust so as to guard against the dangers of paternalism, the Trust, through its building covenants and its tenants' rule books, could establish the guidelines for life on the estate. Furthermore, George and Elizabeth Cadbury continued to promulgate their views amongst the residents. Whenever a new family moved onto the estate, Mrs. Cadbury would usually make a special visit to welcome the newcomers and ensure that they were aware of their communal responsibilities. A card printed with 'Suggested Rules of Health' was issued to each household. Advice was offered on general health, diet and social behaviour. Alcohol, tobacco, pork and aerated bread were to be avoided. Single beds were advocated: 'double beds are now little used in civilised countries'. Cold baths, breathing through the nostrils with the mouth closed, walking and gardening were all recommended. The latter, especially, was fervently promoted.[131]

Clearly, some, though not all, of Cadbury's ideas coincided with the aims and aspirations of many of the early residents, who included some Adult School members. The fact that many took to gardening with relish was apparent. It was evident that the Villagers had a healthier environment than the slum dwellers of Birmingham. George Cadbury continually emphasised the fact that the death rate at Bournville was very low, and this, he believed, gave some indication of the healthiness of the village. In 1904, for example, the death rate at Bournville was 6.9 per thousand compared with 19 per thousand for the city as a whole. Similarly, when comparative tests were carried out, Bournville children were found to be taller and heavier than children of the same age in inner city areas.[132]

Such benefits had a price. Bournville houses simply cost more than most speculative houses in the city. The houses designed by Harvey in the late 1890s in Beech Road cost between £532 and £637 for a pair of semi-detached dwellings.[133] In 1907, it was calculated that there were only 15 houses in the Village available at 4s. 6d. per week.[134] A block of four cottages, designed by Bedford Tylor and built in 1909, was built for £959. These figures were the 'lowest on record'.[135] Unfortunately, relatively few of these economical houses were constructed in the Village in the years just before the First World War.

Despite these efforts, rents at Bournville remained higher than in more central areas. Other factors had also to be borne in mind. Access to the job market, transport costs and the higher price of food and necessities in the suburbs were of consequence to some. Some were reluctant to move from more lively, close-knit communities, despite their obvious environmental drawbacks, but for many 'the attractions of country life are sufficient to overcome any objection ... to living at a distance from the place of employment.'[136] Given the quality of the houses and the environment, those who had the desire to live in such a community and who could afford the higher rents undoubtedly received good value for money at Bournville. It could be said that a process of selection and self-selection was at work in determining who would come to live at Bournville.

The promoters of Bournville were anxious to encourage social mix and develop a balanced community. A few affluent households (mostly members of the Cadbury family) lived in large houses on the fringes of the Estate. While it is apparent that Bournville attracted artisans and factory workers as well as white collar workers and professionals, it is clear that the very poor were never part of the village's social mix. As J.H. Barlow, the Trust's manager, admitted in 1902, 'Bournville did not, as yet, touch the slum dwellers directly.'[137] Indeed, he had to admit that it was difficult to ensure that the 'better class' did not take possession of Bournville. 'Every endeavour was made', Barlow claimed, 'to give preference to *bona fide* working men.'[138]

A list of the 25 tenants who took part in the early Bournville garden tests indicates that the working classes were represented on the Estate. Apart from a jobbing gardener, a labourer and a window cleaner, most were skilled workers: carpenters, brass workers, a blacksmith, engine driver and a glass worker. There were also a number of white collar workers, including two Post Office employees, a policeman and a lodge keeper at the Bournville Works. Approximately 40 per cent of these Bournville gardeners were identified as Cadbury employees (a figure which roughly corresponds to the proportion in the population of the Village as a whole).[139]

Not every Bournville resident was happy at the prospect of cheaper cottages being built on the Estate. Some of the original 999-year leaseholders had objected to the Trust's plans for smaller, cheaper cottages in Bournville Lane in 1901. They claimed that such properties would have a detrimental effect on the value of their own homes. The Bournville Village Trust did not give in to this elitist minority, and Barlow reminded them of the Trust's mission to ameliorate the condition of 'the working classes and labouring population'. Then, as now, there were those who wanted to bolt the gate after they had moved to greener pastures. Barlow admonished those who had been given the chance to live in the Village, despite earlier opposition, but who then wanted to deny the same chance to others:

> When Mr. Cadbury's intention to build Bournville first became known, strong opposition was expressed in various quarters on the ground that it would spoil the country and interfere with the privacy of surrounding residences. Now it is proposed yet further to extend the benefits of the Village the Trustees are disappointed to find similar opposition arising from those who first profited by Mr. Cadbury's action. They trust it may be recognised that the more widely the advantages offered at Bournville are extended and the more the sum of general happiness is increased thereby, the more completely will the purpose of the Donor be fulfilled.[140]

Given the uneasy relationship with some of the 999-year leaseholders, the Trust began to buy back a number of their houses. Generally, they offered the cost price plus 10 per cent. This policy was not pursued for long. By the spring of 1904 the Trustees had concluded that it was better 'at present to use all the available money for building rather than to expend it on buying back houses.' Appleton and Tylor were instructed to 'produce the cheap cottages which [were] so important for securing the fulfilment of the purpose of the Trust'.[141]

In spite of such efforts, later reports tend to confirm the impression that Bournville was 'designed for the skilled artisan'.[142] The demand for the cheaper rented property at Bournville ran ahead of the supply.[143] A number of correspondents wrote to the *Birmingham Daily Mail* to complain about the relatively high rents at Bournville. 'Very few working men get sufficient wages to pay a rent from 6s. 6d. to 12s. a week,' one explained. Another rightly noted that the bigger houses on Acacia Road were not intended for 'the pale-faced dwellers in the slums'.[144] If doubt can be cast on the Trust's ability to make a significant contribution to the solution of the housing problems of the poor, it undoubtedly satisfied the craving for a better environment in the classes above them. Bournville was an attractive, healthy and viable alternative to the average industrial suburb.

George Cadbury suggested that it was not only the residents who benefited from such model estates. He forcefully argued, 'Nothing pays the manufacturer better than to go out into the country'.[145] This view was reinforced by Thomas Adams, the secretary of the Garden City Association, who suggested that Bournville provided the 'best existing illustration of the advantages which accrue to the manufacturer and his employees from a combination of town and country life'.[146] Cadbury clearly sought not only to emphasise the environmental advantages of his venture, he also sought to convince people that the scheme was based on sound economic principles. Not everyone agreed. In July 1908, J.H. Barlow read a paper on 'Housing and Health' at the Annual Meeting of the Royal Institute of Public Health at Buxton. Here was an audience that might have been expected to be sympathetic to Barlow's message about the benefits of life at Bournville. 'Instead of this', he sadly reported, 'the paper, and one by Henry Vivian, M.P. on a similar subject, was sharply attacked and something like a defence set up for one room homes and the existing state of things, while Bournville's were pronounced "Utopian".'[147] While Barlow concluded from this that there was a need for propaganda work among local administrators, it highlighted the difficulty of providing the very poor with decent, healthy and attractive housing.

Bournville and Port Sunlight

As we have noted, industrialists had built factory villages before the Cadbury Brothers began developing their Bournville Estate. Most were, in effect, tied villages. In certain cases, religious beliefs and humanitarian concerns coincided with a desire for an obedient and efficient workforce.[148] The later schemes at Bournville and Port Sunlight were the more advanced products of manufacturers who sought to combine Christianity with Commerce. Dellheim has suggested that they should be considered 'in the context of their founders' urban visions and management philosophies'.[149] This approach helps us to identify the differences between these two contemporaneous schemes.

Jeremy has highlighted some of Lever's 'paternalistic ploys' at Port Sunlight.[150] He notes, however, that George Cadbury 'rejected the traditional concept of the company village as an instrument of employee discipline and control'.[151] These differences of approach are just one of a number of contrasts between the two schemes. The most significant divergence was that Bournville was not built solely for the workers in the adjacent factory. The heavily subsidised Port Sunlight estate was based on Lever's policy of 'prosperity sharing', while Bournville was meant to pay its way and thus prove what was possible 'by well-conceived private enterprise'.[152] The emphasis on 'economy' as well as 'art' at Bournville tended to produce simpler dwellings than the more heterogeneous and highly decorated houses at Port Sunlight. The superimposition of a formal Beaux Arts axis onto the original plan of Port Sunlight in 1910 served to further differentiate these two important low-density planned settlements. Even the memorials on the two estates could be said to reflect the different characters of George Cadbury and Lord Leverhulme. The modest bust of George Cadbury, discreetly placed in a niche on one of the side arms of the Bournville Meeting House, contrasts markedly with the larger and more prominently placed Leverhulme Memorial.

Although Bournville Village was partly the result of the generous donations of George Cadbury, and other members of the family, it was claimed that it was not a 'benevolent autocracy'.[153] Even if members of the Cadbury family kept a close watch on the Estate and its residents, they were always keen to stress that they had no intention of treating the residents of Bournville as recipients of a 'dole'. Indeed, after 1900 it was intended that the Estate should generate a sufficient dividend for the promotion of the objectives of the Trust.

73 The memorial bust of George Cadbury set in a niche in the Meeting House. It looks out over The Green.

The term 'trust' may have had special meaning for George Cadbury and his brother, Richard, who had set up the Bournville Almshouse Trust just before his sudden death. The word implies stewardship and duty, the obligation on the part of the rich to do something to improve the lot of the needy. The establishment of a trust is meant to ensure the continuation of a scheme in perpetuity. Nevertheless, it should be pointed out that the Bournville Village Trust Deed gave George Cadbury, the Founder, extensive powers during his lifetime. He continued to retain a considerable degree of personal control over Bournville until his death in 1922. The other original Trustees, Elizabeth, Edward and George Cadbury Jnr., exerted a strong influence over the development and control of the Estate for a long period of time. In later years, the Society of Friends, the University of Birmingham and the City Council have been represented on the Board of Trustees.

The Family, the Firm and the Village Community

The relationship between the family, the firm and the Village was therefore somewhat ambiguous. George Cadbury paid for the land, and he, and members of his family, provided the finance for a number of buildings on the Estate. Although the Bournville Village Trust, established in 1900, was meant to be a guard against the dangers of paternalism and to distance the management of the Estate from the affairs of the firm, throughout his life George Cadbury retained the sole right to appoint new Trustees, and the firm of Cadbury Brothers were not averse to publicising the quality of the products manufactured in the 'factory in a garden'. The most obvious of these advertisements claimed 'Bournville Cocoa is produced under healthy conditions by British workpeople in the garden village'.[154] Such claims tended to lead to continuing confusion about the nature and status of the settlement. Despite Cadbury's generous gift of the Estate to the Bournville Village Trust, and the fact that Cadbury Brothers' employees accounted for only just over 40 per cent of the residents in the village, many commentators have characterised the settlement as a factory estate rather than an autonomous garden suburb. Despite the counter-arguments of the Trust's representatives, many have continued to link the village to the firm over the years.[155] As late as 1948, Trust staff were coming across people who 'carried a picture of Bournville as a "paradis artificiel" of half-timbered houses and incessant paternal supervision against a background of canny salesmanship'. The continuing presence and high profile of members of the Cadbury family on the Board of Trustees contributed to this perception.

Early descriptions of the Village took into account the splendid facilities and multifarious clubs encouraged and provided by the firm. The fine sports and recreation grounds for Cadbury workers disguised the fact that the Village was, for some years, underprovided with its own facilities for outdoor recreation. The factory possessed a Dramatic Society, Music Society, Camera Club and Garden Club, whose exploits were regularly reported in the *Bournville Works Magazine*. These Cadbury clubs undoubtedly contributed to the developing life of the village, but their contributions should not be over-estimated. Similarly, it should be remembered that the first major public buildings on the Green were not finished until 1905. Although highly valued and much used, there was some delay in providing these facilities. Not surprisingly, therefore, J.A. Dale commented in 1907 on the 'dormitory character' of Bournville.[156]

Dale also suggested that there was 'too little corporate life' in the Village. The overall management of the locality was divided between the District Council and the Bournville Village Trust. There was also a tension between the Trustees' commitment to the Foundation Deed and their desire to promote a sense of civic responsibility among the residents of Bournville. 'This privacy of control secures the continuity of the founder's policy', Dale maintained, 'but it tends to depress public activities.'[157]

The Trustees tried to adopt a careful, but not dictatorial, approach to the running of the Estate. 'The Trustees continue to exercise a close personal interest in the management of the Estate', it was reported in 1903, 'but at the same time anything like undue interference with the independence of the tenants is avoided.'[158] There is little evidence that residents resented George and Elizabeth's continuing interest in the Estate and their concern about the people who lived there.

74   The first Village Council, 1903. Back row: Dr. Richardson, H. Smith, G. Cadbury Jnr., Mr. Harris, Mr. Wood and Mr. Chisholm; Front row: Mr. Wakeman, Mr. Jones, Mr. Bednall and Mr. Pugh.

'The policy of the Trustees from the first has been to avoid needless interference and to foster in every way possible the spirit of independence and self-help,' it was re-affirmed in 1904.[159] From the start they envisaged giving residents a role in the development of the community. A Tenants Committee was operating by the end of 1901.[160] One of its first tasks was to organise a Children's Fête in connection with the Coronation celebrations for Edward VII. This was so successful that it became an annual event. One of the most symbolic and enduring images of life in the new Village was that of young children dancing round the Maypole. It reflects the concern to raise a healthy populace, the interest in the pre-industrial past and the desire to use pageantry and traditional forms to help establish a collective mentality for the young community.[161]

It is interesting to note that advantage was taken at that first gathering of the tenants' children to weigh and measure them, with a view to comparing them with inner-city children of the same age. The comparative statistics gathered then, and later, were used to show the benefits to children of life in the Model Village. The Bournville children were taller, heavier and generally healthier than their counterparts in the Digbeth district of the city.[162]

Other efforts to improve the health of the local community included schemes to test the quality of the milk supplies to Bournville, a matter of some importance when tuberculosis was common. The Tenants' Committee also helped with the first census of the Village, which confirmed the fact that only approximately 40 per cent of the householders on the Estate worked for Cadbury Brothers.[163]

Although the Trustees occasionally came under attack from within and without (usually about rent grievances), it would seem that they enjoyed the support of many residents. A motion was passed at a Village Meeting in 1902 expressing the appreciation of the tenants for the 'unselfish labours and generosity' of George Cadbury and their 'admiration for ... such a village as will allow us to live natural, healthy lives'. They dismissed those critics who, they believed, understood 'little or nothing of the circumstances appertaining to the village'.[164]

Given such support, it was not surprising that a more formal Village Council was established in 1903 to replace the Tenants' Committee, but it was largely concerned with 'the amenities of the place'.[165] This was not an unimportant task, because it did help to establish a sense of social cohesiveness on the estate.

The Village Council, whose members were elected after 'keenly contested' elections, assumed certain duties. Its main responsibility was to act as a conduit between the tenants and the Trust. To help them in this task 'Suggestion Boxes' were placed in the Village. Specific issues were brought to the notice of the Trustees. 'The place grows rapidly', it was recorded, 'and the birth rate strikes one as high.'[166] This led to the demand for school accommodation.[167] The higher density of children led to a certain amount of low-level crime. Such misbehaviour was quickly reported by the residents and action was taken. Trespassers at the Sandpit were reported to the police. When children were seen damaging trees, a member of the gardening staff was sent to the local school to explain to them the error of their ways.[168] The misuse of the Triangle led to a call for a playground in that part of the Estate.[169]

The Village Council looked after the swimming baths, originally provided for the use of employees, organised the playgrounds, took control of the Bath House, and promoted gardening in various ways. its efforts in this direction were said to have 'met with great success'.[170] The Village Council organised the Flower Show, to which were soon added a Chrysanthemum and a Rose Show. It was also responsible for the competition for spring and summer displays in the front gardens in the Village. By 1914 'rapid strides' were said to have been made in this area. More prizes than ever before were given that year. 'This is very encouraging indeed', the Council reported, 'and has given pleasure, not only to the residents, but to thousands of visitors who have come to see the beauties of Bournville.'[171] The co-operative purchase of bulbs, the hire of garden tools and a loan library of gardening books were among the other activities of the Council which underpinned the horticultural activities of the Villagers. By 1904 it had organised a series of lectures during the winter months and excursions during the summer. It also continued to organise the Children's Festival, open-air concerts and excursions for tenants.[172]

The Village Council's remit clearly included the encouragement and organisation of 'rational recreation'. It thus helped to cement together the disparate elements of the newly established village community. One writer commented that the Village Council was 'one of the many illustrations that might be given of the spirit which characterises Bournville'. Others were more sceptical about its real power. 'Its Village Council can never attain true dignity', Dale proclaimed, 'till it has real responsibilities.'[173] Whilst the Village Council never had any statutory powers, its members were represented on the management of two of the Village's cultural and educational institutions. Of particular significance was the decision by the Trustees to go beyond the requirements of the 1902 Education Act and allow the Village Council to

75   Maypole Dancing at the Village Festival, held on the Men's Recreation Ground of the Bournville Works. This custom, encouraged by John Ruskin, has become a central feature of Village life at Bournville over the years.

nominate two managers to the Bournville School Management Committee. The Trustees wanted 'to secure a more distinctly popular element' on the Committee, alongside the two members selected by the Trustees and the two appointed by the local education authority (initially Kings Norton and Northfield Urban District Council). The arrangement was said to have worked well and the representatives of the Village Council were regarded as 'valuable members'.[174] Not surprisingly, the Village Council was also asked to choose two members to sit on the committee which managed Ruskin Hall, the Village's social and cultural centre. Messrs. D. Roy, H.G. Pugh, T.H. Palser and E. Wakeman were among the early residents who gave much time and service to the Village Council. The last named had become Honorary Secretary by 1914, and he was still in that post at the outbreak of the Second World War.[175]

It should also be noted that a Village Council had been established on the Bournville Tenants' estate by 1909. The general aim of this patriarchal body (which consisted of '18 Male members') was 'to promote the Social, Educational, and Recreative life of the village'. Its main tasks were to manage and control the games, to fix and collect fees and ensure that the greens, courts and recreation grounds were adequately maintained. Tom Bryan, the chairman of Bournville Tenants, claimed that garden villages should provide for the development of the aesthetic and physical faculties. He believed that open spaces and recreation grounds contributed to the achievement of those objectives.[176] Elizabeth Cadbury suggested, at the opening of the recreation ground in 1909, that it would also help 'to cultivate the social faculty'. It certainly looks as though the recreation grounds satisfied a need on the part of the local residents. By the autumn of 1913 the Village Council was reporting that it had just had a successful summer season. 'There has been a very good demand for lawn tennis', it was recorded, 'but a greater number of players on the bowling green would be welcome.'[177] The Bournville Tenants Village Council also took over the management and maintenance of the hall in Woodlands Park Road provided for the Tenants by George Cadbury in 1909. This was to be used for a wide range of activities over the years.

It is difficult to quantify the impact of the various educational institutions built at Bournville. The Junior and Infant Schools were welcomed and admired. Ruskin Hall was greatly in demand for social as well as educational purposes in its early years. It served as a temporary infant school until 1910. Art and craft classes soon began to be held there, and residents were able to produce examples of water-colour painting, lacework, woodcarving, silverware and other works. Exhibitions, which were intended to improve the standard of taste, were held at Ruskin Hall. Visitors often commented favourably on the work displayed. 'The best and brightest kinds of furnishings only are used on interior work', reported one interested American, 'and it would be difficult to improve upon even one slightest detail.'[178] In 1911 it was agreed that the Education Committee of the City Council should take over the administration and financing of the classes at Ruskin Hall. The control of the building, however, remained in the hands of the Management Committee.

Clearly, the relationship between the founder, the firm, the village community and the outside world was complex. While it is true to say that Bournville was not a tied village, it is also apparent that the range of amenities provided a network of cultural influences which helped to shape life on the estate, just as surely as did the gardens and the picturesque cottages. They helped to produce a settlement that was attractive, respectable, orderly and (essentially) committed to family values, and one which was in marked contrast to the dirty and disorderly inner city areas. 'After the mad Metropolis, placid Bournville is blessed indeed,' one northern journalist wrote in 1906. He concluded his report:

> In this pretty, peaceful, model town among the fields, it seems impossible to be otherwise than good, in fact there are no inducements to be naughty; and when I saw a policeman strolling along in the shade of the trees I reckoned that that man had struck the safest job on earth.[179]

The Impact of the Model Village and its Cottages

Publicity was important if the model village was to have a wide impact. George Cadbury, J.H. Barlow and, to a lesser extent, W.A. Harvey never tired of publicising and promoting the scheme, giving interviews, meeting visitors, speaking at conferences, writing articles and publishing handbooks. W.A. Harvey, with the Trust's blessing, published a book in 1906 entitled *The Model Village and its Cottages: Bournville*. This provided a full account of the scheme and gave details of the cottages that had been constructed on the Estate.[180] Some five years later, in response to further requests for plans and information from private, municipal and national bodies, the Trust published a set of *Typical Plans*. This was largely the work of Bedford Tylor, although Elizabeth Cadbury oversaw the project.[181] This included illustrations of the cheaper blocks built after 1904. Journals in Britain and elsewhere noted the progress of the village. A range of British publications, from *The Studio* through to the *Economics Journal* and the *Town Planning Review*, commented on the developments at Bournville.[182] Georges Benoit-Levy, the key figure in the French Garden City movement, visited Bournville in 1904. The visit caused the Trust staff some stress. 'This strain has not been suffered in vain', it was reported, 'M. Levy has returned to France full of enthusiasm.'[183] A complimentary article in *L'Universel* followed. A multitude of newspaper articles on the Estate (and the factory) was published. In 1906, George Cadbury arranged for a trainload of journalists to visit Bournville.[184] This alone generated a voluminous amount of publicity, almost all of it favourable. In addition, the Trust had already started to produce its own handbooks and guides, the first of which appeared as early as 1901.[185]

Interested parties came from far and wide. By the early 1900s, the Trust had organised an itinerary for these visitors and arranged for local guides to show visitors around Bournville. A show house in Bournville Lane was fitted out with simple furniture, largely designed by Harvey. Visitors and residents were encouraged to emulate the 'homely' Arts and Crafts style displayed therein, 'it being hoped that such examples might encourage a taste for plain but artistic furniture'.[186]

Prominent among the visitors were housing reformers from Britain and elsewhere. As early as 1902, J.H. Barlow was reporting that 'it is evident that the Village has come to be regarded as the place that ought to be seen by all who are interested in housing and kindred questions'.[187] The Estate continued to be visited by large numbers of people interested in housing and town planning. 'Visitors of practical and professional standing', Tylor claimed in 1911, 'still say that Bournville is the best scheme they have yet seen as an economic example of housing.'[188]

Voluntary organisations and municipal councils sent representatives and professional staff to view the estate, whilst national organisations held conferences at Bournville. 'Almost every newspaper in the land', Ebenezer Howard recalled of the 1901 Garden City Association Conference, 'gave a report of the proceedings.' The conferences of the Co-operative Congress and the National Housing Reform Council in 1906 were also widely reported. [189]

The 1901 Bournville meeting undoubtedly gave an impetus to the Garden City movement. 'It would be impossible to over-estimate the value of the conference at Bournville,' Ralph Neville claimed. Bournville provided the promoters of the First Garden City with an object lesson in estate development. 'A garden village has been built,' Ebenezer Howard observed in 1906, 'a garden city is but a step beyond.'[190]

Bournville and New Earswick

Seebohm Rowntree attended the Garden City Association's conference at Bournville. There, he was not only impressed by the Estate, but he also met Raymond Unwin. The two events were significant for the development of New Earswick, the estate outside York started by Joseph Rowntree in 1901. The Rowntree family not surprisingly turned to the Cadburys for assistance and advice when they decided to develop their own model village. George Cadbury sent A.P. Walker to York to help the Rowntrees choose a site for the new estate. In the end, Joseph Rowntree went against the advice of Walker and bought a low-lying site, adjacent to the River Foss, 2½ miles north of York, in 1901.[191]

When the Joseph Rowntree Village Trust was founded in December 1904, the Cadbury model was more respectfully followed. The Trust Deed was based closely on that of the Bournville Village Trust, and Cadbury's lawyer helped draft the document.[192] The objectives of the Joseph Rowntree Village Trust were similar to those of the Bournville Village Trust. One of the main aims of the Rowntree Trust was

> the improvement of the conditions of the working classes ... by provision of improved dwellings with open spaces ... gardens ... and the organisation of village communities with such facilities for the enjoyment of full and healthy lives'.[193]

There were other similarities between the two schemes. On the advice of Seebohm Rowntree, Parker and Unwin were commissioned to produce plans for New Earswick in 1902. They, like Cadbury and Harvey, were concerned about the 'dreary rows of miserable tenements that we see in all our small suburbs'.[194] They set out to design cottages that would be 'well-built, convenient, healthy and artistic in design'. Parker and Unwin were, like the Bournville architects, expected to consider economy as well as art. On arriving in New Earswick in 1902, Parker and Unwin were informed that the object of the scheme was to 'demonstrate what could be done to improve village and cottage design without exceeding the limits of sound finance'.[195] Clearly, the outlook of these Quaker manufacturers to their model villages was remarkably similar. George Cadbury and Joseph Rowntree wished to promote exemplary schemes, but they recognised that ventures would have to be not only visually appealing but also economically viable if they were to have any influence.

Bournville and New Earswick share certain visual and physical characteristics. Both have informal layouts, with linear parkways laid out alongside the streams that run through the estates. A considerable amount of land is given up in both to recreation grounds and open spaces (although there was no wood on the York site). Gardens were a significant feature at Bournville and New Earswick, and the size of those gardens was determined, on both estates, by calculating 'the amount of land a man could easily and profitably work by spade cultivation in his leisure time'.[196] Housing densities were also low at New Earswick because they followed the Bournville lead in allowing only a quarter of any building plot to be occupied by the dwelling.

Parker and Unwin did not have to conform to rigid bye-laws, as Walker and Harvey had to at Bournville, and this is reflected in the slightly freer layout of certain parts of New Earswick. There you find examples of the quadrangle idea (which Unwin had advocated at the 1901 Bournville Conference) and the chequerboard layout (exhibited at the Northern Art Workers' Guild Exhibition in 1903).[197] The former was to be used a little later at Bournville, but the latter never was.

Although some of Harvey's early houses had the back projections common in bye-law houses of the time, he soon attempted to remove these, wherever possible, and produce simpler and more economical plans for his dwellings, which also allowed more light and air into the houses. This was an approach to house design that was comparable to that of Parker and Unwin. It is interesting to note that Harvey and Parker and Unwin had come to similar conclusions about the design of cottages and site planning by 1906. By that date they had published books and articles about the subject and they had been practically involved in some of the most high-profile schemes of the period. In Harvey's case the practice came before the publications, whereas Parker and Unwin's slightly later Garden City and garden suburb work followed on from their earlier publications.[198] It should be noted that Unwin and Parker continued to write, and their works were important and influential.[199]

The promoters and architects of both schemes were concerned with community development, and provision was made for public facilities in both villages. At New Earswick, a folk hall, a school and shops were provided before the First World War.

Co-partnership

Nearer home, Birmingham people began to call for the city to be ringed with estates like Bournville. A local co-partnership scheme, promoted by Harborne Tenants Limited, was begun in 1906. Supported by J.S. Nettlefold and designed by Martin and Martin, the Moorpool estate was another attractive low-density scheme. Its curvilinear layout diverged from the standard grid pattern, although the estate roads were built to bye-law standards. The houses were constructed largely of brick and tile, although some were pebble-dashed to provide variety and protection. As at Bournville and the contemporaneous Bournville Tenants scheme, natural features were retained (in this case the pool and trees) and recreational facilities were provided. Gardens and allotments were prominent features on this estate too.

Such ventures were usually registered under the Industrial and Provident Societies Act of 1893. They raised capital by the issue of shares and loan stock and there were strict limits on the dividends

76 Part of the Harborne Tenants estate, showing the simple brick and rough-cast cottages and the allotments.

and interest paid on these, usually five per cent. There were also limits on the number of shares an individual could take up. All tenants were required to hold at least two shares, but, if they could afford to, they could purchase more. The co-partnership system made the tenants joint owners with outside capitalists of the houses they occupied. The management of these societies was in the hands of a committee elected by the shareholders. The rules usually stipulated that a certain proportion of the committee should be tenants. Abercrombie pointed to the potential benefits of the system in 1910:

> It is intended that the results of this system shall be both economic and social, a society which is on its commercial side a partnership of capital and tenants, and on its social side a community bound together with strong ties of common interest and a possibility of promoting social and educational life out of the surplus profits which accrue to the tenants, and not as usual heretofore to the landlords.[200]

It is not surprising, therefore, that the co-partnership tenants companies soon became linked with the emerging town planning movement. This came about either through individuals such as Cadbury and Nettlefold or organisations like the Co-partnership Tenants Council or Tenants Co-partnership Limited.[201]

While some, like Nettlefold, promoted co-partnership schemes, others called for local authorities to build 'municipal Bournvilles'.[202] Reform groups throughout the country urged builders to follow the lead set at Bournville and Port Sunlight. In 1904 the Manchester and Salford Citizens' Association proposed that town councils and private builders should 'strive to attain in their building schemes— in the general laying out of the sites as well as in the construction of the houses—the admirable conditions obtaining in Bournville, Port Sunlight, and other places.'[203] Two years later the Garden City Association extended its aims and began to encourage 'the building of Garden Villages, as exemplified by Port Sunlight and Bournville, for properly housing the working classes near their work'.[204]

Garden City and Garden Suburb

The Model Village provided a model and a stimulus to the supporters of the Garden City. As one local newspaper reported at the time of the 1901 Conference:

> The Garden City Association owe a debt of gratitude to Mr. Cadbury. Before their Association was dreamed of he was solving the absorbing social problem with which it seeks to grapple. And in its youthful days he has given it an object lesson more precious than all the talk of a hundred conferences, for he has shown that the 'Garden City' is not a mere ideal fashioned from "the things that dreams are made of", but a reality within comparatively easy grasp of practical reformers.[205]

The debt went further because George Cadbury bought shares in the Garden City Pioneer Company and the Board included Edward Cadbury. He also served on the Board of First Garden City Limited, the company set up to raise capital and develop Letchworth in 1903.[206] Furthermore, the Bournville Village Trust built cottages for the 1905 Cheap Cottages Exhibition and the 1907 Urban Housing and Rural Homesteads Exhibition at Letchworth. The flow of ideas was not just in one direction. The patterns of site layout being developed at Letchworth by Parker and Unwin were taken up in the years before and after the First World War by the Trust architects. The layouts incorporating houses round a green or in culs-de-sac, as at Birds Hill, Westholm and Pixmore, were particularly influential. Bournville had its Green, but it was eventually surrounded by public buildings. Residential blocks set around a grass quadrangle were not constructed at Bournville until 1909-11, when the blocks on Woodbrooke Road, Selly Oak Road and Kingsley Road were being built. Culs-de-sac were not used at Bournville until after 1919, when the building bye-laws were relaxed.

The Bournville Village Trust also invested in Hampstead Garden Suburb. This scheme was described by Henrietta Barnett as the 'grandchild' of Bournville.[207] It was also based, like Bournville, on the notion of 'social mix' and architectural variety. In terms of its layout and its architecture, Hampstead Garden Suburb had more formal elements and more Germanic and Classical features than Bournville.[208]

Industrial decentralisation was a central tenet of the garden city and garden village ideal. Manu-facturers were thus encouraged to emulate George Cadbury and W.H. Lever. A reporter on the *Church Times* explained, 'The importance of Bournville is that it supplies a substantial proof of what can be done, here and now, by hundreds of other manufacturers and landlords'.[209] This writer had to concede, 'Few men are as charitable as the Cadburys'. Despite the publicity given to schemes financed by employ-ers, such as those at Bournville, Port Sunlight, Woodlands (for the Brodsworth Main Colliery Company) and Hull (for Sir James Reckitt) most employers failed to 'blend with their care for dividends ... a little thought for the bodies and souls of those whose labour is essential to their success'.[210] The speculative builder, constructing dwellings at higher densities on uniformly regular bye-law streets, continued to dominate the domestic construction scene before 1914.

Given the contrast between the slums, the long rows of 'tunnel-back' houses and the Model Village, with its low-density cottages, open spaces and easy access to the countryside, it is easy to understand why the latter could be characterised as 'a Modern Arcadia'.[211] While some commenta-tors rhapsodised about their walk through 'fairy land', others recognised Bournville's value as a practical object lesson. It afforded evidence of 'Utopia in practice'.[212] Several commentators saw Bournville as the realisation of Morris's utopia. 'At every turn in the lanes and tree-planted streets', the radical critic George Haw noted, 'I was re-minded of William Morris' picture in *News from Nowhere*.'[213] A local contributor to the *Bournville Works Magazine* went further: 'The Bournville community differs from Morris' dream only in being healthier and truer.'[214]

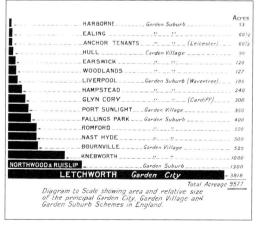

77   The area and size of the principal garden city, garden village and garden suburb schemes in England. From *Garden City and Town Planning*, February 1911.

German Bournvilles

It was not just British commentators who praised the scheme. Visitors from abroad came in significant numbers. German housing reformers seem to have been particularly impressed by the village and its cottages. Herman Muthesius, an authority on the English house, praised Bournville and Port Sunlight, claiming that they provided 'a solution to the problem of the small house and a grouping together of houses to form a residential area that is modern and satisfies all practical and artistic requirements'.[215] A group of German Burgomasters visited Bournville in May 1906.[216] They were followed, in 1909, by over 200 delegates from the German Garden City Association. During their tour of the Village, Bernard Kampffmeyer, the President of the Association, referred to Bournville as 'the first real garden city'.[217] Another band of German Garden City enthusiasts came to inspect Bournville two years later. One of the delegates, Helen Schem Riesz, recalled Elizabeth Cadbury's statement that the cause of housing reform was the cause of women. She agreed with Mrs. Cadbury's view that 'the active sympathy of women should be awakened in a movement which was helping to render the lot of children brighter and happier'.[218]

Certain foreign manufacturers and developers sought to emulate the Bournville model. Two reports describing 'German Bournvilles' appeared in the years before the First World War. Ewart G. Culpin, the Secretary of the Garden Cities and Town Planning Association, wrote an account of the Krupp's Margaretenhöhe estate at Essen in 1911:

> One of the most interesting housing experiments in Germany is that at Margaretenhöhe ... a garden suburb which is being erected by the Margarethe Krupp Trust, under the supervision of Mr. George Metzendorf, the architect, somewhat upon the lines of the Bournville Village Trust.[219]

An even more direct example of the influence of the Model Village was the creation of a small 'Bournville' in Düsseldorf. In 1911, Otto Effey, the manager of a silverware factory in Düsseldorf, visited Bournville and was greatly impressed by what he saw, especially the cottages with their front and back gardens. On his return home, he called a meeting of workers in his factory. He described what he had seen at Bournville and suggested that an attempt should be made to provide similar houses for workmen's families in Düsseldorf. Although Muthesius had publicised *Das Englische Haus*, most German workmen and their families still occupied rooms in tenement blocks, so the idea was new. Nevertheless, it was taken up. An Association was formed, with one of the silver workers as President, and they were able to carry through the scheme with the support of the burgomaster and the financial assistance of the municipality. By the autumn of 1913, 78 houses had been constructed and occupied. The dwellings had small front gardens and larger back gardens. The workers were the owners of the houses, but the municipality had the mortgages on nearly all of them. The houses were bigger than those in Bournville, having 6, 8 or 10 rooms. Most of the householders in this small Düsseldorf 'colony' sub-let rooms, and the rental income from their tenants helped them to pay their mortgages. 'The houses', a visitor reported, 'are well arranged and delightfully clean and trim and the garden evidently gives great delight to their possessors.'[220] Beside these German experiments, commentators from Austria to Russia were also expressing an interest in the Estate at this time.[221]

Bournville and 'the suburb salubrious'

'Bournville is a great-hearted experiment,' was J.A. Dale's assessment in 1907. 'If it disappoints some-times it is because it raises expectations too great.'[222] Harvey himself noted in 1906, 'It would be stating its claims at the lowest that it stands as what a village of the future may be, a village of healthy homes amid pleasant surroundings.'[223] John Burns was said to have been a frequent visitor at the time he was promoting the Town Planning Bill. Delegates from the major R.I.B.A. Town Planning Conference in 1910 visited Bournville. They, like many before them, were impressed, and one delegate complimented George Cadbury on the success of his experiment:

> During the week they had seen many delightful plans, but when visiting the realities they had been a little disappointed. At Bournville, however, it was the reverse, the well-built houses and laying out of the estate being, he considered, unequalled.[224]

Bournville could not provide a complete answer to the housing problems of Edwardian England, but it did provide a viable pattern of suburban development. Writing in 1910, Patrick Abercrombie suggested, 'The keynote of the revival of English town planning which has taken place during the past 20 years has been the creation of suburbs of small houses with a strict limitation on numbers per acre.'[225] George Cadbury, W.A. Harvey and Bournville have an honourable place in that revival. Indeed, the simple, pleasant and informal style introduced at Bournville could be said to have helped to establish the pattern for suburban living for the first half of the 20th century. Henrietta Barnett once told a deputation from the German Garden City Association that Bournville was 'the parent of the whole movement'.[226] The garden suburb became synonymous with British town planning. Rationalising the situation in 1913, E.G. Culpin wrote, 'The Garden Suburb has not to create new conditions, but simply direct an existing flow, and therefore since we as a people are inclined to take the line of least resistance the Garden Suburb succeeds the more quickly.'[227] This was a view shared by the Birmingham reformer, J.S. Nettlefold: 'We cannot hope to make Birmingham into a Garden City, although something can be done towards that end, but we can, if we will, create Garden Suburbs around Birmingham.'[228]

With its emphasis on suburban control, the 1909 Housing and Town Planning Act encouraged the 'suburb salubrious'. George Cadbury and many of his fellow reformers were, however, disappointed with the Act. Birmingham City Council was one of the few local authorities to put forward schemes under the cumbersome procedures of the Act. (Schemes were produced for Harborne and Quinton and for East Birmingham.) John Sutton Nettlefold, one of the leading figures in the town planning movement, locally and nationally, was highly critical of the Local Government Board, the local authority and their planning schemes:

> Under the present regime the preparation of town planning schemes is very largely in the hands of men obsessed with old ideas and old methods. The bye-law official, the rate collector and the old-fashioned lawyer or the mere politician are the very last people who should be entrusted with new and important work of this nature.[229]

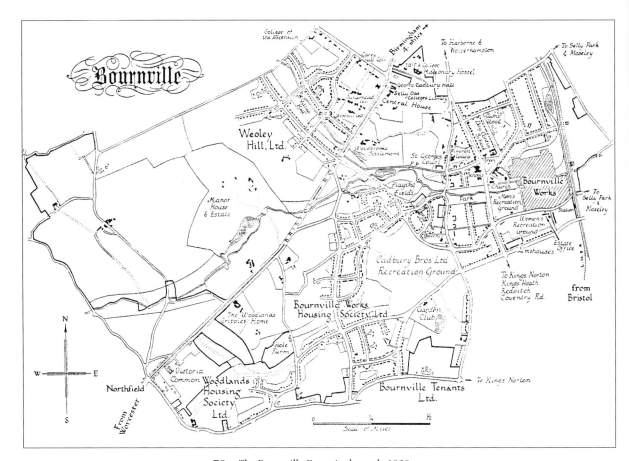

78   The Bournville Estate in the early 1920s.

Not everyone involved with town planning on the City Council could be characterised in this way. George Cadbury Jnr. was on the City's Town Planning Committee, but even he had to admit in 1915 that 'as yet, Town Planning has not advanced far beyond the stage of practical experiment'.[230] Bournville was, of course, one of the most influential of those experiments.

Further advances were, somewhat surprisingly, made during and after the First World War. Some of the wartime schemes to house munitions workers, like those at Well Hall, Gretna and Dormanstown, were the work of leading figures in the young town planning movement.[231] The move of Raymond Unwin into Government circles was instrumental in bringing the best contemporary practice into the public arena. The Tudor Walters' Report and the 1919 *Housing Manual* (which are widely regarded as being mainly Unwin's work) institutionalised the pattern of low-density suburban development.[232] If the emphasis in house design in the inter-war period was more on economy than art, site plans were often more sophisticated than in the early days at Bournville.

Chapter Five

THE INTER-WAR YEARS

Homes for Heroes

The pre-war years had witnessed a 'trenchant debate' about the approach to be adopted when tackling the housing question.[1] Liberals had called for land reform to reduce development costs and minimum wage legislation to allow the payment of an economic rent. Municipal ownership and control of development land was welcomed but the erection of dwellings was to be in the hands of private builders or public utility societies. By 1913 Unionist Social Reformers were proposing 'state aid for housing to spread the burden over the broader shoulders of the taxpayer'.[2] Labour politicians were keen advocates of municipal housing as a means of solving the deep-seated crisis in the Edwardian housing market. The cessation of building during the First World War accentuated the problem in Britain. Increased pressure on the housing stock led to overcrowding and increases in rent. This resulted in unrest and the introduction of rent controls in 1915. Further state interference in the housing market came when the Government provided subsidies for wartime housing schemes for munitions workers. Some of these ventures, such as those at Well Hall and Dormanstown, were innovative, well-planned and attractive, reflecting the advances made in some of the pre-war 'garden city' schemes. In terms of their financing and their design they were important prototypes of the 'homes fit for heroes' promised to the returning soldiers after the Armistice.[3]

During the war, a national housing programme came to be regarded as the keystone of post-war social policy. The war stimulated an interest in the quality of working-class life. The war also revealed, once again, the poor physical condition of many potential recruits. 'You cannot maintain an A-1 empire', Lloyd George argued, 'with a C-3 population.'[4] Better housing would produce a healthier and more efficient nation. Those who noted with fear the revolution in Russia and were anxious at the signs of unrest in Britain came to see a generous housing policy as 'an insurance against revolution'.[5]

There was widespread agreement that there would be a serious shortage of houses at the end of the war and a reluctant acceptance that private enterprise would not be able to provide sufficient housing at rents 'the heroes' could afford. There was also a consensus that 'the comfortless and badly planned house with no garden must be a thing of the past'.[6] The Tudor Walters report and the ensuing 1919 *Housing Manual* marked a dramatic advance in the quality of housing regarded as acceptable for the working classes of Britain.[7] The new standards recommended by the Ministry of Health represented the acceptance of the Bournville model as the norm. The actual wording of the *Housing Manual* was close to that of Harvey's 1906 book:

> By so planning the lines of the roads and disposing the spaces and the buildings as to develop the beauty of the vista, arrangement and proportion, attractiveness may be added to the dwellings at little or no extra cost. Good exterior design in harmony with surroundings and adapted to the site should be secured ... By the choice of suitable local materials, and the grouping of buildings, with well considered variation in design and treatment of prominent parts, good appearance may be secured within the limits required by due economy.[8]

Although clearly bearing Unwin's imprimatur, this statement echoes Harvey's earlier plea for a marriage between 'art and economy'.[9]

With national targets and standards set, the 1919 Housing and Town Planning Act required local authorities to survey the needs of their areas and carry out plans to provide the houses needed. The local authorities were encouraged by the fact that all losses on these schemes above that covered by a 1d. rate were to be borne by the Treasury. In addition, rents on the 'homes for heroes' were to be fixed in line with controlled rents up to 1927, irrespective of the cost of the houses.

In terms of space standards the houses built under the 1919 Act were the best of the inter-war council houses. Shortages of labour and materials helped, however, to push up costs. It was calculated that the average cost of an Addison house was £1,000, four times the pre-war figure, at a time when the general price level had doubled. The ambitious building programme coincided with the awkward transition from a war economy and an inflationary boom. This, however, soon gave way to depression. Government alarm at the high costs of building under the 1919 Act led to the Geddes Axe in 1921 and the curtailment of the programme. By that time, 214,000 houses had been sanctioned under the Act. Whilst they set a new standard for public housing, they were insufficient in number to have an impact on the wider housing shortage. Indeed, the situation had worsened in the post-war years: the shortage had increased from 600,000 to 805,000 by 1921. Nationally, 30 per cent of households were living in dwellings having no more than 3 rooms, whilst 20 per cent were sharing dwellings with at least one other family (compared with 15.7 per cent in 1911), and 9.6 per cent of the population were living at a density of more than 2 adults per room.[10] A similar pattern of events occurred in Birmingham.

Housing Policy 1923-39

Despite the belief in Conservative ranks that state intervention in the housing market would be a temporary measure, the scale of the problem led successive governments to continue with subsidies and rent control. The focus changed and subsidies varied. Whereas the 1919 Act had offered open-ended subsidies, later legislation offered fixed amounts. The targets changed too. The 1923 Chamberlain Act was largely concerned with stimulating private building, whereas the 1924 Wheatley Act once more placed local authorities at the forefront of housebuilding. Whilst Councils could build for 'general needs'

79   A view of Fox Hill on the Weoley Hill estate, from a painting by Michael Reilly reproduced in a 1929 BVT Handbook.

80   A view down Linden Road showing the Junior School and Bournville Green, from a painting by Michael Reilly reproduced in a 1929 BVT Handbook.

under the latter, the emphasis changed after the passage of the 1930 Greenwood Act, which related housing provision to slum clearance. Because of the economic crisis, the programme did not get under way until 1933. A major difference between the 1930 Act and the 1923 and 1924 legislation was that the Greenwood subsidy related to the number of people displaced and rehoused and not to particular properties. As Daunton has pointed out, the 1930 subsidies, like those in 1919, were progressive with need, whereas the effects of the 1920s Acts had been regressive.[11]

Despite the lack of a consistent housing policy and a major recession, the level of building activity between the wars was far higher than it had been before 1914, and compares favourably with the post-war period.[12] A total of 3,998,000 houses were built between the wars, 1,112,000 by local authorities and 2,886,000 by private enterprise (430,000 of which were subsidised). Local authorities were the dominant providers in the 1920s, whilst private builders, erecting houses for sale, were pre-eminent in the 1930s. Both tended to provide low-density homes in the newly developed suburbs. Whilst there was pressure on local authorities to produce 'minimum standard houses', there was a growing convergence of standards between the public and private sectors. By 1939 one-third of Britain's housing stock was new. This represented, as Burnett has pointed out, 'a major change in the age composition and in the standards of amenity of the housing stock'.[13] Unfortunately, one-third of the population still lived in sub-standard properties. Despite a falling birth rate and only slow population growth, there was a rapid increase in the number of households. In 1901, 34.8 per cent of the population was married; by 1931 the figure had reached 42.8 per cent and it was to continue rising after the Second World War to 50.5 in 1951. Although families were getting smaller, there were more of them to be accommodated.[14] The well-built and increasingly well-serviced three-bedroomed house became the standard family home. There is firm evidence of the attachment of the suburbans to their houses and gardens and, despite the criticisms of metropolitan critics and Modernists, it was a widely shared ideal.[15] The suburban semi-detached house sheltered 'the most family minded and home centred' generation in history; it provided 'a vehicle for living out a fantasy' and allowed for 'the exercise of snobbery and social pretension'.[16]

Birmingham 1919-39

There was already a housing shortage in Birmingham in 1914. The almost total cessation of housebuilding during the war and the influx of workers into the city as 'Birmingham became a veritable arsenal' only exacerbated the problem.[17] It was calculated in 1918 that 12,000 new houses were required to make up the backlog in the city. The situation was made worse by post-war shortages of labour and materials. The new Housing and Town Planning Committee reported in 1918 that 5,000 houses had to be built each year for the next 20 years if the city's housing problem was to be tackled successfully.

Remarkably, Birmingham City Council, which had been known for its support of town planning and its opposition to municipal housing, started on a programme which led it to build more council houses than any other local authority in the country. By 1939 the City Council had built over 50,000 council houses, mainly on suburban estates.[18]

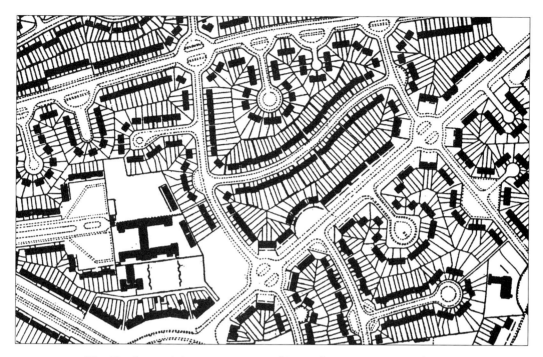

81   The characteristic geometric pattern of Birmingham's inter-war council estates.

The complex, geometric patterns of these suburban council estates are easily recognised. Laid out in pairs or blocks of four and six dwellings, these low-density developments were a marked improvement on earlier working-class housing (even when standards were cut in the 1930s, and non-parlour types came to dominate).[19]

By 1939 municipal estates ringed the city. No less than 15 of these estates contained more than 1,000 houses, with Weoley Castle having 2,718 and Kingstanding 4,802. Contemporary commentators and residents were fulsome in their praise of the well-equipped and better-built houses with their gardens and open spaces. Nevertheless, the provision of communal facilities lagged behind other aspects of estate development. Invidious comparisons were made with the provision of such facilities in historic towns or in the inner-city areas where many used to live. Many bemoaned the lack of schools, shops, libraries, transport and community centres. In 1936, when 1 in 6 of the city's population lived on council estates, only 5 of those had a community hall. The first council-built community centre was not constructed until that year, the others having been the result of local and voluntary effort. George Cadbury Jnr. was instrumental in getting the first purpose-built centre on a council estate erected in 1931 on the Allen's Cross Estate at Northfield. (Of course, by that time a number of community halls had been constructed on the Bournville Estate.)[20]

The lack of communal facilities on the suburban municipal estates was not the only problem faced by some of the new residents. 'From the housing point of view the conditions are almost ideal', a 1935 report concluded, 'but from the economic point of view it seems fairly clear that the tenants on the new housing estates are on the whole in a worse position than they were originally, owing to a natural increase in their expenditure.'[21] Suburban council house rents were higher than those for private-rented property in the older central district. A Bournville Village Trust survey published in 1941 showed that the rents of municipal houses ranged from 7s. 3d. for a two-bedroomed non-parlour house through to 20s. for a four-bedroomed parlour house, whilst the rents of the more numerous three-bedroomed non-parlour houses ran from 8s. 11d. to 14s. 6d. By comparison the rents of three-roomed houses in the more central areas were about 7s. 6d. and five-roomed dwellings were let at about 10s.[22]

Not only were rents usually higher on the suburban council estates, travel costs were greater and food tended to be more expensive. 'One consequence of this', a 1935 report suggested, 'is that some tenants on the new estates have counterbalanced their increased expenditure in other respects by economising in the purchase of foodstuffs, to the consequent detriment of the health of themselves and their families.'[23] Another survey at Kingstanding, four years later, seemed to confirm this view.[24] Whilst many benefited from the pleasant conditions and attractive houses on the new estates, others missed the facilities and rough vitality of the inner wards, and others found their health deteriorating as they found it difficult to afford their new suburban lifestyle.

82   The Weoley Castle estate, built on a site adjacent to the land owned by the Bournville Village Trust, was one of Birmingham City Council's showpiece developments.

Suburban Expansion

The inter-war years saw a significant expansion of the built-up area of the city and quite dramatic changes in the distribution of the local population. Between 1921 and 1938 the central wards lost 22.5 per cent of their population while the middle ring lost 24.1 per cent. During the same period the population of the outer ring of the city increased by 90.8 per cent. It is hardly surprising to find that the majority of the new houses constructed in the city were erected in the outer ring of suburbs. Between 1920 and 1938, 480 new houses were built in the inner ring (413 by the local authority), 9,713 in the middle ring (5,960 of which were municipal properties) and 83,881 new houses in the outer ring. In the suburbs private builders just outstripped the local authority as the major provider of homes, building 42,913 houses to the Council's 40,968. Although the City Council had recommenced building on a substantial scale after 1935 (building about 2,500 houses per year), they were outstripped by the private sector, which was managing to construct houses at the unprecedented rate of 7,000 houses a year between 1935 and 1938.[25] Even though the city's population was growing, its prosperity was apparent and its tentacles were spreading, 'Greater Birmingham', as Gordon Cherry reminded us, 'was no Metroland.'[26]

By 1938, one-third of Birmingham's population was living in dwellings built since the end of the First World War. The rate of building within the city in the late 1930s was striking, yet it was not sufficient to ensure the abolition of the slums, as some had hoped before and after the Great War. An anti-slum campaign had been launched in the 1930s, but the slums remained. Despite increased legislative powers, a modest total of 10,000 old and insanitary dwellings had been condemned in Birmingham and about 8,000 of those were pulled down between 1930 and 1938.[27]

Whilst the slums were a continuing reminder of the past, the new council estates were a signal of the dramatic environmental and tenurial changes that took place in the inter-war period. One other significant change was the very marked increase in the number of houses built for sale by private builders. About 46,700 houses were built by private enterprise in Birmingham from 1920 through to 1938. The privately-owned semi-detached house situated in a newly developed area became a characteristic feature of the Birmingham landscape.[28] In a city which had a share in some of the growth industries of the period (especially car manufacturing and some of the associated industries), there was a growing demand for homes. The period also saw an expansion in the professions and the service sector.[29] Building societies (and, in Birmingham, the Municipal Bank) fuelled this demand for home ownership with low interest mortgages. Small builders erected little estates of relatively low cost houses, each with just enough 'individual' features to make them appealing to those who sought a home of their own in the healthy suburbs. The advertisements for these properties promised 'health and happiness' and 'sunshine and country breezes'. Other promoters offered 'ideal homes' in 'garden villages'. Whilst most offered perfectly sound respectable houses at prices from £400 to £600, virtually none had the kind of landscaping and communal facilities that were to be found at Bournville, whilst a few degenerated into scrappy ribbon developments.[30] By 1936, the *Birmingham Evening Mail* was expressing its concern about the prospect of an 'endless Birmingham'. From 1935 onwards, in co-operation with Birmingham City Council, the National Trust and Cadbury Brothers, the Bournville Village Trust began to acquire agricultural land so as to secure a 'green belt' on the south-west side of Birmingham.[31]

The Bournville Estate between the Wars

George Cadbury had envisaged that the Bournville Estate would be a 'small contribution to the solution of a great problem'.[32] The original Model Village had set high standards of housing design and site planning. Its influence was real and far-reaching. 'Today,' it was noted in 1924, 'the ideals embodied in Bournville are on the statute books.'[33] The Estate continued to expand, but the inter-war developments attracted less publicity than the earlier work. Nevertheless, the Trust's efforts were of sufficient interest and quality to attract the attention of housing and planning experts. Writing in 1949, the City Engineer and Surveyor of Birmingham, Herbert Manzoni, suggested that Bournville's success was 'largely attributable to the careful design of houses and roads and to the landscape treatment'.[34]

Certain aspects of the Bournville Village Trust's activities in the period between the wars can be highlighted. It continued to provide carefully planned and well-sited homes for sale or rent to factory workers and professionals. The Trust's planners continued to explore the relationship between the

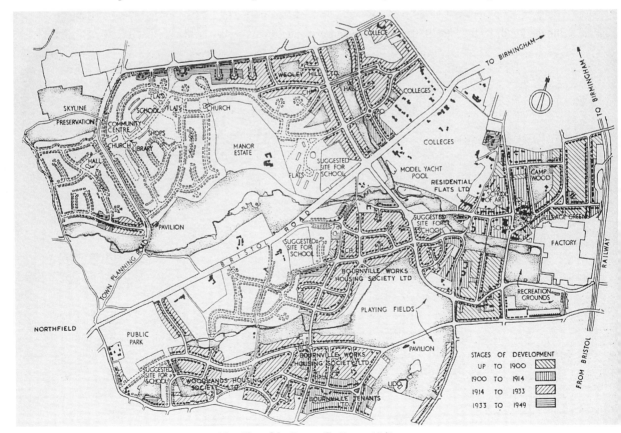

83   Plan of the Bournville Estate, 1949.

houses and the natural features of the Estate. The Trust engaged in a number of housing experiments. It also sought to promote different ways of raising capital for the development of the Estate and the purchase of houses. Public Utility Societies were the main agents of growth in the inter-war period at Bournville. To this extent Bournville differed from most developments elsewhere in the city, where local authorities and private developers funded housing schemes.

After the First World War the Bournville Village Trust made further land purchases. In 1919 land in Hole Farm Lane was bought for £1,710 from the Bayliss Trustees.[35] Ten years later the 80-acre Upper Shenley Fields Farm was purchased for £8,250.[36] By then the Trust had accumulated enough land for the building schemes it promoted both before and after the Second World War.

Little development took place during and immediately after the First World War, although the Weoley Hill estate, beyond the Bristol Road, was started in 1915. By 1921 the first stages of the Bournville Works Housing Society development along Hay Green Lane were also under way. The pace of work soon picked up. By 1923 it was being recorded that 'the work of development on the Estate has been going forward at the maximum rate possible'.[37] By the late 1920s, Weoley Hill and Fox Hill were almost complete and houses were appearing on Middle Park Road. The Bournville Works Housing Society had by this time covered the area bounded by Hay Green Lane, Woodlands Park Road and Bunbury Road. The smaller Woodlands Housing Society had also erected dwellings in Hole Lane, Bunbury Road and Innage Road. By the late 1930s, the Estate had expanded onto Shenley Fields Road and Green Meadow Road to the north and St Laurence Road and Heath Road in the south. The first houses on the Yew Tree Farm estate were built on Meadow Brook Road just before the outbreak of the Second World War.

The Estate witnessed a threefold increase in its housing stock in the inter-war period, from 739 houses in 1919 to 2,197 by 1939. The inter-war schemes were planned separately and the Estate grew in a piecemeal way. The area between the original Village and the Bournville Tenants estate was partially filled, and the Estate expanded westwards. The developing road network and the emerging parkway system helped to link the old and new parts of the Estate.

Public Utility Societies at Bournville

As early as 1910, the Trustees were suggesting that 'when the vacant sites on the Village have been built up, the Trust will probably discontinue further building and will look to developing in future by means of co-partnership and similar societies'.[38] The first had been established in 1906, and four later societies became 'the main developing agents of the Trust' after 1915.[39]

Public utility societies, registered under the Industrial and Provident Societies Acts, could obtain funds from a wide range of sources, especially after the passage of the 1909 Housing and Town Planning Act.[40] Loans could be negotiated with the Public Works Loan Board, local authorities, banks, co-operative societies, employers and pension funds (like Cadbury Brothers). Investors interested in promoting housing societies and willing to accept a low return on their capital, and 'thrifty and responsible' members of the working and middle classes desirous of a home of their own were also significant shareholders in the public utility societies.[41] Members of these societies were not allowed to hold more than £200 in shares and there was a six per cent dividend limit. Income was used to repay loans and interest, together with the costs of management and upkeep. Public utility societies could not only build houses to rent, they were also allowed to lease land and build houses for sale. The societies established at Bournville had distinctive features, but each developed land leased from the Trust and were bound by the general rules laid down in the Trust Deed.[42]

The Bournville Village Trust encouraged such societies, arguing that they would promote house owning and also assist those who wanted to rent good houses. This, however, marked a slight shift in policy for the Trust, as the majority of the houses erected by the Trust before 1914 had been rented properties.[43] 'In response ... to a strong demand', the Trust proclaimed in 1922, 'the system has been restored in a modified form, and houses are now sold and land let for building purposes on 99-year leases.'[44] It could be argued that after 1919 the State and local authorities had taken on the responsibility for housing the poor and that the Trust should now try to satisfy the demand for 'artisan and middle class houses'.[45] By leasing plots for 99 years, the Trust also argued that it could ensure the Estate was developed to a high standard and that the natural beauty of the site was retained.[46]

The effects of this policy can be seen in the work of the second public utility society operating at Bournville, Weoley Hill Limited. This society, which was eventually registered in 1914, sought to develop the Park Cottage Farm estate beyond Bristol Road. Raymond Unwin was approached to produce a plan for the estate; but when he failed to deliver the final plans for the estate, the Trustees turned to their own architect, S.A. Wilmot, who had recently been successful in two town planning competitions. His first plan for the proposed development of the Park Cottage Farm estate dates from the latter part of 1913.[47]

Wilmot's plan followed the contours of the south-facing site and retained many of the existing trees. To conform with the City's plan for South West Birmingham, a wide thoroughfare (Middle Park Road) was included. An attractive double road with a tree-lined central reservation ran up Weoley Hill, and a parkway, tennis courts and playing fields all figured in the plan. Although the early plans for Weoley Hill suggest that short terraced blocks were being considered for all parts of this estate (except Weoley Park Road, where middle-class residences in keeping with those already in the road were planned), the houses eventually built ranged from bungalows through to a number of substantial detached houses. As early as 1922 it was being noted that the Weoley Hill estate had been 'carefully laid out to make the most of its natural advantages, and is now a very delightful garden suburb'.[48]

Although the original idea had been to build workmen's houses for rent, Weoley Hill Limited eventually opted to sell houses on 99-year leases. It did, however, operate in a fairly flexible way. It either leased land to those wishing to employ their own architect and builder, or it leased land and supplied plans and specifications for houses, or used its own direct labour force to build houses on land leased from the Trust, which it then sold. Early brochures claimed that Weoley Hill Limited sought 'to provide residential property of suitable values ... and at the same time to preserve the natural beauties of the locality'.[49] The protection of the estate by the Bournville Village Trust Deed, which only allowed development on garden suburb lines, meant that the society could claim the value of the houses at Weoley Hill were not liable to depreciate because there was no danger of overcrowding or factories being sited nearby.

The first houses on the Weoley Hill estate were constructed at the junction of Witherford Way and Bristol Road in 1915 and 1916. These houses were sold by the society for between £200 and £300. After the First World War the cost of labour and building materials was far higher. For a while the society sold houses on an instalment plan. By the late 1920s that system was suspended and purchasers were encouraged to try the Co-operative Building Society or Birmingham Municipal Bank for loans. By 1928, some 250 houses had been erected on the Weoley Hill estate. On the whole, larger houses than those which qualified for government subsidies were built on this estate. The houses were sold for between £700 and £1,400.[50] By 1939, nearly 500 houses were to be found on the Weoley Hill Estate, and a small number had cost as much as £2,000. One unusual building was the large residential home at the corner of Middle Park Road and Swarthmore Road built for the City of Birmingham District Nursing Association to accommodate their staff in the south-western part of the city.[51] The houses on the Weoley Hill estate were less picturesque than those in the original Village, but they were still varied and the layout was appealing. Although it was essentially a residential area, it did have its own amenities and village hall which added to the attraction of the estate. As the dividends to shareholders of public utility societies were limited by law, the profits of such societies could be spent on such local amenities.

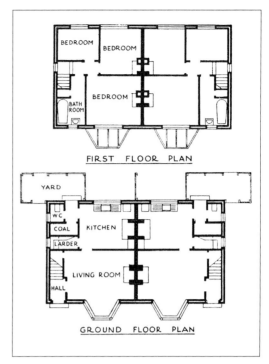

84   Plan of subsidy houses built on the Woodlands estate after 1923. The *Bournville Village Trust 1900-1955*, published in 1955.

The Woodlands Housing Society Limited was formed in 1923. Its aim was to build houses for sale on 99-year leases and lease plots to those willing to employ their own architects and builders. In the latter case, all plans had to be approved by the society and all developments had 'to be carried out on Town Planning lines, preserving as far as possible rural surroundings'.[52] It eventually built 79 houses in the area between Bunbury Road and Hole Lane.

In its first two years of existence, the Woodlands Housing Society built 14 non-subsidy dwellings and 30 houses built with the aid of government subsidies. The more expensive non-subsidy houses cost between £900 and £1,200. Within a few years costs were reduced, and the society's houses began to sell for between £825 and £925. When the society decided to build a further 20 subsidy houses, modifications had to be made to their designs to bring them within the range of the more stringent requirements of the 1923 Housing Act. The Woodlands Housing Society was faced with the alternative of lowering their standards of construction or foregoing the government subsidy. After experimenting

85   The first houses built on the Weoley Hill estate at the junction of Witherford Way and Bristol Road during the First World War.

86   Houses for sale on Middle Park Road, *c*.1930.

with reduced specifications, the society felt it advisable to return to the 'Bournville standard' of building. It is hardly surprising, therefore, to find that the staff of the Bournville Village Trust were complaining about the insufficiently high standard set by the Ministry of Health in the 1923 and 1924 Housing Acts:

> In this respect, Bournville has always advocated really well-built houses, though at the present time these appear to be in advance of what the Minister of Health will allow for subsidy on account of their initial cost. It is clear that Bournville should continue to urge, especially in the case of houses for sale, that without being extravagant, construction should be of the best, both in materials and workmanship.[53]

The Woodlands Housing Society built houses on 99-year leases for sale to its own members. Each leaseholder was required to hold ten ordinary £1 shares in the society. The leaseholders usually obtained mortgages from institutions like the Birmingham Municipal Bank, which offered 'advantageous terms' to prospective buyers. As with other societies leasing land from the Trust, the Woodlands Housing Society Limited introduced restrictive covenants in its underleases. Householders were not to alter the elevations of their houses without approval, carry on a trade or business from the premises or to damage or remove trees from the estate.

87   Bungalows built facing an open, grassed area off Fox Hill.

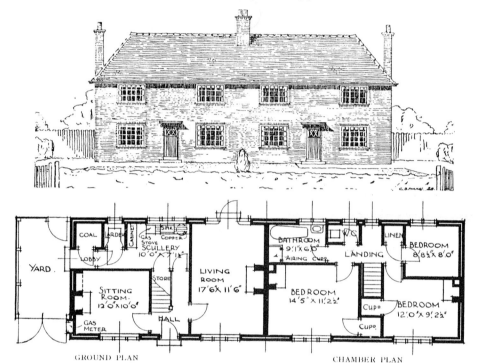

THE WEOLEY HILL ESTATE
SELLY OAK, BIRMINGHAM

Particulars of Houses, Type 3 B6

From the plans it will be seen that the accommodation is arranged upon labour-saving principles. Attention is called to the exceptionally large Living Room, with window at each end, which is a feature of this type of house.

The houses are built with red brick cavity walls, the roofs being of hand-made tiles.

A detailed description of the internal equipment is given in the booklet, "Good Houses," a copy of which may be obtained from the Secretary.

The houses are leasehold for a period of 99 years, with ground rents from £6 per annum, according to the site chosen.

Price—£800 per house, including Legal Expenses in connection with the Underlease, Architect's Fees, planting hedges, making paths, digging over garden, planting fruit bushes and laying lawns at back and front.

For further particulars apply to :—

THE SECRETARY, WEOLEY HILL LIMITED, ESTATE OFFICE, BOURNVILLE.

(Telephone : King's Norton 367 and 368)

or at the Office on the Estate (Telephone : Priory 1602) or after office hours to Mr. H. E. PANKHURST, 75, MIDDLE PARK ROAD (Telephone : Priory 1574).

88   Sale particulars of houses to be erected on Green Meadow Road. The 'through' room proved quite popular.

89   Some of the largest houses on the estate were erected in Weoley Hill. Mature trees were retained as part of the streetscape.

Plot sizes varied from 500 to 1,000 square yards, and a ground rent of 2½d. per square yard was charged. Even in its subsidy houses, the society sought to provide a modern, well-planned house with a good garden. 'Care has been taken', an early handbook noted, 'that plans of a house suit the aspect and the position, and much thought has been given to the internal arrangements with a view to convenience and work saving.'[54] Generally speaking, the Woodlands Housing Society's dwellings were built of red brick with hand-made roof tiles.

In numerical terms, the most significant of the public utility societies operating on the Bournville Estate was the Bournville Works Housing Society Limited. Established in September 1919, it started operations in 1920 and had built 363 houses along Hay Green Lane, Woodlands Park Road and Heath Road by 1939. Like the other societies, it leased land from Bournville Village Trust. Membership of the Works Housing Society was, however, confined to Cadbury Brothers' employees. Every member of the society had to take a £1 share and purchase a set of rules. On being allocated a house, the shareholding immediately had to be made up to £15, and ultimately to £75 (although this was payable in instalments of 6s. per month). As with the other societies, there was a dividend limit of 6 per cent on the shares. Although most of the Bournville Works Housing Society's dwellings were rented properties, the society offered assistance to those who sought to buy their houses. By 1939, it had helped 49 members by offering them 3½ per cent mortgages, to be repaid weekly over 25 years.

90 Houses built on Mulberry Road for the Woodlands Housing Society Ltd.

When the Bournville Works Housing Society Limited was established in September 1919, Cadbury Brothers and the Bournville Works Pension Fund took up loan stock in the Society. A loan from the Public Works Loan Board was also obtained by the Works Housing Society. Their first houses were built by direct labour between February 1920 and September 1921. Unfortunately, building costs were high at that time and the houses cost £1,139 each. They did, however, attract the high subsidies available under the 1919 Housing and Town Planning Act. Over time the situation improved, and by early 1928 similar houses were being built for half the above amount. The Bournville Works Housing Society remained handicapped by the high rate of interest charged on government loans. Cadbury Brothers helped the Society to pay off its Public Works loan, and replace it with one at a lower rate of interest. This move enabled the society to reduce the rents of its properties. In the late 1920s, the rents of the society's properties ranged from 14s. 1d. (including rates) to 15s. 2d. (exclusive of rates).

One third of the dwellings on the Bournville Works Housing Society Estate were of the two-bedroom type. These were often arranged in short terraced groups. An effort was made to ensure that the streetscape did not become monotonous by varying the building line and mixing house plans. The curved roads, open spaces and plentiful trees helped to produce an attractive street scene. As with most of the Bournville buildings of this period, the plans of the Works Society's houses carry the name of the Trust's Chief Architect, S.A. Wilmot. Internal records show that C.B. Parkes was 'specially responsible for the architectural works done for the public utility societies'.[55] The short terraces and semi-detached dwellings designed for the Bournville Works Housing Society, although built of the same materials, were, on the whole, simpler than those erected on the Weoley Hill and Woodlands Estates.

Another public utility society, Residential Flats Limited, was responsible for the erection of St George's Court on Woodbrooke Road between 1922 and 1924. This attractive neo-Georgian block of flats, designed by J.R. Armstrong, provided accommodation for professional and business women in self-contained flats and bed-sitting rooms. In addition the building contained a common room, a dining room, service rooms and a kitchen.

91 Early Bournville Works Housing
Society housing on Hay Green Lane.

92 Works Housing Society
dwellings on Heath Road.

93 St George's Court provided
accommodation for professional
women. From *Bournville Works
Magazine*, December 1951.

The scheme was the brainchild of George Cadbury (who died before the venture really got off the ground) and his wife, Elizabeth. St George's Court attracted considerable attention, and articles appeared in the press and deputations were sent from Welwyn Garden City and London. The flats and bed-sitting rooms proved popular, and an annexe containing a further six bed-sitting rooms was soon added. A long waiting list of prospective members soon grew up. 'Being easy of access from the City', it was noted in 1928, 'it appeals to business women, teachers and others following a profession.'[56] As with other societies, each tenant took at least one £1 share on being allocated accommodation in St George's Court. The rents charged in the late 1920s were 15s. for a bed-sitting room, 25s. for a single flat, and 32s. for a double flat. The rents included rates, certain essential pieces of furniture and cleaning.

St George's Court was an example of the attempt to provide non-standard or special accommodation on the Bournville Estate. This trend was apparent before the First World War, in the Almshouses in Mary Vale Road and the bungalows for older residents (and single women) in Woodbrooke Road. More bungalows were, however, built for Cadbury Brothers on the former Hay Green allotment site in 1923. These bungalows on Cedar Road were only let to single women employees and pensioners of the firm.

Housing Experiments

Like other bodies, Bournville Village Trust was anxious to tackle the housing problem after the First World War. Unfortunately, the high cost of building materials and labour shortages caused difficulties for the Trust just as it did for other developers and builders. The Trust manager reported in 1918:

> The period under review has been of exceptional difficulty for all interested in house property, wages and costs of materials having more than doubled compared with pre-war rates, while rents have remained unchanged.[57]

The prohibitively high building costs had inhibited the work of the Bournville Works Housing Society. In 1920 Cadbury Brothers made a grant to the Trust to investigate the potential of materials other than brick, the usual building material of the district.

The Trust examined over forty different methods of construction before five were selected for an experiment at Bournville. Seven houses were erected on Hay Green Lane 'with the object of ascertaining

94 The timber and brick bungalows on Hay Green Lane constructed as part of the building experiment on the Estate after the First World War.

95 The rammed earth bungalow under construction.

the comparative costs and rates of construction' of the various types of construction. Wooden, brick and rammed earth bungalows, plus two pairs of concrete houses, were erected on the site in the early months of 1920. The experimental houses 'were not erected with the intention of their being considered a pattern or model of what is desired as a workman's cottage'. The main aim was to try 'to discover a method whereby materials other than brick may be properly tried and proved as to whether they can be utilised in assisting to supply in some measure the great need for houses'.[58] The buildings were erected during the early months of 1920, and the winter weather undoubtedly caused some delay in completing the experimental houses.

The three-bedroomed wooden bungalow was designed and erected by Boulton and Paul Limited of Norwich. It was a prefabricated structure, with the various sections brought from the factory and erected on the concrete foundation on site. The chimney stack was constructed of brick and a course of brickwork provided the seating for the wooden structure. The inside walls and ceiling were covered with beaver boards and then plastered. The bungalow, which cost £800, surprisingly took 12 weeks to complete.

The deeper brick bungalow, built alongside, was designed by a local builder, A. Francis of Saltley. The dwelling had a 1½-inch cavity wall. The outer walls were of brick and the inner wall and partitions were of three-inch ash and concrete blocks 'of Mr. Francis' own design'. The blocks took a fortnight to dry and mature and were equivalent to about ten bricks. This slate-roofed dwelling also cost £800, but it was completed in only seven weeks during bad weather.

In addition to these two bungalows, two pairs of houses were erected using different forms of concrete construction. The first was of concrete blocks made on site using hand-operated machinery. The work was carried out by Winget Limited. The outer walls of this pair of houses were constructed of sand and cement blocks, whilst the inner walls were made of ash and cement. There was a two-inch cavity between the outer and inner skins. The floors were concreted and covered with boards or tiles. The roof of the Winget house had red tiles, which, it was claimed, gave it 'a pleasing appearance'.

96   The experimental 'Winget' concrete house.

Because the blocks were left for ten days to dry, then were sprinkled with water and left for three weeks to mature, this semi-detached pair took five months to complete.

The other concrete house was built from 're-con' blocks, using a system developed by John Mitchell. Erected by the Bournville Village Trust under Mitchell's supervision, this house had a four-inch outer wall, a two-inch cavity and a two-inch inner wall. The blocks used throughout this dwelling were made of ash and cement.

The *pise de terre*, or rammed earth, bungalow was generally regarded at the time as 'the most interesting experiment of the whole'. (Unfortunately, it has not survived, unlike the previous examples.) The rammed earth bungalow was designed by Geoffrey Morland and built by the Trust. This L-shaped dwelling required substantial concrete and brick foundations before work could begin. Then experiments had to be carried out to choose suitable earth. In this case a red marl soil was chosen. Shutters were then fixed to the foundations before the earth was rammed down between the shutters. This produced a structure with walls 18 inches thick, the insides of which were plastered and the outside covered with liquid cement. The party walls and the door openings were constructed of three-inch ash and cement blocks.[59]

The use of such alternative building materials was not new. Prizes had been given for timber and concrete house designs at the 1905 Cheap Cottages Exhibition at Letchworth.[60] *Country Life* had promoted a cottage competition (won by W.A. Harvey and H.G. Wicks) in 1914, which drew attention to different forms of construction.[61] During and just after the First World War, Clough Williams-Ellis had built *pise de terre* dwellings for Mr. Strachey at Newlands Corner, near Guildford. After the war, the Board of Agriculture constructed a number of experimental rammed earth cottages at Amesbury. Wooden and concrete cottages were also being built elsewhere 'to satisfy the needs of the moment'. One such venture was that of Sir Charles Ruthen at Newton, Mumbles, near Swansea.[62] Nonetheless, the Bournville experiments aroused a good deal of interest, attracting several thousand individual visitors, deputations from municipalities and delegates from the International Housing Congress. There were, in addition, a significant number of postal enquiries about the cottages.

After reviewing the venture, the Trustees decided that 'no other method was so economical for the district as brick'.[63] Birmingham Corporation, which experimented with the steel frame and concrete 'Dorlongco' system on the nearby estate at Linden Road, came to much the same conclusion.

W.A. Harvey had tried to achieve a marriage between 'art and economy' in his Bournville cottage designs before 1914. His successor, H.B. Tylor, had been encouraged to design cheaper dwellings. After the First World War, the emphasis seemed to be even more firmly on economy. The estate manager, J.H. Barlow, recognised the trend in 1916. 'Economy in design and materials, with the standardisation of windows, doors and fittings', he presciently commented, 'will receive more attention by architects after the war.'[64] Certainly, this was the way in which the public utility societies, under the aegis of the Trust, operated in the inter-war years.

In the early 1920s building actually picked up at Bournville. Nevertheless, shortages of skilled labour ensured that further consideration was given to new methods of house building. In 1924, for instance, some publicity was given to the Triplex Foundry's Iron Plate House. L.P. Appleton, the Trust's new manager, was dismissive of this scheme: 'We do not think that houses like this would be at all desirable.' He urged the Trustees to consider building two short terraces 'of the simplest possible construction of brick and slate or brick and tiles'.[65] Although some simple brick and tile subsidy houses were built by the Woodlands Housing Society, it is very surprising to find that the Trust erected a pair of 'Telford' steel houses of non-parlour type in 1925. These three-bedroomed houses were built on Hay Green Lane and cost £465 each. Although these steel houses were not regarded as 'suitable for adoption as a permanent part of the Bournville Scheme' they were erected 'in order that the merits of any possible contribution towards relieving the housing shortage might not be neglected'.[66] These were to be the last of the experimental houses built on the Bournville Estate, although the Trust and the local housing societies continued to show an interest in the services and equipment of the modern house.

In 1925, a different kind of housing experiment was carried out in a pair of subsidy houses in Hole Lane, built by the Woodlands Housing Society Limited. The aim was to test the practicability of applying electricity for all domestic purposes in a small dwelling house. One of the two houses was equipped with a coal fire to heat the kitchen, cook food and heat the water. The other was an 'All Electric House'. The claim made for the latter was that, because it did not require chimney breasts and coal storage, it would economise on building costs and allow more floor space. It was also argued that it would save housewives work and cut down on the expense of chimney sweeps and redecoration. Because it produced less smoke and dust, the 'All Electric House' was also regarded as being more healthy.

97   The 'Telford' steel house of 1925.

98   The 'All Electric House' experiment, 1925.

Tests were carried out on the costs of running these two houses. Given the high cost per unit of electricity at the time, the experiment was regarded more as a demonstration than as a test. It was anticipated that the one coal-fired house would be more popular, for economic rather than for other reasons. The supporters of the 'All Electric House' pointed out that the savings on construction would go a long way towards covering the cost of wiring and electric fittings. It should be noted that the local authorities at Gateshead, Woolwich and Leeds had built, or were considering promoting, all-electric houses at the time.[67]

In the spring of 1934, 'An Experiment in Furnishing' was tried on the Weoley Hill Estate. Following on from a successful venture at Welwyn Garden City in 1933, the Design and Industries Association furnished a house in Hemyock Road. Their representative, Mrs. H.G. Wright, set out to furnish the house for £200, 'to demonstrate the fact that good design need not necessarily be beyond the means of the average man'. Mrs. Wright made a few alterations to the interior decorations and fittings of the house, and furnished it with pieces loaned by local retailers (like Lee Longlands and Kean and Scott) and things made specially for the exhibition.[68] The show house attracted a good deal of local interest, and some claimed that it reflected 'the modern movement towards simplicity in design and decoration'. Others,

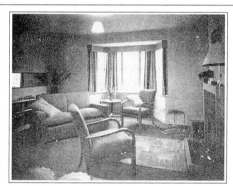
THE LOUNGE.

THE DINING-ROOM RECESS.

ONE OF THE BEDROOMS.

ANOTHER BEDROOM.

THE " £200 HOUSE. "

Three of the rooms in the house at Weoley Hill, furnished for £200 by the Design and Industries Association.

99   The Design and Industries Association 'Experiment in Furnishing', 1934.

noticing the rush-bottomed ladder-backed chairs, possibly remembered the Arts and Crafts pioneers who had influenced the Village's original promoters. Interestingly, Mrs. Elizabeth Cadbury, when opening the house to the public, recalled the early show house at Bournville furnished by W.A. Harvey as an object lesson in home design and economy. She believed that the earlier venture had had 'some influence in the same direction as the present example was designed to have'. Given the dearth of photographs of house interiors, it is difficult to judge the success, or otherwise, of this experiment.[69]

Housing Patterns

These housing experiments undoubtedly kept Bournville in the public eye, even if they were not representative of the Estate as a whole. While more attention was paid to the layout of the kitchen and bathroom, the plans of the inter-war houses were not greatly dissimilar from the earlier Bournville cottages. The majority of Bournville houses continued to be built of traditional materials. The Bournville Village Trust again stressed the need for good quality materials and workmanship as well as the necessity for avoiding extravagance. Despite the pressure to economise and standardise, Trust architects persisted in designing houses that were more varied than those of their local authority counterparts. They could even provide aesthetic justifications for their choice of materials, such as the local stock brick. 'By employing local materials of soft tones', a Weoley Hill brochure announced, 'the building is soon seen to be part of the land upon which they are built, thus providing a harmony not often obtained.'[70] Such a statement reflects the close attention paid by the Trust and its agents to the overall appearance of the estate.

Despite the pressure for economy and standardisation, the Bournville Village Trust continued to insist 'that without being extravagant, construction should be of the best, both in materials and workmanship'.[71] Savings could, however, be made by building in large groups and using the plans drawn up by the Trust staff interchangeably on the plots developed by the different societies.

The Trust tried hard to maintain 'a high standard of house construction', but its dwellings were no longer so obviously in advance of others in the country, because the 'garden city' standard was by the 1920s widely accepted. Even so, when the Bournville Works Housing Society decided to build subsidy houses they were still 'planned with the object of effecting the maximum saving of labour for the housewife'. The smaller subsidy houses built for the Woodlands Housing Society were claimed to be 'probably the best types of subsidy houses erected under the Chamberlain scheme'.[72]

Because of the desire to maintain Bournville standards (and because the local authorities had, to a large extent, taken over as frontline providers of working-class housing) relatively few subsidy houses were built at Bournville. This did not mean that the dwellings at Bournville were uniform. Houses varied in size and plan. Weoley Hill contained houses of all sizes from bungalows to reasonably large detached houses. The former appealed to single women and the elderly, while the latter were presumably occupied by well-paid professionals. There were a significant number of three-bedroomed houses (with and without parlours) built at Bournville between the wars, but the Works Housing Society, in particular, sought 'to provide houses with a minimum of accommodation'. Approximately one third of the Bournville Works Housing Society's dwellings contained only two bedrooms.[73]

The houses provided for the public utility societies, Cadbury Brothers and private individuals, not surprisingly, varied greatly in size, accommodation and standards of fitting. The Weoley Hill Estate attracted most attention. The society claimed that it had been 'developed to ensure the most satisfactory conditions from the artistic and utilitarian points of view'. Particular attention was paid to the siting of the dwellings and it was claimed that they were 'healthful, well-lighted houses'. As with the Woodlands dwellings, the plans of the Weoley Hill houses were said to 'embody the latest ideas of arrangement and the saving of useless steps in the work of the housewife'. Particular attention was paid to the kitchen, 'the workshop of the home'. It had modern sanitary fittings, a gas copper, gas points, electric wiring, kitchen cabinet, etc. The main rooms had open fireplaces, but they too

100   'The Workshop of the Home': a kitchen at Weoley Hill. (Weoley Hill Limited, *Good Houses*, *c*.1922).

contained gas points. Houses on the Weoley Hill Estate were provided with garages or a 10-foot space, for it was argued (in a publicity brochure for the estate) that 'a modern house is not complete without a garage'.[74] Two other features of some of the inter-war Bournville houses that were popular with residents were the covered yard and the 'through' room.[75] The long-standing controversy about the value of the parlour, however, continued to rumble on. (See illustration 88.)

While the plans varied, there was a consistency of style throughout the estate. This was achieved in two ways. Firstly, the designs were either produced, or vetted, by the Trust's architects. Secondly, the walls, roofs and fittings were standardised. A local, red brick was used for the walls, red hand-made clay tiles were employed on the roofs and standard wooden fittings were used for the doors and casement windows. Such uniformity of materials clearly meant that the inter-war estates lacked the variation in styles and materials evident in the original Village. Opinions differed as to the effect of the inter-war developments. Some thought they lacked character, whilst others appreciated the unobtrusiveness of the buildings. Those looking for more varied and impressive architectural forms would suggest that 'economy' had triumphed over 'art'.[76] Even an advocate of Modern architecture, such as J.M. Richards, recognised that such suburban homes were genuinely popular except among 'the cosmopolitan rich, a minority of freaks and intellectuals and the very poor—and even for the latter it is what they would dream about'.[77]

Gardens remained an important feature of the Bournville landscape. As before 1914, the gardens were laid out and planted before people took up residence. The gardens did tend to become more varied in size 'to suit the inclinations and abilities of different occupants'.[78] The gardens continued to be kept extremely well, and practically no cases of neglect were recorded.

Planning and Landscape Treatment

As the Bournville Estate expanded during the inter-war period it clearly progressed from being a 'Model Village' into a larger garden suburb made up of virtually discreet neighbourhoods. It remained an exceptionally good example of 'controlled suburban development', but it was no longer one of a small group of pioneer settlements. Nonetheless, the lessons learned during those experimental early years were applied to the new developments in the areas adjacent to the original Village. Situated between established suburban shopping centres, the new residential estates were deemed not to require a large centre with shops and public buildings. (Indeed, the residents of Weoley Hill overwhelmingly objected to the building of shops in the early 1920s.)[79]

The newer housing developments, although separated from Bournville Village, were linked by a system of parkways and open spaces. A continuous parkland strip, which started at the small, rectangular park in the Village and then followed the valleys of local streams, provided miles of pleasant walks, recreation grounds and rural vistas. The informally laid out parkway varied in width and treatment; some of it was given over to playing fields, whilst other parts remained in a fairly natural state (except for paths and extra planting). The Valley Pool, constructed by the local unemployed in 1932-3, became the focal point of the parkways and a major centre of activity for model boat enthusiasts, young and old.[80]

101 Valley Parkway and the Model Yachting Pool. The pool was constructed by unemployed workmen in 1933. It thus provided work and a valuable amenity on the Estate.

102 Woodlands Park Recreation Ground. Part of the parkway laid out as a recreation ground to the rear of the Bournville Works Housing Society estate.

103 Landscape treatment in Knighton Road on the Woodlands estate.

The inter-war developments at Bournville are of interest not only because of the informal parkway system but also because of the way in which they were planned with reference to the particularities of the site. Wilmot and his team showed a greater appreciation of the natural features and contours of the sites than did the surveyors of the original Village. Groups of trees and individual specimens were incorporated into the layout plans. Roads were also laid out, where possible, in relation to the lie of the land. Some of the new roads, therefore, wend their way around the hilly parts of the Estate and offer glimpses of distant vistas and nearby valleys. Relaxation of the bye-laws meant that road widths could be varied according to their status. Pre-existing routes and wide 'town planning' roads (like Middle Park Road) did restrict the freedom of the Bournville planners, but culs-de-sac and closes did begin to figure more prominently in their site plans.[81]

The Weoley Hill and Woodlands estates were singled out for praise. *Garden Cities and Town Planning* wrote approvingly of Weoley Hill in 1925:

> The layout of this portion of the Bournville Estate is especially worthy of note, for, though it owes much to the original conformation of the ground, by the careful preservation of trees-singly, and in groups, and in old hedge lines-by the covering of banks and raised frontages with gorse, broom and other plants, the building of groups of houses in 'closes', surrounding lawns on three sides, a really beautiful village is being created.[82]

Woodlands was also thought to rival Weoley Hill because of 'the intermingling of types and the preservation of the natural beauties of the site'.[83] Such attractions were clearly of interest to prospective householders.

104   The remodelled Green.

Different patterns of road-side tree planting and treatments for verges and garden fronts were developed on the Estate in the inter-war period. Bristol Road, for example, was lined with tree belts 50-60 feet deep. The smaller roads were successfully planted with a variety of ornamental trees. The Bournville practice reflected the theories of the Road Beautifying Association in its use of flowering trees, and it represented 'a pleasant change from the treatment in the older parts of the estate'. The overall effect of these policies was to create an effect of 'groups of houses among trees'.[84]

It had always been the intention to maintain the rural atmosphere of the Village. By the late 1920s the increased amount of traffic through the centre of the Village led the Trustees to consider alterations to the Green. As early as the summer of 1925 the Trust first considered a proposal to close Hazel Road, the little used road that ran alongside the new Day Continuation Schools. Harvey and Wicks were called in to prepare a layout for the general reconstruction of the Green. The scheme involved a considerable amount of work levelling the ground. The original old trees, those planted at the turn of the century, and the row of lime trees bordering Hazel Road were all retained. A new central paved avenue was placed in relation to the lime trees. The new Linden Road entrance was provided with low stone walls and seats. The walls were linked up with the entrance gates to the Meeting House and the Day Continuation Schools. The hedges in front of the Church and Church Hall were replaced with similar dwarf stone walls. A flight of steps and path from Sycamore Road up to the Rest House was also laid out.

The work on the Green, which began in December 1928, was partly done by chocolate workers who were temporarily not required in the Factory. At first 22 men were involved, but the number involved was later reduced and consequently the job was not completed until 1931. The Estate Forestry Department did much of the levelling and grading work, and this meant that many of the established trees on the Green could be seen to greater advantage. The stonework and paving were executed by two local firms.[85]

At the same time a scheme of decoration for the interior of the Rest House by Harvey and Wicks was started. The ceiling and beams were treated with colour and new seats were provided. A series of panels recording the development of the Works and the Village were introduced. The work was executed by William Bloye, the well-known Birmingham sculptor. Once again art and nature were called into play as the Firm and the Trust recalled the past and looked to the future.[86]

Building a Community

In 1918 the Bournville Estate contained almost 1,000 houses and had a population of 4,570. By 1938 the population had risen to 8,750 and the number of houses stood at 2,400. The more rapid rate of housebuilding reflects the faster rate of household formation and the decline in family size in the country as a whole in the inter-war period.

The Trust tried to ensure that as plans for the expanding Estate were drawn up provision was made for the social, recreational, educational and religious needs of the residents. 'A housebuilding scheme', the Garden Cities and Town Planning Association argued in 1925, 'must also be a community building scheme if it is to fulfil its function completely.'[87] The Trustees concurred with that opinion. 'I cannot stress too strongly', Edward Cadbury told a journalist in 1944, 'the fact that a housing scheme must be more than bricks and mortar—it must have a life of its own.'[88] The Trust consequently gave support, financial and otherwise, to the tenants and owners to form Residents Associations and other social, recreational, sporting and horticultural societies.

Although there was some truth in the claim that the amenities of Bournville were 'available alike to the tenant of the small house and to the wealthier houseowner', there were signs that the different classes were not as well integrated as in the original Village.[89] This separateness was, in part, the result of the physical distance between the estates and the social difference between the Cadbury workers renting properties on the Works Housing Society Estate and the leaseholders at Weoley Hill. A large proportion of the residents on the latter estate were professional people: doctors, university staff and teachers. 'Weoley Hill has tended to develop interests of its own', a Trust writer was forced to conclude, 'and it is doubtful whether its house-owners feel that they are in very close touch with other parts of the estate.'[90]

With the exception of the small Woodlands Housing Society, each of the public utility societies established its own residents' association, based on the original Village Council. Though not statutory bodies, they played a useful role in negotiations with the Trust and the City Council and in organising the social life of their neighbourhoods (a word becoming widely used at that time).

The Bournville Village Council continued its work after the First World War. The Founder's Day Service, the annual meeting of the tenants, the Flower Show, the front garden competition and the annual Children's Festival remained central events in the life of the Estate. The latter, with its plays and Maypole dances (directed for many years by Mrs. Gumbley), was a source of pride and enjoyment to Bournville residents. The Council also continued to organise the Gardeners' Association, manage the Social Centre, provide lectures and liaise with the Trust. E. Wakeman and T.H. Palser continued to serve on the Village Council, while R.H. Barratt, W. Brealey and W.E. Clack were also long-serving officers during the 1920s and 1930s.[91]

The most dynamic of the inter-war associations seems to have been the Weoley Hill Council. It consisted of 12 elected representatives and one nominated by Weoley Hill Limited. George Cadbury Jnr. was the society's nominee on the Council for many years, whilst Huldah Taylor and L.H. Pankhurst figured prominently in its activities during this period. The Village Council was first formed in 1921, and met for

105   The Children's Festival, 1923. The children are performing 'Love's Golden Land' by J.R. Quinton and L. Burton.

some years in a room at Woodbrooke. In addition to acting as a conduit between the residents and the Trust, the Council had a Gardening Sub-Committee to oversee the garden competitions and the annual Flower Show. Gardens remained an important element in the life of Bournville, while the Flower Show became 'the highlight of the Village year'.[92] The Weoley Hill Village Council appointed a special committee to administer the Village Hall, erected by public subscription in 1925. The hall was used on several nights during the winter months for badminton, on Fridays by the Choral Society, and on Saturday evenings for whist drives and dances. It was also used for coming of age parties and wedding receptions. The Weoley Hill Council also assisted the tennis, badminton, cricket and bowling clubs formed in that part of the Estate. The Trust's Secretary was certain about the communal and commercial value of such facilities:

> There is no doubt that the early provision of tennis courts and recreation grounds in the development of an estate materially assists in building up a community spirit, in addition to their advertising value for sales purposes.[93]

The flourishing sports clubs benefited from the fine facilities in the Parkway. A crown green was laid out in 1928 and a cricket field followed the next year.[94] There were also allotments, which were deemed worthy of study as 'an example of communal organisation'.[95] These allotments, which were provided 'largely through the kindness of the Chairman of the Trust', had huts of uniform design, fruit trees and roses and a children's playground alongside.[96] In addition to these sporting and horticultural groups, a dramatic society, a choral society and a Boy Scouts group were formed. In the late 1920s the Weoley Hill Village Council started publishing a small handbook and guide to the estate. By then a local paper was reporting on the 'Happy Community' at Weoley Hill. It noted 'a very healthy communal life on the estate' and commented favourably on the many activities of the local community.[97] By 1932, the Village Council was welcoming 'the increasing spirit of fellowship and goodwill' that was being shown in Weoley Hill.[98]

A Tenant Members' Committee was set up on the Bournville Works Housing Society Estate. The main functions it organised were the Annual Outing, the Annual Social and Children's Party and the Christmas Whist Drive. A Gardening Sub-Committee was also established which arranged talks and shows. From 1925 they worked with the Bournville Village Gardeners' Association, the Works' Allotment Association and the Haygreen Allotments members to arrange a joint Flower Show on the Estate. The amalgamated shows were widely regarded as being very successful.[99]

The religious needs of some of the Weoley Hill residents were permanently provided for when the striking, Dutch-gabled, Presbyterian Church, designed by J.R. Armstrong, was erected at the junction of Green Meadow Road in 1934 on a site provided by the Trust. Up to that time the developing congregation had worshipped in a former YMCA hut, re-erected on a temporary site in Witherford Way.[100] The other inter-war estates at Bournville were not quite so well endowed with facilities, but they fared better than most council estates.

106   The cricket ground on the Parkway at Weoley Hill.

107   Bournville Works Housing Society's Annual Outing in 1926.

By 1938, there were five places of worship on the Bournville Estate. Architecturally, the most significant were the Weoley Hill Presbyterian Church and the Anglican Church of St Francis of Assisi on the Green. The latter, designed by W.A. Harvey in an Italian Romanesque style, opened for worship in 1925. Other groups worshipped in places like the community hall in Woodlands Park Road, which was also home to a private school as well as the usual whist players and social groups.[101]

The new Day Continuation Schools on the Green were also opened in 1925. They were designed by J.R. Armstrong, built by Cadbury Brothers, and leased to the City Education Department. George Cadbury Jnr. was said to be the driving force behind this venture.[102]

As early as 1902, physical training classes were held during working hours at the Bournville Works and in 1906 attendance at evening classes was made compulsory. The City Education Department was later approached by Cadbury Brothers and Morland and Impey Limited (later Kalamazoo Limited) and asked to start day classes for young employees. These classes began at Stirchley Institute in October 1913. By the end of the first year 209 boys and 476 girls had enrolled for classes on one half-day a week.

In 1914 the boys' classes were moved to the Friends Hall and Congregational Church at Cotteridge. The girls remained at Stirchley until 1919, when they transferred to the Beeches at Bournville. By this time most students had begun to attend the Bournville Day Continuation School for one day a week. The aim of the School was not to give a specific technical or professional training, but to continue the general education of the young workers. The curriculum included physical training and English, and students had a choice of subjects in the arts, sciences and crafts. (The arts and crafts classes continued to be held across the road at Ruskin Hall, which itself was extended in 1928.) The intention was that the students should have 'acquired at any rate the rudiments of good citizenship, and shall have discovered some worthwhile hobby or an interest of lasting value'.[103]

The new buildings were a stimulus to the further development of the Day Continuation Schools, which were presided over in the late 1920s by Mr. C.J.W. Bews and Miss A.E. Cater. In 1925 the number of students rose to 1,865. During the Depression the number shrank to 700 in 1930, but they began to climb again as trade recovered. By 1935 five firms and two municipal departments were sending their young employees to the Schools. At their peak some 2,800 students attended the Day Continuation Schools.

In addition to the educational needs of the local population, the material requirements of the Bournville residents had also to be considered. The original Village already had its complement of shops, but the newer estates were only provided with a limited number of retail outlets. The most significant new group of shops was situated at the junction of Woodlands Park Road and Heath Road, and these served not only the needs of the tenants of the Bournville Works Housing Society but also the residents of the Bournville Tenants and the Woodlands Housing Society Estates. There were, however, some complaints from residents about the lack of shopping facilities on the Estate, and many chose, or

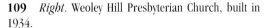

108 *Above*. St Francis' Church, Bournville Green, built in 1925.

109 *Right*. Weoley Hill Presbyterian Church, built in 1934.

110   The Day Continuation School, Bournville Green, built in 1925.

111   A view of Hole Lane on the Woodlands Housing Society estate, from a painting by Michael Reilly reproduced in a 1929 BVT Handbook. Note the rural character of this part of the estate at this time.

were forced, to shop in Stirchley, Cotteridge, Northfield or Selly Oak.[104] Not everyone wanted shops immediately to hand, however, for, as we have noted, the residents at Weoley Hill objected to retail outlets being built on their estate.

The facilities provided by Cadbury Brothers at Rowheath were a major feature of the expanded estate. The 75-acre grounds were mainly laid out for football, cricket and other sports. A further nine acres were given over to the Garden Club, 'a space picturesquely planned, and including tree-shaded walks, a large pool, croquet and clock golf greens, open air stage and bandstand and a pavilion'. The latter provided views of the estate and surrounding countryside as well as changing facilities, showers and a dining hall (which was also available for dances and entertainments).[105] Although targeted mainly at workers in the chocolate factory, these facilities were said to be more frequently used by non-employees than any other Cadbury institution. In 1937, Cadbury Brothers also provided a Lido at Rowheath 'for the happy and healthy recreation of their employees and their families'.[106]

It should be noted that, besides the recreation grounds and the parkways, there were still other natural retreats and informal play areas on the fringes of the developing Bournville Estate. Letitia Haynes has described how the children spent hours exploring the lanes, hedgerows, fields, brooks and ponds beyond Hay Green Lane.[107] Others could remember walking from Weoley Hill across the fields to Clent without seeing a house. Even the wife of the owner of the new garage on Bristol Road offered pony riding sessions on the undeveloped parts of the Estate.[108]

Continuity and Change

The Founder had seen Bournville as an attempt to ameliorate the condition of the working classes. His death in 1922, which was marked by an extraordinarily well-attended Memorial Service on the Green, did not signal any dramatic changes in the make up of the panel of Trustees. Elizabeth Cadbury took over as Chairman. Like her husband, she claimed that a 'religious motive' was the basis for her continuing work in the fields of housing and education. George Cadbury Hall was the appropriate memorial she commissioned in 1927. The Hall, which was designed by Hubert Ledbetter, was intended as a meeting place for the students and staff of the Selly Oak Colleges.[109]

Paul S. Cadbury, the son of Barrow Cadbury, was appointed as a Trustee on the death of George Cadbury in 1922. He was to take a particular interest in the building and leasing of houses in the Selly Oak and Northfield areas of the Estate. He remained a Trustee for 60 years and was to establish himself as a key figure in the debates about the reconstruction of Birmingham after the Second World War.[110]

The years before 1939 did, however, see a shift in policy on the part of the Trustees and this had its effect on the social complexion of the estate. Firstly, they tended to leave the general provision of working-class housing to the local authority, and concentrated their efforts in the field of rented housing on Cadbury workers. Secondly, they encouraged the building of houses for sale on 99-year leases. It was argued that Public Utility Societies would secure the erection of houses 'for the thrifty and responsible members of the artisan and labouring classes', but a review of the Weoley Hill and Woodlands schemes would suggest that the horizon had widened.[111] It remained one of the aims of the Trust to house a wider range of people on the Bournville Estate than in contemporary municipal or private estates. It would appear that the different social groups were still represented on the Estate during the inter-war years, but they were, to a greater degree, being separated by tenure.

The provision of good houses, well-landscaped sites and amenities ensured not only an attractive, but also a desirable, residential area. One measure of its success was its 'remarkably stable' population. A survey of the Works Housing Society tenants during the Second World War showed that one-third of them had not left their houses since they had been built. The average length of a tenancy was almost seven years. Of those who moved, one-fifth transferred to another BWHS property. Interestingly, the average length of tenancy for the society's two-bedroomed houses was nearly nine years, and half the tenants in these cheaper dwellings had remained in them since they were first completed. This was at variance with the expectations of the Committee when the society was formed in 1919. They had thought that there would be more transfers from the smaller houses as families increased in size.[112] Economic factors and a falling birth rate, as well as a desire to stay in Bournville, were among the explanations for such a trend.

The various communities at Bournville developed 'long standing ties of family relationships and friendship'.[113] The stable conditions provided by long-term planning and the fairly generous provision of facilities undoubtedly assisted in the building up, over a period of time, of this community spirit.

Assessments

Despite its relative absence from the planning history literature on the inter-war period, Bournville continued to exert an influence on the housing and town planning scene in the inter-war years. The Estate still attracted many visitors; these ranged from local people to members of the Royal family. The visit of King George V in 1919 was especially significant, given his interest in 'Homes for Heroes'. Two more Royal visits, in 1929 and 1939, gave further recognition to the work of the Trust.[114] Professionals still came to admire the housing and landscaping. Delegates from the International Housing Congress visited Bournville in 1920, and they were followed 14 years later by a prestigious group of members and officials of the Town Planning Institute. Their judgements of the Estate, while not so effusive as in the early years, were still positive.[115] Their views were echoed in a Cadbury publication published in 1928:

> Bournville's special contribution has been, and is, in examples of financing building schemes, particularly through the means of Public Utility Societies. Coupled with this is a high standard of site planning and building construction.[116]

Five years later, J.B. Priestley passed through Bournville on his *English Journey*. He found it 'still infinitely superior to and more sensible than most of the huge new workmen's and artisans' quarters that have recently been built on the edge of many large towns in the Midlands'. This was, in part, because these estates lacked communal provisions, 'whereas at Bournville you see everywhere recreation grounds and halls'. While Priestley admitted that he found 'rather too many public halls of religion and too few frivolous meeting places' for his taste, and would have liked to see more rows, courts and quadrangles, he accepted that the residents preferred to be 'semi-detached'. He recognised that the Bournville Estate was still 'an example of what can be done by some careful planning and an absence of jerry-builder's motives', but he also recognised that it no longer had the impact of George Cadbury's pioneer Model Village. 'Its tree-lined roads, pleasant spaces, villas and gardens are not, of course, the eye-opener they must have been thirty years ago.'[117]

Priestley's pen picture can be complemented by the Mass Observation account of 'Modelville' 11 years later. Bournville struck one of their investigators as 'a pleasant and well-laid out estate, with plenty of green spaces, parks and recreation grounds'. He was also impressed by the wide roads and big gardens, which were 'almost without exception ... well cared for'. The survey showed that Bournville was popular with the residents interviewed, 85 per cent of whom liked their houses and 89 per cent of whom liked the neighbourhood.[118] This view was reiterated in 1944 at a meeting between Trust staff and a group of housewives from the Estate. They concluded that 'the houses already built were giving satisfaction, but it was generally agreed that the new plans were a great improvement on the old'. The only real complaints voiced by the residents of Bournville concerned the lack of shopping facilities on the Estate and the lack of a 'proper bathroom' in some of the oldest houses. To address this latter issue a programme of modernisation of the older houses was begun before the Second World War.[119]

112   The Royal Party passing through the Weoley Hill estate in 1939.

The Mass Observation survey also provides a picture of the changing social structure of Bournville. The majority of the people interviewed in 1942 were of C class. There were even a few from class B, leaving only 18 per cent from class D. Such a social pattern reflected the fact that 23 per cent of the interviewees were buying, or had bought, their houses. The survey not surprisingly showed that an increasing number of Cadbury Brothers' employees were living on the Estate.[120] This confirms the numerical contribution made by the Bournville Works Housing Society (and the lesser contribution of Cadbury Brothers) to the growth of the Estate during the inter-war period.

Although Bournville grew quite rapidly in these years, so did the rest of the suburbs in the city. The City Council built a great many suburban estates between the wars, as did private builders. In the period between 1935 and 1938 building by private enterprise on the outskirts of the city was proceeding at the unprecedented rate of over 7,000 houses per year. The difference between Bournville and the other Birmingham developments may not have been as great as in 1900, but it was still significant. 'It is not unreasonable to state that in the design of housing estates', S.A. Wilmot suggested in 1942, 'the Trust's work is as good as any in the country and vastly superior to the average work of local authority departments.'[121] Interestingly, the Trust's architects began to work for a number of local authorities in the inter-war period, most notably Newcastle-under-Lyme. The Bournville Village Trust's own research in the late 1930s, published in book and film form as *When We Build Again*, was a major contribution to the debate about the rebuilding of Britain after the Second World War.[122] As a result of its housing programmes, the high quality of its landscape planning, its widening consultancy role and its research, the Bournville Village Trust continued to exert an influence on the housing and planning scene in Britain.

Chapter Six

THE POST-WAR YEARS

When We Build Again

The events of the Second World War had convinced the British public of the need for planning: economic planning, social planning and town and country planning were seen as necessary for the creation of a better Britain by the Labour government after 1945. The basis for some of this work had been laid by a series of important parliamentary investigations from the late 1930s onwards. A significant number of articles, books and films had fuelled interest in housing and town planning. Professionals and the public alike were discussing 'the rebuilding of Britain' and expressing a desire for 'a better Britain'. The film version of *When We Build* again emphasised the need to get away from 'the unvarying, unpitying landscape of the slum' and highlighted the benefits of well-planned settlements with plenty of open space and modern houses with gardens. It stressed the necessity of 'listening to the people'. Their own extensive survey of 7,000 people indicated that one third were anxious to move from 'the slums and the monotonous inner suburbs'.[1]

It was against this background that the Bournville Village Trust began its first post-war schemes. It was a period that saw the creation of the first national system of town planning (based on the 1947 Town and Country Planning Act) and the start of the New Towns programme.[2] Significantly, the Ministry of Town and Country Planning approached the Bournville Village Trust for information which would 'throw light on the way in which new towns could be planned and social services and amenities provided'.[3]

The desire to demolish the slums, repair war damage, and make up for the lull in building activity during the war all meant that there was pressure to build quickly. Aneurin Bevan, the Minister of Health, instituted an ambitious housing programme. Although falling short of the target of 200,000 permanent new dwellings a year, over 558,000 houses had been constructed by the end of 1949. In addition, about 125,000 temporary houses were erected and more than 14,000 war-damaged properties repaired. Bevan's policy was to build houses for workers, mainly using the local authorities as his agents. Private building for sale was severely restricted. Despite the difficult economic climate, Bevan insisted on high standards. He encouraged the building of 'spacious homes fitted with all the labour-saving appliances invented by domestic science'.[4] 'After Bevan', Helen Meller has shown, 'no such efforts were made.'[5]

Conservative governments after 1951 pressed for higher numbers of dwellings to be built and lowered standards to achieve economies. Unconventional building types and new layouts were tried, and industrialised building systems were introduced, especially for the increasing number of multi-storey flats.[6]

These trends were apparent in Birmingham. The City Council had plans for the reconstruction of large parts of the inner ring of the city. (Paul S. Cadbury, who was actively involved in the research programmes of the Trust and the West Midlands Group, was also chairman of the City Council's Reconstruction Committee.) As a short-term measure, the City Council erected a significant number of prefabricated dwellings in Birmingham. The interest of senior officers, such as Herbert Manzoni and Sheppard Fidler, in high-rise housing, and the desire to meet demanding housing targets led to a dramatic increase in multi-storey flats as the City's schemes got under way (although they were usually part of 'mixed development' schemes). In 1951 flats formed a mere 3.69 per cent of the annual total of dwellings erected in Birmingham; by 1957 the total had risen to 75 per cent.[7] The search was also on for building land inside (and outside) the city. It was clear that City officials would regard the undeveloped parts of the Bournville Estate as prime residential sites and that the Trust would come under pressure to develop the land itself or let the City Council build houses there. Already before the Second World War negotiations between Manzoni and the Trust had begun about developing the areas to the west of Weoley Hill, at Shenley and Bartley Green.[8] In 1942 Egbert Cadbury and S.A. Wilmot had come to the conclusion that, because of its proximity to the Corporation's Weoley Castle Estate, the Shenley Fields Road site should be developed quickly so as to safeguard the Trust's rights to the land.[9] The talks between the Corporation and the Trust were renewed after the war, when the legislative background had changed.

After the passage of the 1947 Town and Country Planning Act, housebuilding and all other forms of development were constrained by development controls and the statutory development plans that had to be drawn up by the local authorities. The latter not only operated the licensing system, they were also regarded as the main providers of houses. Housing trusts and housing associations were allowed to build houses for rent with state funds, but only for nominees from the local authorities' housing lists.

Bournville during and after the War

Building activity at Bournville was, not surprisingly, discontinued during the war. The Estate did suffer some bomb damage, four houses being destroyed in Bournville Lane and four in Hawthorne Road, but they were all rebuilt after the war. The Trustees were anxious to continue with their researches and ready to plan for the years ahead. The Trust sought to establish certain basic principles for the houses they wished to provide in future. They believed that their properties should be 'designed on up-to-date lines'. The key elements were an upstairs bathroom, a downstairs w.c. and a larder approachable directly from the kitchen. The latter was to be planned 'so that work can be carried out in proper sequence and to save labour'. The Trust also felt that the house layouts should allow for meals to be eaten in the kitchen, or in a dining recess in the living room.[10] These proposals were similar to the recommendations of the Dudley Report and the standards set in the *Housing Manuals* of 1944 and 1949. The latter envisaged a mixture of dwelling types, a course of action long practised at Bournville.[11]

113   The Trustees in 1951. Back row: John Cadbury, G.Norman Cadbury, Major Egbert Cadbury, Paul S. Cadbury and Mrs Ruth Gillett; Front row: Mrs E. Dorothea Hoyland, George Cadbury Jnr., Dame Elizabeth M. Cadbury, Henry T. Cadbury and Laurence J. Cadbury. [Peter Cadbury and G.W. Cadbury were absent.] As with Dame Elizabeth Cadbury, who died in December 1951, most of the Trustees in this photograph served the Trust for a long period of time.

By 1939 development plans for the Estate had been produced. These included the Shenley Fields and Yew Tree Farm areas. This large and undulating area was an attractive site and was planned for development in the late 1930s at a very low density of no more than about six houses to the acre. The original plan did not provide for the erection of schools, a community centre or other buildings. By the post-war period such features were regarded as 'essential to a satisfactory residential unit'.[12]

After the war a new layout plan was prepared. The Trustees took an active role in the preparation of the plans. It was regarded as 'the biggest job they [had] ever done'.[13] In February 1947 Henry T. Cadbury put to the Trustees 'a very rough outline of the potentialities of such a scheme'. Given the proximity of nearby factories and the Manor Park estate, he did not think that workplaces and open spaces need figure prominently in their deliberations. Those issues aside, he urged his fellow Trustees and the Trust staff to use their past experience to develop on the Shenley Fields site 'a village as complete as possible, bringing in all the latest improvements and again leading the way in the housing world'. He believed that a new village with a social centre, a shopping centre, 'the best form of school and educational facilities', a clinic 'on the lines of the Peckham Clinic', a community centre, a community church and (a reminder of the power of the original Deed) 'some centre to take the place of the ordinary public house' would help to generate 'a real community spirit'.

In view of the post-war housing shortage, residential developments were central to the discussions about the future form of the Shenley Fields area. Henry T. Cadbury urged the Trustees to continue 'the building of houses covering the largest possible range of the social scale'. He envisaged the construction of larger houses for businessmen, like those built at Weoley Hill during the inter-war period, through to small workmen's dwellings of the kind built on the adjacent municipal estate at Weoley Castle. He believed that the houses should be varied in form as well as size. He proposed houses in terraces, dwellings built in open squares, bungalows, houses for single women and old people, and workmen's flats. He considered houses with small gardens should be built (for those who could not or did not want to labour there) as well as more typical Bournville houses with reasonably large gardens.

Henry T. Cadbury felt that his proposals were in line with the ideals of the Trust. He believed that the Trustees would be fulfilling their duty if they could push through such an enterprise—a venture which 'could stimulate better housing and a community spirit elsewhere'. Those running the Bournville Village Trust still had a vision of where they wanted to go, and one which still related clearly to the objectives of the Founder.

The context in which the Trustees and the Trust staff worked had, however, changed considerably. The economic situation was difficult and Henry T. Cadbury was aware of 'the serious factors of finance'.[14] The 1947 Town and Country Planning Act had made it the duty of the larger local authorities to produce development plans for their areas. The City of Birmingham did not produce its development plan until 1952, after the Trust had produced its new post-war layout for Shenley Fields area.

The Trust's plan envisaged the estate as one unit divided into two parts by Shenley Lane, 'a town planning road' 120 feet wide. The two sections were to be connected by an underground subway for pedestrians. In the new layout, there were to be open spaces on both sides of the road leading to the centre of each part of the estate. The larger of the two was to contain all the communal buildings, including shops, primary and nursery schools, a community centre and religious buildings. Included in the plan was a promenade on the highest part of the site which was linked to a large open space. Another interesting feature of the plan was a network of tree-planted walks which provided pedestrian access to the main centres.

When the Bournville staff had worked out all the details of this scheme the Trustees expressed themselves very happy with the result. 'We thought we had planned a residential area', they reported, 'which would be one of the most complete and interesting on the Bournville Estate.'[15] The publication of the City Development Plan in 1952 meant, however, that they had to go back to the drawing board. In part, this was because of the rising projected population figures being put forward at the time. *Conurbation*, produced by Sir Patrick Abercrombie and Herbert Jackson and published in 1948 had calculated the future population of Birmingham at 990,000.[16] The Ministry of Town and Country Planning then amended the figure to 1,000,000. The City of Birmingham Public Works Committee, however, based their development plan on a proposed target population of 1,167,000. Given the desire to abolish the slums, the intention to provide spacious sites for schools, and the willingness to provide more amenities than in the past, the implications for those planning estates in the city were significant. There was no alternative but to increase the density of development.[17]

The City's Development Plan provided for two zones, an inner zone with densities from 75 to 120 persons per acre and an outer zone, which included Bournville, with a density of 50 persons per acre. It was calculated that this represented a gross residential density of about 15 dwellings per acre. If the amount of land required for roads and non-residential buildings was subtracted, the density of the land used for housing purposes would be raised to 16 or 17 dwellings per acre. Given that on a large part of the Bournville Estate the density did not exceed 8 houses per acre, it was self-evident that the City's plan would lead to radical alterations to the Trust's second scheme for Shenley Fields, and 'the character of [its] future development'.[18]

It was against this background that the Trust began building its first post-war houses. The Trustees and their officers set to work, as they had done after the First World War, to address the housing famine that faced them. They were aware of the demand from young couples, blitzed families, slum dwellers and the expected post-war increase in population.[19] They realised that the demand for homes was varied. They recognised that there was a very great demand for working-class homes and they concluded that 'the Trust should provide as many low-rented houses as possible'. The Trustees also acknowledged there was still a demand for 'good class houses for sale' and a need for 'special houses' for older couples and single retired persons, especially women.[20]

The Trust gave much thought to the post-war housing problem. Like most bodies preparing large-scale plans they gave some consideration to prefabs. C.B. Parkes, the Trust's architect, and Paul S. Cadbury, a Trustee and City Councillor, produced reports on temporary houses. Parkes visited the Tate Gallery exhibition of prefabricated dwellings, the Ministry of Works Demonstration Houses at Northolt and various experimental housing schemes in Birmingham, Coventry and Redditch. Whilst accepting that prefabs represented 'a good method of meeting the most serious shortage with the minimum delay', he concluded that he had 'not discovered any system that is free from the risk of failure to a greater or lesser extent'. Their conclusions were similar to the ones they had reached after the First World War: 'Our enquiries have so far failed to discover any system which is superior to the normal brick construction in terms of permanence, reliability or appearance.'[21] Parkes and his colleagues were not blind to the advances that had been made in the intervening period, or to the prospect of labour and materials shortages in the immediate post-war period. The best possible solution for permanent houses in Bournville and elsewhere in the Midlands was 'to use the normal construction for the shell of the house, while taking advantage of standardisation and prefabrication in relation to fittings, etc., in order to speed up house production'.[22]

Paul S. Cadbury was rather more enthusiastic about prefabs. He noted the 'popular appeal' of those exhibited at the Tate Gallery and recognised that Birmingham, 'as the second most bombed provincial city', would get a substantial share of the government's proposed programme of prefabricated temporary dwellings. The most urgent issue, he believed, was to decide 'on what sites they will present least problems, from a town planning point of view'. Paul Cadbury considered single-storey prefabs to be unsuitable for areas covered by the City's redevelopment plans and the suburbs. 'Flat-roofed bungalows', he argued, 'would deteriorate the amenities of the new outer suburbs.' Whilst it was not surprising that he urged the Council to build prefabs in the middle ring and central areas not covered by Manzoni's plans, what was more surprising was that Cadbury urged the Bournville Village Trust to consider authorising sites for 50 prefabs.[23] What actually happened was that temporary and permanent houses were erected by the City Council at Bartley Farm and Shenley Lane on land sold and leased to them by the Bournville Village Trust in 1945.

The Trust's own plans included building some houses for Cadbury Brothers on the east side of Shenley Fields Road (a scheme which was regarded as 'sufficient earnest of the Trust's intention to develop this area'), the building of family houses to let, and the erection of houses for sale on 99-year leases. As in earlier decades, the Trust was still anxious to achieve a degree of social mix and architectural variety on the Estate. 'If houses of various sizes are built in these areas, in addition to those which are built for letting', it was reported in the summer of 1945, 'it will give a considerable range.'[24]

It was the clear intention of the Ministry of Health that local authorities would be main agency for housing in the post-war period, and that they would build houses for letting.[25] However, Housing Societies, as with the Trust, could under the 1936 Housing Act negotiate loans at fixed rates of interest with local authorities to construct rented properties. (The local authority would have the right to nominate tenants to the houses so built.) In addition, private houses, under a fixed limit, could be built if the prospective owners succeeded in getting a precious building licence from the City.

At this time the Cadbury Board were also considering the post-war housing needs of Bournville workers. A 1943 survey showed that there were 1,600 Cadbury employees in the armed forces. Many had married since 1939 and 'in very few cases is there a separate home available when the husband returns'.[26] The Cadbury Board decided to build some two and three-bedroomed houses for Cadbury nominees. Eighty-six houses were erected by the Trust and let to Cadbury workers by September 1948.[27]

Discussions about the size and nature of the post-war housing stock were also going on within the Trust. It was evident to the Trustees and their staff that three-bedroomed houses had been built in very large numbers in the inter-war period. Trust surveys showed that over 50 per cent of three-bedroomed houses on the estate were occupied by three persons or less, and yet at the same time there was a strong demand for small houses, especially for older people. 'It seems reasonable', Paul Cadbury suggested in 1943, 'in order to get cheaper and more houses, that the immediate post-war building programme should include a considerable proportion of two-bedroomed houses.' The intention was that older people would be encouraged to vacate the three-bedroomed properties and move to the newly-built smaller dwellings, thus allowing families to move into the former. 'Most of us would prefer to see all houses for young married people built with three or more bedrooms', Paul Cadbury confessed, 'in order to encourage them to have children.'[28]

In order to ascertain just how many residents would be willing to exchange larger for smaller homes the Secretary/Manager undertook a survey of all Bournville Village Trust and Bournville Works

Housing Society tenants in three-bedroomed properties. There was a 73 per cent response to his questionnaire. Of the 423 residents who responded 73 were prepared to transfer, although 13 specified they wanted a bungalow and 33 others made conditions about either the planning of the houses or the level of rent. It was noticeable that, statistically, the Works Housing Society tenants were more willing to transfer than those from Trust properties.[29] As had been anticipated, the numbers willing to transfer were not great. Laurence J. Cadbury was probably correct to claim that 'people do not change their house lightly, especially if they have got a garden in good shape'. He believed that to build two-bedroomed houses for returning Cadbury employees and their families would be a 'lamentable' policy. 'To build two-bedroomed houses not for the average citizen, but specifically as "homes for heroes", is to give those heroes and their wives the strongest possible lead that they are not expected to have more than two children.'[30] As a compromise the Cadbury Board recommended the building of two- and three-bedroomed houses.

It is clear that Trustees and senior staff were aware of many of the housing experiments being carried out, and itself contributed to the vast literature on housing reform during and after the war. Trust staff were actively involved in the researches of the West Midland Group which produced a number of important studies on town and country planning after the war.[31] It is evident that they were aware of the debates about neighbourhood units, community living and the management of Green Belt estates. Trustees and staff also attended conferences at home and abroad on some of these issues. These activities and the continuing work on the Estate meant that Bournville, once again, began to attract substantial numbers of visitors.[32] The majority were councillors or professionals with a social or technical interest in housing and town planning. The most distinguished of the early post-war visitors was Lewis Mumford, the well-known American sociologist and author of *The Culture of Cities* (1938).[33] He was received by Paul Cadbury and some of the Trust staff in the summer of 1946 and given a tour of the Estate. He was reported as being impressed by both the social and physical aspects of the Estate. He was struck by the attention given to amenities and the way in which 'a community composed of people drawn from many different employments' had been built. He was also taken by 'the way in which such natural features as the contours of the developed sites had been made to serve both utilitarian and aesthetic purposes'.[34]

Whilst Mumford might have been impressed by what he saw and heard at Bournville, there is some evidence that Trust staff were not altogether happy with Mumford's message and influence. 'The socio-logical theory of groups has a direct bearing upon plan,' Mumford had pronounced in 1938.[35] His message was starting to reverberate around the planning world, but its effects were not always welcome or clear. 'There was a great deal of amateur sociology, psychology and economics indulged in', wrote a Trust officer of the proceedings at the 18th International Congress for Housing and Town Planning in October 1946. 'The influence of Professor Mumford was pronounced, and may yet prove to be harmful.'[36] Great emphasis was given to the notion of 'liveability' as one of the criteria for design at the Congress, but no clear definition of the term emerged.

Another contemporary meeting, the Human Needs and Planning Conference, also revealed a wide variety of interpretation of many terms used by planners at that time: phrases such as 'neighbourhood unit', 'community feeling' and 'village society'. It seemed apparent that there was a need to investigate the structure of the family and research the extent to which estates of all sorts satisfied the domestic and social requirements of the local population.[37] Planners were beginning to register the fact that their work had to be based on solid research, but that they also needed to consult with those involved and carry them with them. The Trustees compared the way in which they had consulted various parties before they had finalised their Knutsford Plan Exhibition of 1946 (which was concerned with the need to rehouse the overspill of population and industry from large conurbations and the rehabilitation of an old country town) with the situation in Stevenage New Town, where the Ministry's plans met with some opposition.[38]

When it came to the continued development of their own estate the Trust tried, in a number of ways, to get the views of their own tenants and lessees. In this way they became aware of the residents' concerns. Tenants in the older houses wanted their properties improved. They were particularly anxious to have proper bathrooms, and there was a clear preference for upstairs bathrooms. The Trustees had, in fact, begun a modernisation programme before the war, but this had been halted at the outbreak of hostilities. The Trust made a start after the war by modernising property as it came vacant, but in the longer term it expressed a desire to modernise all the older properties.

In line with the Dudley Committee and organisations like the Electrical Association for Women, the Trust's officers also discussed the existing housing stock and future house plans for the estate with a representative group of Bournville housewives. (Six women from Bournville Village, Weoley Hill and the Bournville Works Housing Society were in the group.) They confirmed the impression gained from the earlier questionnaire that the 1930s properties were 'a great improvement on the old' and that generally they were 'giving satisfaction'.[39] There were misgivings about some of the cheaper subsidy houses built before the war. 'Criticism is made of the last small houses built', it was reported, 'in which the accommodation and equipment were cut down to a very low level to reduce the cost and resulting rents in order to obtain the subsidy.'[40] This had been noted at the time, and a decision had been made to revert back to the higher 'Bournville standard'.

In their discussions with the housewives, the Trust architects reviewed plans for post-war houses on the estate drawn up before and after the publication of the Dudley Report. The women expressed their approval of the through living room, the large kitchen which allowed for family meals to be eaten there, the two w.c.s, the fitted wardrobes in the bedrooms, and the covered yard. They did make other suggestions. Most significantly, they recommended that the utility room, a key feature of the Dudley plan, should be omitted. They considered it 'a waste of space'. They also expressed a preference for retaining the open-fired grate with back boiler and oven. They believed that the kitchen should be as light as possible, and that its floor should be tiled not boarded. Their other recommendations included an airing cupboard, heated towel rails in the bathroom, cupboards in the hall for coats, and boxed-in gas and electric meters 'as in the latest plan'.[41]

As a result of the meeting, new plans were drawn up embodying the main suggestions. One significant result of the omission of the utility room was a reduction in the superficial area of the proposed houses from 978 to about 900 square feet. This reduced the cost of the dwellings.[42]

114   Charfield Close was one of the first developments to be constructed after the Second World War.

Having devoted much attention to the type and layout of the houses during the latter part of the war, the Trustees were anxious and ready to start building at its end. The first contract for 58 houses was signed and the construction of the first houses began in 1945. Not surprisingly, given the government's policy, these were all rented properties. Fourteen of these were erected in Charfield Close and the remainder were built in Shenley Fields Road and Gorse Close. They were constructed by C. Bryant and Son. The houses were described as being 'relatively spacious and well equipped'.[43] Externally, they were a good deal simpler than varied houses built before 1914. 'In the later parts of Bournville, this striving after individual difference in each house,' the Trust's manager explained, 'is replaced by an attempt to design groups of houses as architectural units.'[44]

In one of the houses in Charfield Close a 'House and Furniture Exhibition' was held in late August and early September 1946. It was calculated that about 3,000 people came to see the exhibition, a clear indication of people's desire to see a good, well-furnished, new house and of the continuing importance that housing had assumed in the public mind. Comments made by the visitors were favourable. Women were said to be pleased with the amount of space, with the plan, with the design of the kitchen and the provision and design of the cupboards. The light coloured walls and woodwork were universally praised. 'This might possibly be taken', the Trust's officers suggested, 'as a definite indication that public taste

115 'The House and Furniture Exhibition', Charfield Close, 1946. Women were said to be pleased with the design of the kitchen and the fitted cupboards and they praised the light coloured walls and woodwork.

is becoming converted to more open and simple schemes of decoration and design.' It might be recalled that the Trust's first show house and the D.I.A. exhibition in 1934 had tried to achieve a similar objective.

Criticisms of the house's design were made. Some objected to the 'pokiness' of the wardrobes, others disliked the wash boiler in the kitchen, suggesting it might be better in the covered yard. More significant was the fact that over half the people who filled in a questionnaire at the exhibition said they would prefer not to eat their meals in the room in which they were cooked. Families from Bournville itself showed an even greater distaste for meals in the kitchen than those from other areas (despite the pronouncements of the group of Bournville housewives interviewed by the Trust's officers in 1944). It should be remembered that in many cases builders between the wars sacrificed kitchen space to the provision of two living rooms (i.e. the kitchen became a 'kitchenette'). Nevertheless, the criticisms of the kitchen-dining room plan were significant. It meant that the layouts recommended in the Dudley Report and incorporated in the 1944 *Housing Manual* did not satisfy the demands of those many people who seemed to want a large kitchen, a separate dining room and a living room. The cost of such a house would put it beyond the reach of many poorer tenants.[45]

These early post-war houses were built at a time when there were severe shortages of materials, particularly hand-made roofing tiles and facing bricks. As a consequence the houses on Shenley Fields Road were, in the opinion of the Trust, not as good as they might have been.[46]

Building on the Estate proceeded slowly but continuously over the next few years. A group of 12 houses was erected by contract in Bunbury Road before the Direct Works Department was reconstituted. The Department went on to construct small groups of houses in Mulberry Road and Woodbrooke Road, 20 bungalows and maisonettes for old people in Hay Green Lane and a group of eight bungalows in Lower Moor for retired professional people. In addition, houses began to be built in the Shenley Fields area; almost 100 by the autumn of 1952.[47]

One problem facing all developers and builders in the post-war period was the increased cost of building. The government established a Committee of Enquiry into Building Costs under J.G. Girdwood. The Committee found that the typical local authority three-bedroomed house had cost approximately £518 to build in 1939, but by 1946-7 the figure had risen to approximately £1,242. They attributed the rise to a number of factors. These included an increase in the average floor area of the dwellings, the addition of outbuildings, improvements in construction and finish, additional equipment, higher costs of materials, increased wages, a decline in the productivity of the building industry and increased overhead charges.

The Girdwood Committee recommended a limitation in the price fluctuation clauses in housing contracts and suggested that the government review standards of accommodation and equipment in new houses.[48] This was soon to lead to changes. 'There was a time', the Trust reported in 1952, 'when the Minister for Health insisted on an increase in the size of houses—now decreases are the rule.'[49]

The publication of the Girdwood Report led the Trust to embark on a study of the comparative cost of houses built at Bournville before and after the war. Ten houses erected in Idris Close in 1937-9 had cost £539 each, whilst the individual cost of the 10 houses built in 1946-7 in Erica Close was £1,288 and a further eight houses constructed in Mulberry Road in 1947 had cost £1,309 each. It was apparent from the figures that the overall cost increase to the Trust was slightly less than that for the average local authority house (about 135 per cent compared with 140 per cent).[50] It was also clear that Trust houses cost more than local authority houses, both before and after the war, although the gap was closing. The higher costs can be put down to higher specifications and better workmanship and finish. As the Trust often suggested, these higher costs would be offset by lower maintenance costs.

Ways of reducing costs were sought. In the latter part of 1945 the Trust's architects were asked to look for 'possible economies in connection with frontages in future developments and into the desirability of grouping six and eight houses together with long gardens and a group of garages at the back with service roads'.[51] When tenders came in for some new houses in Bunbury Road early in 1947, the estimated cost was £1,531 per house. The Trustees responded by asking the architects to produce an alternative 'austerity plan'.[52] Later that year, the Trust's architects were instructed to ensure that 'the frontage given to each house shall be as small as possible'. Savings were also sought on road construction on the Shenley Estate, although the cost of road work elsewhere on the Estate in the late 1940s remained high. When this happened, the roads were sometimes reserved for houses of a size larger than allowed at that point. This was the case with Innage Road and Dinmore Avenue.[53]

In view of the rising costs (and higher rents which consequently had to be charged), the Trust chose for a while to omit overhead charges when calculating the capital cost of a house. This enabled them to charge lower rents than they might have. This, as they later admitted, amounted to a subsidy from the Trust. By the end of 1948 it was being suggested that the overhead charges should be included in the capital cost of houses built by the Trust and be taken into account when rents for new houses were calculated.[54]

The post-war licensing system, with its stringent cost limits, made it very difficult to construct private houses for sale. 'The present licensing restrictions,' the Trust reported in 1949, 'made it impossible for a good house to be built within the permitted figure.'[55] By 1951-2, after considerable delays, some houses for sale on 99-year leases were constructed. These were followed by 'a few special houses for those ... fortunate enough to obtain a building licence' in Heath Road South, Innage Road, Fox Hill and Dinmore Avenue.[56]

In 1949 a group of bungalows was built in Lower Moor for retired professionals. This was an experimental scheme that had been proposed by Edward Cadbury before his death late in 1948. He believed there were many such people who, while having a reasonable income, still wanted comfortable, easily manageable small dwellings (preferably bungalows) in later life. The scheme, which was sanctioned

116   Bungalows at Lower Moor for retired professionals paid for by the Edward Cadbury Charitable Trust, 1949.

by the Ministry of Health and Birmingham Corporation, was paid for by the Edward Cadbury Charitable Trust. This attractive and relatively expensive group of bungalows did not attract any subsidies. Indeed, they cost £1,000 more than the estimate, and the extra cost had to be borne by the Edward Cadbury and the Bournville Village Trusts.[57] At this time the Bournville Village Trust also began to convert some of its older houses into flats for the elderly.[58]

Another venture of note on the Bournville Estate in the early 1950s was the construction of Brook House, a two-storey terrace of 20 self-contained flats for single women in Cob Lane. This scheme, which was first considered in 1947, was partly financed by Birmingham Soroptimist Club and built by the Birmingham Copec House Improvement Society. Copec was a housing association formed in 1925 as a result of a Conference on Politics, Economics and Citizenship held in Birmingham the year before. At first it was involved in the reconditioning of back-to-back houses. It later started to build new houses, flats and maisonettes on cleared sites. The Bournville Village Trust finally agreed to lease the land in Cob Lane in February 1950, and the flats were occupied a year later. The block, which was designed by the Trust's architect, C.B. Parkes, was built of brick and tile, but had generous metal-framed windows, typical of this period. The roof line was slightly varied and the frontage was punctuated with two-storey bays. There was a lawn in front of Brook House and at the rear were the tenants' gardens. The flats were hidden from the busy Bristol Road by a belt of trees, and for a few years the tenants could watch the cows from nearby Woodbrooke Farm grazing.[59]

The landscaping of the Estate was not forgotten in the immediate post-war period. Good trees were preserved on the new estates, and renewed attention was paid to trees planted alongside the roads of the older parts of the Estate. The Trust produced a colour film, *Street Prospect*, in 1948 and this was followed up the following year with a book, *Landscape and Housing Development*. The book described the Trust's experiments (successful and unsuccessful) in the planning of compact groups of dwellings in settings of trees and grass and well-defined belts of open space. One trend, set by the residents themselves, was beginning to emerge. 'During the last ten years or more', it was reported, 'occupants have begun, quite spontaneously, to remove front hedges and so throw open their front gardens.'[60] This trend, which reflected American patterns, was to become more common in the following years.

In June 1951, Dame Elizabeth Cadbury officially opened the 200th house built by the Trust since the war. This event coincided with the Trust's Jubilee, which was deferred for a year to coincide with the Festival of Britain. The Jubilee began with a Thanksgiving Service held by the United Churches of Bournville on the Green. Other events included an exhibition on the history and work of the Trust at Minworth Greaves, a Jubilee Regatta arranged by the Model Yacht and Power Boat Club at Valley Lake, an old residents' tea party and open-air folk dancing. The celebrations culminated in a greatly expanded Children's Festival, which residents claimed was 'one of the finest efforts they had seen'. A firework display provided by the Firm was the grand finale of the day.

The Jubilee celebrations provided a reminder of Bournville's history and of its current and on-going activities. Further small memorial contributions were made. Flower boxes were placed in front of the shops on the Estate and the annual exhibition of the work of the students at the Bournville School of Art and Crafts was brought forward to Jubilee Week.[61]

117   Brook House was a scheme partly financed by the Birmingham Soroptimist Club and built by the Birmingham Copec House Improvement Society in 1951. It provided self-contained flats for single women.

118   The opening of the 200th post-war house on 27 June 1951. Paul S. Cadbury, Dame Elizabeth Cadbury, C.B.
Parkes (Chief Architect) and F.R. Barlow (Secretary/Manager).

Whilst the Trustees might baulk at the many controls and high costs of development in the post-
war years, they believed that 'it would be wrong for any organisation which has any vacant land at the
present time not to build houses'.[62] This remained their main function. By October 1952, 317 houses
had been constructed on the estate since 1945.[63] (This figure included the re-building of a small amount
of war-damaged property.) While the rate of construction was not as rapid as in the late 1890s or the
1930s, it still bore comparison with the output of many small local authorities.

Some of the post-war developments were on infill sites in the older parts of the estate where lower
densities were the norm. The Trust continued to press the City Council to allow some areas of land to
be devoted to larger houses. 'We feel certain', they claimed, 'that certain parts of Bournville have always
served the needs of those who wish to erect something larger than the minimum house and it would
be a pity if this need could not be met somewhere on the estate.'[64] The likelihood of this happening
increased with the Conservative victory in the General Election of 1951.

If the new targets laid down in the City's Development Plan were to be met, however, densities
elsewhere on the estate would have to be increased. 'We intend to retain the community buildings and
open spaces', it was explained in 1952, 'but we shall have to build the houses closer together and with
smaller gardens, also to build a number of four- and five-storey flats.'[65]

There can be no doubt that the Trust felt itself to be under pressure. The City Council did, in the last resort, have the power to take over any land for housing purposes. The Trustees wanted to continue 'to make a worthwhile contribution to housing and town planning' and therefore sought 'to bring their experience to bear upon development at a higher density'.[66] One way of doing this was to develop a site at a higher density with traditional houses and small gardens. In arrangement with the City, a scheme was prepared for the erection of some 157 houses on the south-west side of Shenley Lane to be built by four builders who undertook to build smaller houses at prices ranging from £1,250 to £1,679. The idea was to satisfy the demand for houses for sale from those people who individually would have little chance of getting a building licence. The houses themselves were designed by the Trust's architects, and, as ever, an effort was made to preserve interesting groups of trees and open spaces. Of course, because of the higher densities, these houses were closer together than earlier houses at Bournville and their gardens were smaller. The Trustees believed that they were helping families to obtain 'convenient and well-planned houses in pleasant surroundings'.[67]

More dramatic than this was the decision to include flats on some sites so as to achieve a density of 50 persons per acre. On land to the north east of Shenley Lane the Trust agreed to erect dwellings which were to be let to families on the Corporation's waiting lists. The development was expected to include terraced houses, maisonettes and three- and four-storey flats. The first phase of this development allowed for 100 dwellings, with another 400 to follow. In 1948 the Trust negotiated the first of a series of 60-year loans to build houses that would let at rents that would qualify for Exchequer subsidies. It was said to be 'one of the few examples on a comparable scale of co-operation between a Housing Trust and a Public Housing Authority'.[68]

Some viewed this development with dismay, but within the Trust the alternative of a municipally planned and managed estate was seen as a less acceptable option. The case for the Trust controlling the scheme was put thus:

> We have the opportunity for controlling the design of the buildings, we can offer the new residents a place in the Bournville community, and since we shall continue to manage the property ourselves, we can continue to have a rather more personal relationship between landlord and tenant than usually exists on Corporation estates.

They did not seem too confident about the artistic merits of some of the dwellings for they suggested that 'success of the scheme from an aesthetic point of view will depend largely upon tree planting and landscaping'. They promised to devote considerable attention to the latter and claimed that 'the starkness and austerity of much of our new building will soon disappear with the weathering of materials and growth of trees'.[69]

Other developments which were to have an impact on the future of the Estate took place in the early 1950s. As a result of the coming into force of George Cadbury's will the Manor Estate came to figure in the planning of the area along Bristol Road. The first result of this was the handing over of the park to the City for public use. In addition, a large area was added to the Bournville Estate for building purposes.

At this time the City's Educational Committee was calling for the establishment of a large number of new schools. Given the rising population in the area and the presence of a number of inviting plots on the Bournville Estate, it was hardly surprising that the Trustees agreed to dispose of five sites to the Education Committee. In view of the interest of most of the Trustees in education, the move was not unexpected. Although not every Bournville resident welcomed such schemes, the schools could be an important element in the community-building process which the Trust wanted to foster. The sites, which covered a total area of about 60 acres, were for a Secondary Modern School in Woodbrooke Road, a Secondary Technical School on Bristol Road, near Hole Lane, a Day Continuation College near the corner of Middle Park Road, a Secondary Modern School on Shenley Lane, opposite Shenley Fields Road, and a Church of England Infant and Junior School between Innage and Bunbury Road.[70]

The need for other facilities was also becoming apparent. The building of a fairly large group of houses in Shenley Fields Road and Green Meadow Road highlighted the need for shopping facilities and a place for meetings. Although there were long-term plans for a group of shops and a community centre, to satisfy the short-term needs of the residents the Trust managed to get permission to erect a temporary hall and lock-up shop in Green Meadow Road.[71] The early post-war residents at Shenley Fields and Yew Tree Farm were undoubtedly happy to get new houses on one of the most prestigious estates in the city. They had to face the advantages and the disadvantages of living on the expanding urban frontier. The countryside was still very close at hand, but so were the new building sites. As yet there was little else.

In Bournville Village, the Council sought to re-establish itself as a useful communal institution. During the war, the Festival had been suspended, but the Social Centre remained open 'to provide a little relaxation for the tenants who wished to go'. A new caretaker was appointed after the war and the Club was improved. A putting green was opened nearby for the summer months. In 1946 the Festival was revived, and Mrs. Gumbley continued her work as trainer of the Maypole dancers. In 1949, the Bournville Village Council published a *Year Book* for the first time since 1941. Several residents who had been voted on to the Village Council before 1939 (like G.L. Barnard, R.H. Barratt, C.L. Chapman, B. Hunter, E. Owen and F. Pugh) continued to give good service in the post-war years. While they were not able to get a new Community Centre, because of the difficult economic circumstances, they were able to embark on a few smaller initiatives. These included new prizes for back gardens on the Estate and a scheme to help the old and infirm with their gardens.[72]

As the Trust looked ahead, in 1952, to the completion of the Shenley Fields and Yew Tree Farm Estates they realised that the schemes depended upon many things, not least the national finances and the supply of building materials and labour.

Chapter Seven

FROM AUSTERITY TO PROSPERITY

National and local trends 1951-64

Conservative governments after 1951 pressed for higher numbers of dwellings to be built. They pursued a policy of 'reluctant collectivism' and encouraged local authorities to build large numbers of houses to replace those lost through slum clearance. The Conservatives sacrificed quality in their quest to build a greater numbers of houses. The proposed economies started with the Ministry of Health's proposals for reduction in the size of houses in 1950.[1] The Trust's response was that they 'did not wish to appear as advocates of reduced standards'. They did consider asking the Ministry for permission to build a three-bedroomed house with a floor area of less than 900 feet 'as an experiment'. (Back in 1942, they had said that the pre-war standard of 760 feet 'was insufficient accommodation for a three bedroom house'.) The Trustees insisted that any plans which were prepared with this end in view 'should not involve any sacrifice of present amenities'.[2]

Further economies were proposed by the Conservative Government during the 1950s. Firstly, they encouraged the building of smaller houses. Then *Houses 1953* (the Third Supplement to the *Housing Manual* of 1949) proposed more ways to reduce housing construction costs. These included frontage-saving houses built in terraces (a modified Radburn layout), the use of corner flats at junctions to avoid waste, more economical layouts, and the reduction in length, width and the standards of roads.[3] Because of the pressure to build at higher densities and Ministry restrictions on the cost of subsidised houses, some of these methods had already been tried at Bournville. The Trustees welcomed the suggestions relating to road construction, but they believed that, just as with the 'People's House', the lower cost figures would become the Ministry norm.[4]

Particular attention was given to the proposals for houses with path access. The Trust believed that such houses could be let, but felt that they would not be saleable. They were aware that it would be difficult to deliver coal and empty dustbins to terraces without access tunnels.[5]

Nationally, unconventional building types and new layouts were tried and industrialised building systems were introduced, especially for the increasing number of multi-storey flats.[6] These shifts were graphically illustrated in Birmingham, where the interest of senior officers such as Manzoni and Sheppard Fidler in high-rise housing and the desire to meet demanding housing targets produced a marked increase in multi-storey flats (though they were usually part of 'mixed development' schemes). In 1951, flats formed a mere 3.69 per cent of the annual total of dwellings erected, but by 1957 the figure had risen to 75 per cent—and this in a city with a traditional commitment to low-rise developments.[7] At this time Bournville Village Trust came under pressure not only to build at higher densities but also to consider high-rise flats.

The Conservatives had somewhat reluctantly encouraged local authority housebuilding, and there were signs in the 1950s that they saw an increased role for the housing trusts and housing associations. They were supportive of the self-build movement. In 1952 Harold Macmillan wrote to the National Federation of Housing Societies, 'I am pleased that your Federation is helping self-build groups, and I want to encourage people who are enterprising enough to build their own houses.' Five years later the 1957 Housing Act provided the legislative framework which allowed housing associations to obtain loans and subsidies for the purchase, conversion and renovation of properties. Although the housing associations were regarded as 'the second best option' by the major political parties, they could 'fill the gaps' left by municipal and private house providers.[8]

As the Trust entered its second half century, it was aware that 'the difficulties of working under modern conditions are very considerable'. Although the Trustees were aware of 'the many controls and high costs which affect private development', they remained committed to building houses on their vacant land and to embarking on small experiments. While they could not be certain as to the function of the Trust in the future, they believed that the Trust had 'a duty to manage its existing properties as well as possible in accordance with the ideals of the Founder and that the Estate should be a community, not just a group of buildings'.

Self-build at Bournville 1950-65

Whilst the majority of the dwellings at Bournville were constructed by either the Trust's Direct Labour Team or private builders, between 1950 and the mid-1960s just over 200 houses were erected by self-build groups.[9] The self-build movement was a response to the problems of the post-war period. It was a time when there were shortages of building materials and labour and when construction projects could only be carried out under government licence. Very few houses were being built for sale and, with the exception of a relatively small amount of building done by bodies such as the Bournville Village Trust, properties for rent were largely being constructed by local authorities. The Councils' waiting lists were long, and young married couples looking to start a family, or with few children, occupied a low place on those lists. One possible answer was self-build, which would give them a house at a lower price than normal.

The first recognised self-build groups had been set up by ex-servicemen in Brighton and Post Office workers in the Sheldon district of Birmingham. Late in 1949 the Trust's manager and architect had visited the Sheldon scheme and they came away impressed by what they had seen.[10] The Trust, therefore, responded favourably to a request by a group of ex-servicemen who worked for Cadbury Brothers to form a housing society with the intention of building their own homes on the Estate. With the help of Cadburys' Legal Department and the Trust the Hay Green Housing Society was formed. It was registered under the Industrial and Provident Societies Acts and affiliated to the National Federation of Housing Societies. Like the other early self-build societies, it was a co-partnership society. At the time this was a legal necessity as only housing societies, building for letting, could erect part of a local authority's housing allocation from central government. Birmingham City Council were supportive and through them Exchequer loans and rent subsidies were available.

It seemed quite natural that the self-build movement should find a home at Bournville. The Trust had long experience of estate development and working with co-partnership and public utility societies and they had land available. Their architects were experienced in house design and could provide them with the necessary professional advice. Because the Trust only leased land, the self-build societies did not have to find the money for the purchase of land at a stage when the society was not fully constituted and able to borrow. In addition, the Trust also developed the land, laid sewers and built roads, the costs of which were later included in the ground rent.

The members of the self-build societies were encouraged by the Trust to subscribe as much as possible to the scheme before building work started. It would seem that £150 was the maximum that most could manage to raise. The Trustees were initially anxious whether amateur builders could build in their spare time to Bournville standards. It was found that the groups who approached the Trust had a nucleus of building tradesmen. In the time it took to get the societies registered, the plans passed and the finances sorted, the rest of the members received training in the building trades. The members of the Hay Green Housing Society Limited were taught in classes organised by the Bournville Works Education Department under the instruction of a master builder and former Government Rehabilitation Building Instructor.

The Hay Green Housing Society leased land from the Trust on a 99-year lease in a new cul-de-sac off Hay Green Lane, known as Cobs Field. After discussions with the members of the society, plans for 24 houses were prepared by the Trust's architects. The dwellings were single-storeyed and contained three bedrooms. Different designs were produced for the bungalows depending on whether they had north or south aspects. In addition, a large store or a garage was to be attached. The site for this low-density development contained a triangular green.

Work started on the site in November 1950, and by February 1952 the first two bungalows had been occupied and another 10 were in various stages of construction. All of the bungalows were completed by Whitsun 1954. These were the only self-build bungalows built on the Estate. The groups which followed built two-storey houses.

The first of these was the Self-Build Housing Association who approached the Trust with a scheme for 50 houses in May 1950. They were mainly workers from the Shaftmoor Lane factory of Joseph Lucas Limited. The Association was formed by a Trust Deed under the terms of the Housing Act of 1948. The Trustees included members of the Association and a Lucas director. A few of the members had building experience, and one of them acted as general foreman.

The Association was offered two sites in the Yew Tree Farm area of the Estate. One was for 12 houses on a service road parallel to Shenley Lane and the other was in Meadow Brook Road, part of which had been developed before the Second World War, and which was being extended to Merritt's Hill at the time. The 50 members and their wives visited the area in July 1950. As it was not possible to find space for bungalows, it was agreed that houses should be built. They were shown various types of post-war houses by the Trust's chief architect, and after discussions a decision was made as to the type of

119   Self-builders working at the site in Shenley Lane.

dwelling required. Three-bedroomed houses with living room, kitchen and dining room (with access from both kitchen and living room) were decided upon. The houses were fitted with a simple radiator system to provide background heating. Each house was also to have a garage. The plans were, of course, prepared by the Trust's Architects' Department. (The architect who worked closely with all the self-build groups was William Muirhead.)

The City Council agreed that the houses, built in groups of 12, were to be part of their housing allocation from the Ministry and that they should qualify for subsidies. The Self-Build Housing Association obtained a loan of £50,000 from the Public Works Loan Board to finance the scheme. Work started in Shenley Lane at the end of October 1950 (that is, before the Hay Green Society) and the first 12 houses were completed by August 1952. A short time before, two members left and the number of houses to be built was reduced to 48. Work continued at the other site in Meadow Brook Road and the scheme was completed in December 1954. The members worked 23½ hours a week, 8 hours on Saturdays and Sundays and 2½ hours on Mondays, Tuesdays and Wednesdays. A points system, similar to that used for municipal houses, was employed by the Association to allocate the houses.

Following the successful formation and progress of the Hay Green Society, another group of Cadbury employees got together to form the Shenley Housing Society Limited. Once again the Cadbury Brothers' solicitors and the Trust provided help in setting up the Society. A loan of £1,000 (at a rate of 4½ per cent for 60 years) was obtained from the Public Works Loan Board. As before, the houses were included in the City's allocation and they also qualified for subsidies. Work commenced in March 1952 and the scheme was completed quickly.

The Shenley Housing Society had 20 members, 12 of whom were Cadbury employees and eight worked in the building trades, one of them for Cadbury Brothers and another for the Bournville Village Trust. Their houses were constructed on Green Meadow Road in the Shenley Fields area of the Bournville Estate. The sites were acquired from the Trust on 99-year leases at a ground rent of £12 10s. per plot. The houses were three-bedroomed semi-detached dwellings and, being on the south side of the road, were planned with the main rooms to the rear. The ground floor accommodation included a living room, dining room and kitchen and, again, each house was provided with a garage. Radiators were installed to provide background heat for the houses.

At much the same time, a group of workers from the Austin Motor Company and a number of building workers asked the Trust for plots for 40 houses. The number was later reduced to 34. The Trust offered them sites on Meadow Brook Road and Verbena Road on the Yew Tree Farm Estate. The land in the area sloped steeply and additional foundation work was required, but the members coped with these difficulties. This site had few natural features and, by Bournville standards, few trees were planted.

The Austin Self-Build Association was formed by Trust Deed and obtained loans and various permissions from the City Council in the same way as the Self-Build Housing Association. Work started in February 1953 and the 34 houses were completed by September 1955. The plans were fairly similar to those prepared for the Self-Build Housing Association, but had stores in place of garages. These stores were later enlarged to form garages, where the site allowed.

The first four self-build societies were, of necessity, of the co-partnership type. They were 'real pioneers'. The members had to learn the building trades before starting years of building. A Trust official, who worked closely with these Societies, felt that their Secretaries deserved 'special praise for their undaunted efforts in a field of housing ... not known to many'.[11] Not only had they to deal with many administrative problems, they also had to cope with licensing difficulties, restrictions and shortages of materials.

During the time that these first four societies were constructing their houses, building restrictions were eased and building licences were abolished. It thus became possible for a self-build society to erect houses with a view to individual ownership—the members of the society coming together only long enough to get their houses completed and transferred to individual ownership. (The later self-build societies at Bournville were rather like the earliest terminating building societies that operated in Birmingham in the late 18th century.) The shift from collective ownership to individual ownership reflected the changing political situation in the country, and the transfer of power from Labour to the Conservatives.

120   The houses on Hay Green Lane built by the members of the Second Independent Housing Association Ltd., most of whom were firemen.

The Yew Tree Housing Society Limited was the first of the new societies. It was made up of a group of 12 building workers. They were offered leases of plots on Long Mynd Road in the Yew Tree Farm area, which was then being filled with houses for sale. Twelve separate plots of land were leased to facilitate transfer on completion. All the houses were three-bedroomed types with garages, similar in plan and size to the earlier self-build houses. Work on the 12 houses started in February 1958 and it took 18 months to complete the scheme.

After this there was a lull in self-build activity on the Bournville Estate until a group of firemen formed themselves into the Second Independent Housing Association Limited in 1961. The Hay Green Lane/Hole Lane area of the Estate was being opened up at that time and 12 plots were leased in the new portion of Hay Green Lane. The Association arranged a loan from a building society and work began in May 1961. The houses were in semi-detached pairs of two slightly different types, each with three bedrooms, living room, dining room, kitchen and attached garage. Heating was provided by radiators, with the heat source being either the back boiler in the living room or a kitchen boiler.

By the early 1960s there was a good deal of pressure to build at higher densities, even at Bournville. It was often suggested at that time that pre-fabricated or industrialised systems might be the answer to the housing problem. For the self-builder the main concern was to save costs, and he could achieve this by contributing time and labour. Consequently, systems aimed at reducing site labour had little appeal to the self-build groups. Traditionally constructed dwellings continued to be erected by these groups. Because of the pressure to build at higher densities the form that the self-build houses took changed. Terraced houses with narrow frontages were designed by the Trust architects for the self-build groups and for sale.

At the very end of 1961 and the beginning of 1962, three self-build groups approached the Trust. They were the Wilway Housing Association Limited, the Presthope Independent Housing Society Limited and the Castle Housing Society. All three groups were made up mainly of building workers. The three groups were offered sites on Presthope Road, a new road being laid out in the Shenley area off Swarthmore Road. All the societies agreed to have the same plan for their houses. The leases were for 99 years and again there were separate ones for each plot so that they could be assigned later to the individual members. The ground rent for each plot was £10. A total of 33 houses on three access footpaths set at right angles to the road were planned. Drives to garages at the bottom of each garden were constructed. The three societies approached a building society for funds, but they were refused a loan because of the unconventional layout and close proximity of the houses. As housing associations they were, however, able to get the funds they required from the Public Works Loans Board. Work began in the summer of 1962 and proceeded satisfactorily on two of the schemes, but there were some difficulties with the Castle Housing Society.

In May 1962, another group approached the Trust. They formed the Presmore Housing Association and were offered plots for 15 houses on the south side of Presthope Road. The houses built for this society

121   Terraced houses with narrower frontages built at right angles to Presthope Road by the Presthope Independent Housing Society Ltd.

were three-bedroomed houses with attached garages, and were similar in style to the houses being built for sale on adjoining sites. The building plots were larger than those on the north side of the road and consequently the ground rents were £11 a year. Given the more conventional nature of the scheme the Presmore Housing Association was able to negotiate a loan with the Co-operative Building Society.

By this time there was an upsurge of interest in self-building in the Midlands. The *Daily Sketch* had produced a series of articles on self-build. They took the matter further, making plans and a design service available. In addition, they formed a Land Bank to provide a central source of information about suitable building plots.

In October 1963 a conference was held at Birmingham Town Hall, at which the National Federation of Housing Societies was represented. The major result of this conference was the creation of a Midland Self-Build Council. Its main objectives were to provide a regional organisation for putting individuals in touch with groups, to act as a centre of information and to help in the search for suitable building land.

Not surprisingly, much interest was generated in self-build. Birmingham Corporation had numerous applications and leased land to a number of societies. Bournville Village Trust also received a great many applications, not unexpectedly as they still had land available; they also had experience of self-build and the recommendation of those who had already built there.

To meet the needs of the societies who had applied to them the Trust designed 70 three-bedroomed houses. All were built to the new Parker Morris standards and had efficient heating systems and a garage. Virtually all the houses were built in terraces but they were designed 'to give some feeling of individuality and variety of arrangement'.[12] The 70 houses were allocated to the first six suitable societies on the Trust's waiting list. Four of the groups were made up mainly of workers in the building trades: the Northoak Independent Housing Association, the Ashford Housing Association, the Shelmore Self-Build Housing Association and the Oakley (Birmingham) Self-Building Housing Association. The other two societies consisted, once again, of firemen: the Third Independent Housing Association Limited and the Fourth Independent Self-Build Association. By mid-1965 work was well under way on these schemes which had been leased sites on Guiting Road and Radford Road.

Even after these 70 plots had been allocated, there was still a significant demand for land. Almost the last portion of building land in the Shenley area, on the east side of Guiting Road, was set aside for self-build societies and designs for 131 houses were provided by the Trust. Eleven groups were involved. The dwellings were all terraced houses and a modified Radburn layout was adopted on some schemes, with footpath access through green spaces to the fronts of the houses and service roads to the backs. Garages were placed either at the bottom of the gardens or in nearby groups. This type of layout is to be most clearly found in Long Leasow and Hollybrow. Again, all the houses were built to Parker Morris standards and provided with gas-fired warm air heating.

Considering their early misgivings the Trust were immensely satisfied with the contribution of the self-build societies to the development of the Estate. As the houses were designed by the Trust's architects they blended in with the rest of the housing stock. It proved impossible to pick out the self-build houses because of differences in workmanship. The Trust believed that the standard of the societies' work was 'as good or better than those produced by building firms specialising in housing work'. The best work was said to have been produced by those societies which had a first-class general foreman. Ironically, the least satisfactory work was produced by societies whose members were all building workers.[13]

Despite the great efforts made by the members of these societies, some of the specialist work was carried out by sub-contractors. The extent of such work depended on the skills of the members of the various societies. Plastering and roof tiling were among the jobs where sub-contractors were more frequently brought in. Most of the societies had electricians and plumbers among their members. It was not uncommon for members' wives to help with the painting and decorating.

Generally, the self-build houses seem to have been built to a standard acceptable to the Bournville Village Trust. As usual plaster cracks and timber shrinkages were noted during the first few months of occupation, but because of careful site management and supervision the problems were few. The worst trouble was experienced by the Shenley Housing Society, where the floors had to be taken up because chemically active hardcore caused the concrete floors to swell.

122 Aerial view of Lower Shenley (or Shenley Manor as it later came to be called). Shenley Lane is at the bottom right of the photograph and the Cranesbill Road flats can be seen in the centre. Some of the self-build schemes can be found in the top right-hand quarter, including the pedestrian access schemes at Hollybrow and Long Leasow.

Although it was generally felt that the societies should 'stand on their own feet', many of them benefited from the help and advice of the Bournville Village Trust. Others had the assistance of the firms for which they worked. Cadbury Brothers, Austin and Lucas helped their workers by providing interest-free loans, arranging for the purchase of materials through their Buying Departments, or even paying for garden work. The later societies generally had to rely on credit from suppliers or additional short-term loans to continue their building programmes. The Trust helped the cash flow of the societies by delaying their request for payment of fees until the housing scheme was completed.[14]

Because of the political and economic constraints at the time, the early co-partnership societies produced subsidised rented houses. While many of their members hoped that, eventually, they might own their own homes, it was not thought that this would happen at the outset. The matter was, however, taken up by the National Federation of Housing Societies and as a result it was made possible for members of these early societies to purchase their houses (without having to pay back the subsidies which had been paid to the societies).[15]

The self-build societies made a significant contribution to the development of Bournville in the 1950s and 1960s. Although some of the schemes were not as well landscaped as other parts of the Estate, the layouts were sometimes more adventurous. Where more care was given to the landscaping and the layout, as at Hollybrow and Long Leasow, the result can be pleasant (although problems have arisen with the garage courts in certain areas). Whether because of the pressure to reduce costs or architectural fashion, the façades of houses in this period were usually without ornament. The earlier self-build schemes (and other subsidised developments) at Bournville were affected by Harold Macmillan's economy drive. By the late 1950s the lower standards introduced by Conservative governments earlier in the decade were at variance with the rising living standards and expectations of many in the population. The later Bournville self-build schemes were built to the more generous standards of the Parker Morris Committee.[16]

Infill and expansion at Bournville

As a consequence of the higher building densities set for the suburbs by the City, the layout for the Shenley Estate had to be revised. The revised Shenley scheme produced in late 1947 made provision for 1,200 houses, compared with 1,000 in the original proposal.[17] The need for higher densities led to the provision of flats and maisonettes on the Shenley Estate, though none were ever more than three storeys high. The Trust officers did consider new constructional methods, but concluded that the savings over brick were not sufficient to offset the poor appearance and lack of variation in design of such schemes. Prefabs were believed to have 'the appearance of army hutments' and were not considered suitable for the Bournville Estate. The potential of prefabricated fittings for post-war houses was recognised.[18]

Although the first houses built at Bournville after the war were constructed by C. Bryant and Son, the Trust's own Direct Labour Department was re-formed in 1945 and went on to do much of the building work on the Shenley Estate. 'On the whole', the Trust concluded in 1953, 'houses built by contract are less satisfactory than houses built by our own labour.' Interestingly, they believed that private builders were suitable for the erection of private houses for sale.[19]

123 Varied housing types at Lower Shenley: houses, bungalows, flats and maisonettes at Green Meadow Road and Black Haynes Road.

By January 1951 the 200th post-war house had been constructed on the Estate. At the end of the year Paul S. Cadbury was expressing the desire that the Shenley area could be more rapidly developed than in the past. In view of the Conservative victory in the General Election, it was considered more likely that a portion of the estate, preferably that part to the south of Shenley Hill, could be developed with houses for sale.[20] In 1952 a further agreement was made with the City Council to construct another 400 houses on the Shenley Estate. By spring 1959 most of these were completed.[21]

By the mid-1950s the Trust was reviewing its housing policy. It reaffirmed its belief that the Trust's aim was 'to provide or help in the provision of the maximum number of houses of a wide range of sizes both for sale and for letting'. It had, of course, to maintain its existing houses. By 1954 there were 908 dwellings under the Trust's control, of which 327 had been constructed after 1945.[22] It envisaged building more houses to let under agreements made with Birmingham Corporation. The Trust wanted to construct more houses to let for single women and the elderly, in part to reduce under-occupation elsewhere on the Estate. The lease of land for houses for sale to be built by private builders was also part of their policy, as was the improvement and conversion of some of their older properties. Grants for the latter were available under the 1949 Housing Act (and the 1953 government proposals in *Houses—the Next Step* also related to the repair of older houses).[23]

A group of bungalows for retired professionals had been built in Lower Moor in 1949. A further development of bungalows and flats in Westholme Croft in 1957 was paid for by the Edward Cadbury Charitable Trust. Rents of 25s. and 30s. were charged for the flats and 45s. for the bungalows. The rents brought in a surplus of £200 which was used for converting further houses into flats.[24]

The Bournville Village Trust considered Lower Moor and Westholme Croft to be valuable additions to the Estate's properties. 'They have little doubt that in the coming years', they rightly asserted, 'the problem of finding lower rented accommodation for old people will be very real.'[25]

124   The staff of the Trust's Building Department, 1951.

The Trust had co-operated with Copec on the Brook House scheme for single women in Cob Lane which had been opened in 1951. Six years later Copec took over Wolseley House, a large dwelling on Weoley Park Road acquired through a legacy, and converted it into 11 one- and two-roomed flats. In 1965, Copec built three bungalows for handicapped persons in the grounds of Wolseley House. The aim was to provide dwellings in which a disabled housewife could be self-sufficient and contribute to the running of the family home. The dwellings were designed by Trust Architects. They produced a design with a fairly open plan and no steps or changes of level. A square hall gave access through wide doors to the living room, three bedrooms, bathroom and toilet. The kitchen was situated off the living room and separated from it by a room divider. The bungalows contained many facilities recommended for the chairbound, including low-level work surfaces, revolving cupboards and cookers with easy controls. Similar detailed attention was paid to the bathroom. Externally the bungalows were made to look as normal as possible, and an ornamental garden (for the able-bodied members of the family) and raised flower boxes on paved terraces were provided so that chairbound tenants could also do some gardening.[26]

Early in 1956 two blocks of maisonettes on the Lower Shenley Farm Estate were completed and let. They consisted of a living room, kitchen, bedroom and bathroom. The maisonettes were let at an inclusive rent of 21s. 9d. Sheds were provided outside, and not only were these useful in themselves, they also provided shelter for the courtyards. The tenants were women living alone or sharing with a relative. They were reported to be 'most satisfactory' tenants. 'They are pleased with their accommodation', it was reported, 'and have made attractive homes.' These tenants did not want much garden, so the Trust turfed most of the space, leaving small beds for the tenants to plant flowers and shrubs. The occupants of the maisonettes soon got to know each other. They also appeared to get on well with the neighbouring families, although there were some complaints about the behaviour of the children. The block at Almond Close and Green Meadow Road was better sited than the one on Veronica Close, because it was far enough back from the road not to be disturbed by children.[27]

The long negotiations between the Trust and the City Education Department about sites for schools finally came to fruition in the early 1950s. The Trust had been happy to lease sites, but was not so happy with the Department's valuation of the plots.[28] Eventually, a number of schools were opened to cater for the growing child population on the Estate. The first of these was Dame Elizabeth Cadbury Secondary Modern School on Woodbrooke Road, which was opened in 1951. In 1954 and 1955 the Bournville Boys' and Girls' Technical Schools followed. Infant and Junior school children were catered for by the construction of Green Meadow School in the Shenley area in 1958 and Northfield Manor Infant and Junior School adjacent to the Weoley Hill Estate in 1962. A Technical College was also planned at the junction of Bristol Road and Middle Park Road in the late 1950s. Sheppard Fidler, the City Architect, explained to the Trustees that 'the proposed scheme shows the logical and economical development of the site for the proposed development'. The Trustees expressed some concerns about the design. Sheppard Fidler was working within strict cost guidelines, but he also favoured a more Modern style.[29] Those who preferred the traditional style normally associated with Bournville could reconcile themselves with the fact that the College was to be screened by the rows of mature trees on Bristol Road.

By 1957 the City Council were bringing further pressure to bear on the Bournville Village Trust. The Chairmen of the City Public Works and House Building Committees called upon the Trust to speed up the production of houses at Shenley Fields and build at higher densities. 'The Council would not have in mind development along the typical lines of pre-war estates', they explained, 'but would envisage the interspersing of flats, most carefully sited, having regard to local features.'[30] They also suggested that the Corporation might build on Trust land. The Trust responded by saying that they were already proceeding in accordance with the densities prescribed in the City's draft development plan (i.e., 50 per acre). Paul Cadbury did point out that 'in adopting a higher density the Trustees had made a departure from their traditional practice'. The members of the Corporation House Building Committee thought that the Trust should adopt even higher densities. The City Architect, who was closely associated with the latter committee, suggested that the Trust build some 'tall slab blocks'.[31] The members of the Public Works Committee, however, did not necessarily see eye to eye with the House Building Committee. The Chairman of the Public Works Committee, Councillor Price, told the Trustees that he was satisfied with their policy. Although he acknowledged the City was desperate for land, he advocated an overspill policy rather than higher densities within the City.[32]

There was pressure on the Trust to develop their land at a faster rate.[33] The Trust could point to the fact that 'the provision of funds had lagged behind the Trust's ability to start work'.[34] At the beginning of May 1959, the City Council requested the Trust to construct a further 200 houses at Shenley (despite the fact that their House Building Committee would have preferred to purchase Trust land and build themselves). The Chief of the City's Housing Management Department claimed, however, that he was 'very satisfied' with the arrangements for the first 500 houses constructed at Shenley. He did suggest that the Trust consider building dwellings at lower rentals, and he indicated that he too was in favour of higher densities.

The Trust did respond to these promptings and constructed 42 low-cost three-storey flats in Cranesbill Road, Lower Shenley. 'For reasons of economy', it was claimed, 'the plan is such that there is only one staircase serving six flats.'[35] Despite such economies, the Trust claimed that the Lower Shenley flats displayed 'improvements in standards of convenience'.[36] Slightly later, more three-storey flats for Corporation nominees were built in Black Haynes Road and Burdock Road.

The pressure to build at higher densities on the Estate did not diminish. Consequently, the Trust agreed to lease land in the Middle Park Farm area to Toran Limited, a subsidiary of Ashworth and Steward, to build flats to let. The flats, mainly three-storey blocks but with two nine-storey blocks, were built to Toran's own designs. Unfortunately, the company got into difficulties and, eventually, the estate was taken over by the City Council.[37]

Some private house building was taking place in the late 1950s and early 1960s, in particular, on the western edges of the Middle Park Farm Estate and on the Yew Tree Farm Estate beyond Shenley Lane. There the Trust, as usual, laid out the roads and the open spaces. Many of the old, established trees were preserved. The Trust architects prepared the plans and specifications and the houses were built by individual builders. The houses were sold on 99-year leases at prices ranging from £1,600 to £2,400. Most houses had garages, or space for one.

It is apparent that after 1945 there was a degree of segregation on the newly developed parts of the Estate. Shenley Lane was just as great a physical barrier as Bristol Road had been. Originally a narrow road it was eventually widened by the Corporation. Narrow or wide, it remained dangerous for pedestrians travelling from the Yew Tree Farm Estate to the emerging neighbourhood centre and the schools. The Corporation agreed to provide an underpass when making the new road. This, and other, wide roads and open spaces were used to form 'a buffer between the private development and the tenanted houses'. It is true that the Trust still encouraged the building of a wide range of houses for sale and for letting. It is equally clear that 'the Corporation nominees [were] kept more or less in one area'. Nonetheless, the Trust continued to argue that 'the Estate as a whole is not by any means a one-class development'.[38]

At this time Cadbury Brothers recognised the need for extra accommodation for their older employees and pensioners. The firm made a donation to the Trust of £5,200 to build and manage 26

125   Green Meadow School from Shenley Green.

126   Houses for sale in Spiceland Road on the Yew Tree Farm portion of the Bournville Estate. Trees and open spaces continued to be important elements in the Bournville landscape.

bungalows to be let at a subsidised rent of 28s. Eight were built in Laurel Grove for the Bournville Works Housing Society (to help release family houses) and 18 in Selly Oak Road for the firm's nominees.[39] These bungalows were provided with a much smaller back garden than usual, because it had become noticeable that the large gardens attached to the inter-war bungalows in Cedar Close were becoming a burden to their ageing tenants. Attention was also paid to the heating of the bungalows. 'The system of closable convector fire with a good back boiler heating the hot water and a radiator in the bedroom', it was asserted, 'is as practical ... as can be installed at the present time.'[40]

By the mid-1960s four blocks of flats for Cadbury Brothers employees had been constructed in Ramsden Close. The rest of the houses in Ramsden Close and the adjoining roads were built for sale.

Heating and insulation

In general, more attention was being paid to heating and insulation at this time. The Trust itself investigated the heating of small dwellings. They recognised that there had been great advances in living standards since the Bournville Estate was started. The first major change came round about 1930 with the replacement of the hob grate or kitchener with the combination boiler. The open fire was frequently supplemented by portable paraffin or electric heating appliances. Paradoxically, the substitution of electric for incandescent gas lighting removed an effective source of background heat in the smaller house.

The Trust accepted that people were beginning to expect a greater degree of warmth in their homes. They also recognised that different households had different needs. The needs of pensioners, young families and working households all varied. Similarly, systems that were appropriate for larger dwellings might not be appropriate for smaller houses. The Trust officers concluded that the traditional central heating system with large pipes and cast iron radiators had 'serious disadvantages for the smaller house'. Small bore systems had been used 'with complete success' in a number of privately built houses at Bournville. Partial whole house heating (using a powerful back boiler) had been installed in some recent small houses built for sale and some larger four-bedroomed houses for letting by the Trust. This seemed a reasonable compromise, but underfloor electric heating (which the Trust installed in a small number of properties) was considered unsatisfactory and expensive. In general, they considered that a solid fuel fire with a back boiler and radiators was satisfactory for 'tenanted family houses'.[41]

By the late 1950s the Trust's houses were also being better insulated. They were being constructed using insulation blocks for the inner skin of external walls. Fibre-glass insulation was being used in the roof space, and in some houses with suspended floors a fibre-glass quilt was put under the floor boards. The Trust's officers expressed the belief that use should be made of double glazing where there were large windows.[42] They argued that their post-war practice was in advance of the standards recommended by the Egerton Committee, and adopted by the Ministry and local authorities.[43]

Just as standards were being improved in one area the Trust were being pushed again to make economies elsewhere. In April 1961 the Trust agreed in principle to build a further 200 dwellings for the Corporation at Shenley. Over 40 one-bedroom dwellings were to be erected, but the remainder were for slum clearance tenants. The Trust were urged to try to get the rents down 'as low as possible'. This put pressure on them. C.B. Parkes, the Trust's Chief Architect, was praised not only because he brought 'fine traditions and high standards' but also because he had been 'a pioneer in new ideas and in meeting the difficulties caused by restrictions in the use of land, materials and money'.[44]

There were moves in the opposite direction. *Homes for Today and Tomorrow*, the report of the Parker Morris Committee, 'marked the last attempt to put the public sector in the vanguard of design'.[45] It called for extra floor space to allow for changes in lifestyle and the greater number of possessions many were beginning to accumulate. 'Homes are being built at the present time', the report claimed, 'which are not only too small to provide adequately for family life but are also too small to hold the possessions in which so much of the new affluence is expressed.'[46] The report was 'not about rooms so much as about the activities that people want to pursue in their homes'.[47] Consequently, a flexible approach to planning the house was advocated. The 'adaptable house' was a common theme of the report.[48] It pressed for major changes in the heating of homes: 'Better heating is the key to the design of homes at the present time, for it provides an extra freedom in meeting individual needs in the areas of the home which at present are too cold to be suitable for daytime and evening use except in summer.'[49] The report also stressed that kitchens should be designed so as to take into account the common practice of taking some meals there.[50]

Externally, the Parker Morris report emphasised the need to separate pedestrians from cars, the necessity for play space and the requirement for good landscaping. It noted several recent 'commend-able efforts at landscaping housing developments'.[51] Bournville was one of the schemes they had in mind. Sir Parker Morris had visited the Estate with the National Federation of Housing Societies in March 1959, and had expressed his admiration of the work of the Bournville Village Trust.[52]

In the years following the publication of the Parker Morris Report, the Trust continued to pay particular attention to the questions of heating and landscaping. Between 1962 and 1965 a heating and double glazing experiment was carried out on the Estate. Double glazing was found to have been most effective in terms of heat conservation in flats with 'expensive heating', like underfloor heating or night storage heaters. 'Whilst generally desirable', the trust officers concluded, 'it may not be economically justifiable to put double glazing into dwellings for rental except in cases of exceptional exposure ... and where the proportion of window to wall is particularly high—say over 40 per cent.' The ratio of window to wall had increased in the post-war houses at Bournville and reached almost 50 per cent in the Cranesbill Road flats.[53]

Landscaping

The Landscaping Department had some catching up to do in the post-war period 'after six years of unavoidable neglect'.[54] The varied patterns of forestry and planting developed in the 1930s were carried forward—the emphasis being on ornamental trees rather than the larger forest-type trees. The efforts of the team were quite widely publicised. A film of their work attracted good audiences on the Estate and elsewhere in the city. *Landscape and Housing Development* was published in 1949. This book, based on the Trust's evidence to the Faringdon Committee, also seems to have aroused interest.[55]

Approaches to landscaping were changing, and the older parts of the Estate began to be seen as 'out of date' (in part because they were almost overgrown). After 1958 an attempt was made to rectify some of the problems. It was seen to be necessary to remove some of the roadside trees, which by then had grown to a great size and were causing problems for residents and traffic. The large old trees were replaced with small flowering trees. The front and dividing hedges of many of the houses in the original Village were removed and the small front gardens were replaced by lawns which could be more easily maintained.[56] This, of course, was the way in which the front gardens were being treated on the new parts of the Estate. Some of the new residents at Shenley requested fences, because they felt the gardens were too open. The Trust fenced in their back gardens, but insisted that the fronts were left open.

127 Commercial developments on the Bristol Road at the junction with Bournville Lane. These buildings, originally occupied by Wagon Repairs and the Central Electricity Board in 1960, were set behind a tree barrier.

128   The plot on Bristol Road recommended to be kept as an open space by the well-known landscape architect, G.A. Jellicoe, in 1961.

Even the most sensitive and spacious of developments has an impact on the landscape. Farms and farmland were disappearing from the Bournville scene. Woodbrooke Farm, at the corner of Bristol Road and Cob Lane, was one such landmark. It was demolished in 1958. It became apparent that there were times when the Trustees had to balance the amenity value of the landscape against the commercial value of certain plots of land. The land opposite the South Birmingham Technical College on Bristol Road was a case in point. The plots had originally been zoned for commercial development, but Herbert Manzoni, the City Engineer and Surveyor, later expressed the view that the plots should instead be kept as open spaces. By the spring of 1960 the buildings for Wagon Repairs and the Central Electricity Board at the end of Bournville Lane were both nearing completion. The Trust were anxious to develop two adjacent plots. If those sites were left undeveloped this would, of course, involve considerable financial loss to the Trust. They argued that these commercial sites could be successfully landscaped, just as the two buildings nearing completion and the nearby College and schools had been.

To help them try to resolve the issue, the Trust called in G.A. Jellicoe, the well-known landscape architect. He was asked 'to advise them upon the most agreeable development, having in mind both the economic and the landscape interests'. Although he felt that the site could be developed in an informal and agreeable way for commercial uses, Jellicoe came down in favour of retaining the open landscape which he considered a potentially important part of this unusually distinguished highway approach to Birmingham'. He concluded:

> I have no hesitation in recommending ... that this land should remain as existing, *provided* it is opened up and becomes part of the scenery of the main road. I would add that it seems to me that this romantic view of Bournville, in contrast to the enjoyable but fleeting glimpse along Bournville Lane, would give the motorist a very happy awareness of a project that was first of its kind in England.[57]

Social Trends at Shenley

By the end of 1956, 119 houses had been completed on the Lower Shenley Farm Estate. The average density was 3.45 persons per dwelling. At that point there were 241 adults, 10 children under 1, 217 between 1 and 10, and 66 aged 10-20 on the estate.[58] By April 1959 Shenley had nearly 500 children aged between 1 and 10 and over 100 between 11 and 15.[59] Young parents and children dominated this new part of the Bournville Estate.

The people who made up the new Shenley community came from all over the city. The largest group came from the redevelopment areas in the city. Many of these 'pioneers' had previously been sub-tenants or lodgers in Council properties or back-to-backs. A number came from older council estates, however, thus releasing cheaper older properties for those who could not afford the higher rents of these new dwellings. The rents of the houses and maisonettes at Shenley ranged from £1 17s. 10d. to £3 3s. 5d. (including rates). The one- and two-person flats were let at rents ranging from £1 3s. 5d. to £1 7s. 3d.[60] Some hesitated to come to Shenley because of the relatively high rents, and the first group of four-bedroomed houses proved difficult to let (although there were no problems with later groups). It should be noted that the estimated rents at Shenley were generally lower than post-war council estates.

Generally, rents were promptly paid at Shenley.[61] The Corporation nominees at Shenley were, however, required to pay their rent weekly, whilst elsewhere on the Bournville Estate rents were usually collected fortnightly. This, the Trust explained, was because there were 'extremely few bad tenants' on the older parts of the Estate and because 'they are not really the type of tenant who needs management of this sort'.[62]

Most of the new residents seemed to like the idea of moving to Shenley and living on the Bournville Village Trust Estate. All the Council's nominees were visited before being offered a house at Shenley. The standard of their homes was said to be good 'in the circumstances'. Most expressed an interest in gardening. The average wages of the new tenants was said to be between £9 and £10.[63]

The earliest tenants moved to Shenley in October 1954 and they soon got their homes established. On the whole, it was felt that the tenants settled down well and soon began to take pride in their houses. Many residents commented favourably on the design and finish of their new houses at Shenley. Some decorated their homes in 'contemporary' style. The through living rooms were generally popular. Nearly all the tenants used their kitchens for meals, although in many cases this could hardly have been comfortable. Most sensed 'the Bournville passion for gardening' and soon made a start cultivating their gardens. Trust officers claimed that the results were quite good, if occasionally unimaginative.[64] By spring 1959 it was being reported that 'a tradition of good cultivation ... has now been established'.[65]

Given that the Shenley estate might well have looked like a 'frontier town', with its unmade roads and nearby fields, the new residents seem to have settled down quite promptly. 'Incoming tenants seem quite quickly to get to know and make friends with neighbours', the female rent collector reported, 'and the general "atmosphere" of the estate is satisfactory.'[66]

The Trust made an effort to incorporate the Council nominees into 'the Bournville community' and to make these 'pioneers' feel that they belonged. Even before the first tenants took up residence, the Trustees were adamant that the nominees 'should be made to feel that they are part of a local community'.[67] They also encouraged the setting up of a residents' association. The Lower Shenley Residents Association was formed in May 1956, and their first meeting place was a room in Yew Tree Farm. The Association was regarded as 'the nucleus of a community movement'.[68] A new prefabricated Community Hall was built, with some difficulty, by the residents themselves in the spring of 1959.[69] The Trust provided the site and made a contribution towards the cost of the building. It proved to be a valuable amenity for this fast-growing settlement.

'Harlow and Stevenage have had their problems', it was noted, 'and Shenley has been a challenge to the B.V.T.'[70] As former city dwellers, many of the new arrivals (the women, in particular) could feel isolated. Initially, it was a considerable distance to the shops and schools. A temporary shop operated from the ground-floor rooms of the old Yew Tree Farm. Mobile stores helped, as did the provision of a school bus by the Education Department.[71] Things got better when Green Meadow School and the shops opened.

129   The Lower Shenley (later Shenley Manor) Community Hall erected by the residents in the spring of 1959. It is still in use.

The area near the top of the hill on the eastern side of Shenley Lane had been designated as the shopping and community centre for the Shenley area. The site was formerly occupied by Lower Shenley Farm, which was demolished in the autumn of 1959. A local reporter noted the transformation:

> The vacant site will be occupied by a shopping centre, and on land nearby where, until recent times, the hares ran through the corn and foxes lay in wait, there will be a church.[72]

The shops with flats over them were quickly constructed, followed in 1961 by the church hall (which was used as both a church and a hall for about eight years). They provided useful local facilities and a focal point for this expanding neighbourhood. The land beyond what had been the old farmyard and the new primary school was largely left open. Playing fields and play areas were provided, with a paddling pool. Bungalows were built on one side of Shenley Green, as the area came to be called. Nearby, on Green Meadow Road, a youth centre was built.

There was a tendency for women 'not tied by children' to go out to work. The money and 'something to do outside the home' were the reasons given for this trend.[73] There were, however, very few elderly people at Shenley in the early days. Many families were said to be missing 'grandma'. Several grandmothers visited the estate to look after either the house or the children while 'Mom' went to work. It was noted by the Trust, and others, that communities without grandparents were not balanced communities.[74] A group of bungalows at Brookside, between Merritts Hill and Shenley Lane, were built and let to elderly relatives of residents in the neighbourhood. Another group was, as we have noted, constructed at Shenley Green. Bungalows for sale to the elderly or handicapped were also erected in Long Leasow and Mulberry Road.

Clearly, the elderly had a part to play in local society. Special provision for the elderly was more noticeable at Bournville than in most other developments. One such scheme was Oak Tree House, built on a plot leased from the Bournville Village Trust and opened in 1964. This block contained 17 unfurnished flats or bedsits for single people, two flats for married couples and quarters for a warden. Lunch was provided for the residents, who were expected to get other meals for themselves. Oak Tree House was built to provide accommodation for retired Quakers and the management was in the hands of a committee appointed by the Warwickshire Meeting of the Society of Friends.[75]

Whilst many women had particular problems to face at Shenley, it should also be noted that the most flourishing section of the new Residents' Association was the Ladies' Section. One of their first tasks was to make curtains for the new Community Hall. At Christmas they organised a party for children and an evening meal at the *Jubilee Inn*, Studley. In summer, they arranged evening trips. Within a few years they expanded their activities to include lectures and craft work.

Given the large number of children on the Lower Shenley Farm Estate, it is not surprising that there were a few problems, though these were usually minor. It was said that Shenley, like many other places, had a 'teenage' problem. It was, however, noted that the older teenagers played a significant part in the construction of the Community Hall, impressing the adults not only with their willingness to help but also the quality of their work. Youth work and sports clubs soon began to figure quite prominently and the Lower Shenley Hall and the nearby Allens Croft Pavilion and sports facilities were extensively used. The Youth Centre on Green Meadow Road was said to have been 'very active in providing for the young people from a wide area'. Indeed, it needed to be extended in the early 1970s.[76]

At Shenley, as elsewhere on the Estate, the Trust controlled the layout and the appearance of the Estate, though increasingly they were subject to national legislation and local authority oversight. Despite the imposition of higher densities and subsidy restrictions, the Trust sought to maintain high building standards and continue its landscaping tradition. Mature trees were retained and fruit tree saplings planted in the rough-dug gardens. Seeing little value in industrialised building systems, they continued to use brickwork and 'suitable external renderings' for external walls and clay tiles for the roofs of their houses. (Marley tiles came to be used more and more on the Estate.) Although more varied types of dwelling came to be built, most were simple rectangular blocks with equally simple rooflines. Whereas wooden windows were the norm before 1939, after the Second World War metal window frames dominated (in part because of timber shortages). If the Trust saw little benefit in adopting industrialised building systems, they were far more interested in the mass production of components. They began to consider developing plans for the interiors of their houses on a modular basis.[77]

The Trust architects continued to design houses to be built and sold on lease to owner occupiers. Unlike the work at Shenley funded by the Corporation, which was constructed by the Trust's Direct Labour Team under Les Pankhurst, most of the private houses were built by a small group of four or five builders, including Holdings and Bryants.[78] No firm, therefore, had a chance to establish a monopoly, and prices were compared with similar work elsewhere in the region (as well as with the Direct Labour Department). Such comparative surveys led the Trust to conclude that 'by and large the customer at Bournville is getting a reasonably fair deal'.[79]

As one would expect, 'consumer society' came to have an impact on Bournville. The residents in both the new and the old parts of the Estate had rising expectations. By the early 1950s there were calls for a community centre in Bournville Village. The long-established Social Centre in Laurel Grove was regarded as being outdated and no longer satisfied the social needs of the residents. At that point it was not possible for the Trust to accede to the requests of the Village residents. In 1958-9 the Bournville Village Trust moved their offices from Bournville Lane to a converted property in Oak Tree Lane. They also took over a building at the rear of the new offices, which contained a hall and two smaller rooms. This was refurbished at the expense of the Trust and the George Cadbury Fund as a Community Centre. It was named Dame Elizabeth Hall in memory of Dame Elizabeth Cadbury, who had died in 1951.[80] The renovated and refurnished hall became a well-used resource. The rooms were suitable for committee meetings and the hall was used for large meetings, entertainments, receptions and parties.

Another manifestation of the changing social scene was that cars began to appear in ever increasing numbers on the Estate. Garage provision became a major issue for the Trust. From the mid-1950s they began to lay foundations and drives for garages and indicated which 'approved designs' they would allow. Garage provision at Bournville was higher than in comparable developments. In 1955 New Towns were providing garages in 10 per cent of new units, whilst at Bournville provision was made for 25 per cent. They were prescient enough to suggest that the figure might eventually rise to 75 per cent.[81]

There was an increasing number of attractions both outside and inside the home. Television was one of the most popular of the new consumer durables, with ownership rising dramatically from 1953. There was concern about the visual impact of television aerials at Bournville. The Trust prided itself on being 'fairly successful in preventing television aerials on the Estate'.[82] Where indoor aerials would not suffice, they expected outdoor aerials to be placed as inconspicuously as possible. A bigger problem for them was that for the new BBC2 service external aerials would be necessary. 'The effect of this', they concluded, 'would be disastrous.' The Trustees, therefore, began to explore the viability of a system of 'piped' television. A survey conducted on their behalf suggested that 70 per cent of dwellings in Bournville could use efficient loft aerials. When the residents were questioned late in 1964, it was clear that a significant majority said they wanted to view BBC2 within the next two years. The Trustees felt that this was sufficient to go ahead with a VHF wired system and they were encouraged by the fact that local dealers seemed willing to co-operate.[83] Given this, they continued to oppose the erection of television aerials.

The Trustees and the Trust staff continued to pay attention to detail as well as the wider pattern. They also recognised that, whereas at the beginning of the century Bournville was 'in the van of the Housing Movement', by the 1960s there were many other housing agencies producing work which was as good as that produced by the Trust. Nevertheless, they still believed that their work was of significance:

> To an increasing extent ... the Estate is achieving importance as a controlled experiment in town development comparable, save that it is a suburban area and that it is on a much smaller scale, to a New Town. By concentrating on the provision of houses of different values for all classes of the community and houses which are of good standard of design, by assisting in the development of community life, by generous provision of parks and playing fields, by careful landscaping and by a reasonable standard of maintenance, the Trustees believe that they are creating something of value.[84]

Chapter Eight

DEVELOPMENT AND REDEVELOPMENT

1964-79

The 1960s saw many development schemes, not least in Birmingham. At this time the city centre was being transformed: the inner ring road was being constructed and the new Bull Ring completed. Beyond the central business district work on the five Central Redevelopment Areas was under way. Terraces, back-to-backs and workshops were demolished to make way for grand 'mixed development' schemes made up of flats, maisonettes and low-rise dwellings. Increased overspill from the Redevelopment Areas meant that the City Council had to build on the periphery of the city and negotiate with neighbouring authorities to take some of Birmingham's excess population. The overspill schemes that came to fruition had little impact on Birmingham's overall housing problems. The need for further building sites led the City Council to look beyond its boundaries for land. In 1959 the Council bought the former Castle Bromwich airfield site. During the mid-1960s the Castle Vale estate, with its large number of high-rise flats, was constructed to house a population of 20,000. In 1963 Warwickshire County Council allowed Birmingham to develop an estate for 50,000 people at Chelmsley Wood. Significantly, far fewer multi-storey blocks were included in this scheme. In the late 1960s the City Council and Worcestershire County Council put pressure on Cadbury Brothers to release covenanted land at Moundsley and Hawkesley for development.[1]

By the late 1960s attitudes towards comprehensive redevelopment were beginning to change. Multi-storey flats were proving expensive, problematic and unloved. The 1968 Town and Country Planning Act brought about the end of the old Development Plan system and shifted the emphasis away from redevelopment and introduced measures to tackle urban decay by means of Action Areas and improvement schemes. The emphasis moved from demolition to modernisation.[2]

In terms of local authority housing provision the changes had been dramatic. A total of 81,270 new homes were built by the City Council between 1945 and 1970.[3] At the same time approximately 55,000 unfit houses had been demolished in the inner areas. A 1971 survey revealed that 26,000 households in Birmingham still lacked a hot water tap and 28,000 did not have a fixed bath.[4] Nevertheless, more and more people were living in the suburbs, in dwellings with more amenities than ever before. Whilst the suburbs were not without their problems, they did generally offer better housing and a greener environment. The movement of the population to the suburbs, however, put further pressure on land and increased the demand for schools, shops and other communal facilities. The break up of old communities and increasingly privatised lifestyles were bound to have an effect in Birmingham as elsewhere.[5]

Whilst high-rise flats had their critics, so too did the suburbs. Ian Nairn was one of the foremost opponents of 'Subtopia', the supposedly dull, boring and modest suburb.[6] Their supporters enjoyed them for their modest pleasures, but rarely composed hymns of praise about their comfortable homes and pleasant surroundings. By the early 1970s, more reasoned and balanced accounts of the suburbs were beginning to appear.[7] Historians and conservationists were also drawing attention to some of the pioneer factory villages and garden suburbs.[8]

Attitudes towards the housing trusts and housing associations began to change in the 1960s and 1970s. There were several reasons for this. Firstly, they had not been involved in the building of large estates of high-rise dwellings. 'Their reputation', the Director of the Joseph Rowntree Foundation noted, 'was untarnished by the failed architecture and planning of ugly estates.'[9] Secondly, housing associations were seen to be doing a useful job 'filling the gaps' left behind by the public sector. The associations gained recognition for their ability to provide housing for groups with special needs, particularly the elderly. It was during the 1960s that sheltered housing became a significant part of housing association work.[10]

Whereas governments in the 1950s had encouraged housing associations to convert and rehabilitate older properties, in the 1960s the associations were given powers and money to build new dwellings. The Housing Act of 1961 encouraged the building of 'cost rent housing'. Inflation and high interest rates soon brought cost renting to 'a dead halt'.[11] The answer seemed to lie in subsidised 'co-ownership' schemes. The Housing Act of 1964 brought the Housing Corporation into being. It provided funds (alongside building society mortgages) for co-ownership schemes. By 1968, 527 co-ownership societies and 471 cost rent schemes had been established (including one at Bournville).[12] Co-ownership has been characterised as 'a short-lived exercise'. As the cost of capital and land rose in the early 1970s production petered out.[13]

In 1970 housing trusts and housing associations owned about 170,000 homes, 74,000 of which had been built before 1939. Over the next 20 years the housing stock of the associations rose to 60,000. The peak years of development were in the late 1970s.[14]

Although there was some criticism of housing associations in the 1970s because of their lack of accountability, they were encouraged in various ways by governments to extend their housing provision. The 1972 Housing Finance Act introduced 'fair rents' and made housing associations eligible for subsidies from the Exchequer. The 1973 government White Paper, *Widening the Choice: The Next Steps in Housing*, proposed 'to widen the range and choice of rented accommodation by the expansion of the voluntary housing movement'.[15]

The Housing Corporation, which was the link between the state and the voluntary sector, was already extending its scope by 1972. It was moving on from co-ownership schemes to supporting schemes let at 'fair rents'. It also began to assume a 'policing' role, registering and monitoring housing associations. The Housing Corporation's powers of lending and control were extended by the 1974 Housing Act, which had the support of the Conservatives and Labour. Additional finance was made available to the Housing Corporation in 1977. These injections of public money fuelled the expansion of the housing association movement in the late 1970s.[16]

Maintenance and development at Bournville

By the summer of 1965, some 5,000 houses had been built by the Trust or lessees on the 1,000 acres they owned within the city boundaries. Over 3,200 of these had been built on land leased by the Trust to individuals, self-build groups and public utility societies. Approximately 700 of the remainder were houses let on short tenancies and built in collaboration with the City Council. There were three unbuilt areas of the Bournville Estate whose development was under active consideration.

It was the hope of the Trustees that further development on the Estate could be carried out using the leasehold system.[17] The Trust was concerned because leasehold enfranchisement was being considered by the Government. They considered leasehold enfranchisement 'would be harmful for the future interests of their properties'.[18]

The alternatives to leasing, as far as the Trust was concerned, were building themselves and renting the houses to tenants, and selling the freehold to purchasers who would build their own houses.

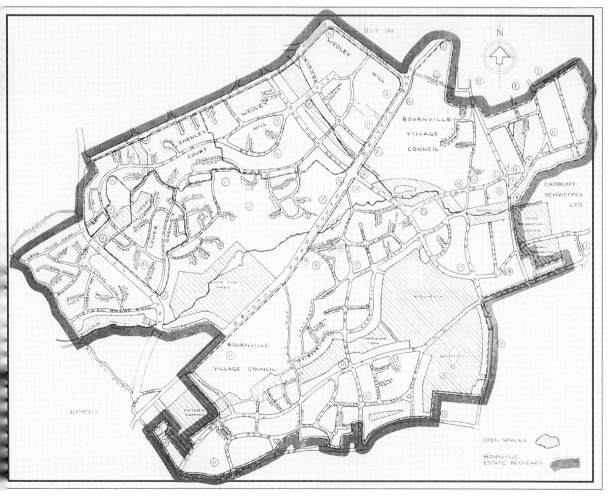

130   Plan of the Bournville Estate, 1970.

The former required considerable amounts of capital both to develop the site and build the dwellings. While further co-operation with the Corporation was a possibility, the Trust did not think that form of expansion was suitable for the whole of their building programme. If the freeholds were sold the Trust feared inappropriate or even inferior developments might be built.

Certainly, over the years the leasehold system had given the Trust, as ground landlord, extensive powers of control over amenities such as the preservation of trees, the maintenance of gardens, outdoor advertising and standards of upkeep and repair. It had also taken responsibility for the maintenance of communal facilities and the smaller open spaces (most of the parkland had been handed over to the City Council). 'It would become much more difficult to preserve the amenities of the Trust's Estate', Laurence Cadbury explained to the Ministry of Housing and Local Government, 'if the lessees became freeholders. For example, the ultimate sanction of forfeiture for breach of covenant will have disappeared.' The Trustees were fighting a losing battle, and they recognised that it was unlikely that housing associations or trusts would be exempted from the forthcoming legislation. Laurence Cadbury enquired whether other powers might be given to landowners:

> If exemption cannot be granted we would ask the Minister of State what alternative powers he would give to large landowners to ensure that Estates are developed and re-developed when leases fall in with full regard to the proper principles of planning.[19]

There was some concern at the time about the oldest properties on the Estate, which had been built at much lower densities than the post-war dwellings (at 16 to 18 persons per acre as opposed to 50). The Trustees envisaged a period some 30 to 40 years ahead when the early properties had become obsolete and needed replacing. Block by block redevelopment, which they considered the appropriate method, would be virtually impossible if the areas were 'pepper-potted with individual freeholds'.

In the event, the Leasehold Reform Act was passed in 1967 and this made provision for lease-holders to buy their freeholds. The response of the Trust was twofold. Firstly, they tried to consolidate their properties, buying and selling houses so as to create pockets of rented, leasehold and freehold dwellings. Secondly, they sought to establish a Scheme of Management under Section 19 of the Lease-hold Reform Act. The Trustees believed that 'the disintegrating effects of leasehold enfranchisement could be checked if the residents could be made to feel that they have a positive contribution to make to a community which had a great deal to offer to the quality of urban life'.[20] The Trust's scheme was finally approved in 1972 and this allowed for some control to be exercised over enfranchised residents. A Scheme Committee of four Trustees and four elected residents (one for each of the areas served by the four Village Councils and Residents' Associations) was provided for. The first elections were held in December 1972.[21] Dr. John Woodward became the first Chairman of the Committee. In its first year the Scheme Committee, which dealt with broad principles of amenity preservation rather than day-to-day matters, discussed a wide variety of issues including the Birmingham Structure Plan, new developments on the Estate, unsatisfactory property repairs, caravan parking and unsightly television aerials.[22]

131 Property in Elm Road, showing the porches added in the late 1960s.

Paradoxically, leasehold enfranchisement improved the immediate cash position of the Trust, even if it seemed to impede its long-term plans.[23] If large-scale redevelopment of Trust properties seemed some way off, the Trust did recognise the need to modernise older properties. The programme begun before 1939 was continued after the war, although progress was not always rapid. Reviewing the bathroom conversion programme in September 1960, G.W. Cadbury argued, 'We have some leeway to catch up and yet the total cost of providing complete bathing facilities for all is pretty small.' Since 1949, 79 bathrooms had been provided in older properties and, although the rate of conversion had improved, 81 properties on the estate were still either without baths or reliant on the old table or cabinet baths provided before the First World War. G.W. Cadbury pressed his fellow Trustees to act on this so that they could 'hold up their charitable heads'.[24]

Certain properties received more extensive treatment. The Bournville Almshouse Trust houses on Mary Vale Road were comprehensively renovated in 1967-8. They were completely modernised at a cost of £1,000 per dwelling, with each being provided with kitchens, bathrooms and central heating. 'The increased rent,' it was reported, 'has been readily paid.'[25]

Elm Road was improved at much the same time. 'It is the nearest section of the Village to Selly Oak', the Trust explained, 'and might have deteriorated as a neighbourhood.' There were improvements both inside and out, and the tenants were said to have taken great pride in the appearance of the road after the work had been completed. The work involved the removal of many overgrown roadside trees. Smaller ones were planted in front gardens, and front hedges and fences were taken out. The Trust laid turf on these gardens where necessary. The rented properties were modernised internally, and some had porches fitted. 'Many tenants have chosen to have a small wood and glass porch built around the front door', the Trust's officers claimed, 'which incidentally greatly improves the external appearance.'[26] Viewed in retrospect, these 1960s additions, though providing a greater degree of warmth and comfort, do not sit happily on the fronts of these Edwardian houses.

Times were changing and there was a growing conservation lobby intent on preserving the original houses intact. By 1970 a number of individual buildings at Bournville had been listed as being of architectural or historical importance under the Town and Country Planning Act of 1962. These included Selly Manor and Minworth Greaves, the Schools, Ruskin Hall, the Rest House, the Meeting House, the Church of St Francis of Assisi, the Almshouses, the Continuation Schools and a small number of the early houses (92-94 Elm Road, Holly Grove, 3-13 Laburnum Road and 10-12 Sycamore Road).

By this time there was a growing belief in the amenity value of groups of buildings. The wholesale demolition of large areas of Birmingham and other cities and the decline in parts of the manufacturing sector fuelled an interest in Britain's architectural heritage. Increasingly conservationists urged legislators to recognise the group value of buildings and introduce laws to protect whole areas. In 1967 the Ministry of Housing and Local Government published *Preservation and Change*, a valuable guide to conservation practice. In the same year the Civic Amenities Act made it a statutory duty for local authorities to determine which areas under their control were of special architectural or historical interest. Thereafter conservation areas began to be created, and in July 1971 Bournville Village and the Bournville Tenants Estate were both designated conservation areas.[27] The older parts of the Estate henceforth enjoyed a greater degree of protection.

Besides conserving and modernising older properties on the Estate, the Trustees were still keen to promote new developments. The schedule of developments for June 1965 showed that 23 houses were being built by Direct Labour for local authority nominees, and 9 bungalows for letting by the Trust at Hawkestone Road, and 39 houses and 20 bungalows for owner occupation, and 131 houses for self-build groups were under construction at Guiting Road. Plans for 30 owner-occupied houses at Eymore and Dowles Closes and 45 cost-rent dwellings, to be built by the Forward Housing Association at Hornbeam Close, had been submitted for approval. Road works were planned for the autumn on the Hole Farm Estate to open it up for the first stage of development in 1966 (when 57 dwellings were to be built for letting by the Direct Labour Department, in addition to 47 houses and bungalows for owner occupation on lease, and 8 bungalows under consideration by the Birmingham Council for Old People).[28]

The Hole Farm Estate, to the north east of Hole Lane and Heath Road South, was developed at this time. Detached, semi-detached and terraced houses were built for sale by Holdings in this area. In addition, a number of bungalows and individual houses were constructed on Heath Road South and Hole Farm Road. The other dwellings erected there were the two- and three-storey flats of the Cornfield Housing Society.

The Cornfield Housing Society was a co-ownership society sponsored by Bournville Village Trust in 1967. The flats, on Garland Way and in the Paddock, were built with money borrowed from the Housing Corporation. The Trustees handed over the running of the society to a Committee of Management in 1970, on completion of the scheme. Rents of the properties varied according to the date of entry of the residents into the scheme. Residents who left took with them a sum relating to the capital appreciation of the property during their period of residence.[29] The flats overlook the stream and pool in the adjacent landscaped valley.

The continuing care of the landscape remained a priority, although the treatment of particular sites occasionally caused a degree of controversy. In 1969 local papers carried stories and correspondence complaining about the Trust's treatment of The Innage. 'Trees, shrubs and flowers cut to make way for the mower', was one headline. The objectors regretted the loss of an area which they saw as 'a bit of country for the children to explore and play in'.[30] Not everyone agreed with the complainants, and other correspondents wrote to say they had 'nothing but praise for the way in which the estate is managed'. One writer made a telling point:

> I should like to point out to those complaining residents that it has been found impossible to have wild areas in suburbia without them becoming tips of unwanted refuse ... The Trust has a long history of planting trees and flowering shrubs throughout the village, and, in this, is practically unrivalled anywhere in the country.[31]

The infilling of pockets of space occasionally brought protests from the residents, especially if the land was to be used for non-residential or non-standard uses. When, for instance, the Education Department announced their plans to expand the Technical College on Bristol Road, concern was expressed about 'a very heavy concentration of buildings and students on such a small site'. It was held that the enlarged College would not be a 'good neighbour' in what was primarily a residential neighbourhood.[32] In 1967 there was some opposition from residents of Witherford Way to a joint proposal by Copec and the Trust to develop land between Weoley Hill and Shenley Fields Road.[33] Eventually, both areas were developed.

Although lifestyles seemed to be becoming more privatised and less localised, the Village Councils and Residents Associations remained important integrating factors in the life of the Bournville Estate. Besides their more formal function in the passage of information to and from residents, they still had a useful recreational role to play (even though their position as leisure providers was challenged by television and commercial companies).[34] There was a feeling that some of the older facilities needed improving and that newly developed areas needed their own meeting places, no matter how small at first. By 1972 the Weoley Hill Council were complaining that their hall was out of date. 'If there is to be a proper communal life at Weoley Hill', they argued, 'facilities must be improved.'[35] Extensions to the hall and further facilities (including a drinks licence) were proposed. Eight years later it was claimed that there was 'a fairly urgent need for some sort of a community room in the Hole Farm and the Priory areas of the Estate', where 358 mixed rented properties had been built between 1976 and 1979.[36]

The community halls (Dame Elizabeth Hall, Woodlands Park Hall, Weoley Hill Hall, Shenley Court Hall and Shenley Manor Hall) continued to be used for meetings, parties and weddings, as well as for various community activities such as playgroups, scouts, cubs and guides packs, dance clubs, sports sections, ladies groups and Darby and Joan clubs.[37] It should be remembered that the local churches also provided useful communal facilities, although they might be for more limited sections of the local population. This was the case with the Serbian Orthodox Church of St Lazar in Cob Lane built in 1968. The striking church was built for political refugees from communist Yugoslavia, and was a replica of a Serbian Byzantine Church.[38]

Seven years before, a multi-purpose hall had been built to serve the new Anglican parish of Shenley Green. In 1968 a vicarage was built and at the end of the year a start was made on the church itself. St David's Church was consecrated in 1970. With its striking copper roof and concrete walls, it is one of the few modern buildings on the Estate (although it was designed by one of the Trust's architects, Peter Carrick).[39] The church has provided a base for a growing number of church-based and secular groups over the years.

There were occasional reports of a lack of community support and under-utilisation of the halls in some areas, and there were regular calls for volunteers to help with the local organisations.[40] Population changes had also to be accounted for. By the late 1970s there was a declining youth population at Shenley, and there was a growing recognition of the need for alternative uses for the community halls. There was increasing pressure to allow bars in the communal and sports facilities on the estate.[41]

The issue of licensing has come up on a number of occasions from the late 1950s. In 1958 Egbert Cadbury had considered the Trustees' opposition to the application for a licence by the CEGB for their premises on the Bristol Road 'the epitome of out-of-date paternalism'.[42] In 1969 the Trust engaged Gallup to conduct a poll on the question among residents. Eighty per cent were in favour of allowing

132   The Serbian Orthodox Church of St Lazar built in Cob Lane in 1968.

133 The church of St David's and the Shenley Centre.

community centres on the Estate to apply for occasional licences. There were greater differences of opinion about whether sports clubs should be allowed to apply for regular licences for members. The overall figures indicated support for such a policy, yet 64 per cent of those living in the vicinity of the sports clubs were against allowing such licences.[43] There was some concern among the Trustees that this might prove 'the thin end of the wedge' or 'the beginning of a flood'.[44] Nonetheless, occasional licences for the Shenley Court and Lower Shenley Halls, and members' licences for the Allen's Cross Pavilion and Weoley Hill Cricket Club, were allowed.

When the extension to the Weoley Hill Hall came up for discussion in 1972 a justice's conditional licence was requested. Whilst there was some relaxation of the rules about drink, no pubs or off-licences were allowed. The strict rules concerning gambling were retained. No gambling machines or games of chance were allowed, and the only card games permitted were bridge and whist.[45]

A consensus of opinion seems to have emerged by the late 1970s. It was still felt that public houses were definitely not required, although there were no objections to table licences. With regard to the community halls, occasional licences, subject to the overall control of the relevant residents' organisation, were thought to be the most appropriate form of permit. Although the Trustees still believed that club licences were generally not desirable, they felt that each application should be considered individually without establishing a precedent.[46] In the spring of 1979 the licensing question came up again for discussion.[47] In June 1979, the clause relating to drink licensing was revised.[48]

Continuity and change

By 1970 there were 6,400 houses on the Estate, which at that time had a population of approximately 20,000. The modernisation programme continued, and the self-build groups were still operating. The latter were regarded as 'one of the Trust's real success stories'. There were still 30 acres of building land on the Estate to be developed (with the further possibility of land being released by Cadbury Schweppes). Although the Trust's balance sheet was strong, they were in a position where their cash flow was temporarily low in relation to the cost of building on undeveloped land. In effect, this meant that new development was likely to be delayed or spread over a considerable period of time. (The prospects for the late

1970s and 1980s looked rosier.) 'There must be doubts as to how far redevelopment will be practicable', it was revealed, 'as a consequence of leasehold enfranchisement.' With only a limited amount of development work ahead, the emphasis was likely to shift towards modernisation and maintenance, rather than planning and design. Of course, the advisory side of the Trust's work could be developed, as it already had a reputation for establishing 'the link between the theoretical and practical in housing and planning'. The Trustees were also aware of 'the overriding importance of the responsibility for human relations on the Estate'.[49] In a changing world, the challenge to the Trustees and their officers (many of whom had served for long periods of time) was great. As one senior officer wrote:

> There is a developing tendency everywhere to rebel against the 'establishment' and our relationships with residents will be more and more tested by this trend. I think we have to convey to the residents that the Estate is not run for the benefit of the 'Estate Office' but for the community as a whole. I am not sure that we have yet fully succeeded in doing this and I think that future Trustees, and particularly a future Chairman, will be required to make contact with residents at a much wider level than before.[50]

Kenneth Pegg, the officer who wrote this memorandum, was appointed to succeed the long-serving F.R. Barlow as Manager of the Trust in June 1972.[51] Barlow had followed in his father's footsteps, which was not unknown at Bournville. Les Pankhurst had also taken over from his father as head of the Trust's Direct Works Department. In 1978, Laurence Cadbury, who had succeeded Dame Elizabeth Cadbury as Chairman of the Trustees in 1951, retired. He was succeeded by his daughter, Veronica Wootten, who had joined the Trustees 10 years earlier. Paul S. Cadbury, however, did not resign from the Trust until 1982, after 60 years of service.[52]

The issue of leasehold reform had resulted in some tension between the residents and the Trust. Dennis Shaw, the secretary of the Bournville Village Council, had suggested there was a 'wide gulf' between the Trustees and the residents. Others felt that the Cadbury family's attitude to Bournville had become unnecessarily paternalistic. Certainly, the Trust's first proposals for a management scheme (which included the right to make internal inspections of households) proved unacceptable to the residents. The Trust recognised that it needed to consult the residents on the Estate. After careful negotiations with the representatives of the four local residents associations a scheme of management was worked out. Dennis Shaw later admitted that the discussions had been 'generally very harmonious once it was made clear that there was to be no dictatorship'. Dr. Frank Pearce, a former Chairman of the Weoley Hill Village Council, was also involved in the negotiations. He concluded:

> You could say that the Trust has stepped out of a long tradition of paternalism and realised that it is possible to work in harmony with people on the Estate. Residents' opinion has been very carefully canvassed.

Some residents clearly felt that things were changing at Bournville. 'I think,' one resident exclaimed, 'that it has been finally realised that we have all come of age and don't need a father figure any more.'[53]

The relationship between Bournville Village Trust and the Firm began to change too. This was especially true after the Cadbury-Schweppes merger. The links between the two began to diminish, although the continued presence of Cadburys on both Boards meant that they were not completely severed. As a local reporter concluded in 1971:

> To hundreds of thousands of people all over the world, the names of Bournville and Cadbury are synonymous in a way that is probably unique, and if the family now wields less direct influence on the management of the Estate and the many organisations housed there, the long term effects of its influence are still evident wherever one turns.[54]

Whilst there were clear signs of continuity at the Trust, there were also signs of change. The Housing Finance Act of 1972 led to the introduction of 'fair rents' on the Estate. These were in effect the maximum rents agreed with the local Rent Officer. Rent allowances for the less well off were provided.[55] By 1972, the Birmingham Structure Plan had been published. Analysis of the City's proposals led the Trust's officers to conclude that the changes envisaged would not be significant 'other than, possibly, in the density to be adopted for such areas as have not yet been developed'.[56] The Structure Plan also envisaged improved transport links and peripheral shopping developments.

The early 1970s saw building developments by Copec and the Trust at Weoley Hill and by Bryants at Rowheath.[57] In the latter case the Trust exercised the right to acquire the lease on completion of the scheme. The residents thus became direct lessees of the Trust.[58] Nearby, Rowheath House was completed in 1977. This was the first of the Trust's new group of sheltered houses. This was followed up by another scheme at Rosefields.[59]

Two blocks of dwellings for groups with special needs were constructed in 1970. Bonner House in Selly Wood Road was a block of 10 self-contained flats for unmarried mothers which was administered by the National Children's Homes. Queen Mother Court contained flats for retired teachers and the

134   Queen Mother Court and the higher density three-storey 'town houses' built in Sellywood Road in the early 1970s.

135   Selly Wood House.

building costs were met by funds from the Teachers' Benevolent Fund.[60] Some ten years later, money from the same source provided part of the funding for the adjacent Selly Wood House, to provide accommodation for those who were old and infirm. The Society of Friends and the Bournville Village Trust also contributed to the cost of the scheme. The accommodation consisted of furnished bed-sitting rooms, and the residents were provided with meals and nursing care.[61]

The rate of building increased in the late 1970s. In 1978 the Trustees put in place a three-year programme to build 300 units of accommodation 'for a range of occupiers that complement those already living there'.[62] The proposed work included Rosefields, the Convent site, flats in Griffins Brook Lane, Selly Wood House and bungalows in Laurel Grove.[63]

An expanded modernisation programme was begun. The Trust took advantage of the larger grants available to housing associations from the Housing Corporation to modernise St George's Court and begin a rolling programme of repairs and renovations.[64] The conversion of St George's Court into self-contained flats for both male and female residents went ahead.[65] Unfortunately, the rolling modernisation programme had barely begun when the new (Thatcher) government cut its funding.[66]

The issue of 'amenity control' seemed to assume more importance in the 1970s. Certain issues were raised regularly with the Trust's Scheme Committee. These included vandalism, children's games in inappropriate areas, television aerials, traffic problems, and unacceptable alterations and additions.[67] The latter became a real concern because of 'a steady stream of applications to alter and extend properties'. The Trustees and their officers were aware of the need to control development, particularly where it involved infill between semi-detached houses. The residents' representatives were also in favour of stricter control of alterations to property on the Estate.[68] The Trust's responses to two cases at this time were typical. When 'incongruous aluminium windows' were used on a house in Woodlands Park Road, the Trust's officers urged the residents 'to make them more in keeping with the character of the area'.[69] When the occupants of a house in Innage Road sought permission from the Trust for an extension, matching bricks, tiles and windows were insisted upon.[70] Although the residents were required by covenant to ask permission of the Trust for alterations and extensions and were expected to submit their plans for approval, not everyone did so. The Trust was usually reluctant to take their lessees and tenants to court. When some aluminium windows were fitted without approval to a property in Hay Green Lane, the Scheme Committee expressed its disapproval and claimed they were detrimental to the character of the property. 'The Committee', they concluded, 'whilst recognising that the Trust would not be justified in taking legal action, expressed their concern that many residents appeared ignorant of their necessity to seek approval for alterations to their properties.'[71] It usually sought to persuade residents to act in a sensitive and acceptable manner. As more and more freeholds were sold, there were more and more signs of a 'privatised' environment, and non-standard doors and windows have increased over the years. It should also be noted that the criteria for what was 'appropriate' or 'suitable' have also changed over time, and if a resident did not carry out work for some time after approval had been given the Trust's officers might find themselves embarrassed at having to allow work which did not meet current standards.[72] As a means of tightening their control over extensions and alterations time limits were introduced. The Trust also considered recommending that other parts of the Estate be considered for Conservation Area status, so as to ensure even stricter control over the area.[73] The Scheme Committee,

136   Varied housing types on the Convent site, which, in 1980, was the most densely developed part of the Bournville Estate.

however, questioned the value of extending such status to certain other parts of the Estate.[74]

If, by the end of the 1970s, the Trust was having some difficulties in retaining the character of some of its older properties, it was also having problems with a number of small contractors on some of its new schemes. The failure of contractors on the second Hole Farm development and the Convent site caused delays and inconvenience.[75] 'The employment of various small contractors has not been satisfactory', it was recorded, 'and they need the closest of attention to ensure that good standards are maintained.'[76] It is clear that close site supervision was central to maintaining the Bournville standard (although it may have contributed to the failure of builders not used to such tight supervision of their work).

There were other problems concerning the costs of the upkeep of the Estate. The key issue here was that the Trust's income from ground rents was stationary and its income from rents was statutorily controlled, whilst the cost of the Estate's upkeep was mounting with annual inflation. By early 1980, the Trust's manager was warning of the need for drastic action. He concluded that 'residents must be made to understand that they could not expect high standards of maintenance unless they were prepared to pay for them'.[77]

At this time, as a result of a Housing Corporation monitoring visit, the Trust were warned that they needed to tighten up their financial and managerial procedures. The Housing Corporation's main recommendation was that 'the Trustees should promulgate clear lines of delegation and authority in the form of Standing Orders and Financial Regulations'.[78] It was apparent that after the Conservatives came to power in 1979 the Housing Corporation began to impose its will on housing associations. Some believed that the Housing Corporation 'had become a controller rather than a nurturer of the housing association movement'.[79]

Chapter Nine

BOURNVILLE 1979-97

External Factors

While Bournville in the late 20th century could no longer be regarded as a unique experiment, it continued to be admired for the quality of its housing, landscaping and management. Its experiments with special needs accommodation and solar housing also attracted a good deal of attention. The Trustees no longer had the same freedom of action that the early pioneers had. They were increasingly constrained by national legislation and the rules of their paymasters (most notably the Housing Corporation). Changes in these areas could lead to variations in policy about rents and lettings and fluctuations in funding.[1] Social and economic changes affected patterns of housing need and housing demand. During this period unemployment levels passed those of the Depression of the 1930s and there was a significant shift from manufacturing to the service sector. Birmingham was not immune from these trends. A 1986 study highlighted the crisis in the industrial heartland, whilst the National Exhibition Centre, the International Convention Centre and Cadbury World epitomised the shift that took place in the local economy.[2]

The changes have been dramatic and sometimes painful. Engineering and car manufacturing, key local industries which had grown in the 1960s, shrank by a third in the 1970s. By 1984, regional unemployment was 17 per cent, but in 10 Birmingham wards it was over 30 per cent and in three over 40 per cent. The housing situation was little better: '22,000 households in Birmingham live in properties which lack one or more of the five basic amenities, and 21,000 families live in overcrowded conditions, living at a density greater than one person per room.'[3]

137   Cadbury World introduces visitors to 'the chocolate experience'. It occupies part of the works site formerly given over to chocolate production. Many jobs were lost at the Bournville Works in the 1980s as elsewhere in the city and region.

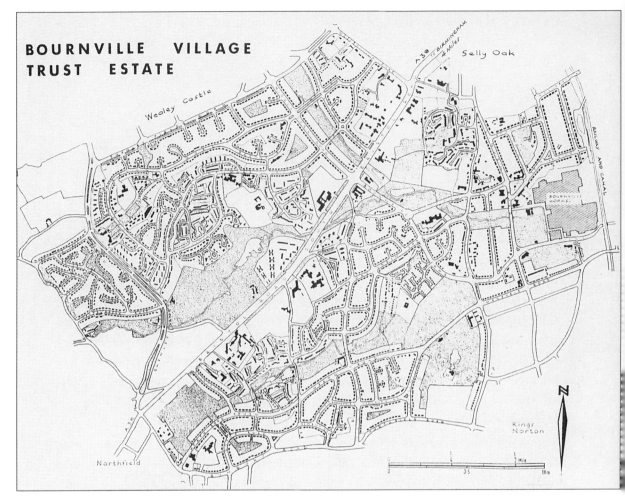

138   Map of Bournville in the mid-1980s.

Even when economic factors did not exacerbate the housing situation, demographic changes caused problems for housing providers. Although the population of Birmingham was falling, the number of households was increasing. This trend arose because of the mounting rate of marital breakdown, the rise in the number of single people seeking their own homes, and the increase in the number of elderly people maintaining an independent household for longer. A National Federation of Housing Associations enquiry into British housing in 1985 concluded:

> There is insufficient suitable housing for specific groups, including elderly people, large families and a range of individuals for whom traditional Council Housing or private rented accommodation is just not available.[4]

By that time the private rented sector had shrunk to 10 per cent of the national housing stock. Housing associations had become the real alternative to the local authorities for those unable to buy.

Local authorities had exceedingly long waiting lists (Birmingham's was 17,000 in 1985) and not everyone could afford to join the 'property-owning democracy' promoted by the Thatcher government. Indeed, the government's 'right to buy' policy dramatically reduced the stock of rented property formerly owned by local authorities and non-charitable housing associations. It was against this background that the Bournville Village Trust restated its commitment to maintaining its rented accommodation. The provision of dwellings to rent for those not in a position to buy their own house remained a matter 'of first importance' to the Trustees. They recognised that, whatever the changes in society, there was still an urgent need for rented accommodation.[5] The Trustees resisted (as local authorities could not) the demand to sell properties, claiming that such a policy would be a negation of the Founder's intentions. When the Conservative government tried to give the 'right to buy' to tenants of housing charities (such as the Trust) in the 1992 Housing and Building Control Bill, there was strong opposition in the House of Lords, and the offending clauses were deleted.[6]

The housing situation in Birmingham and elsewhere did not ease in the early 1990s. Many homebuyers were hit by the recession in the housing market. Clearance programmes (sometimes involving properties built as recently as the 1960s), the right to buy, and a reduction in the number of municipal dwellings built did not help the situation.[7] Many properties were considered to be inadequate or in need of repair. In Birmingham in 1995, it was calculated that 20 per cent of its total housing stock (400,000 properties) was unfit and a further 25 per cent was in need of renovation. The needs of the elderly, ethnic minorities, lone parents and single-person households were apparent. Beyond these there was 'a wide range of client groups requiring various levels of supported accommodation'. Those with multiple needs included the homeless, the mentally ill, those with drug and alcohol problems, the physically handicapped and a wide range of offenders. Given such a situation, it is hardly surprising that housing experts have come to write about 'the residualisation of social housing'.[8] Those providing social housing came to have much less flexibility in choosing their tenants. 'The various "priority need" groups existing under legislation', it has been argued, 'have become something of a tenant selection system in their own right.'[9]

Such issues were further complicated by the low incomes of many of those in greatest housing need. Rent levels were a serious concern for many tenants, and it was apparent that rent arrears were a major problem for providers of social housing.[10] It was estimated that about 1,700 new dwellings a year were required in Birmingham between 1995 and 2001 to meet the needs of the expected changes in population. While the Trust might try to provide for some of those with the greatest housing needs, it is clear that, because of the lack of building land at Bournville and the low turnover of tenants on the Estate, its contribution was bound to be limited. (It should be noted that the Trust was making a contribution elsewhere in the city, most notably in Heartlands.)

In recent years there have been financial pressures on both the residents and the Trust. As those in greatest housing need are now being offered properties at Bournville, it is noticeable that a significant proportion of the new arrivals (60 per cent in 1993) qualified for housing benefit. While this group of tenants (and the Trust) may not have to worry about rents, they are not likely to have much left for other things. Another group on fixed incomes were the pensioners, a group well represented on the Estate. The rent increases, allowed by the 1980 and 1988 Housing Acts, have become a focus of concern for many elderly tenants. 'Without Housing Benefit many older tenants face falling standards of living', it was claimed at the 1997 Annual Meeting of the Park Tenants, 'because pensions only increase at the rate of inflation, but average rent rises have been three or four times greater.'[11] It was a sign of the times that some of those offered the bungalows at Harvey Mews in 1990 needed Housing Benefit to pay the rent.

Changes in grant and subsidy provision could also clearly have an adverse impact. Cutbacks force bodies such as the Trust to draw on their own (often limited) capital or to borrow to maintain their existing properties as well as build new developments.[12] Conservative governments in the 1990s looked to housing associations to provide 'social housing', yet at the same time increasingly expected them to rely more on private financing.

Reductions in government funding also had implications for the tenants and their level of independence. This was apparent in the mid-1990s. 'The decisions taken by the Government on levels of Housing Association Grant for 1994-95', the Trustees explained, 'can only deepen the poverty trap for many tenants and increase their dependency on the welfare benefit system.'[13] If that was happening on the Model Estate at Bournville, the situation on many council estates in Birmingham and elsewhere was infinitely worse.

Bournville did not remain isolated from other trends in society. The mid-1980s saw a rise in crime. Graffiti, vandalism, car crimes, anti-social behaviour and burglary were to a lesser or greater degree found on the Estate. Burglaries were becoming more common by 1985. Bournville was not alone in this trend; it was repeated throughout the West Midlands. 'This part of Birmingham does have the disadvantage', the Community Officer reported, 'and the dubious distinction, of having not only the highest density of residential accommodation in the whole region, but also, unfortunately, the highest burglary rate as well.' An increase in the number of Neighbourhood Watch schemes did lead to a drop in burglary rates in the area.[14]

The open spaces on the Estate and the relative isolation of some of the communal facilities meant that they were vulnerable. 'Vandalism and hooliganism around the Village Hall have increased over the last years', the Weoley Hill Council reported in 1986, 'and have become a drain on both club funds and morale.'[15] Rubbish tipping and dogs defecating near the children's play area were other issues reported regularly to the Council.

Housing Provision and Special Needs Accommodation

Since before the First World War the Trust had provided dwellings for groups with special needs. Although the Trust did build special needs housing itself, many of the schemes were built and managed by other associations who leased or bought the land from the BVT. One such venture was Selly Wood House, completed late in 1980. This was a joint project for full-care accommodation for 39 elderly people sponsored by the Trust, the Teachers' Benevolent Fund and the Society of Friends.

At much the same time the first of a group of single-person flats at Griffins Brook Lane was completed. The whole scheme, which satisfied a little of that growing demand for accommodation from single people, was completed in 1981.

Laurence Court

Most of the special needs accommodation was rented property, and thus catered only for tenants. Little attention was paid for a long time to the needs of elderly owner-occupiers. Generally, they were not seen as a problem, and consequently there was little or no money available from government to encourage the building of dwellings for this group.

A Leasehold Scheme for the Elderly seemed to be the answer to those considering such schemes. In 1979 BVT opened negotiations with the Housing Corporation for the financing of such a venture. Negotiations were long and difficult. Firstly, the Trust had to settle for an equity-sharing scheme, with the Housing Corporation having a 30 per cent share and the leaseholder the remainder. The Trust were also informed that they were precluded from carrying through an LSE scheme because of their charitable status. Consequently, a separate non-charitable housing association, the St Laurence (BVT) Housing Association Limited, was formed in 1981 to carry out the development, and work finally began on the scheme in 1982. (A subsequent High Court ruling in 1983 indicated that charities were entitled to carry out such schemes as 'new initiatives'.)[16]

139   Laurence Court, a leasehold scheme for the elderly, begun in 1982.

The 1.2-acre site was on a plot of land in front of the Priory of the Sisters of Charity. The site contained a number of fine mature trees which were incorporated into the landscaping of the new scheme. As the Trust's own staff were heavily committed to the developments at Rowheath, an outside firm, Nicol Thomas Viner Barnwell, was put in charge of the scheme.

It was originally intended to build a single two-storey block, but in the end a courtyard solution was chosen. The buildings were designed to give the impression of a number of small, cottage-size dwellings linked by balconies. All the entrances face into the courtyard, and this gives a sense of tranquillity and security. The focal point of the courtyard is the pantiled pergola, which is provided with seating. The pergola is surrounded by an ornamental border containing flowering plants and shrubs, and smaller flower beds have been placed outside each flat (which, it was reported, were soon 'adopted' by the residents). Window boxes and hanging baskets add further to the visual impact of the scheme.

A total of 22 flats is to be found at Laurence Court, 18 two-bedroom flats and four one-bedroom dwellings. The architects used five different layouts, and all the upstairs flats have balconies. All the flats were fitted with gas-fired central heating. Internally, the designers sought to provide reasonable sized rooms and reduce the number of passageways. The intention was 'to give the maximum amount of living space in the most convenient way'. As these flats were designed as retirement homes, the stairs to the first-floor flats have been designed so they can be easily adapted to take chair lifts.

The residents had some choice about the colour schemes and fittings in the kitchens and bathrooms. The living room areas were provided with a 'feature' fireplace with a roughcast brick chimney breast and radiant gas fire. It was felt that this would provide a good focal point for the room. In all the rooms the electric, television and telephone sockets have been placed at waist height. Although this was not a sheltered housing scheme, like the nearby Rosefields, a pull-cord alarm system was provided for emergency use.

Laurence Court was financed entirely through the Housing Corporation. The total cost of the development, including the land, was £595,000. The Housing Corporation provided a 30 per cent subsidy for the scheme. The flats were sold by a local estate agent at prices ranging from £20,000 to £24,000. Six garages were included in the scheme, and sold at £1,500. All were taken up by new residents, who were described as being 'fairly active'.

The residents of Laurence Court have to pay a service charge to cover the cost of the maintenance of the building and the grounds, insurance, the emergency alarm systems, external lighting and the communal television system. Every effort was made to keep the charge as low as possible. The initial charge was £33 per month for one-bedroom flats and £35 for two-bedroom dwellings. The residents are not allowed to purchase their freehold and they are also required by their leasehold agreements to re-sell their property through the Association (at a price set by an independent valuer).

The scheme was successful. The flats seem to have been acceptable to the residents and the general layout was much appreciated. In warm weather the pergola in the courtyard has proved to be a pleasant and popular meeting place. It was reported in 1984 that the residents were 'fast becoming a close-knit community' and they quickly established their own residents association.[17]

Solar Energy Projects

Rowheath House and Rosefields

The Bournville Village Trust had from its early days been involved in housing experiments and research. In the late 1970s Tom Greeves, a Trustee and research engineer with Cadbury-Schweppes, was considering ways of reducing energy consumption in housing and believed that a possible test site might be found on the Estate. At that time Rowheath House, a block of sheltered flats for the elderly providing 40 single-bedroomed flats, two two-bedroomed flats, guest rooms, communal day rooms and a Warden's flat, was being constructed on Heath Road. It was a T-shaped block of conventional design and construction, but solar collectors could be placed on its south facing roof. A local heating contracting firm was called in to design and install a solar water pre-heating system. This consisted of aluminium collectors under patent glazing as a structural part of the roof.

As the first project came to fruition another sheltered housing unit, Rosefields, was being constructed in 1979 on the Priory site near the Bristol Road. This project provided for 28 one-person flats, seven two-person flats and eight bed-sitting room flats. As at Rowheath House, guest rooms, communal facilities, staff accommodation and laundry rooms were included. This second purpose-built block of sheltered accommodation gave the Trust the chance to install a more sophisticated solar heating system and carry out further research into energy conservation. Dr. Leslie F. Jesch of the Solar Energy Laboratory at the University of Birmingham was called in as consultant for this scheme. As Rosefields was already half-built Dr. Jesch's design options were somewhat limited. Nevertheless, a more advanced solar water heating system was introduced at Rosefields.

140 Rowheath House, a block of sheltered flats for the elderly, utilises solar energy. The solar collectors can be seen on the south facing roof.

A new British design of collector panel was selected made entirely of plastic. This system was lighter, less likely to break and still reasonably efficient. Two banks of these plastic collectors were installed on the south-east and south-west facing roofs of the L-shaped building. The collector panels were placed on corrugated, anodised sheet metal and treated plywood to ensure a weather-proof roof, even if the collector panels were removed. Each bank was tilted at an angle of 17.5 degrees, thus allowing the collection of solar energy over longer periods of the day than was possible at Rowheath House.

Both schemes had their own meteorological station, so that air temperature, wind and humidity could be measured. Computer control systems were set up to collect information for control and monitoring purposes. These valuable experiments enabled the Trust and its consultants to gauge the effectiveness of these early active systems of solar heating. Early monitoring revealed recognisable daily patterns of hot water use, as well as weekly and seasonal changes due to user behaviour. It also showed that user figures differed from the theoretical values usually recommended for planning purposes.[18]

Active and Passive Solar Energy

It soon became apparent that it was questionable whether such active systems could be paid for in savings. They also required regular maintenance to provide peak performance and they relied on other forms of fossil fuel for back up. Despite such drawbacks, these experiments were not dismissed out of hand. 'They are still very much in their infancy and experimentation period', a Trust officer reported, 'and they, or more likely their derivatives, are vital to our future since known fossil fuel energy will not last forever.'[19]

An alternative to such active systems were buildings based on passive solar design principles. This form of design seeks to reduce energy requirements by close attention to a structure's orientation, insulation, window placement and detailing, and the thermal transfer properties of the materials used. In this way the passively designed, direct-gain building acts as 'an absorber, store and delivery unit in itself'. Such structures use extensive south-facing window areas to maximise their ability to receive solar heat, especially in winter. The buildings contain the maximum amount of good quality, dense masonry materials to act as storage elements within the 'thermal envelope'. Double glazing and weather stripping of all external doors and windows thus become standard features of such structures. The use of blinds or shutters means that heat can be retained during the night and excessive heat avoided during the summer. 'It is by the careful use of these blinds/shutters', it was reported, 'that the reduced use of fossil fuel energy will be most notable.'[20]

Whilst passive solar designs were regarded as less novel, they were more cost-effective. They could produce significant energy savings, they cost little more than traditional buildings and they required less maintenance than active systems. Not surprisingly, when the Trust built its next sheltered housing scheme and started to develop the sites at Rowheath, passive solar design principles were extensively used.

Christopher Taylor Court

This sheltered housing scheme for elderly people was named after a long-serving Quaker Trustee and was constructed in 1985-6. It consisted of 42 flats, a common room, Warden's house and a laundry. Six of the flats were specially designed for wheelchair users, and had extra space and appropriate facilities. All the flats could be entered without using stairs, and access to them was totally enclosed.

The scheme was funded by the Housing Corporation. Once again an outside firm of architects was used. In this case David Clarke Associates produced the plans. The design aimed to utilise passive design principles while keeping in character with the Bournville Estate. The brick and tile-faced building incorporated high levels of insulation and modest sized double glazed windows. The south walls were designed to maximise solar gain. To counter problems of glare, only part of the south façades had conventional doors and windows. The rest was designed as a solar collector. It had a special 'selective surface' which increases the uptake of solar heat and reduces night time heat losses.

Christopher Taylor Court was laid out on a north-facing slope. It has pleasant views towards the Rowheath recreation ground and catches a great deal of sun from the south. The building was constructed around two open-ended courtyards. The vast majority of the flats were in the three south-facing wings. Full-sized doors allowed access onto patios and balconies in good weather, as well as allowing natural

141   Christopher Taylor Court, a sheltered housing scheme for the elderly, opened in 1986. This energy-saving scheme was built around a series of courtyards. It was designed by an outside firm of architects, David Clarke Associates.

ventilation. The flats had corridors placed on the north side, which allowed views of the courtyards or the landscaping from the kitchens. The corridors were daylit, thus reducing lighting costs. The southernmost wing was single-storey to minimise shadows in winter. The south courtyard was consequently narrower and it was also stepped to take account of the slight slope on the site. A block running north to south linked the three wings. It contained the common room, the sitting area, the laundry and boiler room.

It was calculated that the heating required at Christopher Taylor Court would be less than one-third that of a conventional design. A grant from the European Commission contributed to the cost of some of the energy saving features and the monitoring programme which followed its construction.[21] From the thermal point of view the building has lived up to expectations.

Christopher Taylor Court was just one of seven sites in the Solar Village at Rowheath. These developments were started in 1984 on the fringes of the former recreation grounds of Cadbury-Schweppes Limited.

The Solar Village

Cadbury-Schweppes Limited decided to dispose of their recreation grounds at Rowheath in 1981. Vandalism, declining use and the higher cost of upkeep of the facilities led them to take this path. At first it was not clear what the Firm's intentions were. The prospect of the wholesale development of an area of open space of over 60 acres caused consternation. The Birmingham Rowheath Action Group (BRAG) was set up to oppose development in the area. The Bournville Village Council also came out against a large-scale scheme.[22] The issue was discussed in detail by the Estate Management and Scheme Committee. They urged the Trustees to suggest to the Company 'a proposal for the minimum of development sufficient to produce the finance necessary to maintain the remaining facilities either as open space and/or as leisure facilities'.[23] For the Trustees, the Company's decision was both a threat and an opportunity. They feared wholesale development of the area by outside developers, yet if they could come to an agreement that only part of the recreation grounds should be built on this would offer them 'an opportunity to provide additional homes on the Bournville Estate while at the same time preserving that all important balance between housing and open space which is one of the hallmarks of the estate'.[24]

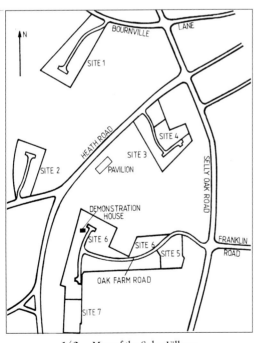

142   Map of the Solar Village.

143   High Heath Close, developed by Lovell Homes Ltd.

As the complicated negotiations went on, it became apparent that there was potential for conflict between 'the interests of existing residents and those still waiting for an opportunity to live in a better environment'.[25] Many residents clearly wanted to keep the Estate the way it was. In the end 'a complex package deal' was put together for the partial development of Rowheath. It included the purchase of 44 acres of open land by the City Council, who then leased it back to the Trust. Despite earlier conflict, support for the Trust's proposals for the development of 19 acres surrounding the open space was expressed at two public meetings.[26]

Approximately 8.5 acres were sold to Lovell Homes Limited for the development of two plots with 54 houses for sale (Sites 1 and 2). Lovell's agreed to follow Trust guidelines, but the houses were independently designed and sold on the open market. All their properties in High Heath Close and Birch Close had garages and central heating.

Another plot on Heath Road (Site 3) was developed by the Trust itself. There, Alan Plested, the Trust's Head of Architectural Services, designed 23 houses and bungalows for the upper end of the market. These brick and tile dwellings at Longwood included one bungalow specially adapted for two disabled people. As with all the Rowheath developments low energy passive solar principles were adopted for this development. It was completed in 1986.

On an adjacent site (Site 4) a 42-unit warden-controlled extra-care scheme for the frail elderly was started in 1985. Lucton House was the result of a joint partnership between the Trust, Servite Housing Association Limited and Birmingham Council for Old People. It was designed by one of the Trust's architects and incorporated passive solar features and had its own power generator for heating

144   Lucton House was a warden-controlled extra-care scheme for the frail elderly started in 1985. it was designed by the Trust's architects and managed by Servite Housing Association Ltd.

145   The energy-saving homes on Oak Farm Road designed by the Trust and developed through the St Laurence Housing Association Ltd. The large south-facing windows maximise solar gain.

the block. (Excess electricity was sold to the Midlands Electricity Board.)[27] This scheme was to be managed by Servite, a housing association with considerable experience in the field.

At the extreme south-west end of Rowheath, on the site of some derelict tennis courts, a leasehold scheme for the elderly was carried through by the Waterloo Housing Association Limited. Once again, the designs for the 20 bungalows in Wyndham Gardens were produced by the Trust's architects.[28] The largest project in the Solar Village was a group of 90 single-family energy saving houses on Oak Farm Road (Site 6). Designed by Alan Plested, the scheme was developed through the St Laurence (BVT) Housing Association Limited. The dwellings were sold on a shared ownership basis (the purchaser being able to buy a 25, 50 or 75 per cent share and pay rent for the remainder, with a view to purchasing the full share later.) The aim was to provide small houses for first-time buyers.

The two- and three-bedroom units were based on three basic designs, but the mixing of garages and carports and the varied positioning of the front doors allows for a degree of variety and choice. As with most passive solar energy schemes, particular attention was paid to the orientation of the houses. They were arranged so that most faced directly south, but monotony was avoided by varying the designs and orienting some houses slightly off due south.[29]

These houses were designed to a thermal standard which exceeded the building regulations. The walls have 100mm brick on the outside, a 100mm cavity filled with polystyrene and 100mm high-density concrete blocks on the inside to ensure heat retention. The dwellings were provided with concrete floors and concrete ground floor partition walls. The houses have large south facing windows to maximise their solar gain potential and minimal glazing to the north, east and west. The timber-framed windows are double glazed and have specially designed insulated roller blinds which are reflective on the outside to reduce radiation. The doors and windows have special seals, and the windows have trickle ventilation slots to eliminate condensation. The kitchens were fitted with humidity controlled extractor fans. The houses have gas central heating systems with small radiators.

Although site planning was dictated by energy conservation, these dwellings are backed by mature trees on parts of this site. Where south-facing windows form the road elevation, pavements were omitted on that side of the road to give greater privacy to the homes.

The focal point of the Solar Village at Rowheath was the Demonstration House. This building, which had both active and passive solar features, was intended as a test house against which the other dwellings could be monitored. It attracted international attention at an Open Day in September 1985.[30]

The passive solar components of the Demonstration House were similar to those of the other houses on Oak Farm Road. One extra passive feature of this house was the sunspace, which provided extra space and collected additional solar energy. This can be transferred to the living room by opening the large sliding patio doors or to the first-floor bedrooms through air bricks.

The active components in the Demonstration House included a solar heated hot water supply, a hot air recovery system, underfloor and ceiling imbedded space heating, and photovoltaic solar power generation. The sophisticated control system allowed energy supply and demand to be matched over

146 Visit by David Hunt, Under Secretary of State for Energy, to the Solar Village in June 1985. T. Greeves, Dr. L. Jesch, David Hunt, M.P. and A. Plested in front of the sunspace of the Demonstration House.

time, either manually or automatically. These active features made the house virtually independent of external supplies for space heating and hot water. 'These features will not be paid for by savings', Tom Greeves, the Trustee most involved in this venture, noted, 'but they will provide valuable data and experience which may lead to some of them becoming cost-effective in the future.'[31]

To learn from the experience of this scheme, the largest solar village in Europe, the performance of the Demonstration House and houses and flats on three other sites was monitored by Franklin Company Consultants and the Solar Energy Laboratory at Birmingham University.[32]

Woodbrooke Meadow

While these developments at Rowheath were under way the Trust began discussions with the City Council about the development of a six-acre site on Woodbrooke Road, adjacent to St George's Court and near the model yachting pool in the Parkway. (The venture involved the exchange of the land in Woodbrooke Road owned by the City Council for two Trust sites in Hole Lane.) The idea was to develop it with a mix of houses for sale and dwellings for rent. The income from the sale of the houses was to finance the building of the rented properties. 'The site will provide much needed bungalows to rent for retired couples on part of the site', it was claimed, 'and the Trust will ensure proper sensitive landscaping of the site, as well as incorporating low energy technology in the buildings.'[33] There was considerable opposition to the development of the meadow on the grounds of its contribution to the visual appeal of that part of the Estate. Many older residents remembered it nostalgically as 'Roy's Field', for it was there that the local baker had formerly taken his horses to graze. The loss of another open space so soon after losing the battle for Rowheath was felt strongly by local residents. Bournville Village Council and Weoley Hill Village Council both expressed their opposition to the scheme.[34] The Trustees were not swayed by the views of the objectors. They believed that with careful landscaping, the need for housing could be met without loss of amenity. In March 1986, Bournville Village Developments Limited, a wholly owned subsidiary of the Trust, was set up to acquire and develop the Woodbrooke Meadow site. The whole scheme was funded by a loan from Lloyds Bank, which, it was expected, would be recouped when the houses were sold.[35] The City Council finally approved the scheme in 1987. Work on the 33 houses for sale and the 14 bungalows for rent began in 1988. Although it was a controversial venture, it did, like the early part of the Estate, mix private and rented properties. (It was perhaps appropriate that one part of the area was called Harvey Mews, after the Trust's first architect.) The dwellings ranged from one-bedroom bungalows to five-bedroom/three-bathroom houses and thus ensured a degree of social mix unusual in the Trust's post-war developments. The Trustees also insisted on 'unprecedented levels of landscaping'.

As with the Rowheath dwellings, careful attention was paid to the energy efficiency of these properties. Each unit was oriented to the sun and was fully insulated. The windows were triple glazed. The properties were fitted with burglar alarms, smoke detectors, fitted kitchens and cable television. The prices of the 'distinctive properties at this prestige location' ranged from £115,000 to £210,000.[36]

Interest in the properties was high as they were going up. Bigwoods, a local estate agent, started to organise a bid system for the properties coming up for sale. Some 400 people wrote to ask for one of the 14 rented bungalows. Unfortunately, by the time the scheme was opened in June 1990 the housing market was plunging into crisis. High interest rates and uncertainty among buyers affected the sales of the Meadow Rise properties.[37]

The properties did eventually sell and the scheme was praised for its innovatory features.[38] The sloping site alongside a popular public space had presented the Trust's architects with a challenge. The landscaping has undoubtedly done much to soften the impact of the scheme. There have, however, been complaints about the quality of the fittings in the more expensive houses, some worries about being overlooked on a sloping site and certain critical comments about the globe-like street lights. When they were surveyed in 1992, the tenants of the bungalows in Harvey Mews expressed a high level of satisfaction with their homes and the neighbourhood. They were especially happy with the quietness of the area and the proximity to parkland. They had some minor complaints about the lack of a bathroom window, the difficulties with ventilation in the single-bedroomed properties, leakages and the absence of a canopy at the front door. Although some tenants found the rent levels for the bungalows high (and needed Housing Benefit to pay the rent) 9 out of 10 thought the properties were good value for money.[39]

147   Woodbrooke Meadow from the Valley Parkway.

148   Harvey Mews, the rented properties in the centre of the Woodbrooke Meadow development.

As with many of their other new properties, the Trust experimented in these bungalows with gas and electric central heating to see which was more acceptable and efficient. The tenants with gas central heating were generally more satisfied with their heating systems than tenants using the electric Economy Seven system as their main form of heating. Their main concerns related to their lack of control over the electric central heating and its higher cost.[40]

The Decade 1988-1998

By the late 1980s the Trust's role on the Bournville Estate was largely a management one, and most of their building activity was concentrated elsewhere. 'There is very little building land now left in Bournville', the Trust reported in 1988, 'but the demand for a decent home still exceeds the supply, and for as long as that situation exists the Trustees will continue to seek ways and means of providing high quality accommodation in pleasant settings for people who need help with their housing.' They did engage in a few small-scale schemes aimed at special groups with particular, and often severe, housing needs. Two examples of the way in which the Trust was trying to diversify its housing stock 'to assist in alleviating some of the wide range of housing needs experienced [at that time]' were completed in the late 1980s.[41]

In the autumn of 1988 two houses in Selly Oak Road (on a site formerly occupied by Birmingham Dairies) were completed for occupation by families that included a member who was physically disabled. They were specially designed to allow a disabled person to occupy one area of the house with all the necessary facilities at one level. The scheme was funded by the City Council and the Trust.

In an ageing community, there has remained a large demand for suitable accommodation for the elderly on the Bournville Estate. In 1991 a group of six bungalows for sale was completed at Summerfield Drive, off Shenley Green. They were constructed on the site of the old Hawkestone Road tennis courts. A rather different experiment was conducted at 27 Elm Road in 1992. There, the Trust, with the Centre for Applied Gerontology of the University of Birmingham and Midlands Electricity plc, set out 'to design the interior of a house to meet the differing needs of the elderly'. The two-bedroomed house was completely gutted and refurbished 'using only products designed by manufacturers with elderly people in mind'.[42] Like many of the Trust's small-scale experimental ventures, the lessons drawn from this scheme add to the Trust's experience and knowledge, and can be used later or disseminated to other organisations.

Another innovative scheme for the elderly was constructed off Tillyard Croft in the late 1980s. This was an Intelligent Buildings Project for Third Age Homes developed on Trust land by Copec. The designers were associated with the Birmingham School of Architecture. Although faced with brick, stained boarding and clay tiles, this pair of dwellings was more adventurous (both externally and internally) than the vast majority of bungalows at Bournville. The accommodation included hall, living room, kitchen, utility room, three bedrooms and a garage or carport. In addition, one bungalow had a conservatory, while the other had a spa pool.[43]

In the 1990s the Trust embarked on two conversion schemes aimed at providing accommodation for tenants with learning difficulties. The first, in 1993, was in Willow Road. The second involved the gutting and conversion of properties in Raddlebarn Road that had been used as a garage into a group home.

Most of the schemes to help the disadvantaged have not caused controversy. One of the Trust's most recent proposals, to provide accommodation for children in care in a new purpose-built block on the site between Charfield Close and Cob Lane formerly occupied by the builder, C. L. Holding and Sons, has disturbed some residents. The presence of the Divisional Police Headquarters nearby does not seem to have reassured the objectors.[44]

149   This innovative scheme for the elderly at Tillyard Croft was an Intelligent Building Project for Third Age Homes developed on Trust land by Copec. The designers were associated with Birmingham School of Architecture.

150   The 'executive houses' built by Wimpey Homes and Berkeley Homes at The Davids.

The Davids

What may be the last significant development on the Bournville Estate took place at The Davids, the former home and grounds of Laurence Cadbury. It seems that the Trustees did initially consider developing the site with houses for sale and rented properties, as they had at Woodbrooke Meadow, but the housing recession had affected the sales at the latter site. This was possibly one of the reasons which led the Trustees to take the decision to sell this well-wooded site near the Bristol Road. The land was bought by Wimpey Homes, who developed the site with Berkeley Homes. The former company built 36 four-bedroom homes, while the latter constructed 12 five-bedroom and 19 four-bedroom houses. The houses themselves were typical of the 'executive homes' produced by commercial builders. Private builders had often before built houses for sale on the Estate, but never has such an isolated group of exclusive properties been erected at Bournville. These relatively expensive houses in a prime location found ready buyers. If the housing at The Davids does not seem to conform to one's expectations of Bournville, the landscaping certainly does. Indeed, the richly planted estate has caused some controversy because it was included in the Scheme of Management area. Its inclusion has added a little to the annual management charge of all the freeholders on the Estate. Whilst some were unhappy about having to pay for what seems like an exclusive private estate, others argued that the extra cost was a small price to pay for ensuring that one of the main thoroughfares through the Estate (Bristol Road) was properly landscaped.[45] The Trustees could also point out that this development meant that £2 million was released for social housing elsewhere in the region (thus enabling them to fulfil one of the basic requirements of the Trust Deed).[46]

Maintenance and Improvement

As the amount of building land on the Estate has dried up, the housing stock has aged and the residents' expectations have risen, so the Trust has had to consider improving and modernising its dwellings. Such a policy was not new, but the scale of the undertaking was. Besides diverting a significant proportion of its rental income to maintaining the Estate, the Trust has also obtained significant amounts from the Housing Corporation not only for new developments but also for its maintenance programmes. In 1986, for example, 27 per cent of the Trust's revenue was spent on repairs and improvements, whilst between 1975 and 1989, the Bournville Village Trust received £7.5 million in public subsidies via the Housing Corporation to provide new homes for rent or shared ownership and repairs and improvements to existing properties.[47]

A major repair programme was started in 1985. In the first year nearly £1 million was spent on problems such as rewiring, heating systems, bath replacements, re-roofing, painting and day-to-day repairs.[48] The properties belonging to the Bournville Almshouse Trust were also re-roofed at this time. In 1986, over £¼ million (all from the Housing Corporation) was spent re-roofing 64 houses in the Woodlands Park Road area.[49]

A somewhat different approach was taken in the late 1980s to heating and energy conservation in older properties. As a result of the concerns of residents about heating (expressed in the 1986 Shenley Survey) the Trustees revised their policy to make generous grants available to tenants wishing to install central heating. Two years later, the success of a cavity wall insulation scheme at Almond and Veronica Close led to an offer of reduced cost insulation to owner occupiers on the Estate. About 400 residents took up the offer.[50]

151   Improvements to many of the older properties on the Estate have been made. These include new timber and tile porches on the post-war houses on Green Meadow Road.

The Trust has continued to use Housing Corporation funds to refurbish property. Such funds were, as we have noted, vulnerable to changes in government policy. In 1979-80 and 1992-3 the level of Housing Corporation funding dropped dramatically. Such a sudden withdrawal of support meant that the Trust had to use its own funds to carry out a minimal programme of necessary work.[51] The financial position of the Trust (and other housing associations) improved after the passage of the 1988 Housing Act which allowed them to increase rents, especially those of assured tenancies. Most of the surplus money generated in this way was accounted for by improvements to the existing housing stock. Further cuts in 1996 made life more difficult for the Trust: 'Cutbacks in funding by the Housing Corporation,' it was reported, 'are forcing all associations to use more of their own money or to borrow to maintain existing properties as well as develop new houses.'[52]

Work has continued on the maintenance and modernisation of the Estate. Recent surveys have shown that the tenants would like to have double glazing, better heat and sound insulation, built-in storage, and kitchen and bathroom improvements.[53] Plans were drawn up to address their main concerns.[54] The replacement UPVC windows installed in Shenley Fields Road were welcomed by the tenants, and the windows do not look incongruous in these simple 1950s terraced and semi-detached houses. Also in the Shenley area, many of the original concrete door canopies have been replaced by timber and tile ones. These have been generally well received, and they add visual interest to the very simple brick and tile post-war houses. A great many new garages, porches and windows have been added to the properties of the leaseholders and freeholders on the Bournville Estate, not always with pleasing results.

From the late 1970s concern was expressed about some of the extensions going up on the Estate.[55] Such work could cause aggravation not only with the Trust but also with neighbours. Disquiet was expressed by one Weoley Hill resident:

> I feel it is so sad that, in this lovely area with its village atmosphere in which we all live, such a lot of bad feeling is being caused by residents putting up erections, aerials, rooms over garages and just about everything else, without consulting amicably with their neighbours to find out if it will affect their home.[56]

The Weoley Hill Village Council urged the Trust to take a stronger line when considering applications for house extensions. It also later opposed some applications which would have involved a change of use for some Weoley Hill properties. After a Theological College was allowed to take over a house in Weoley Hill, the local Scheme representative, Dr. Woodward, expressed the opinion that 'further encroachment at the expense of private residences in our area should be strongly discouraged'.[57] There was 'rock solid' opposition to a proposed office development in Fox Hill in 1993 and the application was rejected by the Village Council and the Trust.[58]

Design Guidance and Conservation

Although the vast majority of Bournville's houses are built of brick and tile and may be loosely described as conforming to the regional vernacular, there are, as one might expect of an Estate that is over 100 years old, certain stylistic variations in the total housing stock. How to maintain the quality and visual integrity of the Estate has been a long-term problem for the Trust, as residents seek to improve and modernise their properties. This is especially important in the Estate's Conservation Areas, but is significant elsewhere (as the residents of Weoley Hill have often argued). Despite the publication of a *Design Guide*,[59] *A Guide to Property Alterations and Repairs for Leaseholders and Freeholders*, and articles in the Trust's quarterly bulletin, *Bournville Outlook*, residents still occasionally make alterations without reference to, or permission from, the Trust. The Trust has continued to inform and persuade residents, rather than adopt a punitive attitude. This gentle approach means that some inappropriate additions have appeared on the Estate. The Trust can, of course, insist on remedial action before a property is sold on (but that may not be for many years in Bournville).

The Trust continues to set guidelines and urges its residents to be aware of their legal and communal responsibilities when contemplating extensions and alterations to their property:

> We, that is the Trust and yourselves, can only preserve and enhance this special environment by ensuring that any new development or alteration work is considered within the context of your neighbours' property, your road, your surrounding area and the Estate as a whole.[60]

As more and more householders have come to replace their windows, this has become a particular area of concern. 'The best maxim to adopt in any replacement programme', the Trustees suggested in their newsletter in 1994, 'is to repeat the original style of the window when your house was first built.'[61] Residents in Conservation Areas were told to consider secondary glazing.

An updated version of the Trust's *Design Guide* was published in 1994 in 'an attempt to introduce more sensitive criteria in recognition of the different features of the various sections of the Estate which make up the whole'. In 1996 Bournville Village was chosen to be one of the first of a series of appraisals of Conservation Areas carried out by Birmingham City Council, in consultation with English Heritage and local residents. As a result, all owners must now get planning consent for certain alterations to their property that might damage the special character of the Village.[62]

Landscape

While it had not been possible after the Second World War to build at the low densities that had prevailed in the early decades, Bournville remained well-known for its parks, open spaces and landscaping. The careful planning and planting of new developments went on alongside renewal programmes for some of the older parts of the Estate. As the developments got under way at Rowheath and Woodbrooke Meadow, an international firm of landscape consultants, Derek Lovejoy and Partners, was called in to try to ensure the quality of the Estate was maintained. Their remit was wide and they were asked to draw up plans for major landscaping schemes on various parts of the Estate.[63] Generally, they advised the Trust to plant in a more dense manner than had previously been the case.[64] Particular attention was given to sensitive sites, like that at Woodbrooke Meadow, where it was recorded that the landscaping cost £2,000 per unit.[65] Specific proposals were put forward for central features like the Valley Parkway, where considerable additional planting, a water garden and an ornamental pool were recommended.

The Trust continued to place great emphasis on the appearance and amenities of the Estate. In 1985, the Trustees set out the guidelines for their landscape policy. The main aims of that policy were:

1. To enhance the street scene and provide a foil to the starkness of the buildings on the Estate.
2. In areas of open public space, to provide an attractive setting for social intercourse.[66]

These broad concepts were reinforced by specific proposals for particular places, such as flatted areas or woodland. A combination of hard and soft landscaping, formal and informal planting, were therefore recommended. It was thought that this would be work which would 'once again ... set Bournville apart as a "special" place in which to live'.[67] Not every proposal was welcomed. A detailed scheme for landscaping and the provision of play areas in the Shenley district was criticised at a public meeting because it was felt that it would lead to 'a likely increase in vandalism and the attraction of external undesirable elements'.[68]

A Landscape Manager was appointed and preliminary work on a major landscape study began in 1986. An interim report was put before the Estate Management and Scheme Committee in the following year. The findings were then presented in audio-visual form at six public meetings in the autumn of

152   The refurbished Garland Way Pool and parkway, with the 1970s flats of Jervoise Drive in the background.

153   Planting of an oak tree during National Tree Planting Week, 1979. Included in the photograph were John Jones (Manager, Bournville Village Trust, Maintenance Dept.), Brian Wood (Chairman, Weoley Hill Village Council, Philip Henslowe (Community Officer, Bournville Village Trust) and Martin Fox (Foreman Gardener, Bournville Village Trust).

154   Barrie Edgar and Peter Seabrook at the 1985 Tenants' Garden Competition Prizegiving.

1987. There was said to have been 'a tremendous response from the residents', once again highlighting the commitment of many in the Bournville community to the maintenance of the quality of their local environment. The Trust officers were instructed then to draw up a Landscape Master Plan, taking into account the views of the residents.[69]

Work on the planned five-year programme got under way in 1988. The two most noticeable projects were the large-scale bulb planting programme on the Green and the major refurbishment of the Garland Way Pool.[70] These were followed by planting schemes in Weoley Hill, Shenley Green and Green Meadow Road.[71] Attempts were made to involve the local community in enhancing and maintaining the pleasant landscape of the Estate. One such effort involved the local residents' representatives and the pupils of St Laurence Junior School during National Tree Week in 1989.[72]

During the late 1980s and 1990s the Garden Competition, which had been such a feature of the early days of the Estate, had a new lease of life. A new Tenants' Garden Competition was started in 1985. The standard of the competition, which was judged by two presenters of television garden programmes, Peter Seabrook and Barrie Edgar, was said to be 'extremely high in all four classes'.[73] In 1993 the Bournville Garden Competition was widened to allow all Bournville residents to take part. A new prize, appropriately called the George Award, was given for the front garden that most enhanced the Estate. The competition continues to elicit an enthusiastic response from the many committed gardeners living on the Estate.[74]

By the mid-1990s the time was ripe for another review of the Trust's landscape policy. Following widespread consultation in 1996, another five-year programme of tree planting and care was drawn up. Over 250 new trees were planted in 1996 alone. The landscape staff, renovating the open space near Green Meadow, have worked once again with the local Junior School to try to encourage an interest in the Bournville landscape among the young residents of the Shenley area.[75]

Traffic

Over the years the Trustees and residents of Bournville have had to come to terms with the motor vehicle. Between the wars a few houses (especially those at Weoley Hill) were designed with provision for a garage. Since that time planners have had to consider the provision of parking spaces, carports or garages in most of their schemes. Nevertheless, a 1997 survey revealed that only a third of those interviewed in Bournville and one fifth of the Shenley interviewees' homes had garages. Other residents (especially at Shenley) did have access to parking facilities in the garage courts, but over 60 per cent of car owners parked their vehicles on driveways or on the road. Not surprisingly, many residents have identified parking as a problem.[76] Whilst the wider roads and bigger building plots insisted upon in the early days have allowed for some accommodation with the car, the narrower roads, culs-de-sac and higher densities of later developments have caused some difficulties as car ownership has increased.[77]

The volume of traffic in the area has risen. The Bournville Estate is crossed by two wide dual carriageways, Bristol Road and Shenley Lane, and the City's outer ring road runs through the heart of the old Village. The Cadbury factory is now served by road transport and Cadbury World brings in thousands of visitors to Bournville from far afield. Unpopular underpasses or bridges provide tenuous pedestrian links between parts of the Estate, while an increasing number of pelican crossings have had to be provided to allow pedestrians to cross the main roads of the Estate. Concern about the levels of traffic was greatest in old Bournville. 'As the area is ... a Conservation Area', the Trust argued in 1989, 'current and possible future traffic levels are not environmentally acceptable.'[78] A traffic survey was carried out in 1990. The report concluded that traffic levels were generally acceptable, but that pelican crossings and waiting restrictions should be introduced. There was some concern expressed about traffic which used Woodbrooke, Sycamore, Acacia and Willow Roads as 'rat runs'.[79] The Trust began negotiations with the City Council in the mid-1990s in the hope of securing limited traffic calming measures at all the entrances to the Conservation Area. The Trust offered a contribution of £30,000 to the cost of the works, and Council representatives accepted that the Trust had an excellent case. Work was delayed in 1998 because of the City's lack of funds. 'Calm at last,' *Bournville Outlook* exclaimed when the measures were finally given the go-ahead.[80]

155   Traffic on the Green in 1997.

Concerns about dangerous junctions and narrow roads elsewhere on the Estate have been expressed over the years. The junctions between Shenley Fields Road and Middle Park Road and Witherford Way and Bristol Road were considered to be especially hazardous. Residents on narrow roads, like Fox Hill and Swarthmore Road, have been anxious to prevent a build-up of traffic in their area.

It should be noted that levels of car ownership are not very high on the Bournville Estate. A 1997 report revealed that 42 per cent of households surveyed in Bournville, and 48 per cent in Shenley, did not have access to a car for private use. Some parts of the Estate were better served by public transport than others; although bus services were not welcomed in certain parts of the Estate. In the early 1980s, there were objections to the bus service which ran up Swarthmore Road. The local residents felt it was 'a further hazard on this busy road'.[81] In the winter of 1993-4, there was a 'revolution in Fox Hill'. The residents were determined to stop the new bus route which ran down Weoley Hill and Fox Hill and 'an ad hoc road blockage was set up by worried residents as a means of voicing their protest'. In the wake of this 'vociferous and determined local opposition', the bus service was re-routed. While it was generally accepted that Fox Hill was inappropriate for full-size buses, 'a more reasonable approach might have been', as one local representative noted, 'to utilise the smaller "community" type buses'.[82] The relative lack of mobility of a substantial proportion of the residents reinforces the continuing need for local facilities and services on the Estate, for both old and young. This was confirmed by the Tenant Satisfaction Surveys in 1991 and 1997.[83]

The Estate and its Residents

By 1980 the Estate covered 1,000 acres and contained approximately 7,000 dwellings.[84] It was estimated that the population was about 21,000 at the beginning of 1984.[85] Approximately half of the houses were tenanted and the remainder were let on long leases, except for those where the freehold had been purchased under the Leasehold Reform Act of 1967.[86] By the end of 1979, 602 Bournville leaseholders had bought their freeholds.[87] The rented property included bungalows, maisonettes, flats and small and large houses. The majority of the housing stock had been designed for general family housing, but smaller dwelling units were being provided in greater numbers. A 1980 housing density survey showed clearly that certain more recent parts of the Estate were built at higher densities than the original Village and inter-war developments. The highest densities were found in those areas with flats and maisonettes, like the Green Meadow Road/ Black Haynes Road area built in the 1960s, the Hole Lane Estate and the Priory area constructed in the 1970s. The actual figures were 7.15 houses per acre for the old Village, 5.85 for Weoley Hill Limited, 14.16 for Green Meadow Road/Black Haynes Road, 15.46 for the Hole Lane Estate and 17.96 for the Priory.[88] By 1991 half of the Bournville Village Trust's housing stock consisted of three-bedroomed properties, whilst one- and two-bedroomed dwellings each accounted for a quarter of the total.[89]

The Trust continued to cater for those with special needs, especially the elderly. They also began to respond to the changing patterns of housing need, whilst continuing to try to provide a good service to their existing residents.

The Trust had from the earliest days set out to encourage 'social mix' and operated in a non-discriminatory manner with regard to politics, religion and race. Within limits they seem to have had some success, especially in the pioneering days when the housing situation was less complex. A number of surveys from the late 1970s through to the 1990s reveal the elements of continuity and change on the Estate.

A 1978 study of 'social mix' came to the conclusion that 'Bournville is now an homogeneous community, not a mixed community'. Sarkissian and Heine went on to explain the reasons for this increased uniformity:

> Our research certainly suggests that homogeneity at Bournville is a result of a strong 'sense of belonging' to the Estate by residents who are aware of its 'history' and 'uniqueness'. These factors combine to create a community interest which, in turn, creates social and behavioural patterns which seem to be generally accepted by all residents.[90]

They also claimed that the level of investment that residents had made in their homes was also a determining factor in their perception of social mix in the neighbourhood. 'Homeowners in Bournville', they concluded, 'appeared to be more tightly bound to their environment than did renters.'[91]

The study by Sarkissian and Heine left one Trustee, G.W. Cadbury, with the impression 'that after the first few years the simple concept of mutual help by association faded away and it was other factors that sustained the community of Bournville'.[92] David Donnison, an expert on housing and planning, concluded:

> In stable British communities most people care much less about social mix, positively or negatively, than about other features of their environment such as the attractiveness of their homes and the neighbourhood in which they stand, and the rents they pay for them. And when they do think about 'mix' the relationships between social classes, which have provoked most of the argument over the years, are probably less important than relationships between different lifestyles, which are only partly a reflection of class, and relationships between different age groups.[93]

The fact that Bournville continued to have a range of housing types, on varying forms of tenure and at different levels of rent or cost, was important. This helps to explain the range of residents on the Estate, but does not necessarily, of itself, lead to social mix or a 'sense of belonging'. Sociologists at the time were increasingly critical of the belief that social integration could be assisted by physical integration.[94] They highlighted the move towards a more home-centred existence and a lifestyle based on social networks. Whilst this might lead to a reduced desire to interact with neighbours and a geographically wider range of interest groups, the importance of neighbours and the locality was still recognised as being significant by some social analysts.[95] One can still identify, in the desire of most residents at Bournville to maintain the quality and 'feel' of the Estate, a community consciousness or local ideology. It may be being challenged by a younger generation or new arrivals (houseowners and tenants), but it is still an important element in the 'self-policing' of the Estate.[96] A review of a local newsletter, like the *Weoley Hill Village News*, provides confirmation of the desire of local residents and their representatives to prevent anything 'which would detract from the present attractive appearance of this part of the Village'.[97]

Life at the end of the 20th century was less likely to depend on the immediate locality than it did when the Estate was founded. The Trustees were aware by the late 1970s that local residents shopped and took their recreation further afield, that they sometimes worked at considerable distances from their homes, and that the communications media brought them in touch with a wider range of stimuli. It was still possible to explain the reasons why people continued to come to Bournville:

> They come because of convenience of location to their work, because transport and other services are good, because the schools satisfy their needs and because of ... good design, both of houses and of overall layout. Good management is also a major factor.[98]

It was apparent that late 20th-century arrivals on the Estate did not often consider the issue of social mix.

Although no detailed demographic study of the Estate has ever been made, one can generally accept the conclusions of an internal report of 1984 that 'it is probably safe to assume that the residents fall almost entirely into the 'B' and 'C' categories, with a few exceptions at either end of the scale'. Respectable working-class and middle-class people have predominated.[99] Changes had, however, been taking place. Large houses, some formerly occupied by members of the Cadbury family, were demolished to make way for residential developments, often for those with special needs. This was the case at Westholme and Selly Wood House. (This process of piecemeal increases in dwelling densities was taking place elsewhere in the city.)[100] This had consequences for the social and demographic structure of the Estate, as had changes in lettings policies. The former led to increased provision for the elderly, while the latter bought in more single young people, the unemployed, single parents, people from ethnic minorities and even the homeless.

The latter groups were rarely present on the Estate in earlier years. There were, however, signs of divisions between the different tenure groups. To a certain extent these were a consequence of the way the Estate had been developed. There were districts, like Weoley Hill, Innage Road and the area to the east of Black Haynes Road, that were entirely made up of leasehold (and freehold) properties, and areas like the City-funded parts of Shenley, Hole Farm and Priory which were filled with rented properties. Signs of a 'them' and 'us' attitude were beginning to be noticed by Trust staff. Reviewing the situation in 1984 one concluded:

> It seems that because of modern market forces, the concept of 'social mix' is not as widespread as it was. Selection and self-selection has led to an unintentional setting up of 'one class' areas on the Estate. There is a marked psychological barrier between the leaseholder/freeholder on the one hand and the tenant.[101]

Such divisions should not be over-emphasised. The most recent Tenant Satisfaction Survey showed that 83 per cent of the tenants in the older Bournville area and 92 per cent of tenants in the Shenley area thought the mix of tenants and householders was about right.[102]

In the same way the Trust had effectively begun to produce 'one class' areas, it also unwittingly created 'one age' areas. Because of the high level of satisfaction of tenants, leaseholders and freeholders with the homes and the areas they live in, many Bournville residents have lived on the Estate for a long period of time. With the arrival of younger tenants and residents with different values, signs of intergenerational tension began to appear. In the early 1980s the majority of complaints received by the community officer came from residents over 50 years of age. These complaints were mostly about their young neighbours and declining standards.

Perhaps the Estate really was becoming like a village; a village where the established residents looked askance at 'incomers', or, at least, took a long time to accept them. Whilst accepting that there might be genuine problems with some newcomers to the Estate, Trust officers were dismayed by the seemingly unfriendly response of some of Bournville's long-established residents:

> Because they have lived in the same house for maybe 35, 40 or even 50 years, they cannot accept that others around them often have a different outlook and sometimes a differing way of life. Therefore they have become very intolerant, wanting everyone to conform to their standards, often becoming aggressive and very argumentative.[103]

There were advantages and disadvantages to being a development that was steeped in tradition and one which had a very low turnover of residents. At its worst, Bournville could be perceived as 'a traditional white middle class closed shop—where "outsiders" [were] not welcome'. There was a need to break down this perceived barrier and put in place policies and procedures that ensured that groups with genuine housing needs were being helped by the Trust.[104]

People from ethnic minorities were often in housing need. In the early 1980s there was growing anxiety in the Housing Association movement about social and racial issues in housing. The Commission for Racial Equality was concerned about the access of black people to housing in the voluntary sector. The Bournville Village Trust was considered for a formal investigation by the Commission for Racial Equality at the end of 1981 because it had such an exceptionally small proportion of black residents. The Trust insisted that its policies were non-discriminatory, but they were left in a position 'of convincing the black community in Birmingham that it was not a racist organisation'.[105] Although there was no evidence of racial bias in its policies, the Trust in association with the Runnymede Trust, commissioned independent research about allocations by Housing Associations to people from ethnic minorities. The Trust also had discussions with the Commission for Racial Equality.

It should be borne in mind that there was a lower concentration of black people in the areas around Bournville than in the city as a whole and that a substantial proportion of those who applied to live at Bournville lived in the vicinity. Whilst it may have been true that the Trust had an 'unwelcoming' image, there was also the possibility that potential applicants might be put off because their fears about cultural and religious isolation and even racial harassment on the Estate.[106] (A very small number of fascists were identified on the Estate.) Although the City Council had nomination rights for some of Bournville's housing stock, the predominant reliance of the Trust on direct applications at the time was said to favour those familiar with the Trust. Applicants to the Trust were more likely to be engaged couples, elderly couples, lodgers, those already with secure accommodation and those who wanted to live in the area because of relations, work or simply because it was pleasant. The applicants were usually retired or in non-manual occupations.[107]

As a result of the meetings between Trust and CRE officials, a number of measures were introduced, aimed at improving the performance of Bournville Village Trust with regard to ethnic allocations. 'This is encouraging', a Runnymede Trust report concluded in 1985, 'but it is not sufficient':

> Until the City Housing Department and Associations keep and monitor ethnic records, and adopt policies and practices which are specifically designed to achieve equal opportunities for ethnic minorities and poorer households, outcomes will remain a matter of chance and management expediency.[108]

The Runnymede Trust report recommended that priority be given to policies for racial equality, that allocation policies be clarified, monitoring be introduced and links be made between housing associations and relevant referral agencies. The Bournville Village Trust responded along those lines. By 1989 it was being reported that 'ethnic minorities were fairly represented throughout the allocation process' (although it was noticeable that 85 per cent of these were allocated flats or maisonettes). Ethnic minority lettings at Bournville increased from 3 per cent in 1984 to 9 per cent in 1988. While this represented a figure above the level of the local ethnic population, it was still below the percentage for Birmingham as a whole (which by 1992 was estimated to be around 21 per cent). For a while it seemed that the Trust could not better this performance.[109] Attempts were made to improve communications with outside organisations and the Trust's policies on race were highlighted. Links were established with organisations representing mainly black and other ethnic minorities. In 1990 the lettings policy was updated (and a points system introduced) and in 1991 the monitoring system was improved. Also in 1991, new procedures for dealing with racial harassment were put in place.[110] These policies seem to have borne fruit in the following years for there was a significant increase in the proportion of ethnic minority tenants housed by the Trust. In 1992, 27 per cent of new lettings were to people from ethnic minorities.[111] More recently the figure has fallen: in 1997 minority ethnic households accounted for 17 per cent of all lettings by the Trust. (This was, however, slightly higher than the figure for 1996.) The Trust were still constrained by the fact that a significant proportion of the nominations for their property came from the City Council and the fact that, while there was some improvement, few ethnic minority applicants applied directly for accommodation.[112]

It was becoming clear to the Trust's officers that while some progress had been made with ethnic minority tenants, certain other areas of housing need and equal opportunity had been largely ignored. A 1990 report on housing need in south-west Birmingham concluded:

> The Trust appears to be helping some special needs groups, predominantly the elderly and, to a lesser extent, disabled people, which is only a small proportion of the total of the special need cases identified in the report.[113]

The report noted that the number of single person households was expected to increase in the 1990s. The largest single group of people looking for accommodation was the under 25s. The percentage of elderly people (particularly the frail elderly) was also expected to rise dramatically. Many people from ethnic groups had serious housing problems (although most still did not seek to live in Bournville). Overcrowding, homelessness and relationship breakdown were the major contributors to housing need. Large numbers of those in housing need were on low incomes and lodging was the predominant form of tenure for this group. A further review of housing needs in the City in 1995 reinforced this picture and pointed to 'a wide range of client groups requiring various levels of supported accommodation'. These included the old, the homeless, the mentally ill, offenders, drug abusers and those with physical problems. While the needs of these groups are great, few residents in Bournville, or elsewhere, have been keen to welcome them as neighbours. The Trust has, however, begun to make small-scale provision for some needy and disadvantaged groups.[114]

The scope for addressing these problems on the Bournville Estate was limited. The number of properties becoming vacant each year was low, and consequently the number of new lettings each year was relatively small. In 1993, for example, there were 167 re-lets. Over half of these were for one-bedroom properties, whilst two- and three-bedroom dwellings accounted for just under a quarter each. Nine out of ten of these lettings were new assured tenancies (at higher rents) and the rest involved transfers by secure tenants. Lettings to ethnic minority tenants comprised 22 per cent of the total. Sixty per cent of the re-lets went to tenants qualifying for Housing Benefit, while 59 per cent went to the homeless or those threatened with homelessness. (Nearly half of those in this category were nominated by the local authority.) Another 17 per cent went to single parent families.[115] During 1997 the Trust let 228 properties. Half of the people housed by them were single people, whilst the second largest group were one-parent families. Almost 40 per cent of those given accommodation were homeless. The Trust may only be helping a small proportion of those in severe housing need, but there is little more they could do given the limited number of void properties available to them each year.

A lettings policy that started to bring those in greatest housing need onto the Estate put extra pressure on the Trust's housing managers and did not necessarily go down well with established residents. In 1985 the Trust's community officer noted 'a somewhat disturbing trend':

> Many newly arrived residents did not appear to be aware, or ignored, the fact that special items and conditions have to be complied with, when coming on to the Estate. This led to the near neighbours of these residents, usually long standing residents themselves, complaining about the behaviour of these new arrivals.[116]

Such problems have not disappeared, nor should one expect Bournville to have escaped the social problems of late 20th-century Britain. The Estate has had its problems with graffiti, vandalism, crime (especially burglary) and even drugs. The anti-social behaviour of a minority has been of concern to the residents of Bournville. Individuals and residents and tenants groups have been urging the Trust (and the police) to develop tougher strategies to deal with such anti-social elements. A 1997 Survey found that just under 50 per cent of the Trust's tenants thought the Trust were too lenient with those who seriously breached their tenancy agreement, whilst a similar proportion thought that they had got it about right.[117] 'Although the Trust has every sympathy with the difficulties some people have in adjusting to life at Bournville,' it was reported in 1996, 'there is no excuse for behaviour that deprives existing tenants and other residents of the quiet enjoyment of their homes.'[118] Generally, the Trust does not want to be seen to be in conflict with any of its tenants and residents; it has, however, evicted some of its tenants for non-payment of rent and serious anti-social behaviour. It is also considering probationary tenancies for certain special needs groups, although its freedom to extend this policy is limited by the regulations of the Housing Corporation.[119]

Problems with neighbours are, unfortunately, a relatively common and unpleasant part of life in contemporary Britain. A recent television documentary series suggested that 1 in 14 householders had reported their neighbours to the police. Noise, pets, hedges, fires and the dumping of rubbish can lead to disputes, rage and despair. Bournville has not been immune from such conflicts. There is evidence of friction relating to garden fires, dumped garden rubbish, house extensions and dogs. The introduction of a dog-free area in the Weoley Hill Parkway was said to have 'polarised attitudes between dog walkers and dog haters to quite a depressing extent'.[120] A long-running legal battle about tall, fast-growing conifers along the boundary between two properties in the area was widely reported in the national media, and was regarded as a classic case of 'Neighbours at War' by the BBC. It seems that some of the local tension stems from a desire to preserve the 'niceness' of the Estate, and this involves social standards as well as environmental quality.[121] In a more individualistic age, and on an Estate with a growing range of social groups and households, the widely held standards and feelings about Bournville have, perhaps, become harder to maintain. What is sometimes apparent is that a few residents have neither the strength, money, skills or inclination to meet Bournville standards and traditions. Whilst the Trust might be expected to do its utmost to maintain the quality of the Estate, it also has the frequently difficult task of encouraging or cajoling a small minority of residents to accept their communal responsibilities.[122]

Despite these changes, Bournville has remained a relatively stable community. Studies in the mid-1980s indicated that the average stay in Bournville properties was 20 years. It concluded that the Trust offered lifetime, permanent housing.[123] A 1991 Survey of the tenants of Bournville, showed that one-third of those interviewed had lived on the Estate for more than twenty years. It is a community where residents are likely to say, 'I have lived here only 20 years.' Not surprisingly, it is an ageing community. The 1991 Survey (which covered one-fifth of the Trust's tenants) indicated that half of those interviewed were over 60, whilst 46 per cent were retired. Of those surveyed 60 per cent had an income of £125 or less a week. Many residents at Bournville are on pensions, and those have been rising more slowly than rents in recent years.[124]

In 1996 preliminary work began on two initiatives designed to address the problem of poverty. This involved support for the creation of local Credit Unions and the setting up of a Hardship Fund. The latter is intended to help tenants in financial difficulties. The Trust set up the fund in 1997 to provide cash grants for major essential purchases like furniture or cookers. By early 1999 the South Central Birmingham Credit Union Limited was finally up and running.[125]

The Trust and the Local Community

Besides its pledge to provide high quality housing and landscaping, the Bournville Village Trust has always tried to encourage community development. It reiterated its commitment to these aims in 1985:

> The Trustees are committed to maintaining high standards in the physical environment of the Bournville Estate. They believe the social environment is no less important.[126]

The Trust had, almost from the very beginning, helped to promote residents' associations.[127] By the 1980s there were four such organisations on the Estate: the Bournville Village Council, Weoley Hill Village Council, Shenley Manor Residents Association and Shenley Court Residents Association. Apart from being a conduit for information between the Trust and the residents on the Estate, the residents' association's role was largely a social one. They had no legal standing. Three of them had their own community halls, whilst the Bournville Village Council had responsibility for the Social Centre in Laurel Grove. (The management of these halls has, at various times, been in the hands of the Trust and the residents associations.) The Bournville Village Council's other main functions included arranging the Annual Festival and the open-air Carol Service and the publication of a Year Book (which in reality was a handbook and local directory). The Weoley Hill Village Council has remained an active and central feature of local life over the years. 'We of the Village Council', Brian Wood claimed in 1980, 'like to think we are at the hub of the Village wheel.'[128] One of its main aims was to promote 'a spirit of community through organised social activities'. Brian Garner and Sue Clay were for many years the main organisers of the social events at Weoley Hill. These included in the 1980s a Village Carnival, a children's holiday scheme, a Senior Citizens' Party, a neighbourhood scheme, a Bonfire Event, a Children's Christmas Party, a Carol Concert, a film show and various outings. The sports clubs utilising the facilities on the Weoley Hill Parkway continued to flourish, but the players were not always local.[129] At various times the Bournville Village Council and the Weoley Village Council have produced newsletters. These publications indicate that the Bournville community still supports a great many social, recreational and sporting clubs for all age groups. They did not always constitute a coherent programme of activities. 'Association-backed activities are therefore few and far between on the Estate', the Trust's community officer concluded in 1984, 'except in Weoley Hill where there is a programme of events throughout the year for local residents.'[130]

156   The Village Council, August 1978.

The social and recreational requirements of the population as a whole have changed dramatically in recent decades, and this has impacted on the local organisations. The associations, their publications and their halls have all had fluctuating fortunes. They have often relied on the hard work and long service of a few officials. Denis Carson was rewarded for his efforts on behalf of the Bournville Village Council (and, more recently, Park Tenants' Association) by having one of the rooms at Dame Elizabeth Hall named after him. Janet McCrindell, Brian Garner, Les Pankhurst, Diane Roe, John Woodward and John Clarke were among the most active of the long-serving Weoley Hill representatives.[131] Pat and Olive Mahon retired in 1988 after 25 years' service on the Shenley Manor Residents' Association. They had both joined when the Association was formed in 1963 and helped in the building of their own hall in Burdock Road. Bob Dalley, the Shenley Manor representative on the Scheme Committee for many years, retired at the same time. Shenley Court Residents' Association was a thriving association in its early days. It put on its own flower show, arranged a bonfire and firework display in the open space off Green Meadow Road, and organised a Christmas party for young children and a trip to a pantomime for the older children. It organised a summer fête with Shenley Manor for a few years in the 1970s. When Doreen Davies joined the Shenley Court Residents' Association in 1970 it had 16 members on the committee. By 1989, the number had fallen to five (including the Scheme representative).[132] It seemed difficult to get 'new blood' on to the committees, and newsletters, such as *Carillion*, *The Three Brooks* and the *Weoley Hill Village News*, have been published intermittently.

The community halls have also had mixed fortunes. 'Changes in national attitudes, together with an increase in expectations and standards', the Trust's community officer reported in 1984, 'have all tended to militate against the use of their local community halls.'[133] Whilst the halls have continued to be booked for everything from children's playgroups to religious meetings, the users are not always locals. The future of the halls has, at times, seemed uncertain. In 1986, it was recorded of the Shenley Manor Hall, 'Lack of support by present day residents and rising costs make its future uncertain.'[134] The Trust has, on occasions, paid for the refurbishment of the halls as they grew older and standards rose. In recent years, the management of most of the halls has been transferred back to local committees under the aegis of the residents' associations.[135] Shenley Court Hall remained the only hall under Trust Management at the beginning of 1998. Local tenants' representatives want the hall refurbished and modernised before they will take it over, while the Trust want evidence of local commitment before committing funds. Such are the difficulties of local groups in this age of mass entertainment and rising standards when people want 'a socially attractive centre'. There is no doubt that there remains some demand for these local facilities. When the Weoley Hill Village Council took over the management of the Village Hall in July 1994 they continued with the original policy of providing a base for local sports and social clubs and the children's playgroup. They were anxious to see more people use the hall for 'suitable purposes', but they had 'no intention of promoting pay-at-the-door discos, raves and so forth, however potentially profitable'. The Council also remained adamant that they did not want a drink licence.[136]

Because the Trust has contributed the creation and the support not only of the residents' associations but also the community halls, it has been suggested that the organisations were not independent

157 The inauguration of the Rowheath Centre Trust (Mrs. Veronica Wootten, Chairman Bournville Village Trust, David Ollivant, Manager, RCT, Mrs. Judith Mackay, Chairman, RCT, Deputy Major, Councillor Bill Sowton, deputy Mayoress, Mrs. Sowton.

or self-sufficient. 'Because they were not formed spontaneously, in response to any perceived need of the residents at the time', one commentator suggested, 'in a way they have had an artificial existence.' Whether they were 'cossetted' or not, the associations, especially those at Shenley, have had their difficulties. 'The lack of a clear role, underfunding and a falling off of support, coupled with a change in recreational and social needs and the proliferation of rival activities and groups', it was conceded in 1984, ' have all led to the problems that the associations face today.'[137] The attraction of television and computers and the fear of crime are among the factors which keep young and old at home, especially on dark nights. Mobile adults on the Estate frequently look further afield for their recreational needs.

While the residents in the old Village complained that they lacked a proper hall until Dame Elizabeth Hall was provided for their use, at Shenley it seemed that there were too many halls, with overlapping activities, competing with each other. In addition to the Shenley Court Hall and the Shenley Manor Hall, St David's Church, the Shenley Green Centre, the Shenley Fields Community Centre (formerly the Allen's Cross Sports Association) and the multi-use community and sports facilities at Shenley Court School all provide facilities for people in the locality and beyond.

The Trust has continued to support these community facilities at the same time as trying to encourage the local communities to sustain and take some responsibility for the amenities. This was shown clearly in relation to the Rowheath Centre Trust, which was inaugurated in 1984. The Bournville

Village Trust sponsored this new company to look after Rowheath Pavilion and the sports grounds. The Centre Trust's key officials were Judith Mackay, the Chairman, and Lyn Chappell, the Secretary. Whilst they were committed to, and enthusiastic about, the venture, they faced some difficulties. An early forecast had indicated the prospect of a heavy annual loss.[138] The Bournville Village Trust and the City Council provided considerable financial support to the Rowheath Centre Trust, but it never quite fulfilled the hopes of its promoters. The Trust had spent £¼ million to make the Rowheath Centre Trust viable by 1986, but it still seemed to lack widespread support:

> Sadly, apart from the heroic efforts of a small group of dedicated people, the majority of the Bournville community seem prepared to let the whole initiative collapse through lack of support and funds.[139]

Despite having one of the few drinks licences on the Estate, and providing a base for the local running club and other sports teams, the Rowheath Centre Trust never prospered. They struggled on for more than a decade before control of the facilities was passed to a religious group at the end of 1997.[140] The new group opened a café for a five-week trial during the summer of 1998. The response was sufficiently promising for them to consider investing in equipment, the decoration of a café-cum-family room and a proper launch for the Pavilion Café.[141]

158   Rowheath Pavilion.

Residents and Management

In the late 1970s there were signs that the traditional, paternalistic style of management of the Trust needed overhauling. A few changes had already been made, such as the establishment of a Scheme Committee in 1972, with four residents' representatives on it. This was a consequence of the Leasehold Enfranchisement Act. In 1978 Laurence Cadbury retired as Chairman of the Trustees. He was succeeded by his daughter, Veronica Wootten. In the following year, the Trust finally established a separate Housing Management Department and appointed a Community Officer.[142]

The Trust began to look to the future. A special conference was held at Barnes Close for Trustees and senior staff in 1980. They were there to take stock and to re-examine their aims and objectives; the intention was 'to restate them in today's terms and begin defining priorities for the next two decades'.[143] In their deliberations, the Trustees and their officers recognised that within the Estate there was 'a unique mix of freeholders, leaseholders and tenants'. They realised the importance of maintaining a close relationship between the trust and its residents. The Community Officer and the Scheme Committee were seen as essential 'in fostering new initiatives and acting as a channel for communication'.[144]

In 1980 the Housing Corporation reported on the Trust. (The Trust had become a Housing Association in 1974 and therefore came under their supervisory control. They did, however, maintain their charitable status.) The Housing Corporation concluded that the Trustees 'should promulgate clear lines of delegation and authority' and establish greater control over financial matters.[145]

159   The Bournville Village Trust Scheme Committee, February 1988.

Changes began to be made from the early 1980s. Other long-serving Trustees, such as Paul S. Cadbury, retired and new officers were appointed: James Wilson replaced Kenneth Pegg. In 1981, the Trustees began 'encouraging new initiatives and responding to change'. The Trust set out to improve its communications, better its services and provide more opportunities for the residents to become involved in planning and running of the Estate. The establishment of a new sub-committee structure led to the creation of an Estate Management Sub-Committee with four Trustees and four representative residents. Its remit included housing management, development and rehabilitation, Estate and property maintenance, development control, renewal of leases, sales and purchases of properties, and community affairs.[146]

The Trust also began revising its lettings policy and procedures in line with the 1980 Housing Act. This led to the introduction of new Tenancy Agreements in 1982 and the publication of information about the Tenants' Charter and consultation procedures. (It also led to a review of, and increase in, rents.) In the following year meetings were held to set up Tenants' Associations, again fulfilling the requirements of the 1980 Housing Act.

Despite these changes, there were still signs of tension between the Trust and the community in the early 1980s. A review of the Trust's relations with the community was undertaken. Its main conclusion was that the Trust had problems that stemmed largely from past management policies. 'Rigidity of attitudes, a cavalier approach, slow response to requests for action', the report concluded, 'all have helped to create the feeling of an unfeeling, increasingly remote bureaucracy.'[147] The community officer felt that the Trust needed to adopt a higher profile and increase levels of communication with the residents. Recent meetings had convinced him of the need for increased dialogue with the people of Bournville. He recognised that times, and the residents, were changing:

> Today's resident on the Estate is a much more demanding person than his forebear ever was. His needs are more complex and far more sophisticated, and his expectations are higher. He requires more of the Trust and will question much more than before. There is a feeling that the standards, set by the Trust in the past, have slipped and that residents' viewpoints and feelings should be taken into consideration more.

Philip Henslowe had to admit that 'they may be partly correct in their assumptions'.[148] The critics were in a minority, but some of their complaints were justified.

Despite the fact that the local associations had sometimes been by-passed by the Trust and were not regarded as being the main line of communication by residents, they continued to receive support and encouragement from the Trust. The new Tenants' Associations were given representation on a Joint Consultative Committee of Tenants and Trustees. In addition, a Residents' Forum was also set up in 1985 to bring together the representatives of the Residents' Associations, the Tenants' Associations and the Trust. 'Meetings are always well attended and comments flow freely,' it was reported.[149] The Residents' Forum was essentially just a 'talking shop', but substantive issues could be referred to the Scheme Committee.

The Trust sought other ways of reaching and informing the residents of new developments and changes of rules on the Estate. In 1984 the Trust's *Annual Report* was given a new format and sent to all residents. It was hoped that this would lead to a 'better understanding' of what was happening on the Estate.[150] It did not entirely stop arguments about new developments, complaints about new tenants and neighbours, or friction about the management charge.

The Trust's main concern in these years was that the rising cost of maintaining the Estate was not matched by equivalent increases in income from lessees and freeholders, and this was putting pressure on its rental income (which was needed to maintain the housing stock). The 1983 *Annual Report* highlighted the situation:

> The viability of the management role of the Trust ... came under close scrutiny during the year as the gap between contributions from owner-occupiers and costs widened. The maintenance of standards of appearance and amenity was only achieved because income from rented dwellings continued to rise faster than inflation. With fair rents levelling out, the future maintenance of the housing stock and of the Estate could become increasingly difficult without either public sector subsidies or a greater contribution from residents.[151]

The Councils and Associations, Rowheath Centre Trust, Selly Manor Museum and other local bodies still continued to receive grant aid from the Trust. The Trustees, in turn, were wanting further contributions (both financial and otherwise) from the residents on the Estate. 'This level of support for the existing community', the Chief Executive revealed in 1984, 'can only be maintained if residents will accept greater responsibility for looking after the environment.'[152]

In late 1988 and early 1989 the Trust established new structures and published a new Statement of Purpose. With regard to community affairs, they re-affirmed their desire to involve residents in the running of the community. One of their first actions was to invite the representatives of the four Tenants Associations (Park, Shenley Manor, Shenley Court and Woodlands) to sit on the Housing Management Sub-Committee. In addition to this further attempt at 'power sharing' they also set up a Tenants' Forum (which replaced the Joint Consultative Committee) and a Bournville Estates Community Forum. Their new Statement of Purpose declared their objective to be:

> To manage their estates in accordance with the best estate and management practice and encourage residents, should they wish, to share in the management decisions affecting them.[153]

In the late 1980s and 1990s there was some restructuring within the Trust to try to achieve these goals.[154] Whilst these changes reflected the growing professionalism and managerialism of charitable bodies, it must be noted that the Trust's efforts to involve residents were of limited success. By 1993 the Trustees were still expressing their concern 'at the apparent failure to reach large sections of the community on the Estate and to share in broad-based participating governance'.[155]

There was still a certain amount of tension between certain sections of the Bournville population and the Trust. The most obvious source of friction was the management charge levied on freeholders to help pay for the protection and maintenance of the Estate. The Trust's officers were, as we have noted, concerned that the cost of maintaining the Estate was rising faster than the increase in contributions from freeholders under the Scheme of Management. The freeholders felt anxious and vulnerable. Some took their concerns to the residents' associations. Dr. Weaver, the Chairman of the Weoley Hill Village Council, summarised their view in June 1989:

Council felt that there was a willingness on the part of residents to contribute to the upkeep of the area in which they have chosen to live. Equally there is a strongly held belief that there is a need for an external constraint on the charges levied.[156]

Not everyone felt aggrieved at the Trust's policy. 'Tenants' rents have been used for many years', Cyril Bezant reminded locals, 'to subsidise owner-occupiers' contributions towards the provision of services, facilities and amenities on the Estate.'[157] Late in 1987 the Trustees resolved to apply to the High Court for powers to make an increase in the contributions made by freeholders (to be based on the actual costs of the previous 12 months).[158] There was continued opposition to the proposed increases in the management charge. Some felt that they had not been properly consulted by the Trust, as promised. In the summer of 1989 the Bournville Freeholders and Leaseholders Action Consortium was set up. While they were still disposed to negotiate, they were also willing to go to court to contest the Trust's application. Ultimately, this was what happened. In 1991 this 'long-running battle over who pays to keep tidy one of Birmingham's most famous model communities' was resolved in favour of the Trust in the High Court.[159] Not surprisingly, the Trust was pleased with the decision, while the freeholders were disappointed. The representative of the latter, Dr. John Woodward, explained that, in future, they would have to be watchful to ensure that the higher charges (of just over £40 a year) were put to good use: 'They will have to scrutinise the way the Trust carries out the maintenance tasks, seeing that they are necessary and carried out efficiently and economically.'[160] To this end a Bournville Freeholders Association was set up in 1992. Interestingly, the Management Charge went down between 1991 and 1993 but this was partly because a number of items previously included in the charge were excluded.[161] The slight increase in the charge, to take account of the development at The Davids in 1996, once again brought the issue to the fore. While many (including the Trustees and their officers) saw the charge as being a reasonable contribution to the maintenance of the whole Estate, some complained that insufficient work was being done in their area, or that particular jobs were being insufficiently well done.

Whilst certain issues seem to disturb the generally good relationship between the Trust and its residents, the Trust itself has continued to try to improve its performance and its links with the local community. More informative and attractive newsletters have been introduced. (A 1991 survey indicated that four out of five tenants interviewed found the Trust newsletter useful.)[162] The *Annual Report* was given another makeover. The new-style report was 'intended to attract investment from private bodies as public money is in the present political and economic climate no longer the main source of revenue for rented housing projects like the Trust's'. As the new and glossy reports were no longer sent to every resident on the Estate, *News from the Trust* became the main link with Bournville's residents.

In 1996 the structure of the housing committees was streamlined. These were 'designed to involve more people in decisions which affect their lives'.[163] New consultative resident advisory boards were set up as part of this overhaul of the Committee structure. Some were not happy about the way in which the changes were introduced. 'Your Council,' the Weoley Hill representatives reported, 'is saddened to see a return to the paternalistic "top down" type of management in which detailed proposals are put forward before consultation.'[164] Trustees and tenants' representatives have responded more positively to these moves, and have made cautiously optimistic predictions about the role of the advisory boards. Other initiatives included the formation of a Junior Forum involving young people from the Estate.[165]

A 1997 survey indicated that tenants felt they should be involved in future decision-making (70 per cent of those interviewed thought it was important that their views should be heard). There was no unanimity about the way in which their views might be registered and taken on board. A third still preferred personal contact with the Trust while another 30 per cent favoured questionnaires. Public meetings, tenants' associations and newsletters were revealed to be less popular forms of communication among the tenants.[166]

An Island of Sobriety?

One issue that has periodically exercised the minds of Trustees and residents has been the drink question. Some relaxation of the rules had occurred in 1979. The matter came up for discussion once again late in 1997 when one of the shopkeepers at Shenley Green applied for an off-licence. The story was deemed newsworthy, and one television company and several newspapers ran reports about the threat to this 'island of sobriety'. The Trust asked the local residents' and tenants' representatives to test local opinion. The request for the off-licence was overwhelmingly turned down. Whilst the Estate is not totally 'dry', there still seems to be no great desire to have off-licences and pubs on the Estate. The Trustees remain aware of the need to encourage and support local shops, but they continue to believe that the sale of alcohol is not the best way forward. Almost ten years after an earlier shopping survey at Shenley in 1989, the Trust has initiated another study to investigate the future of the neighbourhood shops at Bournville.[167]

Resident Satisfaction

Bournville remains a desirable and pleasant place to live. One obvious indicator of its enduring appeal is the fact that many of its inhabitants have lived there for long periods of time. It remains popular with housebuyers. Estate agents recognise the 'Bournville factor'. House prices there are generally higher than in many other suburbs in Birmingham. Well-built dwellings, fine landscaping and good schools are among the factors in the equation. Assessment officers seem to take a similar view, because Bournville properties are often to be found in the higher Council Tax bands (although some adjustments have occasionally been made to take into account the deterioration of small pockets of the Estate).[168]

Tenants and owners seem to be aware of the advantages of the Estate. A survey of the Shenley Manor area in 1986 indicated that both owners and tenants seemed happy with their homes, viewing them favourably in terms of their spaciousness, convenience and location. The respondents had a positive attitude to the Shenley area, valuing it for its 'greenness, quietness, tidiness and spaciousness'. Just over a quarter of them felt, however, that the area had got worse over the previous five years. Some expressed concern about condensation and damp in certain properties, while others expressed fears about vandalism and house security.[169]

A number of surveys in the 1990s have revealed how happy the majority of tenants are with their dwellings and their surroundings. 'There was a high level of satisfaction', a 1991 Tenants Satisfaction Survey concluded, 'with tenants' homes, neighbourhood and standard of service provided by the landlord.' The vast majority (92 per cent) were happy with the condition of the Trust's properties. The small number of dissatisfied tenants complained about problems with windows, draughts, inadequate heating and fixtures and fittings. Four-fifths of those interviewed thought that their present homes were suited to their needs. Almost every interviewee (95 per cent) was happy with the general area around their home. 'The quietness, parklands, open spaces and largely trouble-free neighbourhood', the Trust's Research Officer noted, 'seemed to be the main ingredients for tenant satisfaction.' The situation in some of the Trust's special needs properties seemed equally good. The tenants in warden schemes who were interviewed found them generally suited to their needs and satisfactory.

Certain areas of concern were identified in the 1991 Survey. The tenants were particularly anxious the Trust should try to keep rents low, improve the transfer system and provide good facilities and home improvements (especially for the elderly and disabled). The tenants also had more general worries about security, traffic and landscaping in parts of the Estate (especially around 'flat' areas).[170]

Another survey of the Bournville Village Trust's tenants was carried out by independent housing specialists in 1997. The results were again good, and even indicated that the Trust's services to its tenants had improved. Although the survey covered districts beyond the Bournville Estate, it is possible to identify the responses in the Shenley and Bournville areas. Almost four-fifths of the respondents from Bournville and Shenley were satisfied with the overall condition of their homes. (It is noticeable that tenants of two years or under were less impressed with their accommodation, with about two-thirds of those interviewed in the latter areas expressing satisfaction with the overall condition of their homes.) On the whole, the majority of the tenants thought they were getting good value for money (62 per cent in Shenley and 56 per cent in Bournville).

About two-thirds of the respondents in Bournville and Shenley were concerned about the lack of facilities for teenagers. Almost half of them also recognised the need for more children's play facilities. There were lower levels of concern about noisy neighbours (25 per cent), neglected gardens (about 22 per cent), vandalism (19 per cent), burglaries (14 per cent), nuisance from dogs (nearly 15 per cent) and abandoned vehicles or vehicle repairs (13 per cent). There was a feeling that the area had got worse in the last 18 months. Physical or racial harassment did not figure largely (3 to 4 per cent and 1 to 2 per cent respectively in Shenley and Bournville), but such incidents do cast a longer shadow than their numbers might suggest.

The Trust's power to tackle some of these issues was limited, but it is significant that nearly half of the tenants at Bournville and Shenley thought the Trust should be tougher with tenants who seriously breached their tenancy agreements.

Of the improvements that the Trust could do to renovate their properties, double glazing was the most desired by Shenley and Bournville tenants (57 and 56 per cent). Sound and heat insulation were also regarded as priorities by about half of the respondents, while under one in five of the tenants wanted new kitchens and central heating. Just over one-tenth of the interviewees expressed a desire for a new bathroom.

The survey reinforced the picture of the Trust serving a stable population, with almost half of its entire tenantry having lived in their homes for 10 years or more and nearly 40 per cent of them being over 65 years old. Two-thirds of the entire survey group had no children under 16 years old. Whether because of age, lack of time, money or skill, 32 per cent of interviewees in Bournville and Shenley indicated that they had difficulty in keeping up with their gardens.[171]

Whilst the Trust can take satisfaction from the results of the survey (which a housing expert suggested put them in the top 10 per cent of housing providers and managers), they also point to the issues which the Trust must address if it is to maintain, or improve, its performance in future years.[172]

Retrospect and prospect

The history of the Bournville Estate is a story of continuity and change. The aims of the Trustees have remained broadly the same for a century. 'The Trustees are confident that in a rapidly changing world', Professor Gordon Cherry, the first non-Cadbury Chairman of the Bournville Village Trust, proclaimed in 1993, 'it is possible, and very desirable, to keep faith with the Founder's aims.'[173] The means by which they have sought to achieve those aims have changed, as the values and needs of society have altered. The Estate itself has grown and matured, as have many of its residents. The pioneering Model Village has evolved into a large and well-established garden suburb. The Trust's manager clearly summarised the position in 1960:

> Bournville is no longer a unique experiment. Many larger estates have been built by local authorities and other bodies. Nevertheless, it continues to make its contribution to the solution of the housing problem, especially in the field of good management. The Trustees still lay great stress on the original characteristics of the Estate, and particularly on the planning of pleasant residential roads, with attractive arrangements of trees, grass verges and greens.[174]

The Trust continued to promote schemes in the last quarter of the 20th century, and some of their ventures have attracted attention. As the Trust rapidly approaches its centenary, there is virtually no land left for development on the Bournville Estate.

Looking backwards, it is important to try to understand why the original development at Bournville had such an impact. It is harder these days to recognise how novel and important a venture it was, precisely because the kind of low-density development introduced at Bournville has been widely copied in the intervening period. As David Eversley noted, 'From Bournville ... sprang the Garden Suburb Movement.'[175]

The Model Village was markedly different from the squalid slums and the monotonous bye-law terraces of the later 19th century. Small wonder that this attractive, low-density development was characterised as 'a Modern Arcadia'.[176] Bournville was not an unattainable dream, it provided evidence of 'Utopia in practice'.[177] As one local newspaper remarked, 'Bournville comes, perhaps, as near to the industrial Utopia which the idealist longs to see as it is possible anywhere to find.'[178] Bournville was

160 The May Queen at the Village Festival in 1982. This event has been one of the enduring features of the social life of Bournville.

valued as an object lesson 'more precious than all the talk of a hundred Conferences'.[179] This exemplary scheme managed to combine 'art and economy'.[180] It therefore appealed to the lovers of the picturesque and those who believed such schemes should be run on sound commercial lines.

The original Model Village at Bournville set high standards of housing design and site planning. Many visited Bournville, and some sought to follow its lead. Public reforms also followed in the wake of such private experiments. 'Today,' it was claimed in 1924, 'the ideals embodied in Bournville are on the statute books.'[181] The officials who produced the 1919 *Housing Manual* and the advocates of 'Homes for Heroes' drew on the Garden Suburb prototypes developed before the First World War at Bournville and elsewhere.

The Bournville Estate continued to expand during the inter-war years. The developing scheme was still regarded as being superior to most of the estates built by local authorities and private developers in the period, but it was not, as J.B. Priestley noted, 'the eye-opener' it had been at the beginning of the century.[182] The general quality of the housing and landscaping remained high, and the experimental schemes at Bournville continued to attract attention.

In the 1930s concern mounted about the dangers of suburban sprawl and ribbon development as the area of land covered by the newer low-density developments dramatically increased. Whilst being in the vanguard of the movement to the suburbs, the Trust remained aware of the need to protect the countryside. To this end they bought large plots of land to the south west of Birmingham to provide the city with a valuable 'green belt'. The Trust's own research before and after the Second World War pointed to the need for new towns and satellite settlements when the city's own building land had been used up.[183]

The post-war period saw the creation of a full and more effective planning system. It also brought about significant changes in the way that new developments on the Bournville Estate were funded. The Trust continued to lease land to housing societies as it had done between the wars, but it also began to receive public money (from the local authority and, later, from the Housing Corporation) to build new properties and modernise older dwellings on the Estate. Legislative changes and public funding meant that the Trust had less freedom to develop the Estate and design properties than it had in the past. There was, for instance, pressure to build at higher densities than before. Licensing and subsidy arrangements meant that there were strict financial and design constraints to work within. Stylistic trends reinforced the move towards plainer dwellings. 'Though there have been no revolutionary changes', it was noted, 'there has been an increasing tendency towards simplicity and even severity. The houses have simpler, cleaner lines, and the Estate architects have aimed at planning comfortable houses, each good of its kind, in which household drudgery is reduced to a minimum.'[184] The range of dwellings expanded to accommodate changing needs of Birmingham's population in the late 20th century. This meant the construction of flats, maisonettes, sheltered housing and residential homes as well as bungalows and 'cottages'. The Trust continued to try to encourage the building of sound properties, but increasingly the housing stock on the Estate in the third quarter of the century began to look less distinctive, and more and more like local authority and private developments elsewhere. The landscaping, community provision and management of the Estate remained superior to most public, voluntary and private developments, and resident satisfaction remained high.

Throughout the years the Trust has maintained its commitment to building not only houses but communities. In the early years social balance and architectural variety were achieved by placing dwellings of different size and tenure together. Social cohesion was encouraged by the provision of communal facilities and the encouragement of residents' associations. While the latter policy was continued, from the 1920s onwards the different tenure groups have, to a greater extent, been separated. So while the entire Estate can be said to contain people of different social class and status, particular areas are more likely to be socially homogeneous.

Although the relationship between the Trust and the residents on the Estate has generally been harmonious, there have been moments of tension. Almost from the beginning there have been occasional signs of friction occasioned by the desire of the Trust to meet the needs of the working classes and create a socially mixed community. For many years Bournville attracted residents from the respectable working class and the middle class, and few people from the bottom and top of the social scale lived there (especially when the older members of the Cadbury family left or died and their family homes were demolished or put to institutional use). More recently, because of agreements with the City Council, Housing Corporation rules and changes in their own lettings policy the Trust has begun to house some of the most needy people in the city: the poor, the unemployed, those from ethnic minorities, single parent families, the homeless, people with learning difficulties, the disabled, as well as the elderly and single women they have catered for over a long period of time.

Bournville still has a stable population, but it is an ageing population. The number of new tenancies each year on the Estate is low. Despite the relatively small number of 'newcomers' on the Estate, there is still potential for conflict between the old villagers and the newly arrived residents, especially if the latter do not seem to value their properties and surroundings or subscribe to the ethos of the place. Crime and anti-social behaviour are not unknown. Bournville has not remained immune from the social problems of the large city of which it is a part. These are issues with which the residents, the Trustees, the Community Officer and the Police continue to grapple. These problems should not be overstated, but security and anti-social behaviour remain areas of concern for the residents of Bournville.

In this changing world, the Trustees have tried to remain constant to the basic aims of the Trust Deed. In 1993 they approved a new Statement of Purpose for the Trust. It basically re-affirmed their commitment to the Founder's aims. Their intention was:

> To provide high quality housing developments, distinctive in architecture, landscape and environment, in socially mixed communities, using best management practices to improve the quality of life for those living in such communities.[185]

There can be no doubt that some of the developments in the last 20 years, like the Solar Village, for example, have been successful. The enhancement of the properties and landscape of the Estate has remained a key objective of the Trustees. They have also made it clear that they intend to continue to provide social housing for those with insufficient means to help themselves. Their commitment to provide homes for those with the greatest housing need was reinforced when the Trust negotiated an extension of their nominations agreement with the City Council in 1994. (Fifty per cent of nominations for Trust property now come from the City.)

The Founder and the original Trustees had a clear vision for Bournville. For many years they have maintained a close watch over the Estate. Whilst the Trust sought to encourage communal involvement in the development of the Estate, there was a growing belief among the residents by the third quarter of the century that it was unnecessarily paternalistic. The appointment of a Community Officer in 1978 and administrative changes made in the 1980s were intended to encourage tenant and resident involvement and a more professional approach to management. The Trustees have more recently re-asserted their desire to encourage tenants, leaseholders and freeholders to share in the decisions affecting their community. A small, but active, group of residents can be found on the various committees which advise the Trustees.

In conjunction with the new Statement of Purpose, an ambitious business plan, 'Towards 2000', was launched in 1993. The aim was to set objectives for the Trust, so as to put it in a position 'to make a positive contribution to the housing needs of 21st century'.[186] These involved organisational goals as well as a commitment to enhancing Bournville as a model estate. In addition, a target of 4,000 homes under the Trust's management by the year 2,000 was set. As there are virtually no building plots left in Bournville itself, this has meant that the Trust has become increasingly involved elsewhere, in Birmingham Heartlands and Shropshire.

The business plan illustrates the elements of continuity and change in the Trust's activities. 'Towards 2000' highlighted the Trust's next big challenge, the decision to start building a second Bournville, 'a Mark 2 version for the 21st century'.[187] Discussions between the Trust and the Commission for New Towns and the Urban Villages Forum followed. A site at Lightmoor, Telford, has been selected and a feasibility study and more detailed plans are being worked out. The area has been characterised as 'a brown field site with a green veneer', for natural features have taken hold in this old industrial and mining area. The district also boasts a small experimental housing scheme, but is potentially ripe for development. Bournville Village Trust have argued that their scheme would be a better and more sensitive alternative to a scattering of private developments. To allay the fears of the local defenders of nature, Ove Arup and Partners have been commissioned to undertake an Environmental and Ecological Audit of the area.[188]

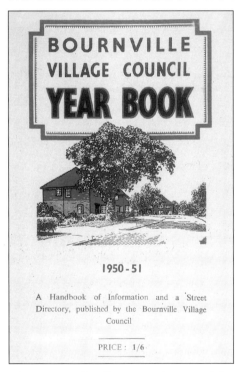

161 *Bournville Village Council Year Book* for 1950-51.

The Trust's proposed scheme ensures that well over half of the total area of the development will remain as open space. In addition, it is their intention to retain as much of the network of lanes and hedgerows as possible. Residential developments and communal and work facilities will be restricted to the poorer land south of Horsehay. Of course, local people in Telford will be allowed to have their say. By the end of 1997, the Lightmoor-based Neighbourhood Initiatives Foundation had begun a series of workshops.[189]

Such a scheme, like the proposal for the original Village, will no doubt have its critics. There is some suspicion about the new venture in Bournville itself. A 1997 Survey confirmed that local residents were still highly satisfied with their homes and surroundings at Bournville, but there was little or no commitment to developments elsewhere.[190] Perhaps they fear that the needs of the original Estate will be lost sight of if the Trust develops its Mark 2 version of Bournville at Lightmoor.

REFERENCES

Abbreviations

BRL	Birmingham Central Reference Library
BT	Bournville Tenants
BVT	Bournville Village Trust
BVT Mins/AR	Bournville Village Trust Manuscript Minute Books (with Reports etc.)
BVT *AR*	Bournville Village Trust [published] Annual Reports and Accounts
BWM	*Bournville Works Magazine*
GCA	Garden City Association
GCTP	*Garden City and Town Planning*
JRIBA	*Journal of the Royal Institute of British Architects*
MHLG	Ministry of Housing and Local Government
MRL	Manchester Central Reference Library
VCH	*Victoria County History*

Introduction

1. G.E. Cherry, *Birmingham: A study in geography, history and planning* (1994), p.236.
2. BVT *AR* (1986).
3. *Ibid.*
4. *Ibid.*
5. BVT *AR* (1993).
6. BVT, *When we build again* (1941).
7. BVT, *Bournville Village Trust 1900-1955* (1955). Shorter recent studies include P. Henslowe, *Ninety Years On* (1985); J. Hillman, *The Bournville Hallmark: Housing people for one hundred years* (1994); P. Broomfield, *A Bournville assortment* (1995)
8. W. Ashworth, *The Genesis of modern British town planning* (1954), pp.132-5; C. and R. Bell, *City Fathers* (1969), pp.268-77; G.E. Cherry, *Urban change and planning* (1972), p.105; C. Chinn, *Homes for people* (1991), pp.23-4; W. Creese, *The search for environment* (1992 edn.), pp.108-24; G. Darley, *Villages of vision* (1978), pp.136-41; A.M. Edwards, *The design of suburbia* (1981), pp.79-82; S.V. Ward, *Planning and urban change* (1994), pp.21-4.
9. See H.E. Meller, *Towns, plans and society in modern Britain* (1997), p.19: 'The social ideas displayed in the design of the village were threefold: A belief in the ideology of the family, the pursuit of the ideal of the community, and a belief in nature, as civilising agents in a harsh world.'
10. M. Durman, 'On the construction of citizenship in Bournville during the period 1895-1914: a critical analysis', unpublished M.A. Dissertation, Middlesex Polytechnic, 1987; J.F. Hoffman, 'Imaging the industrial village: architecture, art and visual culture in the garden community of Bournville, England', Unpublished Ph.D. Dissertation, Yale University, 1993.

11. P. Atkins, 'The architecture of Bournville 1879-1914', in B. Tilson (ed.), *Made in Birmingham, Design and Industry 1889-1989* (1989); J.R. Bryson and P.A. Lowe, 'Bournville: a hundred years of social housing in a model village', in A.J. Garrard and T.R. Slater (eds.), *Managing a conurbation: Birmingham and its region* (1996); D.J. Jeremy, *Capitalists and Christians: Business Leaders and the Churches in Britain 1900-1960* (1990); A. Mayne, *The imagined Slum: Newspaper representation in three cities 1870-1914* (1993).

12. BVT, *Bournville Village Trust 1900-1955* (1955); M. Harrison, 'Bournville 1918-39', *Planning History* vol.17, no.3 (1995); P. Henslowe, *Ninety Years on* (1985); J. Hillman, *The Bournville Hallmark: Housing People for 100 Years* (1994).

13. Archives Department, Birmingham Central Reference Library (BRL) MS 1536. Other useful material is held in the Local Studies department of BRL. The BVT Minute Books and the most recent records are still held by the Trust.

14. A reasonable amount of material relating to the Bournville Estate is held in the Cadbury Archives at the Bournville works. Ken Taylor located some very useful material for me there. A very small amount of material relating to the Estate can be located in the Cadbury Papers held in the Special Collections section of the University of Birmingham Arts Library. (Most of the material in this collection deals with the Cadburys' African links.)

15. P. Broomfield, *op. cit.*; G.L. Haynes, *Milestones of growing up* (1995); *A new home in a model village* (1995); *Old Hay Green Lane* (1995). Denis Carson kindly lent me copies of the books. The author has interviewed over twenty officers of the Trust and Bournville residents.

16. BVT *AR* 1986.

17. *Birmingham Daily Gazette*, 21 September 1901. *See* Chapter Four.

18. BVT Mins/AR 1960. BVT Offices.

19. BVT *AR* 1986.

20. H.E. Meller, *op. cit.*, p.9.

21. G.E. Cherry, *Urban change and planning*, p.84.

Chapter One

1. W.B. Stephens (ed.), *The Victoria History of The County of Warwick Vol.7: The City Of Birmingham* (1964); C. Gill, *History of Birmingham Vol.1: Manor and Borough to 1865* (1952); M.J. Wise (ed.), *Birmingham and its Regional Setting: a scientific survey* (1950); V. Skipp, *A History of Greater Birmingham down to 1830* (1980); *The Making of Victorian Birmingham* (1983); G.E. Cherry, *Birmingham: a study in Geography, History and Planning* (1994); C. Upton, *A History of Birmingham* (1993).

2. Leland, *Itinerary*, cited in *VCH Vol.7*, p.6.

3. Camden, *Britannia*, cited in Skipp, *Greater Birmingham*, p.38.

4. V. Skipp, *Greater Birmingham*, p.46.

5. *Ibid.*, pp.50-2; E. Hopkins, *Birmingham: The First Manufacturing Town in the World* (1989), pp.7-8.

6. Hopkins, *op. cit.*; V. Skipp, *Victorian Birmingham*, pp.54ff.; G.E. Cherry, *Birmingham*, pp.60ff.

7. C. Makepeace, *Manchester as it was* (1972). *See also* G.C. Allen, *The Industrial Development of Birmingham and the Black Country 1860-1927* (1929); V. Skipp, *Victorian Birmingham*, pp.38ff.; *VCH Warwick Vol.7*, pp.125ff.; Cherry, *Birmingham*, pp.60-6.

8. Hopkins, *op. cit.*, p.180.

9. Skipp, *Victorian Birmingham*, pp.150ff.; P.H.J.H. Gosden, *Self-Help: Voluntary Associations in 19th Century Britain* (1973).

10. Skipp, *Greater Birmingham*, pp.74ff.; *VCH Warwick Vol.7* pp.270ff.; Upton, *op. cit.*, pp.78ff.

11. C.W. Chalklin, *The Provincial Towns of Georgian England* (1974), pp.81-9; Skipp, *Greater Birmingham*, pp.69-74; D. Cannadine, *Lords and Landlords* (1980).

12. Allen, *op. cit.*; Skipp, *Victorian Birmingham*, pp.38ff.; *VCH Warwick Vol.7*, pp.125ff.; Cherry, *Birmingham*, pp.60-6.

13. Skipp, *Victorian Birmingham*, p.65.

14. *VCH Warwick Vol.7*, pp.40-1; Cherry, *Birmingham*, pp.62-6.

15. Skipp, *Victorian Birmingham*, pp.56-7;*VCH Warwick Vol.7*, pp.22 and 40; Cherry, *Birmingham*, pp.62-6.

16. *Report by the Board of Trade into Working Class Rents, Housing and Retail Prices* (1908).

17. E.P. Hennock, *Fit and Proper Persons* (1973); Upton, *op. cit.*, pp.150-8; Skipp, *Victorian Birmingham*, pp.153-77.

18. Cannadine, *op. cit.*; R. Granelli, 'Architecture' in A. Crawford (ed.), *By Hammer and by Hand: The Arts and Crafts Movement in Birmingham* (1984), pp.41-60.

19. *VCH Warwick Vol.7*, p.16; Cherry, *Birmingham*, pp.106-7.

20. *BWM* November 1910, pp.404-5.

Chapter Two

1. C.W. Chalklin, *The Provincial Towns of Georgian England* (1974), pp.81-9; S.D. Chapman and J.N. Bartlett, 'The contribution of Building Clubs and Freehold Land Society to working class housing in Birmingham' in S.D. Chapman (ed.), *The History of Working Class Housing* (1971), pp.221-46.

2. *Ibid.*, pp.223-4.

3. *Ibid.*, p.225.

4. Chapman and Bartlett, *op. cit.*, p.226; Skipp, *Greater Birmingham*, pp.71-2.

5. Chapman and Bartlett, *op. cit.*, p.227, quoting *Children's Employment Commission*.

6. *Report by the Board of Trade into Working Class Rents, Housing and Retail Prices* (1908), p.84.

7. Cherry, *Birmingham*, p.43.

8. *Report by the Board of Trade*, p.84.

9. Cherry, *Birmingham*, p.42.

10. Chapman and Bartlett, *op. cit.*, pp.236-37.

11. Skipp, *Victorian Birmingham*, pp.84-5.

12. Chapman and Bartlett, *op. cit.*, pp.242-3.

13. *Ibid.*

14. Hopkins, *op. cit.*, p.122.

15. Skipp, *Victorian Birmingham*, p.139.

16. *Ibid.*, pp.96ff.

17. E. Chadwick, *Report on the Sanitary Condition of the Labouring Population of Great Britain* (1965 edn.), p.89.

18. Chapman and Bartlett, *op. cit.*, p.228.

19. *Ibid.*, pp.229-30.

20. Green and Parton, 'Slums and slum life in Victorian England: London and Birmingham at mid-century' in S.M. Gaskell (ed.), *Slums* (1992), p.42.

21. T.J. Bass, *Down East among the Poorest* (1904); J.C. Walters, *Scenes in Slum-Land* (1901), p.4.

22. *Ibid.*, p.11.

23. A. Mayne, *The Imagined Slum*, pp.86-7; *Report of the Special Inquiry Committee* (1914), p.9.

24. *Daily Post*, 13 October 1914.

25. *Report* (1914), pp.2-6.

26. M. Harrison, 'T.C. Horsfall and The Example of Germany', *Planning Perspectives*, Vol.6 (1991), pp.297-314; *City of Birmingham Housing Committee Reports* (1906); G.E. Cherry, 'Factors in the Origins of Town Planning in Britain: the Example of Birmingham', CURS Working Paper, University of Birmingham (1975), pp.14ff.

27. *Report* (1914), p.17.

28. Cherry, *Birmingham*, pp.66ff.

29. *Report by the Board of Trade* (1908), pp.84-5.

30. *Ibid.*, p.86.

31.   City of Birmingham, *Report of the Special Housing Inquiry Committee* (1914), p.8.

32.   *Report by the Board of Trade* (1908), p.86.

33.   Walters, *Scenes in Slum-Land* (1901), p.4.

34.   See Mayne, *The Imagined Slum* (1993); Chinn, *Homes for people*, p.17.

35.   George Cadbury Jnr., *Town Planning* (1915), p.8.

36.   J. Marsh, *Back to the land* (1982); W.A. Harvey, *The Model Village and its Cottages: Bournville* (1906).

37.   Quoted in W.L. Creese, *The search for environment* (1992 edn.), p.276.

38.   H. Muthesius, *The English House* (1979 edn.).

39.   M.H. Baillie-Scott, *Garden Suburbs, Town Planning and Modern Architecture* 1910), p.83.

40.   *See* Chapter Four. For Unwin *see* M. Miller, 'Raymond Unwin 1863-1940' in G.E. Cherry (ed.), *Pioneers in British Planning* (1981).

41.   *See* J.A. Hudson, *John Ruskin, Social Reformer* (1904), pp.158ff.

42.   Samuel and Mrs. Barnett were involved in the Settlement movement. *See* H. Barnett, *Canon Barnett, his Life, Work and Friends* (1918). *See also* M. Miller and A.S. Gray, *Hampstead Garden Suburb* (1992).

43.   G.R. Searle, *The Quest for National Efficiency* (1971). *See also* the *Report of the Inter-Departmental Committee on Physical Deterioration* (1904).

44.   Gardiner, A.G., *Life of George Cadbury* (1923), p.155; Garden City Association, *The Garden City Conference at Bournville: Report of Proceedings* (1901), p.31.

Chapter Three

1.   Isichei, E., *Victorian Quakers* (1970); D.B. Windsor, *The Quaker Enterprise* (1980). *See also* G. Wagner, *The Chocolate Conscience* (1987); C. Dellheim, 'The Creation of a Company Culture: Cadburys 1861-1931', *The American Historical Review*, Vol.92, no.1 (1987), p.15; D. Jeremy, *Capitalists and Christians* (1990).

2.   Isichei, *op. cit.*, pp.132ff.; Windsor, *op. cit.*, pp.25ff.,etc.

3.   Dellheim, *op. cit.*, p.15; Wagner, *op. cit.*, pp.3-4; I.C. Bradley, *Enlightened Entrepreneurs* (1987).

4.   T.A.B. Corley, 'How Quakers coped with business success: Quaker Industrialists 1860-1914' in D. Jeremy (ed.), *Business and Religion in Britain* (1988).

5.   Isichei, *op. cit.*, xx-xxi; Wagner, *op. cit.*, pp.4ff.

6.   W. Houghton, *The Victorian Frame of Mind* (1957), p.241.

7.   Time and Tide, pp.70ff.; *Unto this Last, Essay 4*, p.77.

8.   Dellheim 'Company Culture', p.14; Jeremy, *op. cit.*, pp.143ff.; pp.414-5.

9.   J.F. Crosfield, *The Cadbury Family*, Vol. 1 (1985), p.90; *see also* A.G. Gardiner, *Life of George Cadbury* (1923), pp.1-11.

10.   Crosfield, *op. cit.*, Vol.1, p.92.

11.   *Ibid.*, p.300.

12.   *Birmingham Daily Mail*, 24 February 1879.

13.   Crosfield, *op. cit.*, Vol.1, pp.94ff.

14.   *Birmingham Daily Mail*, 24 February 1879.

15.   Crosfield, *op. cit.*, Vol. 1, p.311.

16.   *Ibid.*, pp.304-5.

17.   *Chambers Educational Journal*, 30 October 1852.

18.   Crosfield, *op. cit.*, Vol. 1, pp.317-18.

19.   *Ibid.*, p.331.

20.   Gardiner, *op. cit.*, p.18.

21.   *Ibid.*, p.19.

22. Crosfield, *op. cit.*, Vol.1, p.331.

23. *BWM George Cadbury Memorial Issue* (1922), p.20.

24. *Ibid.*

25. Dellheim, *op. cit.*, p.15.

26. Crosfield, *op. cit.*, Vol.1, p.335.

27. I.O. Williams, *The Firm of Cadbury 1831-1931* (1931), pp.15-53; Dellheim, *op. cit.*, p.17; W. Stranz, *George Cadbury* (1973), pp.14-17; *BWM* October 1947, 'The Battle of Bridge Street', pp.179-83; *BWM* November 1947, 'Bridge Street Pioneers', pp.208-12.

28. Williams, *op. cit.*; Gardiner, *op. cit.*; *BWM Memorial Issue*, Stranz, *op. cit.*

29. J.H. Barlow, March 1901, BVT Archive, BRL.

30. W. Ashworth, *The Genesis of Modern British Town Planning* (1954); G. Darley, *Villages of Vision* (1978); W.L. Creese, *The Search for Environment* (1992 edn.); C. and R. Bell, *City Fathers* (1972 edn.).

31. *VCH Warwick Vol.7* (1964), p.16 and pp.132-33.

32. Booklets about the firm of Cadbury Brothers with this title have been produced in many languages over the years.

33. *Midland Echo*, January 1884.

34. Gardiner, *op. cit.*, p.36.

35. *Midland Echo*, January 1884.

36. Dellheim, *op. cit.*; Jeremy, *op. cit.*

37. *BWM* January 1933, 'Bournville in the '90s' [E. Cadbury].

38. *Midland Echo*, January 1884.

39. *BWM Memorial Issue* (1922), p.23.

40. Williams, *op. cit.*, pp.68-9, p.123.

41. *VCH Warwick Vol.7* (1964), p.16.

42. Gardiner, *op. cit.*, p.299 and p.306.

43. *Ibid.*, p.317.

44. *Ibid.*, p.299.

45. *Ibid.*, Stranz, *op. cit.*, Dellheim, *op. cit.*, p.14.

46. J.F. Crosfield, *The Cadbury Family*, Vol.2 (1985), p.458.

47. Gardiner, *op. cit.*, p.314.

48. Crosfield, *op. cit.*, Vols. 1 and 2 ; R. Scott, *Elizabeth Cadbury 1858-1951* (1955); W. Marks and C. Cadbury, *George Cadbury Junior 1878-1954* (n.d.), p.54.

49. Gardiner, *op. cit.*, p.307.

50. *BWM Memorial Issue* (1922), p.30.

51. Isichei, *op. cit.*, pp.261-74; Gardiner, *op. cit.*, pp.39-58; Stranz, *op. cit.*, pp.6-9; *BWM Memorial Issue* (1922), pp.26-8; E. Cadbury, 'Adult Schools' in J.H. Muirhead (ed.), *Birmingham Institutions* (1911), pp.202-31.

52. Gardiner, *op. cit.*, p.55; *BWM Memorial Issue* (1922), p.28.

53. Stranz, *op. cit.*, pp.7-9.

54. Crosfield, *op. cit.*, Vol.2, p.437.

55. *BWM Memorial Issue* (1922), p.28.

56. Crosfield, *op. cit.*, Vol.2, p.437; Isichei, *op. cit.*, pp.265-7, E. Cadbury, *op. cit.*, p.231.

57. Gardiner, *op. cit.*, p.47.

58. Isichei, *op. cit.*, p.266; G.C.A., *The Garden City Conference at Bournville: Report of Proceedings* (1901), p.31.

59. Gardiner, *op. cit.*, p.57.

60. *Ibid.*, p.470.

61. *Ibid.*, pp.53-4.

62.   E. Cadbury, *op. cit.*, p.212.

63.   Isichei, *op. cit.*, p.267.

64.   E. Cadbury, *op. cit.*, p.212.

65.   *Ibid.*, p.215.

66.   Quoted in Dellheim,'Utopia Limited: Bournville and Port Sunlight' in D. Fraser (ed.), *Cities, Class and Communication* (1990), p.48; Corley, *op. cit.*, p.20.

67.   Gardiner, *op. cit.*, p.48; E. Cadbury, *op. cit.*, p.215.

68.   See J. Marsh, *Back to the land* (1982).

69.   Quoted in D. Jeremy, *op. cit.*, p.9; G.C.A. (1901), *op. cit.*, p.31.

70.   See V. Skipp, *The Making of Victorian Birmingham* (1983); E.P. Hennock, *Fit and proper persons* (1973).

71.   Crosfield, *op. cit.*, Vol.2, p.475.

72.   *BWM Memorial Issue* (1922), p.29.

73.   Crosfield, *op. cit.*, Vol.2, p.475.

Chapter Four

1.   V. Skipp, *The Making of Victorian Birmingham* (1983), pp.153ff.; E.P. Hennock, *Fit and Proper Persons* (1973).

2.   *Birmingham Daily Mail*, 21 September 1901.

3.   *BWM* November 1910, p.404.

4.   G. Cadbury to T.C.Horsfall, 24 June 1901, Horsfall Papers, MPL Archives.

5.   Garden City Association, *Garden City Conference at Bournville: Report of Proceedings* (1901), p.54. *See* G.E. Searle, *The Quest for National Efficiency* (1971).

6.   E. Howard, *A Peaceful Path to Real Reform* (1898).

7.   G. Cadbury to T.C. Horsfall, 24 June 1901, Horsfall Papers, MPL Archives.

8.   BVT, *Deed of Foundation* (1900).

9.   W.A. Harvey, *The Model Village and its Cottages: Bournville* (1906), p.2.

10.   *Ibid.*

11.   *BWM* November 1910, p.405.

12.   P. Atkins, 'The architecture of Bournville 1879-1914' in B. Tilson (ed.), *Made in Birmingham* (1989). *See also* Keene, 'Cadbury Housing at Bournville 1879', *Industrial Archaeology* Vol.13, No.1 (Spring 1987).

13.   BVT, *Bournville Village Trust 1900-1955* (1955), p.63. *BWM* also carries details of the purchases.

14.   W. Ashworth, *The Genesis of Modern British Town Planning* (1954), pp.118ff.; C. and R. Bell, *City Fathers* (1972 edn.), pp.237ff.; W.L. Creese, *The Search for Environment* (1992 edn.); G. Darley, *Villages of Vision* (1975), pp.122ff.

15.   D. Cannadine, *Lords and Landlords* (1980).

16.   Creese, *op. cit.*, pp.87-107; M. Girouard, *Sweetness and Light* (1977), pp.160-76; S. Muthesius, *The English House* (1987 edn.), p.31 sees Bedford Park as 'the starting point of the smaller modern house'.

17.   E. Hubbard and M. Shippobottom, *A Guide to Port Sunlight* (1989).

18.   BVT Archives BRL MS 1536.

19.   D. Hardy, *Alternative Communities in 19th Century England* (1979), pp.102-5.

20.   *BWM* November 1934, p.356.

21.   R. Scott, *Elizabeth Cadbury 1858-1951* (1955), p.75.

22.   BVT Archive BRL MS 1536.

23.   *See* original plan in BVT Archive BRL MS 1536.

24.   'Bournville Building Estate': copy in BVT Archives BRL.

25.   Chapman and Bartlett, *op. cit. See* Chapter Two.

26. 'Bournville Building Estate': copy in BVT Archives BRL; A.G. Gardiner, *Life of George Cadbury* (1923), p.15.

27. *See* P. Bailey, *Leisure and Class in Victorian England* (1978); H.E Meller, *Leisure and the Changing City* (1976); J.M. Golby and A.W. Purdue, *The Civilisation of the Crowd* (1984).

28. 'Bournville Building Estate'.

29. Signatures on plans in BVT Archive BRL MS 1536.

30. *BWM* (March 1951), pp.83-4; *JRIBA* (April 1951), pp.247-8.

31. School of Art Archive. I am indebted to Professor John Swift, Department of Art, University of Central England for allowing me to consult these records.

32. *The Builder* Vol.180, 16 February 1951; *BWM* (March 1951), pp.83-4; JRIBA (April 1951), pp.247-8.

33. Muthesius, *op. cit.*; Harvey, *op. cit.*, p.6.

34. *JRIBA* (April 1951), p.247.

35. Harvey, *op. cit.*, p.6.

36. *JRIBA* (April 1951), p.247; *BWM* (March 1951), p.83.

37. L. Weaver, *The 'Country Life' Book of Cottages* (1919 edn.), p.20.

38. The development of the Estate can be followed by consulting the Kings Norton and Northfield building registers and the site plans in BRL Archives.

39. BVT Mins/AR April 1901.

40. *See* n.8.

41. BVT Mins 1901-2: extracts by F.R. Barlow in BVT Mins/AR 1951.

42. Deed of Foundation pp.1-2.

43. *Ibid.*, p.9.

44. *Ibid.*, p.2.

45. *Ibid.*, p.3; M. Cruickshank, *Church and State in English Education* (1963); J. Murphy, *Church, State and Schools in Britain* (1971).

46. *Deed of Foundation*, p.8; Garden City Association (1901), *op. cit.*, p.11.

47. *Bournville Village Trust 1900-1955*, p.14; M. Miller, *Letchworth: The First Garden City* (1989), pp.24-5.

48. BVT Mins/AR April 1902.

49. G.B. Meakin, *Model Factories and Villages: Ideal Conditions of Labour and Housing* (1905).

50. BVT Mins/AR 'Secretary's Report' 30 September 1911.

51. BVT Mins/AR 31 December 1911.

52. BVT Mins/AR 1951; Notes and extracts by F.R. Barlow from 1901-2.

53. BVT Mins/AR 'Annual Report' 1901. *See also* Bournville Village Trust (1901) [Handbook by J.R. Barlow].

54. BVT Mins/AR 'Secretary's Report' 30 September 1908.

55. BVT Mins/AR 4 September 1902.

56. BVT Mins/AR 'Secretary's Report' August 1902.

57. BVT Mins/AR 'Annual Report' 1901.

58. BVT Mins/AR 'Annual Report' 1901; Garden City Association (1901), *op. cit.*, p.35.

59. Creese, *op. cit.*, pp.87-107; Girouard, *op. cit.*, pp.160-76.

60. *See* plans in BVT Archive BRL MS 1536.

61. *See* Harvey, *op. cit.*, plates 1, 31 and 33.

62. *Ibid.*, p.59.

63. *Oxford Chronicle*, 28 November 1902

64. Creese, *op. cit.*, p.99, Fig. 37.

65. *See* the Cottage at Bishop's Itchington, near Warwick, 1888, illustrated in *British Architect*, Vol.30 (1888), p.407 and Perrycroft, Colwall, near Malvern, 1894, illustrated in *Builder's Journal and Architectural Record and British*

Architect, Vol.42 (1894), p.5. *See* J. Brandon-Jones *et al.*, *C.F.A. Voysey: architect and designer 1857-1941* (1978) London, p.38 and p.43.

66.   *See* A. Saint, *Richard Norman Shaw* (1976), p.24ff.

67.   *See* Muthesius, London; P. Davey, *Arts and Crafts Architecture* (1974).

68.   *See* plans in BVT Archive BRL MS 1536.

69.   J.H. Whitehouse, 'Bournville: A study in housing reform', *The Studio* Vol.24 (1902), p.168.

70.   J.A. Dale, J.A., 'Bournville', *Economic Review* (January 1907), p.26.

71.   Harvey, *op. cit.*

72.   cf. W.L. George, *Labour and Housing at Port Sunlight* (1909); Hubbard and Shippobottom, *op. cit.*

73.   Harvey, *op. cit.*, p.6.

74.   BVT Mins/AR 'Building Department Report' 9 October 1903; Harvey, *op. cit.*, p.21.

75.   *Ibid.*, p.20.

76.   *Ibid.*, p.21.

77.   *Ibid.*, p.17.

78.   *See* C. Chinn, *Homes for people* (1991), p.37.

79.   Harvey, *op. cit.*, p.5.

80.   Garden City Association, *Garden City Conference at Bournville: Report of Proceedings* (1901), p.71.

81.   BVT Mins/AR 'Secretary's Report' 31 December 1903.

82.   BVT Mins/AR 1904.

83.   BVT Mins/AR 'Architects Department Report' 25 March 1909.

84.   BVT Mins/AR 'Quarterly Report' 30 September 1909.

85.   BVT Mins/AR 'Architects Department Report' 29 September 1910.

86.   BVT, Typical Plans (1911).

87.   Harvey, *op. cit.*, p.6.

88.   *Ibid.*, p.31.

89.   M.G. Day, 'The contribution of Sir Raymond Unwin and R. Barry Parker' in A. Sutcliffe (ed.), *British Town Planning: the formative years* (1981).

90.   J.H. Barlow, 'The development of new areas on town planning lines', *Proceedings of the National Advisory Town Planning Committee* (1913).

91.   *See*: *Typical Plans*.

92.   BVT Mins/AR 'Secretary's Report' 30 September 1903.

93.   Harvey, *op. cit.*, p.17.

94.   *The Gardener*, quoted in BVT Mins/AR 'Secretary's Report' 30 September 1903.

95.   Harvey, *op. cit.*, pp.9-10.

96.   *Ibid.*; BVT Mins/AR 'Secretary's Report' 30 September 1903.

97.   *Ibid.*; Harvey, *op. cit.*, p.10. *See* review of Harvey's book in St George Vol.9 (April 1906), pp.136-8.

98.   Dale, *op. cit.*, p.17.

99.   Barlow, *op. cit.*

100. W. Miller, *What England Can Teach Us About Gardening* (1913), p.139. See Creese, *op. cit.*, p.118.

101. Dale, *op. cit.*, p.17; Harvey, *op. cit.*, p.68.

102. BVT Mins/AR 'Garden Department Report' 30 September 1903.

103. Dale, *op. cit.*, p.24.

104. BVT Mins/AR 'Garden Department Report' 30 September 1903.

105. *BWM* November 1904, pp.3-5.

106. M.A. Broomfield, *A Bournville Assortment* (1995), pp.50-1.

107. G.L. Haynes, *A New Home in a Model Village* (1995), p.51.

108. *BWM* (1902).

109. N. Pevsner and A. Wedgwood, *Warwickshire* (1966), pp.158-9; Broomfield, *op. cit.*, pp.17-19.

110. *BWM* November 1951 [Cover photograph].

111. *See* plans in BVT Archive BRL MS 1536.

112. *Report of Proceedings*, pp.61-8; Miller, *Letchworth*, pp.74-5.

113. Broomfield, *op. cit.*, pp.64-6.

114. *Ibid.*, pp.66-9; Scott, *op. cit.*, pp.114-5.

115. Dale, *op. cit.*, p.15; BVT, *Sixty Years of Planning: The Bournville Experience* (n.d.) p.39: ref. 'Cohesion and orderliness'.

116. Weoley Hill Village Council, *Weoley Hill Village* (1927 and 1932); BVT, *Bournville Village Trust 1900-1955* (1955), pp.119-21.

117. *Labour Co-partnership*, July 1906, p.110. For Bournville Tenants *see*, *Bournville Tenants Limited* [Prospectus] (n.d. *c.*1906); *BWM* (July 1906), p.314; *BWM* (December 1906), pp.42-3; Bournville Tenants, *Report and Accounts* (1907, 1909 and 1913); Bournville Tenants Limited (*c.*1909) [Brochure] Plans and Photographs in BRL Archives MS 1536.

118. *See* plans in BVT Archive BRL MS 1536.

119. *Birmingham Post*, 1 October 1913.

120. *Bournville Tenants Limited* [Prospectus].

121. *Birmingham Post*, 10 July 1910.

122. BVT Mins/AR 'Secretary's Report' 30 September 1911.

123. *Ibid.*

124. *Ibid.*

125. BVT Mins/AR 'Secretary's Report' 31 December 1911.

126. BVT Mins/AR 31 December 1912.

127. BVT Mins/AR 13 January 1914; 'Secretary's Report' 30 September 1913.

128. BVT Mins/AR 1906; Labour Co-partnership (July 1906), p.110; *BWM* (December 1913), p.402; *Birmingham Post* 31 October 1913.

129. *Birmingham News*, 8 November 1913.

130. *Birmingham News*, 8 November 1913; *GCTP* (July 1925), p.163; M. Miller and A.S. Gray, *Hampstead Garden Suburb* (1992), pp.47ff.

131. 'Suggested Rules of Health' reprinted in J. Hillman, *The Bournville Hallmark* (1995).

132. A.G. Gardiner, *Life of George Cadbury* (1923), pp.154-5.

133. *See* streetscapes among the plans in BVT Archive BRL MS 1536.

134. Dale, *op. cit.*, p.17.

135. BVT Mins/AR 1909.

136. City of Birmingham, *Report of the Special Housing Inquiry Committee* (1914), p.8.

137. BVT Mins/AR 1902; cf. Dale, *op. cit.*, p.20.

138. *Manchester Evening News*, 4 March 1903.

139. *See* list in BVT Archives; cf. *Report of Proceedings*, p.32; Dale, *op. cit.*, p.17.

140. BVT Mins/AR 'Secretary's Report' May 1901.

141. BVT Mins/AR 'Secretary's Report' 31 March 1904; BVT Mins/AR 'Secretary's Report' August 1902.

142. Dale, *op. cit.*, p.20.

143. BVT Mins/AR 'Secretary's Report' 31 December 1911.

144. *Birmingham Daily Mail*, 25 February 1902.

145. Report of Proceedings, p.33.

146. *Municipal Reformer*, June 1901; for Adams *see* M. Simpson, *Thomas Adams and the Modern Planning Movement* (1985).

147. BVT Mins/AR 'Secretary's Report' September 1908.

148. S. Pollard, *The Genesis of Modern Management* (1968), pp.231-44.

149. C. Dellheim, 'Utopia Limited: Bournville and Port Sunlight' in D. Fraser (ed.), *Cities, Class and Communication* (1990), p.45.

150. D. Jeremy, *Capitalists and Christians* (1990), pp.1-4. *See also* D. Jeremy, 'The Enlightened paternalist in Action: William Hesketh Lever at Port Sunlight before 1914', *Business History*.

151. Jeremy, *Christians and Capitalists*, p.143.

152. Whitehouse, *op. cit.*, p.150.

153. 'The Village of Bournville' Ms. May 1904 in BVT Archives BRL.

154. Dale, *op. cit.*, p.18.

155. This is still quite common. The mother of a long-serving senior member of the Trust staff continued to believe that he worked for Cadbury Brothers. Interview with J. Dakin. See BVT Mins/AR 1948.

156. Dale, *op. cit.*, p.21.

157. *Ibid.*

158. BVT Mins/AR 'Quarterly Report' 31 March 1903.

159. 'The Village of Bournville', p.12.

160. BVT Mins/AR 1901.

161. *St George* Vol.10 (1907), pp.141-2. Founders Day was also celebrated in this manner. *See* P. Wright, *On living in an old country* (1985) p.253.

162. BVT Mins/AR 1901-2 recorded by F.R. Barlow, April 1951.

163. *Ibid.*

164. *Birmingham News*, 28 April 1902.

165. Dale, *op. cit.*, p.19.

166. *Ibid.*, p.24.

167. BVT Mins/AR 17 October 1901.

168. BVT Mins/AR 1901-2 recorded by F.R. Barlow April 1951.

169. BVT Mins/AR 'Garden Department Report' 31 December 1903.

170. 'The Village of Bournville' May 1904, p.11.

171. Bournville Village Council, Year Book (1914).

172. Ibid.; 'The Village of Bournville' May 1904, p.12.

173. Dale, *op. cit.*, p.21.

174. 'The Village of Bournville' May 1904, p.12a.

175. Bournville Village Tenants Village Council, Constitution (1909).

176. *Birmingham Post*, 10 July 1909.

177. *Birmingham Post*, 1 October 1913.

178. *Mount Morris Index* (1902)

179. *Manchester Evening Chronicle*, 26 September 1906.

180. Harvey, *op. cit.*

181. BVT, *Typical Plans* (1911).

182. Whitehouse, *op. cit.*; Dale, *op. cit.*; P. Abercrombie, 'Modern Town Planning in England: A Comparative Review of 'Garden City' Schemes in England', *Town Planning Review* Vol.1 (1910-11), pp.18-38 and 111-28.

183. BVT Mins/AR 'Quarterly Report' 1904

184. Book of cuttings in Cadbury Archives.

185. *BWM* December 1911 quotes a Russian article from 'Golos Moskoy' on 'the homely and artistic' Bournville with its

'invariably sympathetic and vividly variegated English architecture'. Similar approving comments from a correspondent in Austria were noted.

186. 'Notes for Guides' in BVT Archive BRL.

187. BVT Mins/AR 'Secretary's Report' August 1902.

188. BVT Mins/AR 'Architects Department Report' 30 June 1911.

189. *Brotherhood* (1901). National Housing Reform Council, *Conference on the Proper Planning of New Housing Areas* (1906); *Sporting Gazette* 30 June 1906, *Report of the Co-operative Congress: Visit to Bournville* (1906).

190. R. Fishman, *Urban Utopias in the 20th Century* (1977), p.61.

191. L.E. Waddilove, *One Man's Vision: The Story of the Joseph Rowntree Village Trust* (1954), pp.3ff.

192. *Ibid.* See Abercrombie, *op. cit.*, pp.37-9.

193. Waddilove, *op. cit.*, pp.4-11; Day, *op. cit.*, pp.168-9.

194. *Ibid.*, p.170.

151. *Ibid.*, p.169.

196. *Ibid.*, p.172.

197. Ref. M. Harrison, 'Housing and town planning in Manchester before 1914' in A. Sutcliffe (ed.), *British Town Planning: the Formative Years* (1981), p.118.

198. Harvey, *op. cit. See* W.L. Creese (ed.), *The Legacy of Raymond Unwin* (1967).

199. R. Unwin, *Town Planning in Practice* (1909).

200. Abercrombie, *op. cit.*, pp.24-5 and 119-20. *See* Harborne Tenants Limited, *Reports and Accounts* (1907-13), BRL Local History Library.

201. *Ibid.*, pp.24-6; Harrison, *op. cit.* (1981), pp.123-5; The Co-partnership Tenants' Housing Council, *Garden Suburbs, Villages and Homes: All about Co-partnership Houses* (n.d.)

202. *Manchester City News* 29 March 1902. *See also, St George* Vol.9 (April 1906), p.138: 'The next step in social reform is to compel municipal authorities to care for the beautiful and healthy development of their suburbs.'

203. T.R. Marr, *Housing Conditions in Manchester and Salford* (1904).

204. S.M. Gaskell, '"The suburb salubrious": town planning in practice', in A. Sutcliffe (ed.), *British Town Planning: the Formative Years* (1981), pp.39-40; Abercrombie, *op. cit.*, p.20.

205. *Birmingham Daily Mail*, 21 September 1901.

206. Miller, *Letchworth*, pp.24-7.

207. E. Cadbury, 'Adult Schools' in J.H. Muirhead (ed.), *Birmingham Institutions* (1911), p.214.

208. Harvey, *op. cit.*, p.3; M. Miller and A.S. Gray, *Hampstead Garden Suburb* (1992), pp.37ff.; Abercrombie, *op. cit.*, pp.30-3.

209. *Church Times*, 8 August 1902.

210. *Ibid.*; for Woodlands and Hull *see* Abercrombie, *op. cit.*, pp.110-12 and 114-15.

211. *Dewsbury Reporter*, 8 September 1902.

212. *Church Times*, 8 August 1902.

213. *Our Day* Vol.21 (April 1902); *The Clarion*, 11 November 1909.

214. *BWM* November 1913

215. Muthesius, *op. cit.*, p.211.

216. *BWM* August 1909, pp.319-20.

217. *BWM* December 1911, p.381.

218. *Ibid.*

219. *BWM* September 1911.

220. BVT Mins/AR 30 September 1913; Letter from Mrs Horace Groser, Barnet, 'A small "Bournville" in Düsseldorf', October 1913.

221. *BWM* December 1911, p.382.

222. Dale, *op. cit.*, p.27.

223. Harvey, *op. cit.*, p.15.

224. *BWM* (November 1910), pp.404-5.

225. Abercrombie, *op. cit.*, p.18.

226. Gardiner, *op. cit.*, p.158.

227. E.G. Culpin, *The Garden City Movement up-to-date* (1913), p.12.

228. Quoted in G.E. Cherry, 'Factors in the Origins of Town Planning in Britain: The Example of Birmingham 1900-14', CURS Working Paper No.36, University of Birmingham (1975), pp.9-10.

229. J.S. Nettlefold, *Practical Town Planning* (1914).

230. G. Cadbury Jnr., *Town Planning* (1915), p.x. *See also* G. Cadbury, Jnr., 'Town Planning', *The British Friend* (December 1912).

231. M. Swenarton, *Homes fit for Heroes* (1981); Pepper and Swenarton, 'Home front: Garden Suburbs for Munitions Workers', *Architectural Review*, pp.364-76.

232. Day, *op. cit.*, pp.189-93; Swenarton, *op. cit.*, pp.136-61.

Chapter Five

1. M.J. Daunton (ed.), *Councillors and Tenants* (1984), p.5.

2. *Ibid.*

3. *Ibid.*; M. Swenarton, *Homes fit for Heroes* (1981); J. Burnett, *A Social History of Housing 1815-1970* (1978); S. Pepper and M. Swenarton, 'Home Front: Garden Suburbs for Munitions Workers 1915-18', *Architectural Review*, Vol.CLXIII, No. 976, June 1978, pp.366-76; C.H. Whittaker *et al.*, *Housing Problems in War and Peace* (1918).

4. Quoted in B.B. Gilbert, *British Social Policy 1914-39* (1970), p.15.

5. Swenarton, *op. cit.*, pp.81-7.

6. R. Reiss, *The Home I Want* (1918).

7. Burnett, *op. cit.*, pp.218-21; Swenarton, *op. cit.*, pp.88-111; M. Miller, 'Raymond Unwin 1863-1940' in G.E. Cherry (ed.), *Pioneers in British Planning* (1981), pp.88-91; M.G. Day, 'The contribution of Sir Raymond Unwin (1863-1940) and R. Barry Parker (1867-1947) to the development of site planning theory and practice' in A. Sutcliffe (ed.), *British Town Planning: the Formative Years* (1981), pp.189-93.

8. Quoted in Burnett, *op. cit.*, p.221; cf. W.A. Harvey, *The Model Village and its Cottages* (1906), pp.17-18.

9. *Ibid.*, p.6.

10. Burnett, *op. cit.*, p.217; Swenarton, *op. cit.*, pp.112-13; Daunton (ed.), *op. cit.*, pp.9-11.

11. Daunton (ed.), *op. cit.*, p.22; Burnett, *op. cit.*, pp.227-43.

12. H.W. Richardson and D.H. Aldcroft, *Building in the British Economy between the Wars* (1968), p.322, claims that 4,359,000 houses were built between 1920-38 compared with 5,418,000 between 1947-65.

13. Burnett, *op. cit.*, pp.242-43.

14. *Ibid.*, p.257.

15. P. Oliver, I. Davis and I. Bentley, *Dunroamin: The Suburban Semi and its Enemies* (1981); J.M. Richards, *Castles on the Ground: The Anatomy of Suburbia* (1973 edn.). For a recent study of the move to suburban estates and expanded towns *see* M. Clapson, *Invincible green suburbs, brave new towns* (1998).

16. Burnett, *op. cit.*, pp.258-61; J.J. Stevenson, *Social History of Britain between the Wars* (1984), p.467.

17. Cherry, *Birmingham*, p.110.

18. *Ibid.*, pp.110-24; H.J. Manzoni, *The Production of 50,000 Municipal Houses* (1939); C. Chinn, *Homes for People: 100 Years of Council Housing in Birmingham* (1991), pp.31-74.

19. *See* Manzoni, *op. cit.*, and Chinn, *op. cit.*, for plans.

20. Chinn, *op. cit.*, pp.57-8; Common Good Trust, *New Birmingham* (n.d.).

21. *New Birmingham*, p.3.

22. BVT, *When we build again* (1941), pp.57-8.

23. *New Birmingham*, p.3.

24. Cherry, *Birmingham*, p.116.

25. Cherry, *Birmingham*, pp.116ff.

26. Cherry, *Birmingham*, p.117.

27. *When we build again*, pp.32-3.

28. Cherry, *Birmingham*, pp.117-8; City Development Department, *Developing Birmingham 1889-1989* (1989), pp.52ff.

29. *See* Cherry, *Birmingham*, pp.125ff.; Barbara Smith, in *VCH Warwick Vol.7*, pp.141ff.

30. Cherry, *Birmingham*, pp.117-8; *Developing Birmingham*, pp.54-8; C.M.H. Carr and J.W.R. Whitehand, 'Birmingham's inter-war suburbs: origins, development and change', in A.J. Garrard and T.R. Slater (eds.), *Managing a Conurbation: Birmingham and its Region* (1996).

31. *Developing Birmingham*, p.54; *Bournville Village Trust* 1900-1955, pp.105-12.

32. *BWM Memorial Issue* (1922), p.30.

33. BVT Mins/AR 'Secretary's Report' 29 September 1924.

34. 'Foreword' in BVT, *Landscape and Housing Development* (1949), p.1.

35. BVT Mins/AR 8 April 1919.

36. BVT Mins/AR 17 September 1929.

37. BVT Mins/AR.

38. BVT Mins/AR 1901-23, Secretary's Report 31 December 1910 (BRL).

39. BVT, *Bournville Housing* (1928), p.17; BVT Mins/AR, 'Quarterly Report' July 1923; GCTP, July 1925, p.156.

40. K. Skilleter, 'The role of public utility societies in early British town planning and housing reform, 1901-36', *Planning Perspectives* 8 (1993), pp.125-65.

41. *GCTP*, July 1925, p.156.

42. *Ibid.*, p.160; Bournville Housing (1928), p.6 and pp.18-9.

43. *See* Chapter Four.

44. BVT, *Bournville Housing* (1922); Weoley Hill Ltd., *Good Houses* (1922).

45. *GCTP* (July 1925), p.156.

46. BVT, *Bournville Housing*, p.21.

47. BVT, *Bournville Village Trust 1900-1955* (1955), p.25; BVT Mins/AR 'Annual Report' 1913, Secretary's Report 31 March 1913 and 31 March 1914; *BWM* (December 1913), pp.402ff.

48. *Bournville Housing* (1922), p.23; *Good Houses* (1922), p.5.

49. *Good Houses*, pp.21-2.

50. *Bournville Housing* (1928), p.24; BVT, *An Account of its Planning and Housing Schemes in Suburban and Rural Areas* (1938), pp.23-5.

51. P. Broomfield, *A Bournville Assortment* (1995), p.69.

52. BVT, *Bournville Housing* (1922), p.33.

53. *Bournville Village Trust 1900-1955*, p.25; *Bournville Housing* (1928), p.20 and 26; *GCTP* (July 1925), pp.160-3; *Woodlands Housing Society Limited* (n.d.); BVT Mins/AR 'Report on the role of the BVT', 29 September 1924.

54. *Bournville Housing* (1922), p.33.

55. BVT Mins/AR 'Annual Report' 1921.

56. *Bournville Housing* (1928), p.37.

57. BVT Mins/AR 'Annual Report' 1918.

58. BVT Mins/AR 'Annual Reports' for 1918 and 1919; Cadbury Brothers, *Experimental Houses* (1920). *See* BVT Archive at BRL (MS.1536): boxes 2 and 16 contain reports and cuttings on this experimental scheme. Further reports in BWM. *Bournville Housing* (1928), p.45 notes that 'the history of Bournville is largely a record of experimental work of this kind'.

59. Cadbury Brothers, *Experimental Housing* (1922); *BWM* May 1920.

60. Garden City Association, *The Book of the Cheap Cottage Exhibition* (1905). *See also* M. Miller, *Letchworth: The First Garden City* (1989), pp.61-8.

61. L. Weaver, *The 'Country Life' Book of Cottages* (1919 edn.), pp.39ff.

62. *Architects Journal*, 31 December 1919.

63. *Bournville Village Trust 1900-1955*, p.103; BVT, *Bournville Housing* (1928), p.45.

64. BVT Mins/AR 'Manager's Quarterly Report' September 1916. *See also* 'Manager's Quarterly Report' 31 December 1923.

65. BVT Mins/AR 'Manager's Quarterly Report' 29 September 1924.

66. *Bournville Housing* (1928), pp.45-6.

67. *Ibid.*, pp.46-8; BVT Mins/AR notes 'great interest'. *See* Open University, *British Design* ('The Electric House') A 305, Unit 20 (1975).

68. *Design for Today* (May 1934), pp.177-83; *BWM* (May 1934) pp.146-8.

69. *Ibid.*

70. *Good Houses*, p.7.

71. BVT Mins/AR 'Manager's Report' 30 September 1916; BVT Mins/AR 29 September 1924.

72. BVT Mins/AR 29 September 1924; *GCTP* (July 1925), p.161.

73. *GCTP* (July 1925), pp.160-1; *Bournville Housing* (1928), p.48.

74. *Good Houses*; *Bournville Housing*, p.48.

75. *Bournville Village Trust 1900-1955*, p.50.

76. *The Ideal Home* (May 1930); *Good Houses*; *Bournville Village Trust 1900-1955*, p.50.

77. J.M. Richards, *Castles on the Ground* (1973 edn.), p.15.

78. BVT, *Landscape and Housing Development* (1949), p.31; *GCTP* (July 1925), pp.166-7; *Bournville Village Trust 1900-1955*, pp.95-8.

79. *Ibid.*, p.71.

80. *Landscape and Housing Development*, pp.9-10.

81. *Ibid.*, pp.6ff.; *Bournville Housing*, p.48.

82. *GCTP* (July 1925), pp.160-2.

83. *Ibid.*

84. *Bournville Village Trust 1900-1955*, pp.77-8 and p.101; *Landscape and Housing Development*, p.11.

85. *BWM* January 1932, pp.1-6.

86. *Ibid.*

87. *GCTP* (July 1925), p.166.

88. E. Cadbury, 'Factors in Town Planning', DIA 1944.

89. *GCTP* (July 1925), pp.166-8.

90. *Bournville Village Trust 1900-1955*, p.89.

91. *See* Bournville Village Council, *Year Books* 1920, 1925, 1929, 1935, 1941.

92. Broomfield, *op. cit.*, p.168.

93. BVT Mins/AR 'Secretary's Quarterly Report' 31 December 1923.

94. Broomfield, *op. cit.*, 169-70.

95. *GCTP* (July 1925), pp.160-2.

96. BVT Mins/AR 'Annual Report' 1922.

97.   *The News* 29 November 1927; Weoley Hill Village Council, *Weoley Hill Estate* (1927). This, and other material relating to Weoley Hill, was kindly lent to me by John Clarke.

98.   Weoley Hill Village Council, *Weoley Hill Village* (1932), p.5.

99.   *BWM* April 1928, p.119.

100. Broomfield, *op. cit.*, pp.172-3.

101. Interview with John Bridgeman.

102. *BWM* January 1954, pp.15-17.

103. *Ibid.*, p.15.

104. *BWM* June 1928; *BWM* January 1932; Mass Observation, *op. cit.*; BVT Mins/AR 21 November 1944.

105. *GCTP* (July 1925), p.167.

106. *BWM* August 1937, pp.244ff.

107. Haynes, *op. cit.*, p.68.

108. Interview with Les Pankhurst.

109. *BWM Memorial Issue* (1922); Weoley Hill Village Council, *Weoley Hill Village* (1936), p.25.

110. See Crosfield, *op. cit.*, Vol.21, pp.375ff.

111. *BWM* December 1913 and May 1915 p.164: 'the range of classes to whom the new scheme will appeal is a large one'.

112. BVT Mins/AR 'Bournville Works Housing Society Ltd.' September 1942.

113. *Bournville Village Trust 1900-1955*, p.79.

114. *BWM Souvenir Number: Royal Visits to Bournville 1919-1929-1939* (1939).

115. Cadbury Brothers Limited, *Town Planning Institute Visit to Bournville* (1934).

116. *Bournville Housing* (1928), p.6.

117. J.B. Priestley, *English Journey* (1977 edn.), pp.90-1.

118. Mass Observation, *People's Homes* (1943), pp.30-2. *See also* W. Sarkissian and W. Heine, *Social Mix: The Bournville Experiment* (1978).

119. BVT Mins/AR 'Report of Meeting with Housewives' 21 November 1944; 'Quarterly Report' 18 July 1944.

120. *People's Homes*, p.31.

121. BVT Mins/AR 'The Work of the Architects' Department' 9 December 1942.

122. BVT, *When We Build Again* (1941); *Bournville Village Trust 1900-1955*, pp.103-4.

Chapter Six

1.   BVT, *When we build again* (1941); *Picture Post* 4 January 1941 'A Plan for Britain'; G. Boumphrey, *Town and Country Tomorrow* (1940); T. Sharp, *Town Planning* (1940); E. Simon, *Rebuilding Britain—A Twenty Year Plan* (1945).

2.   J.B. Cullingworth, *Environmental Planning 1939-1947, Vol.1, Reconstruction and Land Use Planning 1939-1947* (1975); *Environmental Planning, Vol.3, New Towns Policy* (1979); P. Hall, *et al.*, *The Containment of Urban England, Vol.2, The Planning System: Objectives, Operations, Impacts*, (1973); G.E. Cherry, *Cities and Plans* (1988), pp.136ff.; S.V. Ward, *Planning and Urban Change* (1994), pp.86ff.; H. Meller, *Towns, plans and society in modern Britain* (1997), Ch.5.

3.   BVT Mins/AR 15 February 1949

4.   P. Jenkins, 'Bevan's fight with the B.M.A.', in M. Sissons and P. French, *Age of Austerity* (1963), p.241; P. Addison, *Now the War is over* (1985), Ch.3.

5.   H. Meller, *Towns, plans and society in modern Britain* (1997), p.78.

6.   *Ibid.*, pp.79ff; A Ravetz and R. Turkington, The Place of Home (1995) pp.29ff, S. Muthesius and M. Glendinning, *Tower Block* (1994).

7. H. Meller, *op. cit.*, p.79; A. Sutcliffe, *Multi-storey living* (1974), pp.181-206; *Developing Birmingham 1889-1989* (1989).

8. BVT Mins/AR 1 November 1938. *See also* BVT Mins/AR 4 April 1946.

9. BVT Archive BRL Box 25: Memo from S.A. Wilmot to L.P. Appleton, 2 December 1942.

10. BVT Mins/AR 'Report on Kitchen Planning and Equipment', 20 November 1942.

11. HMSO, *Report of the Design of Dwellings Sub-Committee of the Central Housing Advisory Committee and Sub-Group of the Ministry of Town and Country Planning* (1944) [Dudley Report]; Ministry of Health, *Housing Manual* (1944); Ministry of Health, *Housing Manual* (1949).

12. BVT Mins/AR 'Future Development of the Bournville Estate' 28 October 1952, p.5 [S.A. Wilmot].

13. BVT Mins/AR, H. T. Cadbury, February 1947.

14. *Ibid.*

15. *Ibid.*

16. West Midland Group, *Conurbation: a planning survey of Birmingham and the Black Country* (1948).

17. BVT Mins/AR 'Future Developments', p.6; BVT Mins/AR 1951 'Zoning of the Bournville Estate' [C.B. Parkes]. *See also* BVT Mins/AR 29 November 1943 'Post War Houses at Bournville' [P.S. Cadbury].

18. BVT Mins/AR 'Future Developments', p.6.

19. BVT Mins/AR 14 June 1944.

20. BVT Mins/AR 14 June 1945.

21. BVT Mins/AR 'Post War Housing' 14 June 1944.

22. BVT Mins/AR, P.S. Cadbury, 25 May 1944.

23. *Ibid.*

24. BVT Mins/AR 'Suggestions for Future Development' 14 June 1945.

25. BVT Mins/AR 'Housing Affairs Bulletin' 11 February 1946.

26. BVT Mins/AR 'Post-war Houses at Bournville', 1943.

27. BVT Mins/AR 21 September 1948.

28. BVT Mins/AR 'Post War Houses at Bournville' 29 November 1943 [P.S. Cadbury]. *See also* memo by L.J. Cadbury, 2 December 1943.

29. BVT Mins/AR 'Quarterly Report' 12 July 1944.

30. BVT Mins/AR memo [L.J. Cadbury] 2 December 1943.

31. Cherry, *Birmingham*, pp.149-54; BVT Mins/AR 'Research and Reconstruction' 14 November 1940.

32. BVT Mins/AR 'Report on work being done by T. Burns' November 1946.

33. L. Mumford, *The Culture of Cities* (1938).

34. *BWM* August 1946, p.171.

35. Mumford, *op. cit.*, p.483.

36. BVT Mins/AR Report, 14 October 1946 [T. Burns].

37. BVT Mins/AR 11 February 1946. *See also* the later reviews of the literature and research by R. Frankenburg, *Communities in Britain* (1971); H.J. Gans, *People and Plans* (1968); R.E. Pahl, *Patterns of Urban Life* (1970); W. Sarkissian and W. Heine, *Social Mix: The Bournville Experience* (1978).

38. BVT Mins/AR 'Notes on Knutsford Exhibition Opening' September 1946.

39. BVT Mins/AR Report of Meeting 31 Oct 1944.

40. BVT Mins/AR 'Quarterly Report' 12 July 1944.

41. BVT Mins/AR 'Report on Meeting with Housewives' 21 November 1944. *See also* 'Report on Kitchen Planning and Equipment' 20 November 1942 [S.A. Wilmot].

42. BVT Mins/AR 'Quarterly Report', 31 Oct 1944.

43. BVT Mins/AR 'Future Developments' 28 October 1952, p.1.

44. Bournville Village Council, Year Book 1949, p.7.

45. BVT Mins/AR 'Notes on the House and Furniture 1946 Exhibition at No. 5 Charfield Close, Questionnaire on House and Furniture Exhibition, 5 Charfield Close, August 1946'.
46. BVT Mins/AR 'Future Developments' 28 October 1952, p.2.
47. *Ibid.*
48. For a summary see BVT Mins/AR 11 November 1948.
49. BVT Mins/AR 'Future Developments' 28 October 1952, p.3.
50. BVT Mins/AR 'Building costs', 11 November 1948.
51. BVT Mins/AR November 1945.
52. BVT Mins/AR 10 December 1947.
53. BVT Mins/AR 15 November 1949.
54. BVT Mins/AR 18 October 1949.
55. BVT Mins/AR 1949.
56. BVT Mins/AR 'Future Developments' 28 October 1952.
57. BVT Mins/AR 21 November 1950.
58. BVT, 'The Conversion of Older Houses' (n.d. [1956]).
59. F.M. Fenter, *Copec Adventure* (1960), pp.56-7.
60. *BWM* May 1949, p.120.
61. *BWM* June 1951, p.20ff.
62. Bournville Village Council, *Year Book* 1952-3, p.9.
63. *BWM* April 1959, pp.128-30; BVT Mins/AR 'Future Developments' 28 October 1952.
64. *Ibid.*, p.9.
65. *Ibid.*, p.7.
66. BVT Mins/AR 'Zoning of Bournville Estate' 1951 [C.B. Parkes].
67. BVT Mins/AR' Future Developments' 28 October 1952, p.8.
68. BWM, April 1959 p.129.
69. BVT Mins/AR 'Future Developments' 28 October 1952, p.4.
70. *Ibid.*, p.10.
71. M.A. Broomfield, *A Bournville Assortment* (1995), pp.140-1.
72. Bournville Village Council, *Year Books* 1949, 1950-1, 1952-3.

Chapter Seven

1. A. Ravetz with R. Turkington, *The Place of Home: English Domestic Environments 1914-2000* (1995), pp.29-32; H. Meller, *Towns, plans and society in modern Britain* (1997), Ch.6; E.R. Scoffham, *The Shape of British Housing* (1984).
2. BVT Mins/AR 'Report on Kitchen Planning and Equipment' 20 November 1942; 18 April 1950.
3. MHLG, Houses 1953 (1953).
4. Ravetz with Turkington, *op. cit.*, p.30.
5. MHLG, Houses 1953 (1953).
6. Meller, *op. cit.*, pp.79ff.; Ravetz with Turkington, *op. cit.*, pp.29ff.; A. Sutcliffe (ed.), *Multi-storey living* (1974); M. Glendinning and S. Muthesius, *Tower Block* (1994).
7. City of Birmingham Development Department, *Developing Birmingham 1889 to 1989: 100 Years of City Planning* (1989); C. Chinn, *Homes for People: 100 Years of Council Housing in Birmingham* (1991); A. Sutcliffe and R. Smith, *Birmingham 1939-1970* (1974).
8. R. Best, 'Housing Associations 1890-1990' in S. Lowe and D. Hughes (eds.), *A New Century of Social Housing* (1991), pp.148-9 and p.178.

9. For this section *see* W. Muirhead, 'Self-build in Birmingham', *Quarterly Bulletin of the National Federation of Housing Societies*, No.11 (Spring/Summer 1965); BVT Mins/AR 1967 contains a further account of 'self-build in Bournville'. Interview with William Muirhead. *See also* BVT, 'The Growth of Bournville in the 1960s' BVT Archive BRL MS 1536 Box 24.

10. BVT Mins/AR 20 December 1949.

11. 'Self-build in Birmingham', pp.2-3.

12. *Ibid.*, pp.3-4.

13. BVT Mins/AR 'Self-build in Bournville' 1967.

14. 'Self-build in Birmingham', p.5.

15. BVT Mins/AR Self-build in Bournville' 1967.

16. Ravetz with Turkington, *op. cit.*, pp.36ff. MHLG, *Homes for Today and Tomorrow* (1961).

17. BVT Mins/AR 10 December 1947.

18. BVT Mins/AR July 1945.

19. BVT Mins/AR 'Annual Report' 1953.

20. BVT Mins/AR 20 November 1951.

21. BVT Mins/AR 1 May 1959; BWM (April 1959), pp.128-30.

22. BVT Mins/AR 'Annual Report' 1954.

23. MHLG, *Houses: The Next Step* (1953).

24. BVT Mins/AR 14 January 1957. See also BVT, *The Conversion of Older Houses* (n.d.[1956]).

25. BVT Mins/AR 21 January 1957.

26. W. Muirhead, 'Bungalows for the Handicapped', *Quarterly Bulletin of the National Federation of Housing Societies* (Spring/Summer 1965), pp.5-6.

27. BVT Mins/AR 'Report on Lower Shenley Farm Estate' November 1956.

28. BVT Mins/AR 20 June 1950; 19 December 1950 [Arbitration].

29. BVT Mins/AR 'A.G. Sheppard Fidler to Trustees' 24 April 1958.

30. BVT Mins/AR 'Report of Meeting' 1957.

31. BVT Mins/AR 1 August 1958.

32. BVT Mins/AR November 1957.

33. BVT Mins/AR 5 June 1959.

34. BVT Mins/AR November 1957.

35. BVT Mins/AR 2 May 1960; 7 November 1960.

36. BVT Mins/AR March 1960; cf. U.N. study on 'utilisation of space in dwellings'.

37. BVT, 'Bournville in the 1960s'.

38. BVT Mins/AR 19 July 1955.

39. BVT Mins/AR November 1959.

40. BVT Mins/AR 2 May 1960.

41. BVT Mins/AR April 1959.

42. *Ibid.*; see also 9 January 1961.

43. BVT Mins/AR 7 November 1960.

44. BVT Mins/AR 21 April 1961.

45. Ravetz with Turkington, *op. cit.*, p.31; MHLG, *Homes for today and tomorrow* (1961).

46. *Ibid.*, p.2.

47. *Ibid.*, p.4.

48. *Ibid.*, p.9.

49. *Ibid.*, p.14.

50. *Ibid.*, p.18.

51. *Ibid.*, p.5.

52. BVT Mins/AR March 1959. BVT, *Visit of the Council of the National Federation of Housing Societies, 18th March 1959.*

53. BVT Mins/AR 'Report upon the heating of smaller dwellings, with particular reference to new housing development by the Bournville Village Trust' April 1959.

54. BVT Mins/AR 'Report of Landscaping Department' December 1959.

55. BVT, Landscape and Housing Development (1949); BVT Mins/AR 23 March 1949.

56. *See* R.G. Salter, *Roadside Planting in Urban Areas* (1953); BVT Mins/AR 1967

57. BVT Mins/AR: G.A. Jellicoe, 'An Opinion upon the property adjoining Bristol Road for the Bournville Village Trust, February 1961'.

58. BVT Mins/AR 21 January 1957.

59. *BWM* (April 1959), p.130.

60. *Ibid.*, p.129.

61. BVT Mins/AR December 1955.

62. BVT Mins/AR 14 March 1956.

63. BWM (April 1959); BVT Mins/AR December 1955.

64. Ibid.; BVT Mins/AR 21 January 1957.

65. *BWM* (April 1959), p.130.

66. BVT Mins/AR December 1958.

67. BVT Mins/AR 14 January 1954.

68. *BWM* (April 1959), p.129.

69. *Ibid.*; information from Jim Wilson.

70. BWM (April 1959), p.129.

71. BVT Mins/AR December 1955: the school bus was 'warmly welcomed'.

72. *BWM* September 1959, pp.222-3.

73. BWM (April 1959), p.130.

74. *Ibid. See also* 'Bournville in the 1960s'.

75. M.A. Broomfield, *A Bournville Assortment* (1995), pp.150-2.

76. BWM (April 1959), p.129.

77. BVT Mins/AR 'Report on Industrialised Building Systems and Components Exhibition' July 1964.

78. Interview with Les Pankhurst.

79. BVT Mins/AR 'Report on speculatively built houses in the Midlands' July 1964.

80. Bournville Village Council, *Year Book* 1960-3.

81. BVT Mins/AR 4 November 1955.

82. BVT Mins/AR 20 July 1964.

83. BVT Mins/AR 4 December 1964.

84. *Bournville Village Trust; Visit of the Council of the National Federation of Housing Societies, 18th March 1959*, p.41.

Chapter Eight

1. Birmingham City Council Development Department, *Developing Birmingham 1889 to 1989: 100 Years of City Planning* (1989), pp.79-80; C. Chinn, *Homes for People: 100 Years of Council Housing in Birmingham* (1991), pp.116-20; A. Sutcliffe and R. Smith, *Birmingham 1939-1970*, Chs.7 and 13; P.S. Cadbury and W.J. Wise, *The Expansion of Birmingham into the Green Belt Area* (1968).

2. *Developing Birmingham*, p.125.

3. *Ibid.*, p.80. *See also* A. Sutcliffe (ed.), *Multi-storey living* (1974) and M. Glendinning and S. Muthesius, *Tower Block* (1994).

4. *Developing Birmingham*, p.109.

5. *Homes for people*, pp.112-16. *See* A. Coleman, *Utopia on trial* (1985).

6. I. Nairn (ed.), 'Outrage', *Architectural Review* Vol.117, No.702 (1955), pp.363-460. For a recent and thorough review of the literature on suburbs *see* M. Clapson, *Invincible green suburbs, brave new towns* (1998).

7. N. Taylor, *The Village in the City* (1973); D. Thorns, *Suburbia* (1973).

8. Creese, *The Search for Environment: The Garden City Before and After* (1966 edn.); G. Darley, *Villages of Vision* (1978); K. Pugh, *Estate Villages. Who Cares?* (1983).

9. R. Best, 'Housing Associations 1890-1990' in S. Lowe and D. Hughes (eds.), *A New Century of Social Housing* (1991) p.152.

10. *Ibid.*, pp.148-50.

11. *Ibid.*, p.150; P. Balchin, *Housing Policy: An Introduction* (1995 edn.), p.143.

12. *Ibid.*

13. Best, *op. cit.*, p150.

14. *Ibid.*, p.143; Balchin, *op. cit.*, pp.143-4.

15. *Ibid.*, p.144.

16. Best, *op. cit.*, pp.153-4.

17. BVT Mins/AR 1 June 1965.

18. BVT Mins/AR 'Letter to MHLG, 1 June 1965'.

19. *Ibid.*

20. BVT Mins/AR September 1970.

21. BVT Mins/AR 'Report of Meeting' 13 November 1972; copy of memorandum to residents, 10 November 1972.

22. BVT, *Bournville Village Trust* [Tenants Brochure] (May 1972).

23. BVT Mins/AR 'Annual Report' 1970.

24. BVT Mins/AR 'Report of Meeting' 26 September 1960; 20 February 1961.

25. BVT Mins/AR 'The experience of the Bournville Village Trust in the area of Urban Renewal' January 1968, p.2.

26. *Ibid.*

27. BVT Mins/AR 27 April 1970; M. Ross, *Planning and the Heritage*: Policy and Procedures (1991) pp.28ff. *See also* the leaflets on the two Conservation Areas.

28. BVT Mins/AR 'Schedule of development as at 14 June 1965'. *See* BVT 'The Growth of Bournville in the 1960s', BVT Archive BRL MS 1536 Box 24.

29. BVT Mins/AR 'Annual Report' 1970.

30. *Birmingham Post*, 20 December 1969.

31. *Ibid.*

32. BVT Mins/AR 18 September 1964.

33. BVT Mins/AR 27 February 1967.

34. Thorns, *op. cit.*, p.155; R.E. Pahl, *Patterns of Urban Life* (1970), pp.100ff.

35. BVT Mins/AR 20 September 1972.

36. BVT Mins/AR 'Report of Community Officer' 1980.

37. BVT Mins/AR 'Annual Report' 1970; BVT 'The Growth of Bournville in the 1960s'.

38. BWM July 1968, pp.204-5.

39. St David's Church, Shenley Green, *A Brief History of the Parish and Guide to the Church* (n.d.). I am indebted to Rev. Chris Jackson, who gave me a copy of this pamphlet. Peter Carrick was the architect in charge of the project.

40. BVT Mins/AR 'Report on Community Centres' 1979; 14 June 1980.

41. BVT Mins/AR 11 September 1978.

42.   BVT Mins/AR 17 September 1958.

43.   BVT Mins/AR 'Bournville Estate Licensing Enquiry, July 1969'.

44.   BVT Mins/AR 12 January 1969.

45.   BVT Mins/AR 20 September 1972.

46.   BVT Mins/AR 13 November 1978.

47.   BVT Mins/AR 2 April 1979.

48.   BVT Mins/AR 23 June 1979.

49.   BVT Mins/AR September 1970.

50.   BVT Mins/AR 16 November 1970 [K. Pegg].

51.   BVT Mins/AR 27 June 1972.

52.   Crosfield, *op. cit.*, Vol.2 pp.379-80; pp.676ff.

53.   *Warwickshire and Worcestershire Life* (August 1971), pp.32-3.

54.   *Ibid.*, p.32.

55.   BVT Mins/AR 26 March 1973.

56.   BVT Mins/AR 15 January 1973.

57.   *Ibid.*

58.   BVT Mins/AR 12 December 1977.

59.   BVT Mins/AR 12 April 1978.

60.   M.A. Broomfield, *A Bournville Assortment* (1995).

61.   *Ibid.*, p.153.

62.   BVT Mins/AR 'The Years Ahead' 31 May 1978.

63.   BVT Mins/AR 15 June 1978.

64.   BVT Mins/AR 'Secretary and Manager's Report' 1978.

65.   BVT Mins/AR 25 February 1980.

66.   BVT Mins/AR 31 March 1980; 'Secretary and Manager's Report' 1979.

67.   BVT Mins/AR 15 June 1973; 16 July 1973.

68.   BVT Mins/AR 13 November 1978.

69.   BVT Mins/AR 14 May 1979.

70.   BVT Mins/AR 30 July 1979.

71.   BVT Mins/AR 13 October 1980.

72.   BVT Mins/AR 12 May 1980.

73.   BVT Mins/AR 29 October 1979.

74.   *Ibid.* The east end of Witherford Way was suggested as a Conservation Area.

75.   BVT Mins/AR 12 December 1977.

76.   BVT Mins/AR 8 January 1979.

77.   BVT Mins/AR 12 May 1980.

78.   BVT Mins/AR 'Housing Corporation Report on Monitoring Visit, September 1980'.

79.   Balchin, *op. cit.*, p.150; Best, *op. cit.*, p.149.

Chapter Nine

1.   *See* P. Balchin, *Housing Policy: An Introduction* (1995 edn.); R. Best, 'Housing Associations 1880-1990' in S. Lowe and D. Hughes (eds.), *A New Century of Social Housing* (1991).

2.   K. Spencer, *et al.*, *Crisis in the Industrial Heartland* (1986).

3.   City of Birmingham, *Housing Strategy Statement 1982*, quoted in BVT *AR* (1982).

4.   NFHA Inquiry into British Housing, July 1985, quoted in BVT *AR* (1985).

5.   M.J. Daunton, *A Property Owning Democracy?* (1987); Balchin, *op. cit.*; A. Thornley, *Urban Planning under Thatcherism* (1991); BVT *AR* (1986).

6.   BVT *AR* (1986); Balchin, *op. cit.*, p.151.

7.   *Ibid.*, pp.281-2.

8.   BVT, *Housing Needs Review of Birmingham* (1995) [S. Maneffa]; Lowe and Hughes, *op. cit.*, p.181.

9.   *Ibid.*, p.189.

10. *Housing Needs Review of Birmingham* (1995).

11. *Bournville Outlook* (Summer 1997).

12. BVT *AR* (1996).

13. BVT *AR* (1993).

14. BVT *AR* (1985). *See, Weoley Hill Village News* February 1980; June 1983; June 1986; September 1986.

15. *Weoley Hill Village News* June 1986.

16. BVT *AR* (1981 and 1982); *Voluntary Housing* Vol.16, No.10 (October 1984).

17. *Ibid.*

18. BVT, 'Solar Energy Projects' (1981), p.5.

19. BVT, 'Solar Heating: An Architect's View' (n.d. [1984]), p.2.

20. *Ibid.*, p.3.

21. The Franklin Company Consultants Ltd., *The Making of a Solar Village and a Demonstration House in Bournville* (1985), pp.5-6; BVT, *Christopher Taylor Court* (n.d. [1986]).

22. See *Weoley Hill Village News* October 1981; February 1982; June 1982; March 1983.

23. BVT Mins 13 July 1981.

24. BVT *AR* (1981).

25. BVT *AR* (1982).

26. BVT *AR* (1984).

27. *Solar Village*, p.5; BVT *AR* (1984).

28. BVT *AR* (1984 and 1985).

29. *Solar Village*, p.7; 'Solar Heating', pp.3-4; BVT *AR* (1984).

30. BVT *AR* (1985)

31. *Solar Village*, pp.3ff.

32. *Ibid.*, p.21; BVT *AR* (1986).

33. BVT *AR* (1983).

34. *See, Weoley Hill Village News* June 1983; March 1984; June 1984; September 1985.

35. BVT *AR* (1985); BVT AR (1986).

36. BVT *AR* (1989)[A, Shrimpton].

37. *Ibid.*

38. *Ibid.*

39. BVT, *Tenant Satisfaction Survey—Harvey Mews* (1992).

40. *Ibid.*

41. BVT *AR* (1985).

42. BVT *AR* (1992).

43. Thanks to John Clarke for allowing me to consult this plan.

44. Interviews with J.Wilson and Gloria Gain. There had been some criticism of a proposal to extend a house in Weoley Hill in 1987 to accommodate young people recovering from mental illness. *See, Weoley Hill Village News* June 1987.

45. *Bournville Outlook* (Summer 1997); J. Hillman, *The Bournville Hallmark* (1994).

46. BVT *AR* (1993).

47.   BVT *AR* (1989).

48.   BVT *AR* (1985).

49.   BVT *AR* (1986).

50.   *Ibid.*; BVT *AR* (1988).

51.   BVT *AR* (1980).

52.   BVT *AR* (1996).

53.   BVT, *Tenant Satisfaction Survey* (1991); CWA (Consultancy) Limited, *Bournville Village Trust: Findings from the Residents Survey 1997.*

54.   *Bournville Outlook* (Winter 1997). Concern has been expressed about the suitability of certain extensions and 'improvements' since at least 1979.

55.   *Weoley Hill Village News* June 1979.

56.   *Weoley Hill Village News* February 1982; December 1982.

57.   *Weoley Hill Village News* March 1986.

58.   *Weoley Hill Village News* Winter 1993-94.

59.   BVT, *Design Guide* (1985 and later editions).

60.   *Design Guide* (1985 edn.), p.2.

61.   *News From The Trust* No.17 (Summer 1994).

62.   BVT *AR* (1996).

63.   BVT *AR* (1982 and 1983)

64.   *Weoley Hill Village News* December 1982; Interview with J. Wilson.

65.   M.A. Broomfield, *A Bournville Assortment* (1995), p.146.

66.   BVT *AR* (1985).

67.   *Weoley Hill Village News* March 1984; BVT *AR* (1985).

68.   *Weoley Hill Village News* March 1984.

69.   BVT *AR* (1987).

70.   BVT *AR* (1988 and 1989).

71.   BVT *AR* (1989 and 1992).

72.   BVT *AR* (1989).

73.   *Weoley Hill Village News* December 1985.

74.   BVT *AR* (1985, 1993 and 1996). *See also*, *Weoley Hill Village News* December 1985; *Bournville Outlook* (Winter 1997; Winter 1998).

75.   Interview with J. Taylor.

76.   *Residents Survey 1997.*

77.   *Weoley Hill Village News* February 1980; June 1980; March 1990; Winter 1993-4; Spring 1996; *Tenant Satisfaction Survey* (1991).

78.   BVT *AR* (1989).

79.   *The Three Brooks* March 1990.

80.   *Bournville Outlook* (Summer 1997; Summer 1998).

81.   *Weoley Hill Village News* February 1980; June 1980.

82.   *Weoley Hill Village News* Winter 1993-4; Spring 1996.

83.   *Tenants Satisfaction Survey* (1991), p.11; *Residents Survey 1997*, p.31 and pp.42-5.

84.   BVT *AR* (1980).

85.   BVT Mins: 'Interaction with Communities' (1984) [Report by Community Officer].

86.   BVT *AR* (1980).

87.   BVT Mins/AR 'Secretary and Manager's Report for 1979'.

88. BVT Mins 'Estate Housing Densities and Areas of Various Use' (1980).

89. *Tenants Satisfaction Survey* (1991).

90. W. Sarkissian and W. Heine, *Social Mix: The Bournville Experience* (1978), p.96.

91. *Ibid.*

92. BVT Mins 'Social Mix: A paper by G.W. Cadbury' (September 1978).

93. D. Donnison, 'Introduction' in Sarkissian and Heine, *op. cit.*, p.13.

94. R. Pahl, *Patterns of Urban Life* (1970), p.128.

95. *Ibid.*, pp.100ff.

96. Interviews with J. Wilson and G. Gain.

97. *Weoley Hill Village News* December 1982.

98. G.W. Cadbury *op. cit.*

99. 'Interaction with Communities', p.1.

100. J.W.R. Whitehand, 'Making sense of Birmingham's townscape' in A.J. Gerrard and T.R. Slater, *Managing a Conurbation: Birmingham and its Region* (1996), pp.237-8.

101. 'Interaction with Communities', p.2.

102. *Residents Survey 1997.*

103. 'Interaction with Community', p.2.

104. BVT, 'Review of Ethnic Records and Racial Equality within BVTG Allocation Process' (May 1992), p.13.

105. BVT *AR* (1981).

106. BVT *AR* (1992).

107. P. Niner in collaboration with V. Karn, *Housing Association Allocations: Achieving Racial Equality. A West Midlands Case Study* (1985).

108. *Ibid.*, p.122.

109. 'Review of Ethnic Records'.

110. *Ibid.*

111. BVT *AR* (1992). BVT Performance Update 1998.

112. 'Review of Ethnic Records', pp.12 and 19.

113. BVT, *Housing Need in the South West of Birmingham* (March 1990) [S. Maneffa], p.10.

114. BVT, H*ousing Needs Review of Birmingham* (January 1995) [S. Maneffa]. *See, Weoley Hill Village News* June 1987 for correspondence about proposed accommodation for those recovering from mental illness.

115. BVT *AR* (1993).

116. BVT *AR* (1985).

117. *Residents Survey 1997. See also, Weoley Hill Village News* February 1979; June 1979; September 1980; May 1981; September 1986. Shenley Manor Tenants' Association 1998 AGM highlighted the issue of nuisance neighbours and the Shenley Court Tenants' Association complained about the anti-social behaviour of some tenants at its 1998 AGM. *See, Bournville Outlook* (Summer 1998, Winter 1998).

118. BVT *AR* (1996).

119. *Ibid.*; Interview with J.Taylor.

120. *Weoley Hill Village News* February 1979; June 1979; September 1980; May 1981; September 1986.

121. BBC, *Neighbours at War* (1998); B. Headey, 'Indicators of Housing Satisfaction' (1972).

122. Interview with G. Gain and Deputy Housing Manager.

123. Niner and Karn, *op. cit.*, p.66.

124. *Tenant Satisfaction Survey* (1991). Recent editions of *Bournville Outlook* have identified members of the 'Fifty plus club', i.e. residents who have lived on the Estate for fifty years or more.

125. BVT *AR* (1996).

126. BVT *AR* (1985).

127. *See* Chapter Four. The Bournville Village Council was formally set up in 1903.

128. *Weoley Hill Village News* February 1980.

129. BVT *AR* (1986).

130. 'Interaction with Communities', p.4.

131. *See also, Weoley Hill Village News* for reports on the activities of the members of the Weoley Hill Village Council. Its temporary successor, *The Three Brooks*, provides some information about the Shenley Court and Shenley Manor Associations as well as Weoley Hill.

132. *The Three Brooks* June 1989.

133. *Ibid*. For the problems with the halls *see, Weoley Hill Village News* March 1986; Spring 1996.

134. BVT *AR* (1986); *The Three Brooks* March 1990; *Weoley Hill Village News* Spring 1996.

135. BVT *AR* (1993 and 1994).

136. *Weoley Hill Village News* Spring 1996.

137. 'Interaction with Communities', *op. cit.*, p.4.

138. *Weoley Hill Village News* June 1983.

139. *Weoley Hill Village News* June 1983; BVT *AR* (1986)

140. Interview with J. Wilson.

141. *Bournville Outlook* (Winter 1998).

142. BVT Mins/AR 1978; BVT AR (1980); 'Interaction with Communities', p.5. *Weoley Hill Village News* February 1983 noted some improvement during the period when Kenneth Pegg was Manager. BVT Mins/AR: 'BVT The Years Ahead. Report of the Sub-Committee to consider this matter' (August 1978), p.3.

143. BVT *AR* (1980)

144. BVT *AR* (1980). BVT Mins/AR: 'BVT The Years Ahead. Report of the Sub-Committee to consider this matter' (August 1978), p.3.

145. BVT *AR* (1980).

146. BVT *AR* (1981). *Weoley Hill Village News* February 1982 noted that the new Community Officer had 'improved communications considerably'.

147. 'Interaction with Communities', p.6. *Weoley Hill Village News* March 1985 indicates concern about the maintenance charge.

148. 'Interaction with Communities', p.6.

149. *Weoley Hill Village News* September 1986. Interest in the representative bodies could be patchy. 'Although Weoley Hill is fully committed to the [Estate Management Sub] Committee, there has been some lack of interest by the other Associations.' *Weoley Hill Village News* June 1984.

150. BVT *AR* (1984).

151. BVT *AR* (1983).

152. BVT *AR* (1984).

153. BVT *AR* (1988).

154. BVT *AR* (1989).

155. BVT *AR* (1993).

156. *The Three Brooks* December 1988; June 1989.

157. *The Three Brooks* December 1988; June 1989; *Weoley Hill Village News* Spring 1992; Spring 1994.

158. BVT *AR* (1988); Broomfield, *op. cit.*, pp.157ff.

159. *Ibid*., p.160; *Birmingham Post*, 11 October 1991.

160. Broomfield, *op. cit.*, p.160; *Weoley Hill Village News* Spring 1992; Spring 1994.

161. *Weoley Hill Village News* Spring 1994.

162. *Tenants Satisfaction Survey* (1991); *The Three Brooks* No. 8, 1990.

163. BVT *AR* (1996).

164. *Weoley Hill Village News* Spring 1996.

165. *Bournville Outlook* (Spring 1997; Spring 1998).

166. *Residents Survey 1997.*

167. *Bournville Outlook* (Spring 1998); *Weoley Hill Village News* Spring 1996.

168. Interview with J. Taylor.

169. BVT *AR* (1986). See also *Weoley Hill Village News* June 1986.

170. *Tenants Satisfaction Survey* (1991).

171. *Residents Survey 1997.*

172. *Bournville Outlook* (Winter 1997).

173. BVT *AR* (1993)

174. *Bournville Village Trust* (1960) [Residents' Handbook]

175. D. Eversley, *The Planner in Society: the changing role of a profession* (1973), p.38.

176. *Dewsbury Reporter*, 8 September 1902.

177. *Church Times*, 8 August 1902.

178. *Birmingham Weekly Post*, 28 September 1901.

179. *Birmingham Daily Gazette*, 21 September 1901.

180. W.A. Harvey, *The Model Village and its Cottages: Bournville* (1906), p.6.

181. BVT Mins/AR 'Secretary's Report' (1924).

182. J.B. Priestley, *English Journey* (1977 edn.), p.90.

183. BVT, *When we build again* (1941).

184. BVT, *Sixty Years of Planning: The Bournville Experiment* (n.d.).

185. BVT *AR* (1993).

186. BVT, *Towards 2000* (1993).

187. BVT *AR* (1993).

188. *See, Bournville Outlook* (Winter 1997; Spring 1998).

189. *Bournville Outlook* (Winter 1997).

190. *Residents Survey 1997.* Interview with J. Wilson.

BIBLIOGRAPHY

Archives

Bournville Village Trust:
Original Minute Books and recent material and photographs.

Birmingham Central Reference Library Archives:
Bournville Village Trust Archive MS 1536 includes:
Original House Plans and Maps;
84 Boxes of documentary material;
Photographic Prints (including BVT prints from c.1900, C.L. Holdings photographs, and the Max Jones Collection produced for the Estate's centenary).

Cadbury Limited Archives:
Photographs, printed material and ephemera relating to the Cadbury family, Bournville Works and Village, the Bournville Village Trust, housing and housing loans, the Society of Friends and local history.

Birmingham University Library Special Collections:
Cadbury Papers (mainly relating to their operations in Africa).

Published material

Abercrombie, P., 'Modern Town Planning in England. A Comparative Review of 'Garden City' Schemes in England', *Town Planning Review*, Vol. 1 (1910-11), pp.18-38 and pp.111-128

Adams, T., *Playparks*, Coronation Planting Committee: London (n.d.)

Addison, P., *Now the War is Over*, BBC: London (1985)

Aldridge, H.R., *The Case for Town Planning*, London (1915)

Allen, G.C., *The Industrial Development of Birmingham and the Black Country 1860-1927*, Frank Cass and Co. Ltd.: London (1966 edn.)

Archer, J.H.G., 'Edgar Wood: A Notable Manchester Architect', *Lancashire and Cheshire Antiquarian Society* (1963-4)

Ashworth, W., *The Genesis of Modern British Town Planning*, Routledge and Kegan Paul: London (1954)

Association for Planning and Regional Reconstruction, The, *Housing Digest: An Analysis of Housing Reports 1941-1945*, Art and Educational Publishers: London (1946)

Atkins, P., 'The Architecture of Bournville 1879-1914', in Tilson, B. (ed.), *Made in Birmingham, Design and Industry 1889-1989*, Brewin Books: Studley (1989)

Atkins, P., 'Cadbury Buildings at Northfield', *The Birmingham Historian*, 4, (Spring/Summer, 1989), pp.19-22

Balchin, P., *Housing Policy: An Introduction*, Routledge: London (1995 edn.)

Barlow, J.H., 'The development of new housing areas on town planning lines, with limitation of the number of houses per acre, and with especial reference to the provision of cottages with gardens, to be let at rents within the means of workmen', *Proceedings of the National Advisory Town Planning Committee, National Housing and Town Planning Council*, London (1913).

Beevers, R., *The Garden City Utopia: a critical biography of Ebenezer Howard*, Macmillan: London (1988)

Bell, C. and R., *City Fathers: the early history of town planning in Britain*, Penguin Books: Harmondsworth (1972 edn.)

Best, R., 'Housing Associations 1890-1990', in Lowe, S. and Hughes, D. (eds.), *A New Century of Social Housing*, Leicester University Press (1991)

Bidlake, W.H., 'Birmingham as it might be', in Muirhead, J.H. (ed.), *Birmingham Institutions*, Cornish Brothers: Birmingham (1911)

Birchall, J., 'Co-partnership housing and the garden city', *Planning Perspectives* 10 (1995), pp.329-58

Blatchford, R., *Merrie England*, Journeyman Press:London (1976 edn.)

The Book of the Cheap Cottages Exhibition, County Gentleman and Land and Water Ltd.: London (1905)

Boumphrey, G., *Town and Country Tomorrow*, Thomas Nelson and Sons Ltd.: London (1940)

Bournville Outlook (1997-)

Bournville Village Council, *Annual Report* (1914)

Bournville Village Council, *Year Book* (1920, 1924, 1926, 1929, 1935, 1938, 1949, 1950-1, 1952-3, 1955-8, 1960-3)

Bournville Village Trust, *An Account of its Planning and Housing Schemes in Suburban and Rural Areas*, Bournville (1938)

Bournville Village Trust, *Annual Report and Accounts* (1980-96)

Bournville Village Trust, *Bournville Housing*, Bournville (1922 and 1928)

Bournville Village Trust, *Bournville Village 1912*, Bournville (1912) [for the use of guides]

Bournville Village Trust, *Bournville Village Trust*, Bournville (1974) [Residents Handbook]

Bournville Village Trust, *Bournville Village Trust*, Bournville (1901) [Barlow, J.R.]

Bournville Village Trust, *The Bournville Village Trust 1900-1955*, Bournville (1955)

Bournville Village Trust, *The Conversion of Older Houses*, Bournville (n.d.[1956])

Bournville Village Trust, *Christopher Taylor Court: Sheltered Housing*, Bournville (n.d.[1985])

Bournville Village Trust, *A Design Guide*, Bournville (1985)

Bournville Village Trust, *Housing Needs Review of Birmingham*, Report by Maneffa, S. (January 1995)

Bournville Village Trust, *Housing Need in the South West of Birmingham*, Report by Moore, S. (March 1990)

Bournville Village Trust, *Landscape and Housing Development*, Batsford: London (1949)

Bournville Village Trust, *Review of the Ethnic Records and Racial Equality within BVTG's Allocation Process*, Report by Maneffa, S. (May 1992)

Bournville Village Trust, *Sixty Years of Planning: The Bournville Experiment*, Bournville (1941)

Bournville Village Trust, *Solar Energy Projects*, Bournville (1981)

Bournville Village Trust, *Tenant Satisfaction Survey*, Report by Maneffa, S. (August 1991)

Bournville Village Trust, *Tenant Satisfaction Survey—Harvey Mews*, Report by Maneffa, S. (October 1992)

Bournville Village Trust, *Typical Plans*, Bournville (n.d.[1911])

Bournville Village Trust, *When we build again*, George Allen and Unwin: London (1941)

Bournville Works Magazine, Cadbury Brothers: Bournville (1902-)

Bradley, I.C., *Enlightened Entrepreneurs*, London (1987)

Brandon-Jones, J., *C.F.A. Voysey: architect and designer 1857-1941*, Lund Humphries: London (1978)

Briggs, A., *History of Birmingham, Volume 2: Borough and City 1865-1938*, Oxford University Press (1952)

Briggs, A., *Victorian Cities*, Penguin Books: Harmondsworth (1963)

Broomfield, M.A., *A Bournville Assortment*, The Ebor Press: York (1995)

Bryson, J.R. and Lowe, P.A., 'Bournville: a hundred years of social housing in a model village', in Garrard, A.J. and Slater, T.R. (eds.), *Managing a Conurbation: Birmingham and its Region*, Brewin Books: Studley (1996)

Burnett, J., *A Social History of Housing 1815-1970*, Methuen: London (1980 edn.)

CWA (Consultancy) Ltd., *Bournville Village Trust: Findings from the Residents Survey 1997*, Milton Keynes (1997)

Cadbury, E., 'Factors in Sound Town Planning', *Art and Industry* (April 1944)

Cadbury, G. Jnr., *Town Planning, with special reference to the Birmingham Schemes*, Longmans Green: London (1915)

Cadbury, P.S., *Birmingham—Fifty Years On*, Bournville Village Trust: Birmingham (1952)

Cadbury, P.S., *The Expansion of Birmingham into the Green Belt Area*, Cadbury Brothers: Bournville (1968)

Cadbury Brothers Ltd., *Bournville: A Review*, Bournville (1921)

Cadbury Brothers Ltd., *Experimental Houses*, Bournville (1920)

Cadbury Brothers Ltd., *Industrial Challenge: the experience of Cadburys of Bournville in the post-war years*, Bournville (1962)

Cadbury Brothers Ltd., *Industrial Record 1919-1939*: a review of the inter-war years, Bournville (1945)

Cannadine, D., *Lords and Landlords: the aristocracy and towns 1774-1967*, Leicester University Press (1980)

Carr, C.M.H. and Whitehand, J.W.R., 'Birmingham's inter-war suburbs: origins, development and change', in Garrard, A.J. and Slater, T.R. (eds.), *Managing a Conurbation: Birmingham and its Region*, Brewin Books: Studley (1996)

Chalklin, C.W., *The Provincial Towns of Georgian England*, Arnold: London (1974)

Chapman, S.D. and Bartlett, J.N., 'The Contribution of Building Clubs and Freehold Land Society to Working-Class Housing in Birmingham', in Chapman,S.D. (ed.), *The History of Working Class Housing*, David and Charles: Newton Abbot (1971)

Cherry, G.E., *Birmingham: A Study in Geography, History and Planning*, John Wiley and Sons: Chichester (1994)

Cherry, G.E., *Cities and Plans: the shaping of urban Britain in the 19th and 20th centuries*, Edward Arnold: London (1988)

Cherry, G.E., 'Factors in the Origins of Town Planning in Britain: The Example of Birmingham 1905-14', Working Paper No. 36, CURS, University of Birmingham (1975)

Cherry, G.E. (ed.), *Pioneers in British Planning*, The Architectural Press: London (1981)

Cherry, G.E. (ed.), *Shaping an Urban World*, Mansell: London (1980)

Cherry, G.E., *Town Planning in Britain since 1900*, Blackwell: Oxford (1996)

Cherry, G.E., *Urban Change and Planning*, G.T. Foulis and Co. Ltd.: Henley-on-Thames (1972)

Chinn, C., *Homes For People: 100 Years of Council Housing in Birmingham*, Birmingham Books: Birmingham (1991)

Chinn, C., *Poverty amidst prosperity: the urban poor in England 1834-1914*, Manchester University Press (1995)

City of Birmingham Development Department, *Developing Birmingham 1889 to 1989: 100 years of city planning*, Birmingham City Council (1989)

Clapson, M., I*nvincible green suburbs, brave new towns*, Manchester University Press (1998)

Clark, K., *Ruskin Today*, Penguin Books: Harmondsworth (1964)

Coleman, B.I. (ed.), *The Idea of the City in the 19th Century*, Routledge and Kegan Paul: London (1973)

Cooper, A.B., 'Mr George Cadbury at home', *Sunday at Home*, No.40 (February 1909), pp.241-50

Co-operative Congress, *Report of Co-operative Congress: Visit to Bournville*, Leicester (1906)

Co-partnership Tenants' Housing Council, *Garden suburbs, Villages and Homes: All about Co-partnership Houses*, London (1906)

Corley, T.A.B., 'How Quakers coped with business success: Quaker industrialists 1860-1914', in Jeremy, D.J.(ed.), *Business and Religion in Britain*, Gower: Aldershot (1988), pp.164-87

Crawford, A. (ed.), *By Hammer and Hand: The Arts and Crafts Movement in Birmingham*, Birmingham Museums and Art Gallery: Birmingham (1984)

Creese, W.L. (ed.), *The Legacy of Raymond Unwin*, M.I.T. Press: Cambridge, Massachusetts (1967)

Creese, W.L., *The Search for Environment: The Garden City Before and After*, The Johns Hopkins University Press: Baltimore and London (1992 edn.)

Crosfield, J.F., *The Cadbury Family, Vol.1* [private publication] (1985)

Crosfield, J.F., *The Cadbury Family, Vol.2* [private publication] (1985)

Cullingworth, J.B., *Environmental Planning 1939-1947, Vol. 1, Reconstruction and Land Use Planning 1939-1947*, HMSO: London (1975)

Cullingworth, J.B., *Environmental Planning 1939-1969, Vol.3, New Towns Policy*, HMSO: London (1979)

Culpin, E.G., *The Garden City Movement Up-to-date*, London (1913)

Culpin, E.G., 'A German "Bournville"', *Bournville Works Magazine* (September 1911), pp.265-7

Dale, J.A., 'Bournville', *Economic Review*, (January 1907), pp.13-27

Darley, G., *Villages of Vision*, Paladin: London (1978)

Daunton, M.J. (ed.), *Councillors and Tenants: Local Authority Housing in English Cities 1919-39*, Leicester University Press (1984)

Daunton, M.J., *The House and Home in the Victorian City: Working Class Housing 1850-1914*, Edward Arnold: London (1983)

Daunton, M.J., *A Property-Owning Democracy?*, Faber and Faber Ltd.: London (1987)

Dellheim, C., 'The creation of a company culture: Cadburys 1861-1931', *The American Historical Review*, Vol.92, No.1 (1987), pp.13-46

Dellheim, C., 'Utopia Limited: Bournville and Port Sunlight', in Fraser, D. (ed.), *Cities, Class and Communication: essays in honour of Asa Briggs*, Harvester: London (1990), pp.44-57

Dowling, G., Giles, B. and Hayfield, C., *Selly Oak Past and Present*, Department of Geography, University of Birmingham (1987)

Durman, M. and Harrison, M., *Bournville 1895-1914: The Model Village and its Cottages*, The Article Press: Birmingham (1995)

Dyos, H.J. and Wolff, M. (eds.), *The Victorian City: images and realities*, 2 Vols., Routledge and Kegan Paul: London (1973)

Edwards, A.M., *The Design of Suburbia*, Pembridge Press: London (1981)

Englander, D., *Landlord and Tenant in Urban Britain 1838-1918*, Oxford University Press (1983)

Eversley, D., *The Planner in Society: the Changing Role of a Profession*, London (1973)

Fenter, F.M., *Copec Adventure*, Copec: Birmingham (1960)

First Garden City Ltd., *Where Shall I Live? A Guide to Letchworth and Catalogue of the Urban Housing and Rural Homesteads Exhibition*, London (1907)

Forty, A. and Moss, H., 'A housing style for troubled consumers: the success of the neo-vernacular', *Architectural Review* (1980)

Frankenberg, R., *Communities in Britain: Social life in town and country*, Penguin Books: Harmondsworth (1969)

The Franklin Company Consultants Ltd., *The Making of a Solar Village and a Demonstration House in Bournville*, Birmingham (1985)

Gans, H.J., *People and Plans*, Penguin Books: Harmondsworth (1972)

Garden City Association, *The Garden City Conference at Bournville: Report of Proceedings*, Garden City Association: London (1901)

Gardiner A.G., *Life of George Cadbury*, Cassell and Company Ltd.: London (1923)

Gaskell, S.M., *Building Control: National Legislation and the Introduction of Local Bye-laws in Victorian England*, Bedford Square Press: London (1983)

Gaskell, S.M., *Model Housing from the Great Exhibition to the Festival of Britain*, Mansell Publishing Limited: London (1987)

Gaskell, S.M. (ed.), *Slums*, Leicester University Press (1992)

Gaskell, S.M., '"The suburb salubrious": town planning in practice', in Sutcliffe, A. (ed.), *British town planning; the formative years*, Leicester University Press (1981)

George, W.L., *Labour and Housing at Port Sunlight*, London (1909)

Gerrard, A.J. and Slater, T.R. (eds.), *Managing a Conurbation: Birmingham and its Region*, Brewin Books: Studley (1996)

Gilbert, B.B., *British Social Policy 1914-1939*, London: Batsford (1970)

Giles, B.D., 'High status neighbourhoods in Birmingham', *West Midlands Studies*, Vol.9 (1976), pp.10-33

Gill, C., *History of Birmingham, Vol.1: Manor and Borough to 1865*, Oxford University Press (1952)

Girouard, M., 'Sweetness and Light': *The Queen Anne Movement 1860-1900*, Yale University Press (1977)

Glendinning, M. and Muthesius, S., *Tower Block: Modern Public Housing in England, Scotland, Wales and Northern Ireland*, Yale University Press (1994)

Green, D.R. and Parton, A.G., 'Slums and slum life in Victorian England: London and Birmingham at mid-century', in Gaskell, S.M. (ed.), *Slums*, Leicester University Press (1992)

Greve, J., *People and their Houses*, Cadbury Brothers Ltd.: Birmingham (1960)

Gumbley, E., *Bournville: A Portrait of Cadbury's Garden Village in Old Picture Postcards*, S.B. Publications: Market Drayton (1991)

Hall, P. *et al.*, *The Containment of Urban England*, George Allen and Unwin: London (1973)

Hardy, D., *Alternative Communities in 19th Century England*, Longman: Harlow (1979)

Harrison, M., 'Bournville 1919-1939', *Planning History*, Vol.17, No.3 (1995), pp.22-31

Harrison, M., 'Thomas Coglan Horsfall and The Example of Germany', *Planning Perspectives*, Vol.6 (1991), pp.297-314

Harvey, W.A., *The Model Village and its Cottages: Bournville*, Batsford: London (1906)

Haynes, G.L., *A New Home in a Model Village*, BCS: Bournville (1995)

Haynes, G.L., *Milestones in Growing Up*, BCS: Bournville (1995)

Haynes, G.L., *Old Hay Green Lane*, BCS: Bournville (1995)

Hennock, E.P., *Fit and Proper Persons: Ideal and Reality in 19th Century Government*, Arnold: London (1973)

Henslowe, P., *Ninety Years On*, Bournville Village Trust: Birmingham (1985)

Hickman, D., *Birmingham*, Studio Vista: London (1972)

Hillman, J., *The Bournville Hallmark: Housing People for 100 Years*, Brewin Books: Studley (1994)

Hopkins, E., *Birmingham: The First Manufacturing Town in the World 1760-1840*, Weidenfeld and Nicolson: London (1989)

Hopkins, E., 'Working class housing in Birmingham during the Industrial Revolution', *International Review of Social History*, Vol.31, No.1 (1986), pp.80-94

Hopkins, E., 'Working class life in Birmingham between the wars, 1918-1939', *Midland History*, Vol.15 (1990), pp.129-50

Horsfall, T.C., *The Improvement of the Dwellings and Surroundings of the People: The Example of Germany*, Manchester University Press (1904)

Howard, E., *Garden Cities of Tomorrow*, Faber and Faber Ltd.: London (1965 edn.)

Hubbard, E. and Shippobottom, M., *A Guide to Port Sunlight*, Liverpool University Press (1989)

Ikin, C.W., *Hampstead Garden Suburb: Dreams and Realities*, The New Hampstead Garden Suburb Trust: London (1990)

Isichei, E., *Victorian Quakers*, Oxford University Press (1970)

Jeremy, D.J., *Capitalists and Christians: Business Leaders and the Churches in Britain 1900-1960*, Oxford University Press (1990)

Jeremy, D., 'The Enlightened Paternalist in Action: William Hesketh Lever at Port Sunlight before 1914', *Business History* (1989)

Jones, G.S., *Outcast London*, Oxford University Press (1971)

Jones, J.T., *History of the Corporation of Birmingham, Vol.5, 1915-35*, City of Birmingham (1940)

Keating, P. (ed.), *Into Unknown England 1866-1913*, Fontana: London (1976)

Keene, T., 'Cadbury Housing at Bournville 1879', *Industrial Archaeology*, Vol.13, No.1 (Spring 1978), pp.43-7

Kellett, J.R., *The Impact of the Railways on Victorian Cities*, Routledge and Kegan Paul: London (1969)

Kornwolf, J.D., *M.H. Baillie-Scott and the Arts and Crafts Movement*, Yale University Press (1972)

Land Enquiry Committee, *The Land, Volume 2: Urban*, London (1914)

Lees, A., *Cities Perceived: Urban Society in European and American Thought 1820-1940*, Manchester University Press (1985)

Little, B., *Birmingham Buildings*, David and Charles: Newton Abbot (1971)

Lowe, S. and Hughes, D. (eds.), *A New Century of Social Housing*, Leicester University Press (1991)

Macmorran, J.L., *Municipal Public Works and Planning in Birmingham 1852-1972*, City of Birmingham (1973)

Madge, J., *The Rehousing of Britain*, London (1945)

Manzoni, H.J., *The Production of 50,000 Municipal Houses*, City of Birmingham (1939)

Marr, T.R., *Housing Conditions in Manchester and Salford*, Citizens Association: Manchester (1904)

Marsh, J., *Back to the Land: the pastoral influence in Victorian England from 1880 to 1914*, Quartet Books: London (1982)

Mass Observation, *People's Homes*, John Murray: London (1943)

Mayne, A., *The Imagined Slum: Newspaper Representation in Three Cities 1870-1914*, Leicester University Press (1993)

Meakin, G.B., *Model Factories and Villages: Ideal Conditions of Labour and Housing*, London (1905)

Meller, H.E., *Towns, plans and society in modern Britain*, Cambridge University Press (1997)

Miller, M., *Letchworth: The First Garden City*, Phillimore: Chichester (1989)

Miller, M., 'Raymond Unwin 1863-1940' in Cherry, G.E. (ed.), *Pioneers in British Planning*, The Architectural Press: London (1981)

Miller, M. and Gray, A.S., *Hampstead Garden Suburb*, Phillimore: Chichester (1992)

Ministry of Health, *Design of Dwellings: Report of the Design of Dwellings Sub-Committee of the Central Housing Advisory Committee* [Dudley Report], HMSO: London (1944)

Ministry of Health/Ministry of Works, *Housing Manual 1944*, HMSO: London (1944)

Ministry of Health, *Housing Manual 1949*, HMSO: London (1949)

Ministry of Housing and Local Government, *Flats and Houses 1958: design and economy*, HMSO: London (1958)

Moss-Eccardt, J., *Ebenezer Howard*, Shire Publications: Aylesbury (1973)

Muirhead, J.H. (ed.), *Birmingham Institutions*, Cornish Brothers: Birmingham (1911)

Mumford, L., *The Culture of Cities*, Secker and Warburg: London (1940 edn.)

Muthesius, H., *The English House*, BSP Professional Books: Oxford (English edn. 1987)

Muthesius, S., *The English Terraced House*, Yale University Press (1982)

National Housing Reform Council, *Midland Conference on the Better Planning of New Areas*, Birmingham (1906)

Nettlefold, J.S., *Practical Housing*, Garden City Press: Letchworth (1908)

Nettlefold, J.S., *Practical Town Planning*, St Catherine Press: London (1914)

Nettlefold, J.S., *Slum Reform and Town Planning*, N.H.R.C./G.C.A.: London (1907)

Niner, P. in collaboration with Karn, V., *Housing Association Allocations: Achieving Racial Equality. A West Midlands Case Study*, The Runnymede Trust: London (1985)

Obelkevich, J. and Catterall, P. (eds.), *Understanding Post-War British Society*, Routledge: London (1994)

Oliver, P., Davis, I. and Bentley, I., *Dunroamin: The Suburban Semi and its Enemies*, Barrie and Jenkins: London (1981)

Page, D. and Muir, T., *New Housing for the Elderly*, Bedford Square Press: London (1971)

Pahl, R.E., *Patterns of Urban Life*, Longman: London (1970)

Pawley, M., *The Private Future*, Pan: London (1974)

Pollard, S., *The Genesis of Modern British Management*, Penguin Books: Harmondsworth (1965)

Pooley, C.G., *Local Authority Housing: Origins and Development*, Historical Association: London (1996)

Priestley, J.B., *English Journey*, Penguin Books: Harmondsworth (1977 edn.)

Ravetz, A. with Turkington, R., *The Place of Home: English Domestic Environments 1914-2000*, E. and F. N. Spon: London (1995)

Richards, J.M., *Castles on the Ground: The Anatomy of Suburbia*, John Murray: London (1973 edn.)

Rodger, R., *Housing in Urban Britain 1780-1914*, Macmillan: London (1989)

Rowntree, B.S. and Pigou, A.C., *Lectures on Housing*, Manchester University Press (1914)

Royal Institute of British Architects, *Town Planning Conference*, R.I.B.A.: London (1910)

Saint, A., *Richard Norman Shaw*, Yale University Press (1977)

Salter, R.G., *Roadside Planting in Urban Areas*, Bournville Village Trust (1953)

Sarkissian, W and Heine,W., *Social Mix: The Bournville Experiment*, Bournville Village Trust and South Australian Housing Trust: Birmingham (1978)

Scoffham, E.R., *The Shape of British Housing*, George Goodwin: London (1984)

Searle, G.R., *The Quest for National Efficiency*, Basil Blackwell: Oxford (1971)

Short, J.R., *Housing in Britain: the post-war experience*, Methuen: London (1978)

Silverstone, R. (ed.), *Visions of Suburbia*, Routledge: London (1997)

Sissons, M. and French, P., *Age of Austerity*, Oxford University Press (1963)

Skipp, V., *A History of Greater Birmingham down to 1830*, Victor Skipp: Birmingham (1980)

Skipp, V., *The Making of Victorian Birmingham*, Victor Skipp: Birmingham (1983)

Skilleter, K., 'The role of public utility societies in early British town planning and housing reform, 1901-36', *Planning Perspectives*, 8 (1993), pp.125-65

Smith, D., *Conflict and Compromise: Class Formation in English Society 1830-1914*, Routledge and Kegan Paul: London (1982)

'Special Bournville Number', *Garden Cities and Town Planning*, Vol.15, No.7 (July 1925), pp.156-68

Special Housing Inquiry Committee, *Report*, City of Birmingham (1914)

Spencer, K. *et al.*, *Crisis in the Industrial Heartland: a study of the West Midlands*, Oxford University Press (1986)

Stedman, M.B., 'The townscape of Birmingham in 1956', *Transactions of the Institute of British Geographers*, Vol.25 (1958), pp.225-38

Stephens, W.B. (ed.), *A History of the County of Warwick, Vol.7, The City of Birmingham*, Oxford University Press (1964)

Stevenson, J., *British Society 1914-45*, Penguin Books: Harmondsworth (1984)

Stranz, W., *George Cadbury: An Illustrated Life*, Shire Publications: Aylesbury (1973)

Sutcliffe, A. (ed.), *British Town Planning: the formative years*, Leicester University Press (1981)

Sutcliffe, A. (ed.), *Multi-Storey Living: The British Working Class Experience*, Croom Helm: London (1974)

Sutcliffe, A., *Towards the Planned City: Germany, the United States and France 1780-1914*, Blackwell: Oxford (1981)

Swenarton, M., *Homes fit for Heroes: the politics and architecture of early state housing in Britain*, Heinemann: London (1981)

Tarn, J.N., *Five Per Cent Philanthropy*, Cambridge University Press (1973)

Taylor, N., *The Village in the City*, Temple Smith: London (1973)

The Three Brooks 1988-90

Thorns, D., *Suburbia*, Paladin: London (1973)

Thornley, A., *Urban Planning under Thatcherism*, Routledge: London (1991)

Timmins, S. (ed.), *Birmingham and the Midland Hardware District*, Frank Cass and Co. Ltd.: London (1967 edn.)

Unwin, R. and Parker, B., *The Art of Building a Home*, London (1901)

Unwin, R., *Cottage Plans and Common Sense*, Fabian Society: London (1902)

Unwin, R., *Nothing Gained by Overcrowding*, London (1912)

Unwin, R., *The Town Extension Plan*, Manchester University Press (1912)

Unwin, R., *Town Planning in Practice: an introduction to the art of designing cities and suburbs*, Fisher Unwin: London (1909)

Upton, C., *A History of Birmingham*, Phillimore: Chichester (1993)

Waddilove, L.E., *One Man's Vision: The story of the Joseph Rowntree Village Trust*, George Allen and Unwin: London (1954)

Wagner, G., *The Chocolate Conscience*, Chatto and Windus: London (1987)

Walters, J.C., *Scenes in Slum-Land*, Birmingham Daily Gazette (1902)

Ward, S.J., *Planning and Urban Change*, Paul Chapman Publishing: London (1994)

Weaver, L., *The 'Country Life' Book of Cottages*, Country Life: London (1919 edn.)

Weoley Hill Village Council, *Weoley Hill Estate* (1927)

Weoley Hill Village Council, *Weoley Hill Village* (1932)

Weoley Hill Village Council, *Weoley Hill Village* (1936)

Weoley Hill Village Council, *Weoley Hill Village* (1947)

Weoley Hill Village News, 1976-88; 1991-96.

West Midland Group, *Conurbation: a planning survey of Birmingham and the Black Country*, The Architectural Press: London (1948)

Whitehand, J.W.R., *The Changing Face of Cities: a study of development cycles and urban form*, Blackwell: Oxford (1987)

Whitehand, J.W.R., 'Making sense of Birmingham's townscapes', in Garrard, A.J. and Slater, T.R., *Managing a Conurbation: Birmingham and its Region*, Brewin Books: Studley (1996)

Whitehouse, J.W., 'Bournville. A Study in Housing Reform', *The Studio*, Vol. 24 (1902), pp.162-172

Whittaker, C.H. *et al.*, *The Housing Problem in War and Peace*, American Institute of Architects: Washington (1918)

Williams, I.O., *The Firm of Cadbury 1831-1931*, Constable and Co.: London (1931)

Windsor, D.B., *The Quaker Enterprise*, Frederick Muller: London (1980)

Wise, M.J. (ed.), *Birmingham and its Regional Setting: a scientific survey*, British Association of the Advancement of Science: London (1950)

Woods, R., 'Mortality and sanitary conditions in late 19th century Birmingham', in Woods, R. and Woodward, J. (eds.), *Urban Disease and Mortality in 19th Century England*, Batsford: London (1984)

Videotapes

BVT, *The Bournville Story: The First 100 Years of Housing* (1995)

BVT, *When we build again* (1941) [The Trust has videotaped copies of the film based on the 1941 book.]

INDEX

Numbers in **bold** refer to page numbers of illustrations.

THE WEOLEY HILL ESTATE
SELLY OAK, BIRMINGHAM

Particulars of Houses, Type 3B6

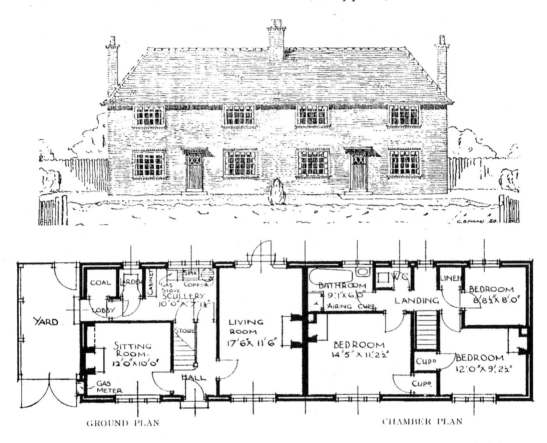

GROUND PLAN   CHAMBER PLAN

From the plans it will be seen that the accommodation is arranged upon labour-saving principles. Attention is called to the exceptionally large Living Room, with window at each end, which is a feature of this type of house.

The houses are built with red brick cavity walls, the roofs being of hand-made tiles.

A detailed description of the internal equipment is given in the booklet, "Good Houses," a copy of which may be obtained from the Secretary.

The houses are leasehold for a period of 99 years, with ground rents from £6 per annum, according to the site chosen.

Price—£800 per house, including Legal Expenses in connection with the Underlease, Architect's Fees, planting hedges, making paths, digging over garden, planting fruit bushes and laying lawns at back and front.

For further particulars apply to :—

THE SECRETARY, WEOLEY HILL LIMITED, ESTATE OFFICE, BOURNVILLE.
(Telephone : King's Norton 367 and 368)

or at the Office on the Estate (Telephone : Priory 1602) or after office hours to Mr. H. E. PANKHURST, 75, MIDDLE PARK ROAD (Telephone : Priory 1574).